THE FUTURE OF JUSTICE

This open access book explores how courts and judges from common and civil law jurisdictions should address the following challenges that affect all of humanity – the ever-rapid development of AI and big data, the dangers of disinformation and misinformation, and the irreversible harmful effects of climate change.

The book is divided into four parts. Part I examines the impact of AI on judiciaries, in areas such as machine-generated evidence, access to justice and the ethical implications of AI. Part II delves into the topic of data protection and privacy in the era of big data and AI, focusing on the legal and regulatory issues relating to the processing of data. Part III addresses truth decay and the courts' role in ascertaining facts in an uncertain world. Part IV explores climate change litigation in various domestic courts around the world and the approaches and techniques that have been taken to address this dynamic and challenging area of the law.

This book is primarily for judges: how should they approach these topics when raised in their courts? What capacity-building is necessary for judges to stay current? Should judiciaries play a role, or is it solely or primarily the government's responsibility to formulate the relevant policies and laws? To what extent can and should impartial judges be proactive on these issues?

The book is, however, also addressed to legal academics, law students, and laypersons interested in the implications of these significant challenges on the integrity of our justice systems: how should our civil justice systems respond?

HART PUBLISHING
Bloomsbury Publishing Plc
Kemp House, Chawley Park, Cumnor Hill, Oxford, OX2 9PH, UK
1385 Broadway, New York, NY 10018, USA
Bloomsbury Publishing Ireland Limited, 29 Earlsfort Terrace, Dublin 2, D02 AY28, Ireland

HART PUBLISHING, the Hart/Stag logo, BLOOMSBURY and the Diana logo are trademarks of Bloomsbury Publishing Plc
First published in Great Britain 2026

1

A catalogue record for this book is available from the British Library.

A catalogue record for this book is available from the Library of Congress.

Library of Congress Control Number: 2026944328

ISBN: HB: 978-1-50998-439-8
ePDF: 978-1-50998-441-1
ePub: 978-1-50998-440-4

Typeset by Lumina Datamatics Ltd

For product safety related questions contact productsafety@bloomsbury.com

To find out more about our authors and books visit www.hartpublishing.co.uk. Here you will find extracts, author information, details of forthcoming events and the option to sign up for our newsletters.

FOREWORD

Society is facing formidable challenges today. Prominent amongst them are the growing use of artificial intelligence (AI), problems concerning data protection and privacy, an increasing inability to identify what is fact and what is not (which has been described as 'truth decay'), coupled with the facility to spread disinformation widely and at little financial cost, and climate change. In common with so many of our existing institutions, our systems of justice are bound to be tested by these issues.

There is a risk that, faced with issues of such scale and gravity, we might feel ourselves powerless to influence the future and so fail even to try. But that is not an option. As those who initiated the Judicial Roundtable on the Future of Justice (Roundtable) recognised, we can, and clearly must, look at our own areas of practice and consider what challenges confront us and how we should respond to them. It is vital that we do this at an international level, because the issues are not confined within national boundaries. The Roundtable provides a particularly valuable opportunity for judges, academics and policymakers from around the world to come together, away from the daily pressures of their working lives, to discuss the problems and contemplate possible solutions.

So it was that senior judges, academics and policy experts met at the Fourth Roundtable held at Durham Law School in the spring of 2024 to reflect upon how civil and commercial judges should respond to technological developments and climate change. Those who have contributed to this book have done us a great service. In setting down the essence of the discussions that took place at the Roundtable, they have crystallised the debate and opened it to a far wider audience. Each chapter provides a unique insight into the relevant issues and will, inevitably, provoke much thought and, it is to be hoped, discussion about them.

Throughout my own career in the law, there have, of course, been technological developments. Younger readers will not have known a world without domestic computers, but I remember making the transition from my electric typewriter to a computer, albeit not venturing beyond word processing at the start. A bit later on, there were emails, but they were initially considered rather daring, and paper documentation remained the norm. Just as we have learned to cope with developments such as these, and with the problems that attend them, so we must learn to deal with recent technological developments and with climate change. AI, for example, must be accommodated within the practice of law and within our justice systems, with a role as a valuable tool, but without it becoming our master.

Whilst our existing justice systems, laws and procedures will need to evolve to serve societies in the new circumstances, this book demonstrates that even now they contain within them the seeds of useful approaches. Our legal systems already have experience of international jurisprudence and international courts, and we can build upon this existing practice to address new global challenges. Expertise and methodology developed in the courts for assessing evidence may be of assistance in approaching the problem of truth decay. Existing legal constructs, such as trust concepts, can be developed so that they can be deployed in new areas, as has occurred in relation to climate change. This Foreword is not the place for detail. These are only examples of the wealth of material to be found in this book, which benefits hugely from the insights of contributors from different national and cultural backgrounds, who have brought their extensive learning, skills and experience to bear in discussing their subject matter.

Jill Black
Former Justice of the Supreme Court of the United Kingdom
June 2025

PREFACE

I have the pleasure of providing the preface for this very timely book that brings together contributions of leading senior judges of key jurisdictions on the common challenges their courts are facing. Durham University had the privilege of hosting the Fourth Judicial Roundtable (Roundtable) in the spring of 2024. This prestigious forum that features serving and retired judges from both civil and common law jurisdictions has been working together since 2016, meeting in different locations, primarily in Asia.

In 2024, the Roundtable ventured for the first time out of Asia and convened in Durham. Under the leadership of Sundaresh Menon and Anselmo Reyes (the latter is now the first overseas member of the Advisory Board of Durham Law School), the Roundtable brought together senior judges, academics, policy experts and Durham Law School faculty, including its distinguished alumna, Jill Black of the UK Supreme Court. The Roundtable explored urgent challenges for the courts and the judiciary, notably artificial intelligence (AI), as well as issues relating to data protection and privacy and climate change within the broader context of contemporary 'truth decay', which is to say declining social trust in previously respected sources of factual information.

The proximity of the University's Norman Castle and the 900-year-old Cathedral may have served as a reminder that the topic of the future of justice is a historically recurring one, and that truth decay is not a new phenomenon. Yet the sheer volume of information and the speed of AI automation, demand the deep and collaborative consideration displayed at the meeting and in this volume. While the law should aim at truth, the large language models underpinning many AI systems may or may not be aligned with the human values of truth-seeking and justice. The law itself will have a paradoxical role in regulating the very tools that have huge potential to enhance the capacities and decision-making of legal professionals.

Durham University has for some years been engaged in advancing sustainability, freedom, the rule of law, and the governance of AI, with a distinct methodological approach towards global dialogue. We have done this with a particular commitment to dialogue across jurisdictions to achieve the shared aspirations set out in the preamble of the United Nations Charter and the Sustainable Development Goals. Our International Dispute Resolution Institute was set up a few years ago in this spirit, and we continue to develop our innovative work at the interface between the law, disruptive technologies and climate change.

The key insights of the Roundtable, reflected throughout this volume, are too rich to encapsulate in this preface, but I wish to highlight a few areas:

First, while the use of AI may bring faster, more efficient decision-making, broader access to justice, and data-driven insights in judicial work, integrating AI into judicial processes must be done with careful oversight, ensuring that bias is mitigated and transparency is maintained. As Anselmo Reyes and Adrian Mak point out in their chapter, AI will work best when embraced as a collaborative partner. Automation bias may be suspect, but 'automation aversion' is no longer an option. In all cases, what matters is that human judgement remains the ultimate arbiter of justice.

Second, in a world where truth is increasingly contested, the legal forensic process offers a foundation for reasoned discourse and informed social and political debate. Yet, as David Goddard points out, the particular epistemological modality inherent in the common law court model – establishing facts to a desired level of confidence through the testing of evidence – is under unprecedented pressure. Internet and social media uniquely engage people's propensity to believe statements based on multiple repetitions and mobilise a strong sense of group identity around those beliefs. To tackle disinformation, there is an urgent need for safeguards to protect the integrity of public discourse and to rebuild trust in public institutions. There is, moreover, a fundamental distinction between viewing information as property and seeing it as a human right – an underlying difference that shapes how different legal regimes approach data protection and privacy. In that case, what authority does a national court have to compel the production of documents stored in a multi-region cloud environment spanning data centres across multiple jurisdictions? And how should a court navigate the issuance of an injunction intended to have worldwide effect, particularly in light of jurisdictional limits and principles of international comity?

Third, while environmental justice as we know it is largely confined to national and domestic jurisdictions, climate justice has expanded this to become a global issue. Given the varied approaches adopted in the Global North and Global South, and the recent advisory opinion of the International Court of Justice on the obligations of states in respect of climate change, it is now time for jurisdictions worldwide to work together and coordinate their responses effectively to address this existential global threat.

Reading through the contributions and thinking about this preface remind me of a famous quotation from the Analects (Book VII):

'Devote yourself to the Way, ground yourself in virtue, rely on benevolence, and delight in the arts.' 志于道，据于德，依于仁，游于艺.

The above Confucian line encapsulates a timeless model of moral and intellectual aspiration. It serves as a fitting tribute to the contributors of this volume – many of whom are senior judges who, despite the demands of their judicial responsibilities, remain deeply committed to reflection, writing, and engaging with the law not merely as a system of rules, but as a living expression of ethical and cultural values. This volume, therefore, celebrates legal minds who, while navigating the practical challenges of judging, continue to enrich our understanding of rapidly evolving issues facing human society, through thoughtful analysis and a shared commitment to the public good. It affirms that law is not only a profession, but also a lifelong process of cultivation – a path (道) grounded in virtue (德), infused with compassion (仁), and elevated by arts (艺).

I hope for this contribution to have the widest audience, and I look forward to Durham University continuing our close cooperation with the Roundtable.

Karen O'Brien
Vice-Chancellor and Warden of Durham University
August 2025

CONTENTS

PART III
TRUTH DECAY

PART IV
CLIMATE CHANGE

ACKNOWLEDGEMENTS

This book arises from the discussions that took place during the 4th Judicial Roundtable at Durham Law School from 23 to 26 April 2024. The editors thank Durham Law School, the Durham International Dispute Resolution Institute (DIDRI), and the Singapore Courts for organising the Roundtable, and the Singapore Academy of Law (SAL) and Kabushiki Kaisha Anselmo Reyes for their sponsorship. We acknowledge the contributions and insights of all who participated in the Judicial Roundtable. Their names are listed at the end of this book.

We are grateful to Dean Volker Roeben of Durham Law School for his hospitality and support of the Judicial Roundtable and to the many Durham Law School student volunteers whose transcription of the Judicial Roundtable's proceedings was indispensable to this book's preparation. We also extend our gratitude to the Secretariat from the Singapore Courts and Kabushiki Kaisha Anselmo Reyes for their invaluable assistance in coordinating the Judicial Roundtable, and to the many others at Durham Law School, the Singapore Courts, and the SAL who assisted with the Judicial Roundtable's logistics and the subsequent compiling of this book. We do not name each individually but express our deepest appreciation for their help.

Finally, we thank the Hong Kong-based artist Brian Chan Kwan-Lok for creating a painting for this book's cover which captures the themes canvassed at the Judicial Roundtable.

The Editors
1 May 2026
Singapore and Kyoto

LIST OF CONTRIBUTORS

James Allsop AC is an International Judge of the Singapore International Commercial Court and was formerly Chief Justice of the Federal Court of Australia.

Andrew Bell AC is Chief Justice of New South Wales and President of the Judicial Commission of New South Wales.

Dhananjaya Y Chandrachud is a former Chief Justice of India. He is an arbitrator and consultant; author and an academic.

Du Weike is the Deputy Chief Judge of the Intellectual Property Court of the Supreme People's Court of the People's Republic of China.

Gao Xiaoli is a Vice-President of the Supreme People's Court of the People's Republic of China.

David Goddard is an International Judge of the Singapore International Commercial Court, a Professorial Fellow at the University of Melbourne Law School, and Special Advisor to the Chief Justice of New Zealand on Digital Technologies. He was formerly a Judge of the New Zealand Court of Appeal.

Goh Yihan is a Deputy Attorney-General of Singapore.

Dirk Hartung is an Assistant Professor of Law at the Yong Pung How School of Law, Singapore Management University.

Philip Jeyaretnam is President of the Singapore International Commercial Court.

Godfrey Lam is a Justice of Appeal of the Court of Appeal of Hong Kong SAR.

Adrian Mak is a founding member of Anselmo Reyes KK and a fellow at the Stanford Law AI Initiative.

Sundaresh Menon is Chief Justice of Singapore.

Hri Kumar Nair is a Justice of the Court of Appeal of the Supreme Court of Singapore. He was formerly a Deputy Attorney-General and a Member of Parliament.

David Neuberger is an International Judge of the Singapore International Commercial Court and was formerly President of the Supreme Court of the United Kingdom.

Matthew S R Palmer is a Judge of the Court of Appeal of New Zealand.

Nallini Pathmanathan is a former Judge of the Federal Court of Malaysia.

Anselmo Reyes is an International Judge of the Singapore International Commercial Court.

Arjan Sikri is an International Judge of the Singapore International Commercial Court and a former Judge of the Supreme Court of India.

Jacob Turner is a barrister at Fountain Court Chambers.

Yeong Zee Kin is Chief Executive of the Singapore Academy of Law and Senior Fellow with the Lee Kuan Yew School of Public Policy and the Future of Privacy Forum; he is also a member of OECD's Network of Experts on AI (ONE AI).

INTRODUCTION

SUNDARESH MENON*

Law and order have been the foundations upon which our societies have organised themselves since time immemorial. By providing a fair and predictable framework for disputes to be resolved effectively, efficiently and proportionately, our legal and judicial systems have enabled communities to live together, to agree on systems of societal governance, to protect spaces for individual interests within limits that also protect the wider society, and to transact with one another in a range of settings. These systems have promoted the public good while also allowing the rights and interests of individuals to flourish.

The success of this venture depends on several factors. But of particular interest is the vital need to ensure that the *systems* that administer justice, the substantive body of *laws*, the *procedural architecture*, and the *people* who advocate, interpret and apply these laws are all in step with the realities of the milieu in which they are to operate. When these are not in step – either because the systems, laws and processes to regulate critical issues are not in existence, or because the people called upon to apply those laws have no real appreciation or understanding of the issues that these laws are designed to address – the system cannot and will not function well.

Some examples of how our legal systems and laws have had to change to adapt to the times will illustrate the point.

I. The Rise of Specialised International Commercial Courts

The first is the pioneering establishment of the London Commercial Court (LCC) in 1895. The creation of the LCC was primarily driven by the London mercantile community's desire for swifter and more cost-effective dispute resolution mechanisms.[1] To better meet these needs, the LCC was set up as a *specialised* commercial court with several unique and innovative features for its time. These included flexible processes that could be tailored to each case, and a practice where all interlocutory applications were heard by judges who could take control of cases from the outset, instead of having these dealt with by Masters.[2]

* The author is deeply grateful to his colleagues, Assistant Registrars Wee Yen Jean, Ong Kye Jing and Bryan Ching, for all their assistance in the research for and preparation of this chapter.

[1] Lord Hamblen of Kersey, 'The Commercial Court: Past, Present and Future', Annual Combar Lecture 2020 (13 October 2020) 3.

[2] ibid 6.

More recently, the advance of globalisation and the proliferation of cross-border trade and investment have led to a growing demand for sophisticated *neutral* forums that are capable of resolving international commercial disputes fairly, efficiently and effectively. This has resulted in the rapid growth of other international commercial courts (ICCs) in addition to the LCC, especially over the last two decades. These ICCs have had to adapt themselves to address the unique demands of international parties seeking a dispute resolution mechanism that *combined* the best practices in international commercial arbitration with the advantages of a domestic court-based system. This was precisely the approach we took in structuring the Singapore International Commercial Court (SICC), which celebrated its tenth anniversary in 2025. Some notable features of the SICC include these:[3]

(a) First, to resolve disputes proportionately and efficiently, cases in the SICC are dealt with based on a bespoke set of procedural rules that draws and builds upon the best practices in both arbitration and international litigation, including those of other commercial courts, while remaining flexible and adaptable to best suit the parties' needs and preferences.[4]
(b) Second, unlike in the domestic courts, questions of foreign law can be addressed through submissions by foreign lawyers of the parties' choice who are registered with the SICC, even if they are not qualified to practice in Singapore.[5]
(c) Third, the SICC bench comprises a diverse and global panel of specialist commercial judges who are experts in commercial law and who are involved in robust case management from the outset. Unlike in arbitration, where there is a long-standing practice of party-appointed arbitrators, judges in the SICC are assigned to their cases directly by the Court and this avoids any possible concerns over their neutrality.

II. The Development of US Constitutional Jurisprudence

Apart from legal institutions, laws too need to adapt to societal changes, and this can be seen, for example, in the development of the constitutional jurisprudence in the United States (US).

One prominent example is the dramatic change in stance of the US Supreme Court towards President Franklin Roosevelt's New Deal in the 1930s. The New Deal

[3] S Menon, 'The Transnational System of Commercial Justice and the Place of International Commercial Courts', lecture in Bahrain (9 May 2023) paras 55–69. Other key features of the SICC are: (a) the SICC can join third and related parties without their consent, which is vital in multi-party and multi-contract disputes; (b) generally, hearings are conducted in open court and written reasoned judgments are published, therefore enhancing public accountability, legitimacy and the development of international commercial law; and (c) matters before the SICC may be appealed against to the Court of Appeal and this avenue for error-correction promotes trust and confidence in the process. However, in line with party autonomy, the appellate mechanism may be excluded or limited by contract.

[4] Singapore International Commercial Court Rules 2021 (SICC Rules).

[5] SICC Rules O 16, r 8(1). This may be contrasted with the traditional common law approach of evidential proof, where evidence on foreign law is often given by legal experts of the foreign law in question, who are then subject to cross-examination.

comprised a series of social and economic legislative measures that were regarded by the Roosevelt administration as necessary to lift the US out of the Great Depression, and which represented a significant expansion of the role of government in the economy. However, a series of US Supreme Court decisions had struck down various aspects of the New Deal as being unconstitutional,[6] such as minimum wage legislation which the Court considered to have interfered impermissibly with the 'liberty' of employers and employees to negotiate the terms of employment contracts, within the meaning of the Due Process Clauses in the Fifth and Fourteenth Amendments.[7] This threatened to derail the President's agenda to such an extent that he sought to increase the number of seats on the Supreme Court through a Bill which has been famously referred to as the 'court-packing plan'.[8] Central to this Bill was a provision that granted the President the power to appoint an additional member of the Court, up to a maximum of six, for every member that was above the age of 70 and who had declined to retire.

This seemingly intractable situation was eventually resolved when the Supreme Court in *West Coast Hotel v Parrish*[9] departed from the legal position that had prevailed until then and upheld the constitutionality of minimum wage legislation. In doing so, it recognised that the legislature had a 'wide field of discretion' to impose regulations to protect 'health and safety' and to ensure 'wholesome conditions of work and freedom from oppression'.[10] It remains a matter of debate as to the extent to which the Supreme Court's decision in *West Coast Hotel* was influenced by the court-packing plan, which eventually failed to pass the Senate.[11] Nonetheless, in deciding *West Coast Hotel*, the Court expressly referred to the need to consider the issue afresh in light of the 'economic conditions which have supervened' and the 'unparalleled demands for relief' which arose during the Great Depression.[12] This was a direct recognition of the reality that the law must evolve in response to changing economic and societal demands.

Yet another example from the US is the evolution of the constitutional jurisprudence on the issue of racial segregation in public schools. In 1896, the Supreme Court upheld in *Plessy v Ferguson* the constitutionality of racial segregation laws, so long as the educational facilities provided to each race were substantially equal in quality, in what came to be known as the 'separate but equal' doctrine.[13] About half a century later, the Supreme Court unanimously held in *Brown v Board of Education* that separate educational

[6] The most famous of these cases are arguably the trio of decisions which were issued by the US Supreme Court on 27 March 1935, which has been referred to as 'Black Monday': see *A.L.A. Schechter Poultry Corp. v United States* 295 US 495 (1935); *Louisville Joint Stock Land Bank v Radford* 295 US 555 (1935); and *Humphrey's Executor v United States* 295 US 602 (1935).

[7] GE White, '*West Coast Hotel's* Place in American Constitutional History' (2012) 122 *Yale Law Journal Online* 69.

[8] Judicial Procedures Reform Bill of 1937.

[9] *West Coast Hotel Co. v Parrish* 300 US 379 (1937).

[10] ibid 393.

[11] See White (n 7) 71–73. The contemporary narrative was that the Supreme Court's shift in *West Coast Hotel* was driven by the need to preserve the judiciary's integrity and independence, in the face of the proposed court-packing plan. This gave rise to the phrase 'the switch in time that saved nine'. This narrative has been questioned in later historical accounts. Internal court papers revealed that Justice Owen Roberts (who was the swing vote) had indicated his vote to sustain the legislation in question before the public announcement of the court-packing plan.

[12] *West Coast Hotel* (n 9) 390 and 399.

[13] *Plessy v Ferguson* 163 US 537 (1896).

facilities were *inherently* unequal, and therefore violated the Equal Protection Clause of the Fourteenth Amendment.[14] For present purposes, what is of note is that the court in *Brown* acknowledged that its decision was influenced by changing societal attitudes towards the importance of education as well as new psychological research on the detrimental effects of segregation.[15]

III. The Perfect Long Storm: Unprecedented Challenges

These examples share a common feature. They reflect changes that came to be realised over time – in some cases, a considerable period of time – as the acceptance emerged that change was needed in order to enable society to function well.

But we are now in an era that is marked by several key features, the confluence of which is unprecedented. Inevitably, this has consequences for the custodians of our justice systems. To begin with, the world is more connected now than ever before. This is well-illustrated by the rapid spread of COVID-19 across the whole world and the hold it took on our lives within an astonishingly short period of time. A global pandemic was declared by the World Health Organisation within just three months of the virus being detected for the first time.[16] As hard as it might now be to imagine this, it was just a few short years ago that borders were completely shut and the world at large turned inwards. And the looming threat of future global public health crises arising from diseases such as Mpox is a vivid reminder both of our interconnectedness and of our shared vulnerability.

Further, we are living at a time defined by several other world-altering events. For example, as technology permeates every aspect of our lives, and as its capability and sophistication grow at an alarming pace, we are confronted with the need to think about whether and how we will regulate its use. The launch of new artificial intelligence (AI) models that are said to have developed *reasoning* capabilities holds great promise in areas such as science and mathematics, and potentially even the law.[17] But it begs the question of how we can ensure that these increasingly powerful models are to be deployed for the benefit of *all* of humanity, and not just for those able to access, operate and take the best advantage of these models. Apart from this, are there areas where we need to forbear from resorting to AI? And what about the impact that technology has had on the flow of information in societies? The creation of alternative channels of mass communication has undoubtedly changed the ways in which we share and receive our information, and it has also affected its reliability. Perhaps because of this, we have seen the growing use of these channels to foment violence in societies. How are values such as free speech to be understood in this new reality?

These are just some of the many questions that present themselves with the rise of technology. And technology is, of course, not the only global challenge that we have

[14] *Brown v Board of Education of Topeka* 347 US 483 (1954).

[15] ibid 493–494.

[16] World Health Organisation, 'Coronavirus Disease (COVID-19) Pandemic', available at www.who.int/europe/emergencies/situations/covid-19.

[17] OpenAI, 'Introducing OpenAI o1-preview' (12 September 2024), available at www.openai.com/index/introducing-openai-o1-preview.

witnessed in recent times. In the geopolitical space, we are witnessing some of the most serious wars and conflicts since the end of the Second World War, in particular, those in Ukraine and the Middle East. Then, there are the rising tensions between the major superpowers. There are also other challenges which confront us and require urgent responses, including the existential threat of climate change; cybersecurity issues that arise especially from the profound impact of quantum computing; the proliferation of disinformation and misinformation; and the problem of inequality and less inclusive growth. Taken together, these form a 'perfect long storm' of global challenges,[18] which are best understood as *an unprecedented confluence of long-term, complex and structural shifts in the world order* that will have a direct bearing on legal and judicial systems.[19]

IV. The Judicial Roundtable on the Future of Justice

It was in these circumstances that the need was felt for a unique forum that would bring together senior judges, legal academics and policy-makers from both civil and common law jurisdictions. The object of this forum is to imagine the emerging issues that the law will need to address, and to think about how the law should respond to these changes that are impacting us at a rate and scale that is simply astounding. To capture its mission, we called it the Judicial Roundtable on the Future of Justice (Roundtable), and the case for its existence rests on the essential premise that it is worth thinking about these issues and our possible responses to them in a relatively unhurried setting before we are forced to encounter them in the courtroom. The work of the Roundtable will maintain a particular emphasis on commercial courts and international commercial dispute resolution, but it will not be limited to this.

A charter has been prepared to capture the mission of the Roundtable and the modality of its operation. The Roundtable has entered into anchor partnerships with the Singapore Management University Yong Pung How School of Law, the Durham Law School and the Singapore Judicial College, and its agenda is steered by an advisory board that includes in its membership respected and experienced judicial leaders.

The Roundtable traces its origins to 2016, when it was first run as part of a course offered at the University of Hong Kong Faculty of Law. Its subsequent evolution saw the Supreme Court of Singapore becoming a collaborator in this project in 2019. The Third Roundtable, hosted remotely by the Supreme Court of Singapore in 2021 and jointly organised with the Shanghai University of Political Science & Law and the University of Hong Kong Faculty of Law, resulted in a book published by Hart Publishing, entitled *Transnational Commercial Disputes in an Age of Anti-Globalism and Pandemic*.[20]

The Fourth Roundtable took place in April 2024 at the Durham Law School in England, and it focused on how civil and commercial judges should respond to

[18] T Shanmugaratnam, 'Responding to a Perfect Long Storm', speech delivered at the IMAS-Bloomberg Investment Conference (9 March 2022).

[19] S Menon, 'The Role of the Judiciary in a Changing World', inaugural Supreme Court of India Day Lecture (4 February 2023) paras 6–7.

[20] S Menon and A Reyes (eds), *Transnational Commercial Disputes in an Age of Anti-Globalism and Pandemic* (Oxford, Hart Publishing, 2023).

technological developments and climate change. The intention was that the fruits of those discussions should be made as widely available as possible.

Hence, the publication of this book, which captures the discussions that took place among a group of around 25 senior judges and a similar number of academics and policy experts at the Durham Law School. The book is organised in four parts. The first three parts cover three related topics under the overarching theme of technology, namely, *AI*, *data protection and privacy*, and *truth decay* (which refers to the devaluation of truth in societies). The fourth and final part of the book relates to *climate change*. Each part of the book is divided into various chapters and begins with a chapter that sketches out the discussion covered in the chapters that follow and which contains a synthesis of the key points and conclusions reached during the Roundtable. In this way, these introductory chapters serve as a useful primer for the remaining chapters, which are intended to function not only as a record of our deliberations, but also as potential roadmaps for navigating some of the complex legal issues that we will face in our rapidly changing world. It is in the spirit of mutual learning and collaboration that we invite you, the reader, to join us as we explore and shape *The Future of Justice*.

PART I

Artificial Intelligence

1

Introduction to Artificial Intelligence

ANSELMO REYES AND ADRIAN MAK

Justice systems worldwide are on the brink of transformation, driven by the rise of AI. Once confined to science fiction, AI – particularly large language models (LLMs), machine learning (ML), and agentic AI – now holds the potential not just to automate tasks but to redefine justice, fairness, and human judgement. This chapter introduces the role of AI in the legal system and sets the stage for deeper exploration in the following sections.

Beyond automating repetitive tasks, AI is becoming a collaborative partner, offering insights, recognising patterns, and providing alternative interpretations of legal texts. However, this potential brings challenges, including bias, transparency, and the balance between human judgement and machine autonomy. This chapter lays the foundation for further discussion on the integration of AI into dispute resolution, legal practice, and judicial systems, focusing on how to responsibly harness these technologies to ensure equity, transparency, and accountability.

I. Key Terms and Concepts

Before exploring the transformative impact of AI on dispute resolution, it is crucial to establish a shared vocabulary. The field of AI is rapidly evolving, often outpacing the development of clear and consistent terminology. This section aims to provide conceptual clarity by introducing key terms and concepts that are central to understanding the discussions in subsequent chapters.

(a) **Artificial intelligence or AI** refers to computer systems designed to perform tasks that typically require human intelligence.[1] These tasks encompass a wide range of capabilities, including visual perception, speech recognition, decision-making, and language translation. AI can be understood as the tangible real-world capability of non-human machines or artificial entities to perform, task solve, communicate, interact, and act logically as it occurs with biological humans.

[1] See, eg, International Organization for Standardization and International Electrotechnical Commission, 'ISO/IEC 22989:2022(E)' (2022); E Lim and P Morgan (eds), *The Cambridge Handbook of Private Law and Artificial Intelligence* (Cambridge, Cambridge University Press, 2024).

(b) **Machine learning or ML** is a subset of AI that focuses on the development of algorithms and statistical models that enable computer systems to improve their performance on a specific task through experience.[2] ML allows systems to learn from data without being explicitly programmed. Key aspects of ML include pattern recognition, data-driven predictions, and automated decision-making.

(c) **Deep learning (DL)** is a specialised subset of ML that uses artificial neural networks with multiple layers to model and process complex patterns in data.[3] DL algorithms are particularly effective in tasks such as image and speech recognition, natural language processing and autonomous systems.

(d) **Large language models or LLMs** are a specific type of AI system that focuses on natural language processing and generation.[4] They are massive neural networks trained on vast amounts of text data, capable of understanding and generating human-like text. LLMs represent one of the most advanced applications of DL in the field of natural language processing.

(e) **Natural language processing (NLP)** is a branch of AI focused on enabling computers to understand, interpret, and generate human language.[5] NLP is crucial for applications like machine translation, chatbots, and text analysis. It combines computational linguistics with statistical, ML, and DL models to process and analyse large amounts of natural language data. NLP technologies are fundamental in bridging the gap between human communication and computer understanding.

(f) **Reinforcement learning** is a type of ML where an agent learns to make decisions by interacting with an environment.[6] The agent performs actions, receives rewards or penalties, and adjusts its behaviour to maximise cumulative rewards.

(g) **Agentic AI** represents a significant advance in AI, introducing new capabilities for autonomous decision-making and goal-oriented behaviour.[7] These AI systems can operate independently, making decisions based on their programming and available information. These systems pursue complex objectives, navigating multi-step processes in dynamic environments. They can adjust strategies and behaviours in response to feedback and changing circumstances.

(h) **Prompting**, in the context of LLMs, refers to the technique of providing input or instructions to guide the model's output.[8] For example, **chain-of-thought**

[2] See, eg, S Brown, 'Machine Learning, Explained' (*MIT Sloan School of Management*, 21 April 2021), available at mitsloan.mit.edu/ideas-made-to-matter/machine-learning-explained.

[3] See, eg, G Ras et al, 'Explainable Deep Learning: A Field Guide for the Uninitiated' (2021) arXiv:2004.14545 [cs.LG].

[4] See, eg, H Naveed et al, 'A Comprehensive Overview of Large Language Models' (2024) arXiv:2307.06435v8 [cs.CL]; V Rawte et al, 'The Troubling Emergence of Hallucination in Large Language Models – An Extensive Definition, Quantification, and Prescriptive Remediations' (2023) arXiv:2310.04988 [cs.AI].

[5] See, eg, F Yu et al, 'Natural Language Reasoning, A Survey' (2023) arXiv:2303.14725 [cs.CL].

[6] See, eg, M van Otterlo and MA Wiering, 'Reinforcement Learning and Markov Decision Processes' in M van Otterlo and MA Wiering (eds), *Reinforcement Learning. Adaptation, Learning, and Optimization*, vol 12 (Berlin, Springer, 2012).

[7] See, eg, Y Shavit et al, 'Practices for Governing Agentic AI Systems', available at cdn.openai.com/papers/practices-for-governing-agentic-ai-systems.pdf.

[8] See, eg, D Carlander et al, 'Controlled Chain of Thought: Eliciting Role-Play Understanding in LLM Through Prompts' (5 August 2024), available at www.semanticscholar.org/paper/Controlled-Chain-of-Thought:-Eliciting-Role-Play-in-Carlander-Okada/4149c7033deee384ba8efd8152cc0750422dbc4c.

(CoT) reasoning is a type of prompting technique used with LLMs to enhance their problem-solving and reasoning capabilities.[9] It involves encouraging the AI model to break down complex problems into step-by-step reasoning processes.

(i) **Retrieval-augmented generation (RAG)** is a technique that enhances the capabilities of LLMs by incorporating external knowledge sources during the generation process.[10] This approach aims to improve the accuracy, credibility, and up-to-date nature of the information produced by LLMs.

(j) **Context window** refers to the amount of text or information that a language model can consider when generating or processing text.[11] It is the maximum number of tokens (words or sub-words) that the model can process at once. The size of the context window is the model's 'short-term memory' and can affect its ability to handle long-range dependencies and maintain consistency in extended conversations or documents.

Having established key AI concepts, we turn to explore how AI represents not just a tool for promoting efficiency, but a paradigm shift that challenges the structure of judicial decision-making.

II. AI as a Paradigm Shift in Judicial Systems

Traditionally, legal systems have relied on human judges and lawyers to interpret laws, evaluate evidence, and render decisions. However, AI – particularly autonomous AI agents – introduces the possibility of automating complex legal tasks, thus forcing us to rethink how justice is dispensed.

The significance of this technological disruption is apparent from the attention judiciaries around the world have placed on it. In particular:

(a) Sundaresh Menon of Singapore acknowledges that AI developments are reshaping conversations about future societies and systems, with courts standing 'on the cusp of seismic shifts' that will affect justice systems.[12]

(b) In his 2023 Annual Report, Chief Justice John Glover Roberts Jr of the US Supreme Court underscored the potential of AI in law while warning of its risks. Unlike past technologies, AI demands a careful human-machine balance, particularly in reasoning. He emphasised that nuance – key to legal decisions – cannot be fully replicated by machines.[13] The challenge is defining what level of nuance humans, instead of AI, should handle and ensuring ongoing expert oversight and accountability.

[9] See, eg, J Wei et al, 'Chain-of-Thought Prompting Elicits Reasoning in Large Language Models' (2022) arXiv:2201.11903 [cs.CL].

[10] See, eg, P Lewis et al, 'Retrieval-Augmented Generation for Knowledge-Intensive NLP Tasks' (2020) arXiv: 2005.11401 [cs.CL]; Y Gao et al, 'Retrieval-Augmented Generation for Large Language Models: A Survey' (2023) arXiv:2312.10997 [cs.CL].

[11] See, eg, A Athar and S Teufel, 'Context-Enhanced Citation Sentiment Detection' (2012) *Conference of the North American Chapter of the Association for Computational Linguistics: Human Language Technologies* 597.

[12] S Menon, 'Judicial Responsibility in the Age of Artificial Intelligence', keynote speech at the Inaugural Singapore-India Conference on Technology (13 April 2024) para 5.

[13] JG Roberts Jr, '2023 Year-End Report on the Federal Judiciary' (31 December 2023), available at www.supremecourt.gov/publicinfo/year-end/2023year-endreport.pdf.

(c) Chief Justice Zhou Qiang of the Supreme People's Court in China has expressed support for incorporating AI in the judicial system. Gao Xiaoli and Du Weike's chapter (chapter four) highlights how under Chief Justice Zhou's leadership and that of his successors, the Supreme People's Court has actively promoted the use of AI and other technologies in the judicial system, including launching the 'Smart Courts' (智慧法院), which aims to create a networked, transparent, and intelligent informational system for all courts in China.

(d) Under Chief Justice Dhananjaya Yeshwant Chandrachud's leadership, the Supreme Court of India has already begun implementing AI in various ways. As discussed in DY Chandrachud's chapter (chapter six), since February 2023, AI has been used to translate judicial documents, conduct legal research, automate processes, and transcribe oral arguments. The Supreme Court has translated over 30,000 judgments into Hindi and over 17,000 into 16 other regional languages using AI. AI-powered live transcription services have been introduced, capable of translating judicial proceedings into 18 regional languages and Hindi.

Another way of conceptualising this paradigm shift is through understanding the metaphors and stories through which we describe the changes that are occurring.[14] A common metaphor used to describe AI's role in the legal profession is that of a junior associate or law clerk. Many suggest that LLMs could be deployed in legal settings to perform simple repetitive tasks, much like an entry-level lawyer. For instance, AI could be used to summarise case law, draft basic legal documents, or conduct preliminary legal research.

This analogy, while useful in some contexts, is misleading. If AI is only viewed as a tool for completing individual legal tasks, the profession risks losing sight of the value humans and machines can create together. By reducing AI's role to performing repetitive or routine task-oriented functions, we fail to recognise AI's potential to revolutionise legal workflows and reshape legal reasoning.[15]

A more apt metaphor would be to consider AI as a collaborative partner capable of unlocking legal knowledge embedded in written text but also in contextual experience and historical precedent. Properly integrated, AI systems can enhance human decision-making by providing insights, identifying patterns that have escaped human notice, and offering alternative interpretations of legal texts.

For example, as discussed in Dirk Hartung's chapter, GPT-4 passed the New York Bar exam with scores comparable to experienced legal professionals, demonstrating its ability to handle complex legal reasoning. A caveat is that LLMs are adept at gaming evaluation benchmarks such as a bar exam designed to test human understanding.[16] LLMs use pattern recognition and prior exposure to similar questions to achieve high scores. This would not constitute a contextual understanding of the law or its nuances in real-world practice.

Thus, while achievements to date are impressive, they should not be mistaken as evidence that AI can fully replace human expertise. Instead, AI models are better

[14] G Morgan, *Images of Organization* (Beverly Hills, SAGE Publications, 1986).

[15] Dr M Ma, keynote speech at the 2024 MIT Computational Law Workshop (29 January 2024), available at law.mit.edu/pub/2024-iap-workshop/release/3.

[16] S Yang et al, 'Rethinking Benchmark and Contamination for Language Models with Rephrased Samples' (2023) arXiv:2311.04850 [cs.CL].

viewed as collaborative tools that can augment the capabilities of legal professionals by enhancing efficiency and broadening the scope of legal analysis.

III. Scaling Laws, CoT Reasoning, Reinforcement Learning, Inference-Time, Larger Context Windows, RAG, Multimodality and Agentic AI

The pace at which AI is evolving demands that we engage in serious discussion now about its role in judicial systems, rather than wait until AI reaches more advanced stages such as Artificial General Intelligence (AGI) or so-called 'sentience'.[17] AI is already reshaping legal reasoning and decision-making through several key developments that go beyond basic automation.

A. Scaling Laws

A fundamental driver of recent AI progress has been the discovery of scaling laws, which reveal that AI model performance improves predictably as three key factors increase: model size (the number of parameters), dataset size (the amount of training data), and computational resources used for training.[18] Research has demonstrated that larger models trained on more data with greater compute consistently produce more capable systems, following mathematical relationships that allow researchers to forecast improvements with remarkable accuracy.[19] For judicial systems, scaling laws suggest that AI tools will continue improving in their ability to understand complex legal language, identify relevant precedents, and analyse intricate factual patterns. However, this predictable progression also heightens the urgency of establishing robust governance frameworks across the judiciary, society, and beyond, before AI capabilities outpace our regulatory and ethical safeguards.

B. CoT Reasoning

One advance is CoT reasoning, a technique employed by reasoning models like OpenAI o1 (o1), DeepSeek R1, and Gemini 2.5 Pro.[20] This approach allows AI systems to mimic human reasoning processes by breaking down complex legal problems

[17] D Hendrycks et al, 'A Definition of AGI' (2025) arXiv:2510.18212 [cs.AI].

[18] J Kaplan et al, 'Scaling Laws for Neural Language Models' (2020) arXiv:2001.08361 [cs.LG].

[19] J Hoffmann et al, 'Training Compute-Optimal Large Language Models' (2022) arXiv:2203.15556 [cs.CL]; T Henighan et al, 'Scaling Laws for Autoregressive Generative Modeling' (2020) arXiv:2010.14701 [cs.LG].

[20] OpenAI, 'Learning to Reason with LLMs' (12 September 2024), available at www.openai.com/index/learning-to-reason-with-llms; DeepSeek-AI et al, 'DeepSeek-R1: Incentivizing Reasoning Capability in LLMs via Reinforcement Learning' (2025) arXiv:2501.12948 [cs.CL]; K Kavukcuoglu, 'Gemini 2.5: Our Most Intelligent AI model' (*Google DeepMind Blog*, 25 March 2025) available at blog.google/technology/google-deepmind/gemini-model-thinking-updates-march-2025/#gemini-2-5-thinking.

into smaller, manageable components.[21] For example, when tasked with analysing a complex legal dispute, reasoning models can 'think' through the problem step by step, refining their strategies and correcting errors before providing a final decision. This method enhances the ability of reasoning models to handle intricate legal matters with a potential for greater reliability and increased transparency, since humans can review the AI's reasoning process. However, doubts remain about whether the steps LLMs write out truly reflect their internal reasoning, raising questions about the authenticity of their thought process.[22]

C. Reinforcement Learning

Reinforcement learning (RL) – where AI models learn through rewards and penalties – enables systems to improve their reasoning skills independently. RL allows AI to adapt and refine its decision-making over time by learning from interactions with its environment. A significant development in this area is reinforcement learning from human feedback (RLHF), which combines traditional RL with human input to guide the AI's learning process. This human oversight helps address complex, nuanced tasks in areas where defining an objective reward function is challenging, such as legal reasoning.

Similarly, approaches such as reinforcement learning from AI feedback (RLAIF) and imitation learning extend this alignment process by leveraging both model-generated evaluations and demonstrations from expert systems.[23] These methods enable iterative refinement of AI behaviour through scalable feedback loops, allowing judicial reasoning models to internalise nuanced interpretive patterns and emulate expert decision-making with greater consistency and transparency.

By integrating human expertise, model-generated evaluations and demonstrations from expert systems into the learning process, RL ensures that AI systems align more closely with judicial standards and ethical considerations, making them increasingly well-suited for the sophisticated reasoning required in judicial applications.

D. Scaling Up Inference-Time

Beyond training, scaling up inference-time – the time AI models are allowed to process a query – can significantly enhance their performance.[24] For instance, models like OpenAI's GPT-4o can essentially be upgraded into o1 by simply giving them more time to think. By allowing the model to take 30 seconds or more to process

[21] ibid; Wei et al (n 9).

[22] M Turpin et al, 'Language Models Don't Always Say What They Think: Unfaithful Explanations in Chain-of-Thought Prompting' (2023) arXiv:2305.04388 [cs.CL].

[23] See, eg, H Lee et al, 'RLAIF vs. RLHF: Scaling Reinforcement Learning from Human Feedback with AI Feedback' (2023) arxiv.org/abs/2309.00267 [cs.CL]; M Zare et al, 'A Survey of Imitation Learning: Algorithms, Recent Developments, and Challenges' (2023) arXiv:2309.02473 [cs.CL]; I Chrysomallis and G Chalkiadakis, 'Imitation Learning in the Deep Learning Era: A Novel Taxonomy and Recent Advances' (2025) arXiv: 2511.03565v1 [cs.CL].

[24] C Snell et al, 'Scaling LLM Test-Time Compute Optimally can be More Effective than Scaling Model Parameters' (2024) arXiv:2408.03314 [cs.LG].

difficult queries, the AI effectively engages in extended 'thinking time'.[25] This additional computational effort boosts their accuracy by enabling deeper analysis. In the judiciary, this extended 'thinking time' could help AI tackle complex legal issues with greater precision and reliability.

E. Larger Context Windows

Recent advances in AI context windows – the ability to process and analyse larger volumes of information – are particularly impactful for the judiciary. In legal contexts, where judges must sift through vast amounts of case law, statutes, and legal precedents, this capability is crucial. Traditional AI models struggled to handle extensive legal briefs or complex case documents in their entirety due to smaller context windows. However, newer models, like Claude 4.5 Sonnet, with a one million-token context window,[26] and Google's Gemini 1.5 Pro, with a two million-token capacity (equivalent to more than 3,000 pages),[27] can now process larger datasets.[28] This enables them to deliver more comprehensive, nuanced, and contextually accurate legal analyses, assisting judges in efficiently handling complex cases with extensive documentation, ultimately improving the depth and precision of judicial decision-making.

F. RAG

RAG has the potential to significantly enhance the accuracy of legal analysis in judicial systems by integrating case-specific documents such as pleadings, witness statements, and procedural filings into the AI's decision-making process.[29] By querying a vector database that stores these documents in mathematical representations, RAG allows an LLM to retrieve relevant case details, much like a journalist consulting a librarian for specific books.[30] This retrieval process enables the LLM to generate context-specific and legally coherent responses, ensuring that the AI's analysis is grounded in the precise facts and legal arguments of a case.

While RAG enhances legal accuracy by grounding AI responses in specific documents like case pleadings and witness statements, its effectiveness depends on the

[25] SM Kerner, 'OpenAI o1 Explained: Everything You Need to Know' (*TechTarget*, 17 September 2024), available at www.techtarget.com/whatis/feature/OpenAI-o1-explained-Everything-you-need-to-know.

[26] Claude Docs, 'Context Windows' (September 2025), available at docs.claude.com/en/docs/build-with-claude/context-windows. Anthropic, 'Claude 3.5 Sonnet' (21 June 2024), available at www.anthropic.com/news/claude-3-5-sonnet.

[27] L Kilpatrick et al, 'Gemini 1.5 Pro 2M Context Window, Code Execution Capabilities, and Gemma 2 are Available Today' (27 June 2024), available at developers.googleblog.com/en/new-features-for-the-gemini-api-and-google-ai-studio.

[28] Deepset, 'Long-Context LLMs and RAG' (20 August 2024), available at www.deepset.ai/blog/long-context-llms-rag.

[29] N Shaik et al, 'The Nexus of AI and Vector Databases: Revolutionizing NLP with LLMs' (2024) 8 *International Journal of Scientific Research in Engineering and Management* 1.

[30] W Xie et al, 'WeKnow-RAG: An Adaptive Approach for Retrieval-Augmented Generation Integrating Web Search and Knowledge Graphs' (2024) arXiv:2408.07611 [cs.CL].

quality and governance of the retrieved data.[31] Incomplete or biased documents can lead to flawed outputs, and while RAG reduces hallucinations, it does not entirely prevent them.[32] Proper data management and oversight remain essential to ensure the AI's analysis is both reliable and fair.

G. Multimodal AI

Recent advances in multimodal AI enable systems to process and reason across multiple types of data simultaneously, including text, images, audio, and video.[33] Multimodal LLMs can analyse photographs, interpret diagrams, transcribe audio recordings, and extract information from video footage.[34] For judicial systems, this capability is transformative. Legal disputes often involve diverse evidence types beyond written documents: surveillance footage in criminal cases, medical imaging in personal injury claims, architectural plans in construction disputes, financial charts in securities litigation, and photographs in property cases. Multimodal AI could enable more comprehensive legal analysis by reasoning across diverse evidence types within a single system, expanding its judicial applications.

H. Agentic AI Systems and Automated Design of Agentic Systems (ADAS)

Another promising development in AI-human collaboration is the rise of agentic systems. These are AI models designed to operate autonomously toward goals, capable of planning, taking actions, and reasoning over extended tasks in dynamic environments.[35] What sets agentic systems apart is their ability to self-reflect – to evaluate their own outputs and adjust their strategies based on feedback.[36] This capability allows AI systems to improve their performance recursively, ensuring that they remain useful as legal standards evolve.[37] In practice, this means that an AI agent could be designed to specialise in handling small claims, managing complex commercial disputes, or analysing constitutional law cases. For example, in Hri Kumar Nair's discussion of AI in the judicial system (chapter five), he emphasises the potential for AI to significantly reduce

[31] C Idemudia et al, 'Enhancing Data Quality Through Comprehensive Governance: Methodologies, Tools, and Continuous Improvement Techniques' (2024) 5 *Computer Science & IT Research Journal* 1680.

[32] IBM Technology, 'RAG Explained' (7 May 2024), available at www.youtube.com/watch?v=qppV3n3YlF8&t=10s.

[33] S Yin et al, 'A Survey on Multimodal Large Language Models' (2024) 11 *National Science Review* nwae403.

[34] See, eg, OpenAI, 'GPT-4 Technical Report' (2024) arXiv:2303.08774 [cs.CL]; Gemini Team Google, 'Gemini 1.5: Unlocking Multimodal Understanding Across Millions of Tokens of Context' (2024) arXiv:2403.05530 [cs.CL].

[35] Y Jiang et al, 'Understanding the Planning of LLM Agents: A Survey' (2023) arXiv:2309.00647 [cs.CL].

[36] N Shinn et al, 'Reflexion: an autonomous agent with dynamic memory and self-reflection' (2023) arXiv: 2303.11366.

[37] Z Ji et al, 'Towards Mitigating Hallucination in Large Language Models via Self-Reflection' (2023) arXiv: 2310.06271.

the burden on human judges by automating time-consuming tasks like drafting initial judgments or synthesising legal precedents.

An exciting frontier in agentic AI development is the ADAS. A novel research idea, it enables AI to design its own agents.[38] By automating the design of these agentic systems, ADAS could enable judicial systems to remain agile and adaptive. This flexibility and self-designing capability could allow AI to adapt to the changing needs of the judiciary, with each AI system optimally configured to support human judges in their decision-making.

The implications of these developments are profound. With CoT reasoning, RL, larger context windows, and AI agents, AI systems are approaching a point where they can not only assist with legal research but also engage autonomously in complex legal reasoning that was once the exclusive domain of human judges and lawyers. In Dirk Hartung's chapter on the administration of justice (chapter two), he explores how AI is transforming judicial workflows, particularly in procedural justice. This reshapes the role of judges and legal professionals, allowing them to focus on higher-level tasks that require human judgement and moral reasoning.

The progress of AI, especially in autonomous AI agents, means judicial systems cannot wait until AI becomes more capable. Courts must engage with these technologies now and develop frameworks for collaboration between human judges and AI systems. This collaboration will enhance efficiency while maintaining fairness, justice, and empathy as core human values of legal decision-making.

While these advances offer significant potential, they also introduce challenges, particularly around bias, transparency, and human oversight. These need to be addressed as AI becomes integrated into judicial systems.

IV. Challenges of AI: Bias, Transparency, and Trust

As AI becomes increasingly integrated into legal systems, addressing its challenges is paramount. These challenges align with broader priorities for science- and evidence-based AI policy, which emphasise the need to understand AI risks, increase transparency, monitor post-deployment harms, develop mitigation mechanisms, and build trust.[39] The judiciary and dispute resolution community are central to this process, particularly given the recognition by the Artificial Intelligence Act of the European Union (EU) of legal evaluation in dispute resolution as a high-risk AI application.[40]

A. Understanding AI Risks

AI's reliance on historical data introduces risks of bias, particularly in judicial decisions related to race, gender, or socioeconomic status. As detailed in Hri Kumar Nair's chapter (chapter five), these biases can perpetuate unjust outcomes. AI models trained

[38] S Hu et al, 'Automated Design of Agentic Systems' (2024) arXiv:2408.08435.

[39] R Bommasani et al, 'A Path for Science- and Evidence-based AI Policy', available at understanding-ai-safety.org.

[40] Regulation (EU) 2024/1689 (Artificial Intelligence Act) [2024] OJ L 2024/1689, Annex III.

on biased data may reinforce existing inequalities. RLHF can exacerbate these biases if human annotators unintentionally reinforce stereotypes.[41] To mitigate this, a deeper understanding of the unique risks posed by AI in legal contexts is essential.

B. Increasing Transparency

The black-box nature of many AI systems – referring to how the internal workings of AI systems are invisible to users[42] – poses significant challenges for the legal profession. As detailed in Jacob Turner's chapter (chapter three), without transparency in how AI models are designed and trained, it is difficult to assess their reliability.

Techniques have improved the accuracy of LLM models. These include advances in explainable AI, RAG approaches and prompting techniques which partially mitigate the problems just mentioned.[43] Yet, the continued pervasiveness of hallucinations demonstrates how LLMs present a challenge for legal systems that rely on transparency and explainability.[44]

Increasing transparency is crucial so that AI models used in judicial systems can be held accountable. This may include disclosing training data, model size, and capabilities, as well as establishing a registry for capable models to facilitate effective risk assessment. As Turner points out, AI-generated evidence must be accurate and open to scrutiny, especially when it is used in high-stakes legal decisions.

C. Monitoring Post-Deployment Risks

Effective use of AI in legal systems requires continuous monitoring to detect potential harms. Post-deployment mechanisms for adverse event reporting and real-time monitoring are essential for identifying misuse or bias in AI-driven legal outcomes, especially when LLMs are deployed in judiciaries. Early warning detection systems can help identify vulnerabilities before they lead to significant harm, so that AI systems remain safe and reliable in real-world applications.

D. Developing Mitigation and Defence Mechanisms

To address these risks, it is critical to develop mitigation and defence mechanisms. This includes creating technical safeguards to prevent AI misuse and exploring new approaches to AI alignment so that AI systems respect legal and ethical standards.

[41] GK Liu, 'Perspectives on the Social Impacts of Reinforcement Learning with Human Feedback' (2023) arXiv:2303.02891 [cs.CY].

[42] S Bagchi and The Conversation US, 'Why We Need to See Inside AI's Black Box' (*Scientific American*, 26 May 2023), available at www.scientificamerican.com/article/why-we-need-to-see-inside-ais-black-box.

[43] See, eg, Gao (n 10).

[44] M Dahl et al, 'Hallucinating Law: Legal Mistakes with Large Language Models are Pervasive' (11 January 2024), available at hai.stanford.edu/news/hallucinating-law-legal-mistakes-large-language-models-are-pervasive?fbclid=IwAR3OINcdoxptTBKLI85p9iyls_YFkDdQ_NcM7FggUdy9M7Wm3B6tuB2zA2o.

Defensive systems should also be put in place to protect judicial systems from cybersecurity risks and other AI-driven threats.[45]

E. Building Trust and Reducing Fragmentation

Building trust in AI systems is vital for their integration into judicial processes. The fragmentation within the AI community – between those advocating for strong regulation and those prioritising innovation – poses a challenge to creating a unified approach.[46] The judiciary and legal professionals must collaborate with AI researchers, policymakers, and industry experts to foster a cohesive AI policy framework. By doing so, the legal community can help shape the future of AI governance, ensuring that AI systems are safe and innovative.

In Dirk Hartung's chapter (chapter two), he emphasises that while AI can improve efficiency in legal processes, it can also undermine public trust if its decision-making processes are not transparent. Hartung argues that the integration of AI into legal systems must be accompanied by robust safeguards to ensure that AI-generated outcomes are explainable and accountable.

V. Human-AI Collaboration in Judicial Systems

Addressing these challenges – such as bias and the black-box problem – requires more than just technical solutions. It calls for active human oversight. In the next section, the potential for human-AI collaboration to create the necessary checks and balances to ensure fairness and accountability in judicial systems is explored.

A. Human Oversight and Accountability

While AI can provide significant support in judicial decision-making, human oversight remains essential to ensure that AI-generated outputs are consistent with legal principles and ethical values. A key concern surrounding the use of AI in judicial systems is the risk of automation bias – the tendency for humans to place too much trust in the decisions or outputs generated by automated systems. In the legal context, this could lead to situations where judges or lawyers rely too heavily on AI-generated recommendations without critically evaluating them or not sufficiently relying on them. On the other hand, automation aversion is also a concern; that is, a general distrust and preference for human recommendations over algorithmic ones.[47]

[45] See, eg, Y Xie et al 'Cybersecurity Risks and Threats in Avionics and Autonomous Systems' (2023) *IEEE Intl Conf on Dependable, Autonomic and Secure Computing, Intl Conf on Pervasive Intelligence and Computing, Intl Conf on Cloud and Big Data Computing, Intl Conf on Cyber Science and Technology Congress* 0814.

[46] See, eg, the debate surrounding California's SB 1047 AI Bill; H Dempsey, 'SIA Letter, SB 1047' (29 September 2024), available at subscriber.politicopro.com/f/?id=00000190-efa9-d94b-a79f-efab876b0000.

[47] D Pruss, 'Ghosting the Machine: Judicial Resistance to a Recidivism Risk Assessment Instrument' (2023) *ACM Conference on Fairness, Accountability, and Transparency* 312.

To deal with this, checks and balances in human-AI collaboration are necessary. AI-generated legal analyses or judgment drafts should always undergo human review, with judges trained to recognise AI's limitations, including potential bias or errors, and encouraged to apply their own judgement. In Jacob Turner's chapter (chapter three), he highlights the importance of transparency in AI-generated evidence, emphasising that judges must understand how AI models reach their conclusions. This collaborative approach ensures that AI provides insights, but human judges remain the final decision-makers.

For example, as detailed in Hri Kumar Nair's chapter (chapter five), one of the most immediate applications of AI-human collaboration lies in case management and decision support. By handling repetitive administrative tasks like document review, case scheduling, and evidence organisation, AI frees up human judges to focus on higher-level decisions that require nuanced legal reasoning and moral judgement.

Another key area where AI can support human judges is in legal research and document-drafting. In Dirk Hartung's chapter (chapter two), he emphasises that AI tools can be particularly valuable in jurisdictions where the volume of cases and legal documents is overwhelming. By automating routine legal research and drafting tasks, AI enables judges to spend more time on the substantive aspects of a case, ensuring that justice is both swift and thorough.

B. Supervisory AI Agents

A key development in AI-human collaboration is the concept of supervisory AI agents – autonomous systems designed to continuously monitor AI outputs, flagging potential biases or errors, and deferring important decisions to human experts. This 'AI monitoring AI' concept introduces a framework of self-regulation within AI systems. As detailed by CodeX, a partnership between the Law School and the Department of Computer Science of Stanford University, supervisory AI agents act as intelligent alarm systems, so that AI-generated legal analyses or decisions are subject to real-time review and human oversight.[48] These agents can play a pivotal role in maintaining accountability and fairness in the judiciary, enabling deviations from ethical or legal standards to be promptly identified and corrected.

C. Scalable Oversight

To ensure the responsible use of AI in judicial systems, a framework of scalable oversight is essential. Supervisory AI agents could operate at a granular level, continuously monitoring AI outputs for errors, biases, or inconsistencies in real time, while humans maintain oversight at a higher level. These AI agents can handle the constant flow of data and flag issues that might otherwise be missed by human reviewers due to volume or

[48] M Ma and J Nay, 'A Supervisory AI Agent Approach to Responsible Use of GenAI in the Legal Profession' (25 January 2024), available at www.law.stanford.edu/2024/01/25/a-supervisory-ai-agents-approach-to-responsible-use-of-genai-in-the-legal-profession.

complexity, with humans intervening when critical legal or ethical concerns arise. Such a multi-layered system, implemented by organisations such as Google's DeepMind, is designed to address the problem of monitoring and controlling increasingly complex AI systems as they grow in capability and autonomy.[49]

D. AI Literacy

Lastly, the legal profession must also prioritise AI literacy. As highlighted by Sundaresh Menon, judges, lawyers, and legal professionals need to understand how AI systems work and how they can be used responsibly in legal contexts.[50] Institutions such as the Singapore Judicial College are providing continuous education on AI, but global collaboration is needed to ensure that legal professionals worldwide are equipped to work with AI systems. Dirk Hartung argues that interdisciplinary collaboration between technologists, legal professionals, and policymakers is essential if AI is to be implemented in a way that aligns with legal values. Only through collaboration can we ensure that AI enhances, rather than undermines, justice.

Different jurisdictions are taking varied approaches to implement these principles. For example, Gao Xiaoli and Du Weike's chapter (chapter four) highlights how the Supreme People's Court of China has issued guidelines emphasising principles of security, fairness, human oversight, transparency, and ethical standards. These frameworks offer insights into balancing technological advancement with ethical considerations in large-scale judicial systems.

VI. Application of Human-AI Collaboration in Access to Justice

AI offers transformative capabilities, but human judgement must remain central to ensure fairness and accountability. One area where this balance between AI and human oversight can play a pivotal role is in expanding access to justice, particularly for marginalised groups.

This is discussed in DY Chandrachud's chapter (chapter six), where the focus is on adapting AI to India's diverse landscape. The chapter emphasises the need for AI models to accommodate a wide array of data inputs reflecting India's varied linguistic, cultural, and regional perspectives. It discusses the challenges of standardisation in such a diverse environment and the importance of contextualising AI design to ensure inclusivity and fairness. The chapter also explores strategies for mitigating biases and promoting transparency in AI systems to enhance their effectiveness and acceptance in India's complex societal context.

AI can significantly expand alternative dispute resolution (ADR) by offering innovative ways to resolve conflicts outside traditional courtrooms. As has been noted, 'AI will

[49] K Wiggers, 'Google DeepMind forms a new org focused on AI safety' (*TechCrunch*, 21 February 2024), available at www.techcrunch.com/2024/02/21/google-deepmind-forms-a-new-org-focused-on-ai-safety.

[50] Menon (n 12).

make EQ more important than IQ.'[51] While AI excels in cognitive tasks, it is emotional intelligence, interpersonal skills, and wisdom that will become increasingly critical – qualities that are essential in processes like mediation, where empathy and understanding play central roles in resolving disputes.[52] This shift towards mediation reflects the ability of AI to handle the technical aspects of legal disputes, allowing humans to focus on interpersonal dynamics and creative problem-solving. For instance, AI is already assisting mediators by generating creative solutions that parties might not have considered on their own.[53] By augmenting human decision-making and offering fresh perspectives, AI not only enhances the efficiency of mediation but also improves access to justice, making dispute resolution more affordable and accessible to a wider range of people.

Gao and Du's chapter (chapter four) highlights the People's Court Mediation Platform as a key advancement in ADR. This platform integrates various mediation resources, courts, mediation organisations, and mediators, facilitating numerous online mediations daily. This approach demonstrates how AI-enhanced systems can promote early conflict resolution and improve access to justice at the grassroots level.

Another exciting possibility is the development of AI-driven dispute resolution systems, where parties increasingly turn to AI for preliminary advice. While we do not yet fully understand the precise effects of AI on the legal dispute market, history suggests that technological revolutions often lead to the creation of new jobs and industries. The Jevons Effect supports this, indicating that as AI becomes cheaper and more useful, it will spur new applications and job opportunities.[54] For example, as Hartung mentions in his chapter (chapter two), more individuals may become aware that their issues are legal problems and turn to AI to resolve them. This increased demand could lead to the establishment of a human-tier appeal for reviewing AI decisions, combining AI's efficiency with the nuance and empathy of human judgement. This shift would not only expand access to justice but also create new roles for legal professionals in overseeing and refining AI-generated outcomes.

VII. A Roadmap Through AI and Justice: The Chapters Ahead

Having explored the foundational concepts, capabilities, and challenges of AI in judicial systems, the chapters that follow provide deeper examinations of specific dimensions of this transformation. Each chapter addresses critical questions about how AI is reshaping and should reshape the administration of justice.

[51] W Daniel, 'Larry Summers, Now an OpenAI Board Member, Thinks AI Could Replace 'Almost All' Forms of Labor. Just Don't Expect a 'Productivity Miracle' Anytime Soon' (*Fortune*, 28 March 2024), available at www.fortune.com/asia/2024/03/28/larry-summers-treasury-secretary-openai-board-member-ai-replace-forms-labor-productivity-miracle.

[52] See, eg, K Cloke, *The Dance of Opposites: Explorations in Mediation, Dialogue and Conflict Resolution Systems Design* (Dallas, GoodMedia Press, 2013).

[53] A Achar, 'Practical Applications of AI in Mediation: CPR Committee Meeting Highlights' (28 June 2024), available at www.cpradr.org/news/practical-applications-of-ai-in-mediation-cpr-committee-meeting-highlights.

[54] M Giampietro and K Mayumi, 'Unraveling the Complexity of the Jevons Paradox: The Link Between Innovation, Efficiency, and Sustainability' (2018) 6 *Frontiers in Energy Research* 26; R York and JA McGee, 'Understanding the Jevons paradox' (2016) 22 *Environmental Sociology* 77.

A. Chapter Two: Managing Legal Complexity Through AI

Dirk Hartung's chapter confronts a fundamental challenge: the unprecedented growth in legal complexity. Through empirical analysis, Hartung demonstrates how legal systems in major jurisdictions have experienced dramatic increases in the volume, interconnectivity, and hierarchical structure of legal rules. This growth has outpaced traditional human capacity to manage cases effectively. He examines how natural language processing and machine learning can address this complexity crisis while analysing the cognitive biases (automation bias and algorithm aversion) that influence how legal professionals interact with AI tools. His analysis provides essential context for understanding why AI integration is increasingly necessary for maintaining access to justice.

B. Chapter Three: AI-Generated Evidence in the Courtroom

Jacob Turner's chapter examines how courts should treat evidence generated by machine learning systems. Using a detailed case study of ML-based market manipulation detection, Turner reveals layered challenges: the quality of training data (the 'garbage in, garbage out' problem), the opacity of ML systems (the 'black box' issue), and the standards courts should apply when evaluating such evidence. While ML-generated evidence may be admissible under existing rules, Turner demonstrates that its effective use requires rigorous scrutiny and suggests courts may need new evidential standards, while legal professionals require enhanced technical literacy.

C. Chapter Four: AI in Practice – The Chinese Judicial Experience

Du Weike and Gao Xiaoli's chapter examines how one of the world's largest judicial systems has integrated AI across multiple dimensions of court operations. Their analysis details AI applications spanning case management, document automation, legal research, mediation, and decision support, from intelligent sentencing assistance to copyright dispute analysis. The chapter describes the institutional framework governing AI use, including principles of security, fairness, human oversight, transparency, and ethical standards established by the Supreme People's Court. This comprehensive implementation at scale demonstrates both possibilities and considerations for other jurisdictions, while highlighting how context and institutional structure shape AI deployment.

D. Chapter Five: Practical Considerations for Judicial Implementation

Hri Kumar Nair's chapter provides a framework for thinking through fundamental implementation questions: What types of cases suit AI assistance? What level of human oversight is necessary? How should we balance efficiency against fairness concerns? Nair distinguishes between 'Complementary AI' (augmenting human decisions) and 'Substitutive

AI' (replacing them), analysing challenges specific to each. His comparative approach examines diverse jurisdictions from the United States to Malaysia to China, illustrating different regulatory strategies through cases like *State v Loomis*.[55] The chapter connects AI's promise for enhancing access to justice through automated guidance and reduced processing times with the concrete considerations guiding responsible implementation.

E. Chapter Six: Ethical Implications and Justice System Values

DY Chandrachud's chapter confronts the most fundamental questions: What are the ethical implications of using AI in justice systems, and how can deployment align with core values of fairness, dignity, and equal treatment? Drawing on India's experience with extraordinary diversity, Chandrachud examines how ethical principles must guide AI implementation, emphasising 'contextualisation': designing systems with deep awareness of specific social, cultural, and institutional contexts. He explores critical issues including bias in training data and algorithms, AI's potential to perpetuate inequalities, and the importance of transparency for maintaining public trust. His framework of 'augmented intelligence', where AI enhances rather than replaces human judgement, connects to earlier discussions while grounding them in ethical principles and establishing that ultimate accountability must remain with human decision-makers.

F. Chapter Seven: Gen AI and the Legal Endeavour

Finally, Sundaresh Menon considers the role that Gen AI might play in advancing and enhancing the legal endeavour. He first provides an overview of the legal endeavour as well as of the legal method. Although Gen AI does not and cannot employ the legal method, he suggests that Gen AI can nonetheless go a long way towards addressing two of the most complex challenges affecting our legal systems: the problem of access to justice and the growing complexification of disputes. The chapter concludes with two key strategies to usher Gen AI into our legal systems, namely, the transformation of legal education and the adoption of an incremental and measured approach in incorporating Gen AI. As far as judiciaries are concerned, Menon proposes a matrix framework that could possibly guide how AI tools are introduced in our courts.

G. Connecting the Chapters

These chapters work together to provide a comprehensive examination from multiple angles:

(a) **Hartung** establishes necessity: legal complexity demands new approaches.

(b) **Turner** examines technical challenges: how do we evaluate AI outputs, particularly as evidence?

[55] *State of Wisconsin v Eric L Loomis* 881 NW 2d 749 (2016).

(c) **Du and Gao** demonstrate implementation: what does large-scale AI integration look like in practice?
(d) **Nair** analyses practical considerations: what questions must judiciaries answer during implementation?
(e) **Chandrachud** grounds everything in ethics: how do we ensure AI serves justice?
(f) **Menon** highlights the significant potential of Gen AI to address the challenges of access to justice and complexification and proposes concrete strategies that would allow us to maximise the capabilities of Gen AI in the most appropriate areas.

Together, they cover the theoretical (why AI is needed and what it can do), the practical (how it is being used and what governs its use), and the ethical (what values should guide deployment). This progression mirrors the journey judiciaries themselves must take: understanding the technology, learning from implementation experiences, and ensuring alignment with fundamental principles of justice.

VIII. Conclusion

As we stand on the brink of a new era in judicial innovation, it is clear that AI will not merely assist but also reshape the fabric of our legal systems. The promise of faster, more efficient decision-making, broader access to justice, and data-driven insights is tangible. Yet, as explored in this chapter, these developments come with significant responsibilities. The integration of AI into judicial processes must be done with careful oversight, ensuring that bias is mitigated, transparency is maintained, and human judgement remains the ultimate arbiter of justice.

The vision of AI as a collaborative partner – capable of self-reflection and continuous improvement through supervisory agents – offers a hopeful path forward. Supervisory AI agents and scalable oversight mechanisms serve as critical tools to ensure that AI systems operate within ethical and legal boundaries. However, even as AI systems grow more autonomous, they must not be allowed to replace essential human qualities of nuance, empathy, and moral reasoning in legal contexts.

The future of justice will be defined by how wisely we navigate the tension between AI's capabilities and justice's timeless values, between efficiency and wisdom, and between what machines can do and what humans must do. The chapters in this Part will explore these evolving dynamics, anticipating a future where technology and human values coalesce to elevate the administration of justice.

2

Artificial Intelligence in the Administration of Justice

DIRK HARTUNG

I. Introduction

> We have moved from being a society governed by the rule of law to being a society governed by the law of rules. We have become so completely seduced by the notion, borrowed from criminal law, that process ensures justice, that we have come to believe that process is justice. Yet to members of the public who find themselves mired for years in the civil justice system's process, process may be the obstacle to justice. It may be time – again – to rethink how civil disputes are resolved.[1]
>
> Rosalie Silberman Abella
> Justice, Court of Appeal for Ontario, 1999[2]

Justice systems around the globe currently face a challenging combination of developments: an increasingly globalised world witnessing the breathtaking advancement of digital technology, while geopolitical tensions run high and a majority of people lack meaningful access to justice. While some of the technological developments, such as the increase in processing power known as Moore's Law, and – to some degree – the decrease of the price for storage known as Kryder's Law have shaped the world for several decades,[3] the digitalisation of the legal profession discussed under the term 'legal tech' has really picked up speed only since 2010. It has meaningfully affected the business of legal service providers, in-house legal departments and courts.[4] Billions of dollars of venture capital have been poured into the legal tech space in the last couple of years,

[1] RS Abella, 'The Law Society of Upper Canada Professionalism Revisited', opening address at the Benchers' Retreat in Hockley Valley (Ontario, 14 October 1999).

[2] Appointed to the Supreme Court of Canada in 2004.

[3] See G Moore, 'Cramming More Components Onto Integrated Circuits' (1965) 38 *Electronics Magazine* 114 and C Walter, 'Kryder's Law' (2005) 293 *Scientific American* 32 respectively.

[4] C Veith et al, *How Legal Technology Will Change the Business of Law* (Hamburg, The Boston Consulting Group, 2016); C Veith et al, *Legal Operations: Getting More from In-House Legal Departments and Their Outside Counsel* (Hamburg, The Boston Consulting Group, 2018); D Hartung et al, *The Future of Digital Justice* (Hamburg, The Boston Consulting Group, 2022).

and more recently even into individual transactions.[5] The admittedly overinclusive TechIndex maintained by CodeX – the Center for Legal Informatics at Stanford Law School – currently lists over 3,000 legal tech companies.[6] The landscape of legal services has become more diverse with the advent of alternative legal service providers (ALSPs), including captive ALSPs that are owned by law firms.[7] Technology has influenced the business model, value proposition and operating model of legal service providers and changed the work of lawyers at all levels of seniority as well as altered the role of other professionals in law firms dealing with operations, information technology, finance, human resources and business development, marketing and communications.

In many regions, the judiciary has not kept pace with technological advancements seen in other sectors. With a few exceptions, such as Singapore, Austria, and the Civil Resolution Tribunal in British Columbia, Canada, many court systems lag behind the private sector and consumer expectations.[8] Extensive bureaucracies, outdated procurement processes, and antiquated procedural laws are just some of the obstacles encountered by innovative judges, clerks, and administrators. Additionally, the comprehensive inclusion of large populations, often dispersed across extensive territories and comprising diverse cultural identities and languages, presents a further challenge to the digitalisation of public infrastructure, including the judiciary.

More than half a decade ago, the World Justice Project estimated that over 5 billion people worldwide had unmet justice needs.[9] Nearly half of the people surveyed had encountered a legal problem within the preceding two years. However, only 17 per cent of these individuals sought resolution through an authority or third party, and just 29 per cent sought any form of advice. This low engagement was partly because less than a third of people recognised that their issue was legal in nature. Additionally, 17 per cent of individuals simply abandoned their efforts to resolve the problem, even when it persisted, with financial constraints or concerns being the primary reasons. This represents a global issue of societal proportions, and nearly half of those surveyed reported that these legal issues had negatively impacted their lives, leading to physical and stress-related health problems, or the loss of their job or home. This situation indeed paints 'a grim picture of the state of health of the global justice system, and none of us whose lives centre on the work of administering justice should be able to rest easily in this light'.[10]

[5] J Um, 'The Current State of Play in Legal Innovation: A New Era of Evolution in the Making (109)' (*Legal Evolution*, 11 August 2019), available at www.legalevolution.org/2019/08/the-current-state-of-play-in-legal-innovation-a-new-era-of-evolution-in-the-making-109; Clio, 'Clio Announces US $900M Investment at US $3B Valuation to Transform the Legal Experience for All' (23 July 2024), available at www.clio.com/about/press/series-f.

[6] techindex.law.stanford.edu.

[7] J Armour and M Sako, 'AI-enabled Business Models in Legal Services: From Traditional Law Firms to Next-generation Law Companies?' (2020) 7 *Journal of Professions and Organization* 27.

[8] Hartung et al (n 4).

[9] For all figures in this paragraph, see World Justice Project, *Measuring the Justice Gap – A People-Centered Assessment of Unmet Justice Needs Around the World* (2019), available at worldjusticeproject.org/our-work/publications/special-reports/measuring-justice-gap and World Justice Project, *Global Insights on Access to Justice – Findings from the World Justice Project General Population Poll in 101 Countries* (2019), available at worldjusticeproject.org/our-work/research-and-data/global-insights-access-justice-2019.

[10] S Menon, 'Judicial Responsibility in the Age of Artificial Intelligence', speech at the inaugural Singapore-India Conference on Technology (13 April 2024) para 23.

In some regions, these challenges are further exacerbated by demographic factors. In Germany, for example, significant portions of the judiciary are set to retire over the next decade, with some areas projected to lose half their judges by 2030.[11] This trend similarly affects the legal profession, creating *legal deserts* in rural and less populated areas, which in turn impacts out-of-court legal services such as wills, contracts, and negotiations.[12] Even in regions where populations are growing and more individuals are entering the legal profession, the outlook remains bleak. The complexity of legal rules tends to increase exponentially with population size, making it increasingly difficult to administer justice and manage legal issues in larger communities, as empirical research has shown.

More broadly, the general growth of legal complexity may be a key factor behind many of the developments hindering more effective access to justice.[13] Complexity often obscures the legal nature of a problem or conflict, and risks overwhelming and intimidating society's most vulnerable members. This complexity manifests in various forms, including statutes,[14] regulations,[15] court decisions,[16] and even the intricate structure of legal arguments.[17] While this growth is driven by an increasingly interconnected and globalised world, it significantly amplifies the volume and complexity of information that courts must process to render legal decisions. Unfortunately, the analogue tools available to manage this complexity – such as file systems, reasoning techniques, and methods for procuring and handling evidence – were often not designed to cope with such vast amounts of information. As a result, legal proceedings are often prolonged, leading to frustration among those seeking justice and burnout among those responsible for administering it.[18]

Digital technology, including tools applying machine learning and in particular *natural language processing (NLP)* – in other words, *artificial intelligence (AI)* – can be used to solve the central challenge posed by the combination of lack of access to justice, demographics and increasing legal complexity: the incapacity to handle all requests for justice appropriately due to insufficient time or expertise. The key is to increase productivity and enable the administrators of justice to process large amounts of information

[11] Legal Tribune Online, 'Richtervereinigungen warnen vor Personalmangel im Osten' (3 April 2023), available at www.lto.de/recht/justiz/j/justiz-personal-engpass-pensionierungswelle-ostdeutschland-brandenburg-sachsen-richter-staatsanwaelte-referendariat-jobs-karriere.

[12] For an introduction to legal deserts, see J Teufel and M Gallo, 'The Minimum Number of Lawyers Needed to Eliminate Legal Deserts in the United States (345)' (*Legal Evolution,* 11 December 2022), available at www.legalevolution.org/2022/12/the-minimum-number-of-lawyers-needed-to-eliminate-legal-deserts-in-the-united-states-345, who point to the American Bar Association, 'ABA Profile of the Legal Profession' (2020), available at www.americanbar.org/content/dam/aba/administrative/news/2020/07/potlp2020.pdf.

[13] See JB Ruhl, DM Katz and MJ Bommarito, 'Harnessing Legal Complexity' (2017) 355 *Science* 1377 for a brief introduction to the topic and area of research.

[14] DM Katz et al, 'Complex Societies and the Growth of the Law' (2020) 10 *Scientific Reports* 18737.

[15] C Coupette et al, 'Measuring Law Over Time: A Network Analytical Framework with an Application to Statutes and Regulations in the United States and Germany' (2021) 9 *Frontiers in Physics* 658463.

[16] A Phang, Y Goh and J Soh, 'The Development of Singapore Law – A Bicentennial Retrospective' (2020) 32 *Singapore Academy of Law Journal* 804.

[17] C Coupette, D Hartung and DM Katz, 'Legal Hypergraphs' (2024) 382 *Philosophical Transactions of the Royal Society A* 20230141.

[18] See SL Lustig et al, 'Inside the Judges' Chambers: Narrative Responses from the National Association of Immigration Judges Stress and Burnout Survey' [2008] *Georgetown Immigration Law Journal* 23, 57 for one such example in a particularly challenging societal context.

as efficiently as possible. This means drastically rethinking the administration of justice, turning courts from physical places into digital services,[19] and understanding justice as a digital, societal platform.[20]

AI holds the promise of substantial gains in efficiency within the administration of justice, offering a much-needed boost to productivity as the legal landscape becomes increasingly complex – a development that risks preventing society's most vulnerable from accessing justice. While many of the issues immediately affecting this group are individually rather simple and often involve repetitive fact patterns arising in a limited number of areas, their sheer volume and relatively low value mean that traditional sources of help are often not viable, as courts risk becoming overwhelmed by caseloads and legal professionals may be disincentivised from engaging in such work due to limited economic viability. At the same time, disputes in areas of greater complexity involving higher-value, lower-volume cases are absorbing judicial resources that are then lacking for more routine matters. If implemented correctly, AI has the potential to expedite legal proceedings, thereby creating a more favourable environment for businesses and meeting critical legal needs for both companies and citizens. However, achieving this requires a precise understanding of the underlying macro-trends, a thorough knowledge of the current capabilities of AI in the legal domain, a clear vision of what constitutes success, and the skilful integration of AI into a manageable and enforceable legal framework.

The remainder of this chapter is therefore structured as follows. The next section presents the imperative for heightened productivity in the administration of justice by outlining the significant increase in legal complexity. This is followed by an overview of the current capabilities of machine learning, particularly NLP tools, within the legal domain, advocating for their more rapid and comprehensive implementation in justice systems. The chapter then introduces two relevant cognitive heuristics – automation bias and algorithm aversion – and explores strategies to mitigate these biases. The final section distils a set of regulatory principles and practical solutions from the literature and existing frameworks for the deployment of AI in courtrooms across various countries. The chapter concludes with a brief discussion that encourages open-mindedness and offers an optimistic vision for the future of justice, enhanced by the thoughtful integration of AI.

II. Background: An Unprecedented Increase in Legal Complexity

The relentless global growth of digitally stored information is so widely acknowledged that it risks becoming a truism to state that the majority of the world's data has been generated in just the past few years.[21] However, this trend in itself holds limited signifi-

[19] For a comprehensive framework, see R Susskind, *Online Courts and the Future of Justice* (Oxford, Oxford University Press, 2019).

[20] An introductory review is provided by J Tashea, 'Justice-as-a-Platform' (*MIT Computational Law Report*, 7 December 2021), available at law.mit.edu/pub/justiceasaplatform.

[21] While the details differ from source to source, see www.statista.com/statistics/871513/worldwide-data-created for a rough estimate.

cance for legal professionals, as much of this data surge stems from areas with little or no overlap with the legal system, such as social media videos or sensor data from Internet of Things (IoT) devices. To assess the impact on the justice system and legal professionals, a thorough, domain-specific analysis is necessary, focusing primarily on legal data. Further complicating the issue, not all legal data holds equal relevance from a practitioner's perspective. A robust model of how information growth influences both the private and public legal systems must consider the degree of interconnection between different pieces of legal information, the cost and effort required to navigate them, and the mutual influence of various components of the legal system. Complexity science, which examines complex and sometimes adaptive systems,[22] has been identified as a valuable and productive approach to addressing these challenges.[23] Just as concepts like rational choice or efficiency and wealth maximisation provide a framework for the field of law and economics, complexity theory serves as the foundation for the emerging field of computational legal studies.[24]

Although various methods are available for studying complex systems, these systems are often analysed using *network analysis*. In this framework, nodes represent components, while edges represent the interactions between them. This network-based approach is particularly valuable for assessing the impact of increasing legal information on the legal profession, including within court systems. By conceptualising and analysing legal systems as networks, researchers can utilise network analytics – a sophisticated and comprehensive set of tools – to obtain reliable empirical insights.[25] However, due to the vast diversity and often limited accessibility of legal data worldwide, a comprehensive global analysis of the development of legal information and the resulting legal complexity has yet to be accomplished.

Using these tools, an analysis of the entire collection of federal statutes in the US and Germany over a period from 1994 to 2018 revealed significant growth in volume (measured by the number of words), interconnectivity (measured by the number of cross-references), and hierarchical structure (measured by the number of elements such as chapters or sections) in both countries, ranging from 51 to 83 per cent.[26] Over these 25 years, the volume of statutory law increased by a factor of more than 1.5, making it significantly more challenging to disentangle and navigate. Consequently, the existing taxonomy of thematic categories became overburdened, as legislation increasingly affected and regulated multiple areas due to the likely greater diversity of products and behaviours. Some of the largest and fastest-growing areas – such as healthcare, pensions, and consumer protection – directly concern some of society's most vulnerable. Others

[22] For an introduction, see complexityexplained.github.io.

[23] JB Ruhl and DM Katz, 'Harnessing the Complexity of Legal Systems for Governing Global Challenges' in V Galaz (ed), *Global Challenges, Governance, and Complexity: Applications and Frontiers* (Cheltenham, Edward Elgar Publishing, 2019).

[24] R Whalen (ed), *Computational Legal Studies: The Promise and Challenge of Data-driven Research* (Cheltenham, Edward Elgar Publishing, 2020) contains an overview of the field.

[25] See, eg, JH Fowler et al, 'Network Analysis and the Law: Measuring the Legal Importance of Precedents at the US Supreme Court' (2007) 15 *Political Analysis* 324; an older overview is provided in R Whalen, 'Legal Networks: The Promises and Challenges of Legal Network Analysis' [2016] *Michigan State Law Review* 539; a comprehensive introduction – in German only – can be found in C Coupette, *Juristische Netzwerkforschung: Modellierung, Quantifizierung und Visualisierung relationaler Daten im Recht* (Germany, Mohr Siebeck, 2019).

[26] All results of this paragraph can be found in DM Katz et al (n 14).

exert more indirect effects, for instance, through increasingly complex tax regimes that may undermine the financial sustainability of mechanisms ensuring access to justice. Given that both countries already had mature regulatory regimes, including a busy judiciary, in the early 1990s, the burden of managing this increase likely fell heavily on legal professionals, including judges and clerks.

An even more comprehensive picture emerged when federal regulations, drafted by agencies rather than Parliament, were included in the analysis for both countries over a comparable time frame.[27] The growth pattern observed in statutes also held true for regulations in both countries. However, in the US, the growth among regulations outpaced that of statutes across all three metrics – volume, interconnectivity, and hierarchical structure. Furthermore, the absolute amount of information contained in regulations was two to three times larger (depending on the metric) than that in statutes in the US. The workload for those tasked with analysing and applying these rules, including courts, has increased accordingly. The inclusion of regulations in the analysis further characterised the key drivers of growth. Housing, workplace, and health safety, data protection, and procedural law played a particularly significant role, all of which are directly relevant to access to justice. Taken together, the growth in both statutes and regulations may obscure the legal nature of a given problem or conflict and overwhelm and intimidate the vulnerable.

While these two studies confirm an ever-increasing workload for legal practitioners primarily from a structural perspective – focusing on cross-references and hierarchical elements – the content of the rules is equally critical. Another examination centred on the US Code – the compilation of all federal statutes – revealed additional factors contributing to this growing burden.[28] The analysis detected increases in duplications, the length of individual sections, ambiguity, the size of reference chains and trees, overly broad references, and sometimes an excessive reliance on natural language in the literal description of times, time periods, percentages, and monetary amounts, rather than using numbers and formulas. These content-related issues exacerbate the challenges of maintaining, applying, and interpreting legal rules, thereby contributing to an increased workload for legal practitioners from a substantive perspective. As a result, it is not only the structural complexity but also the intricacies within the content of legal texts that have made the task of legal professionals more demanding over time.

The increase in legal complexity is not confined to statutes and regulations but is also evident in court decisions themselves. Although court decisions have been extensively studied using network science,[29] the growth in complexity has not been as comprehensively demonstrated as it has for statutes and regulations.[30] Moreover, while some justice systems, particularly well-studied ones like Singapore's and specific parts of others,[31]

[27] All results described in this paragraph can be found in Coupette et al (n 15).

[28] C Coupette et al, 'Law Smells: Defining and Detecting Problematic Patterns in Legal Drafting' (2023) 31 *Artificial Intelligence and Law* 335.

[29] See, eg, Fowler et al (n 25).

[30] Though growth is a recurring theme in many macro-level analyses, see T Smith, 'The Web of Law' (2007) 44 *San Diego Law Review* 309.

[31] J Soh, 'A Network Analysis of the Singapore Court of Appeal's Citations to Precedent' (2019) 31 *Singapore Academy of Law Journal* 246.

such as the US Tax Court,[32] have shown a marked increase in complexity, this trend is not universal. For instance, studies have demonstrated that the US Supreme Court does not exhibit the same level of complexity growth, suggesting that the phenomenon is not consistent across all courts.[33]

Finally, courts are not alone in facing the pressures of increased legal complexity. Publicly traded companies in the US are required under the Securities Exchange Act of 1934 to file annual, standardised reports detailing their financial performance. These Form 10-K reports, mandated by the US Securities and Exchange Commission (SEC), include comprehensive information on the regulatory risks that companies face. Companies and their legal counsel are incentivised to present an accurate regulatory risk profile, as both overstatement and understatement could adversely affect their share price and expose them to liability if these risks materialise. An empirical analysis of these filings, from 1994 to 2016, using the SEC's Electronic Data Gathering, Analysis, and Retrieval (EDGAR) system, has revealed a significant increase in the number of regulatory acts overall and per filing.[34] As companies have been shown to face increasing regulatory exposure across a growing number of dimensions, their regulatory risk profiles have become more diverse, reflecting a more complex regulatory ecosystem. This trend towards greater legal complexity impacts not only companies and their legal advisors but also the courts, when some of these risks inevitably result in litigation.

III. State of the Art of AI in the Legal Domain

As justice systems confront increasing legal complexity alongside often adversarial demographic dynamics, their administrators cannot afford to sit on their hands. A significant, proactive enhancement in the justice system's capacity to manage this growing complexity is essential. Without such improvements, case backlogs will likely grow, and the duration of legal proceedings will extend, ultimately eroding public trust and diminishing civic engagement.

Given that the most straightforward solution – hiring additional public servants – is often unavailable due to financial and demographic constraints, it is essential to enhance the capacity for managing legal complexity at both systemic and individual levels. When increasing headcount is not an option, productivity can be improved through two key strategies: the adoption of more advanced tools and the optimisation of work processes. In this context, AI has the potential to serve both as an enhanced tool and a catalyst for reorganising work processes. While digital solutions in support processes, office management, and infrastructure have already been successfully implemented and are

[32] MJ Bommarito, DM Katz and J Isaacs-See, 'An Empirical Survey of the Population of US Tax Court Written Decisions' (2010) 30 *Virginia Tax Review* 523.

[33] G Goelzhauser, BJ Kassow and D Rice, 'Measuring Supreme Court Case Complexity' (2022) 38 *The Journal of Law, Economics, and Organization* 92; R Whalen, 'Modeling Annual Supreme Court Influence: The Role of Citation Practices and Judicial Tenure in Determining Precedent Network Growth' in R Menezes, A Evsukoff and MC Gonzalez (eds), *Complex Networks* (Heidelberg, Springer Berlin, 2013).

[34] MJ Bommarito II and DM Katz, 'Measuring and Modeling the US Regulatory Ecosystem' (2017) 168 *Journal of Statistical Physics* 1125.

not the focus of this chapter,[35] recent advancements in NLP, particularly the development of *large language models* (LLMs), have brought the development of substantive legal solutions within reach. These technologies hold promise for assisting in the factual and substantive handling of legal proceedings and the application of law. However, their actual effectiveness will depend primarily on their specific technical capabilities in dealing with the complexities of legal work.

To provide a first, intuitively understandable framework for evaluation, a recent study conducted an experiment in which GPT-4, an LLM developed by OpenAI, solved all three parts of the Uniform Bar Exam, a standardised test created by the National Conference of Bar Examiners and currently employed in one way or another in 41 of the 56 US jurisdictions as a requirement to be admitted to legal practice.[36] The results were quite impressive and a significant improvement over previous models, with an average accuracy of 75 per cent in the multiple-choice (MBE) section and reaching an average score of 4.2 of 6.0 in the essay (MEE) and practical application (MPT) parts. If this performance were graded in the same manner as a human test taker, the results would be approximately 297 points, which is not only sufficient for passing the bar in all jurisdictions but also actually surpasses most human test takers and falls within a high percentile (68th to 90th) of overall results.[37] This result was astonishing, and it demonstrates that the current generation of models has reached a level which was nearly unimaginable just a few years ago.[38]

Obviously, testing a machine on an exam designed for human beings has severe conceptual limitations. Technical evaluation mechanisms for machine learning models, known as *benchmarks*, are usually employed to address these limitations. Many of the most popular NLP benchmarks are geared towards general language and therefore contain tasks from a great variety of domains. As a result, they are only of limited use for evaluating domain-specific performance for legal use cases. To mitigate this, legal domain-specific benchmarks have been created, with two currently standing out as particularly popular: LexGLUE[39] is the narrower, yet more widely used European one, while LegalBench[40] is a collaboratively built, much larger American benchmark specifically built for measuring legal reasoning in LLMs. While a variety of models have been tested on these benchmarks globally, there are currently no independent results for the latest generation of models on these benchmarks. The proprietary nature of these models, their extensive and ongoing training on all available data from the internet, and the general lack of the typical open-source availability make it challenging to evaluate

[35] For an overview, see Hartung et al (n 4).

[36] DM Katz et al, 'GPT-4 Passes the Bar Exam' (2024) 382 *Philosophical Transactions of the Royal Society A* 20230254, which contains the results presented in this paragraph.

[37] E Martínez, 'Re-evaluating GPT-4's Bar Exam Performance' [2024] *Artificial Intelligence and Law* 1 demonstrated the lower bound of the percentile range indicated and compared the results to those of another cohort of test takers than the original paper. The actual successful passing was confirmed.

[38] The finding seems to be somewhat generalisable, see S Schweitzer and M Conrads, 'The Digital Transformation of Jurisprudence: An Evaluation of ChatGPT-4's Applicability to Solve Cases in Business Law' [2024] *Artificial Intelligence and Law* 1–26.

[39] I Chalkidis et al, 'LexGLUE: A Benchmark Dataset for Legal Language Understanding in English' in S Muresan, P Nakov and A Villavicencio (eds), *Proceedings of the 60th Annual Meeting of the Association for Computational Linguistics (Volume 1: Long Papers)* (Dublin, Association for Computational Linguistics, 2022).

[40] N Guha et al, 'LegalBench: A Collaboratively Built Benchmark for Measuring Legal Reasoning in Large Language Models' (2024) *Advances in Neural Information Processing Systems 36* (there are currently 40 authors).

these models using established academic best practices. The international research community is gradually adapting to this new paradigm of commercially proprietary models, recognising the need for new methodologies and standards to assess these advanced AI systems effectively. The LegalBench dataset is part of both the more general Holistic Evaluation of Language Models (HELM) Lite[41] benchmark by the Center for Research on Foundation Models at the Stanford Institute for Human-Centered Artificial Intelligence and the offering of a commercial provider for evaluations of LLMs called vals.ai.[42] Both provide regularly updated leaderboards and rankings, which are currently populated by different versions of models from commercial companies such as Meta, OpenAI, Claude, Google, Mistral AI, Writer, Alibaba and occasionally smaller commercial and open-source projects.[43] These rankings can be an indicator of model relative performance, but evaluating models for practical use requires a different approach, capable of integrating additional functionalities of commercial products beyond *foundation models.*

Since entrusting legal tasks solely to these models, without additional supervision, remains highly error-prone at this stage,[44] most commercial offerings incorporate the capabilities of foundation models – primarily in detecting user intent and generating semantically coherent texts – with validation of the results against a database. This approach, intended to mitigate errors generated by foundation models (somewhat misleadingly called *hallucinations*[45]), is known as *Retrieval-Augmented Generation* (RAG). RAG integrates robust information retrieval techniques with interactions from LLMs,[46] ensuring that the responses generated by the model are grounded in a specific set of documents, typically sourced from domain-specific legal databases. The implementation of these approaches varies considerably in detail, including the timing, frequency, and methods used for processing both the user's input and the model's output before presenting the final results.

The evaluation of these approaches has recently caused some controversy, as an academic paper claimed a much higher error rate for two popular products than was advertised by their commercial vendors.[47] However, as vendors were quick to point

[41] crfm.stanford.edu/helm/lite.

[42] www.vals.ai.

[43] See P Colombo et al, 'SaulLM-54B & SaulLM-141B: Scaling Up Domain Adaptation for the Legal Domain' in A Globerson, L Mackey, D Belgrave, A Fan, U Paquet, J Tomcza and C Zhang (eds), *Proceedings of the 38th International Conference on Neural Information Processing Systems* (Canada, Association for Computing Machinery, 2024).

[44] M Dahl et al, 'Large Legal Fictions: Profiling Legal Hallucinations in Large Language Models' (2024) 16 *Journal of Legal Analysis* 64.

[45] A well-founded critique of these *wishful mnemonics* – unhelpful anthropomorphisms employed by researchers in machine learning – can be found in M Mitchell, 'Why AI is Harder Than We Think' in F Chicano (ed), *Proceedings of the Genetic and Evolutionary Computation Conference (GECCO '21)* (New York, Association for Computing Machinery, 2021).

[46] For a technical survey see R Shui et al, 'A Comprehensive Evaluation of Large Language Models on Legal Judgment Prediction' in H Bouamor, J Pino and K Bali (eds), *Findings of the Association for Computational Linguistics: EMNLP 2023* (Singapore, Association for Computational Linguistics, 2023).

[47] V Magesh et al, 'Hallucination-Free? Assessing the Reliability of Leading AI Legal Research Tools' (2025) 22 *Journal of Empirical Legal Studies* 216.

out,[48] the study itself was not without methodological shortcomings. These shortcomings included the evaluation of a tool not designed for legal research on legal research tasks and an overly broad definition of *hallucinations* – a term traditionally reserved for plausible but false or misleading responses generated by AI.[49] The study's expanded definition, which included factually correct statements that merely lack additional document references, diverged from established best practices in computer science and therefore complicated the comparison of results with other research. This approach, while yielding a higher error rate, does so at the expense of clarity and casts doubt on the objectivity of the study.[50] The contentious discussion underscores the urgent need for objective information about model performance in the legal industry.[51] Given the substantial financial and personal stakes involved, the only viable path forward is the development of open-source, community-driven benchmarks that are continuously and independently updated in alignment with established best practices.[52]

In summary, the current capabilities of AI tools demonstrate that they can handle legal tasks at an unprecedented technical level. While vendors may sometimes over-promise, and viable solutions will likely require a significant degree of human oversight, the latest generation of tools is capable of effectively managing legal language. This represents immense progress, making these tools ready for practical use in the legal field for the first time. This practice-readiness, even if not perfect or fully comprehensive, marks the crossing of a significant threshold and likely signals the beginning of a new phase in legal practice.

Effectively processing natural language – including the identification of intent, accurate interpretation of factual representations, and preparation for the application of legal principles – is critical for the successful integration of AI within the legal domain. However, this capability is likely only one component of a broader engineering solution. To truly enhance productivity and manage legal complexity, the development of comprehensively engineered software systems is essential. Many aspects of legal complaint handling and litigation may not primarily depend on machine learning but rather on the implementation of optimised workflows, user-centric and intuitive interfaces, and the reliable, rapid, and secure processing of large-scale data. In short, the advancement of AI does not diminish the need for comprehensive, state-of-the-art software engineering and cutting-edge technical capabilities within the justice system; on the contrary, it actually amplifies their importance.

[48] See industry news coverage at R Tromans, 'Stanford GenAI Study Debacle – Thomson Reuters + LexisNexis Both Reply + HAI Comment' (*Artificial Lawyer*, 24 May 2024), available at www.artificiallawyer.com/2024/05/24/stanford-genai-study-debacle-thomson-reuters-replies.

[49] Hallucinations are an inevitable result from the Generative Pretrained Transformer (GPT) architecture behind all latest-generation LLMs, see AT Kalai and SS Vempala, 'Calibrated Language Models Must Hallucinate' in *Proceedings of the 56th Annual ACM Symposium on Theory of Computing* (New York, Association for Computing Machinery, 2024).

[50] The paper was accompanied by an attention-grabbing article titled 'AI on Trial: Legal Models Hallucinate in 1 out of 6 (or More) Benchmarking Queries', available at hai.stanford.edu/news/ai-trial-legal-models-hallucinate-1-out-6-or-more-benchmarking-queries.

[51] The conclusion of the discussion leaves both industry and media somewhat unsatisfied, see R Tromans, 'The GenAI TR/Lexis Study – Stanford HAI Says "We Were Denied Access"' (*Artificial Lawyer*, 25 May 2024), available at www.artificiallawyer.com/2024/05/25/the-genai-tr-lexis-study-stanford-replies-we-were-denied-access.

[52] For an example see J Thiyagalingam et al, 'Scientific Machine Learning Benchmarks' (2022) 4 *Nature Reviews Physics* 413.

Furthermore, the true potential of these tools is realised when human decision-makers are seamlessly integrated with digital systems within a socio-technical legal framework, as they complement each other very productively. Achieving this integration requires not only meticulous engineering but also the development of new competencies among humans, including data literacy, technological proficiency, and digital intuition. Calibrating the interaction between humans and AI is an exceedingly difficult task, and research on human-AI coevolution and interaction is still in its early stages.[53] In addition, it is clear that significant challenges still lie ahead, both on the technical front and in the human domain. Some of the challenges related to the latter will be discussed in the following section.

IV. Biases and Mental Models: Lessons from Human-Computer Interaction

As just outlined, the purposeful and successful use of AI in the administration of justice requires both a thorough understanding of the technology and extensive familiarity with the legal system. While legal practitioners such as judges, clerks, and court administrators are expected to have deep knowledge of the legal system, their understanding of AI technology is generally less developed. Additionally, the proper mental modelling of AI is often complicated by several conceptual misunderstandings and cognitive biases related to technology.[54] Research in the field of *Human-Computer Interaction* (HCI) has uncovered many of these misunderstandings and developed a series of mitigation techniques to address them. One of the most significant challenges is that users – particularly those with limited prior exposure to AI tools and a limited understanding of the technology – tend to rely on certain heuristics once they become aware that AI is involved. This reliance makes their understanding highly subjective and shaped by media portrayals.[55] These heuristics are often based on outdated and overly simplistic ideas about technology, such as the belief that machines produce consistent and objective results based on a pre-programmed process.[56] While this belief may be more accurate for rules-based AI approaches, it is less applicable to machine learning and data-driven models. To illustrate how these heuristics influence both the debate and implementation of algorithmic decision support systems, it is useful to develop a more detailed understanding of two frequently encountered biases that operate in opposite directions: *automation bias* and *algorithmic aversion*.

[53] D Pedreschi et al, 'Human-AI Coevolution' (2025) 339 *Artificial Intelligence* 104244.

[54] For an introduction to cognitive biases, see A Tversky and D Kahneman, 'Judgment under Uncertainty: Heuristics and Biases: Biases in Judgments Reveal Some Heuristics of Thinking under Uncertainty' (1974) 185 *Science* 1124.

[55] See SM Jones-Jang and YJ Park, 'How do People React to AI Failure? Automation Bias, Algorithmic Aversion, and Perceived Controllability' (2023) 28 *Journal of Computer-Mediated Communication* 1 and in particular J Banks, 'Optimus Primed: Media Cultivation of Robot Mental Models and Social Judgments' (2020) 7 *Frontiers in Robotics and AI* 62.

[56] This so-called *machine heuristic* was originally described in SS Sundar, 'The MAIN Model: A Heuristic Approach to Understanding Technology Effects on Credibility' in MJ Metzger and AJ Flanagin (eds), *Digital Media, Youth and Credibility* (Cambridge, MA, MIT Press, 2008).

Automation bias refers to the human tendency to overly rely on automated decision-making or decision support systems, often leading to the improper disregard of, or failure to seek, relevant information from other sources.[57] This bias was first conceptualised in the 1990s and has been empirically demonstrated to some extent in specific fields, such as among airline pilots[58] and healthcare professionals.[59] However, whether the concept can be fully transferred to other areas of knowledge work remains unclear. Despite its popularity among scholars studying automated decision-making in public services,[60] automation bias has not yet been empirically confirmed in this context. Instead, there is evidence that public servants may actually exhibit a tendency to consciously act against decision support tools, particularly when they have been made aware of automation bias, for example, through a public scandal.[61] This suggests that in public services, rather than an over-reliance on automated systems, there may be a conscious effort to question or even reject the outputs of these tools, especially when concerns about their reliability or fairness are heightened.

The emphasis on automation bias by reputable scholars and scientific outlets, particularly within the legal field, highlights a related issue in interdisciplinary research and practice: the illusion of explanatory depth. This empirically observed phenomenon refers to the tendency to believe that one understands complex topics more deeply than they actually do, often because simplified explanations seem adequate.[62] Given that the concept of automation bias has been discussed for over 25 years, there is a possibility that it might be applied to the implementation of AI technology in the justice system without sufficient evidence of its presence in this context. While the notion that judges might subconsciously follow technological assistance is compelling, it remains to be conclusively demonstrated in practice. Furthermore, robust mechanisms such as judges' training and heightened awareness of potential biases may play a significant role in mitigating this risk.

Algorithmic aversion, on the other hand, refers to the phenomenon where people are reluctant to use or trust the results of technical tools, even when these tools have been demonstrated to outperform human decision-making.[63] While this aversion applies to machine-made decisions and predictions in general, it has also been shown to specifically influence attitudes toward AI.[64] The reasons for algorithmic aversion have been the subject of ongoing debate. Early studies pointed to factors such as the desire for perfection, which

[57] See en.wikipedia.org/wiki/Automation_bias for a high quality, entry-level introduction.

[58] LJ Skitka, KL Mosier and M Burdick, 'Does Automation Bias Decision-making?' (1999) 51 *International Journal of Human-Computer Studies* 991.

[59] D Lyell and E Coiera, 'Automation Bias and Verification Complexity: A Systematic Review' (2017) 24 *Journal of the American Medical Informatics Association* 423.

[60] H Ruschemeier and LJ Hondrich, 'Automation Bias in Public Administration – An Interdisciplinary Perspective from Law and Psychology' (2024) 41 *Government Information Quarterly* 101953.

[61] See for both the lack of empirical confirmation and the potential explanation in the content of the Dutch childcare benefits scandal: S Alon-Barkat and M Busuioc, 'Human–AI Interactions in Public Sector Decision Making: "Automation Bias" and "Selective Adherence" to Algorithmic Advice' (2023) 33 *Journal of Public Administration Research and Theory* 153.

[62] L Rozenblit and F Keil, 'The Misunderstood Limits of Folk Science: An Illusion of Explanatory Depth' (2002) 26 *Cognitive Science* 521.

[63] For an introduction see en.wikipedia.org/wiki/Algorithm_aversion, for a more comprehensive review of the literature see E Jussupow, I Benbasat and A Heinzl, 'Why Are We Averse Towards Algorithms? A Comprehensive Literature Review On Algorithm Aversion' (2020) *Proceedings of the 28th European Conference on Information Systems (ECIS), An Online AIS Conference, June 15-17, 2020.*

[64] Jones-Jang and Park (n 55).

machines cannot fully satisfy; the perception that machines lack the ability to learn from experience or integrate sufficient context; and a general ethical discomfort with decisions being made by non-human entities.[65] Algorithmic aversion tends to increase when users witness technology making mistakes, which has led researchers to attribute this phenomenon to a difference in error tolerance: people are often less forgiving of errors made by computers than by humans.[66] More recent research suggests that one confounding factor in algorithmic aversion is a reluctance to accept counter-normative decision procedures.[67] In other words, one driver of opposition to technology-based decisions may be the degree to which society accepts the use of such technology for specific decisions. Therefore, as official sanctioning of machine-prepared or machine-made legal decisions increases social acceptance, individual psychological resistance to them is likely to decrease.

When legal decision-makers ponder the integration of AI into justice systems, they must remain cognisant of the biases and psychological tendencies that can influence their judgement. These biases often arise from heuristics that have evolved to assist in decision-making under conditions of incomplete information or other suboptimal circumstances. By recognising these tendencies, appropriate measures can be implemented to mitigate their impact, thereby ensuring that the final decisions are as well-informed as possible.

One important countermeasure is education for algorithmic literacy. Training and awareness have been demonstrated to reduce automation bias and commission errors when the training occurs early and ideally before extensive experience with the automated system.[68] An explanation of the function of decision support systems and their reasoning processes has equally increased appropriate use and reduced automation bias.[69] When users approach decision support tools with realistic expectations about performance and risks based on previous education, they are less likely to exhibit algorithm aversion.[70]

Introducing, increasing, or emphasising human accountability in decisions made with the assistance of AI systems could be another effective strategy to mitigate the influence of cognitive biases. However, empirical evidence on this matter remains inconclusive. Some studies suggest that strict external accountability is crucial,[71] while others indicate that users' perception of their own accountability plays a more significant role.[72] Notably, even allowing users modest modifications of AI-generated

[65] RM Dawes, 'The Robust Beauty of Improper Linear Models in Decision Making' in JI Krueger (ed), *Rationality and Social Responsibility: Essays in Honor of Robyn Mason Dawes* (New York, Psychology Press, 2008).

[66] BJ Dietvorst, JP Simmons and C Massey, 'Algorithm Aversion: People Erroneously Avoid Algorithms After Seeing Them Err' (2015) 144 *Journal of Experimental Psychology: General* 114.

[67] JE Bogard and SB Shu, 'Algorithm Aversion and the Aversion to Counter-Normative Decision Procedures' (2022). Preprint only.

[68] LJ Skitka, K Mosier and MD Burdick, 'Accountability and Automation Bias' (2000) 52 *International Journal of Human-Computer Studies* 701; KL Mosier et al, 'Automation Bias and Errors: Are Teams Better than Individuals?' (1998) 42 *Proceedings of the Human Factors and Ergonomics Society Annual Meeting* 201.

[69] MT Dzindolet et al, 'The Role of Trust in Automation Reliance' (2003) 58 *International Journal of Human-Computer Studies* 697.

[70] JW Burton, MK Stein and TB Jensen, 'A Systematic Review of Algorithm Aversion in Augmented Decision Making' (2020) 33 *Journal of Behavioral Decision Making* 220.

[71] MD Burdick et al, 'The Ameliorating Effects of Accountability on Automation Bias' (1996) *Third Annual Symposium on Human Interaction with Complex Systems* 142.

[72] KL Mosier et al, 'Automation Bias: Decision Making and Performance in High-Tech Cockpits' in D Harris and WC Li (eds), *Decision Making in Aviation* (London, Routledge, 2017).

results can significantly enhance their acceptance and willingness to use decision support tools,[73] as can other human-in-the-loop designs.[74] Furthermore, aligning algorithmic outputs with human decision-making processes tends to increase the usage of such tools by preventing conflicts between the decision maker's intuitive and rational processes and the AI's output. Despite promising initial efforts,[75] comprehensive models that adequately capture both intuitive and rational (or rationalised) decision-making processes are still lacking.[76] Nevertheless, legal use cases are particularly suitable for human intervention due to their inherent flexibility. Additionally, research has shown that algorithm aversion is stronger for tasks perceived as subjective and inherently human, such as dating, compared to more objective tasks like financial advice.[77] To enhance trust in and the adoption of automated tools, these systems could be limited to aspects of the legal decision-making process that are naturally perceived as objective, such as fact-finding or calculations. More effective, however, would be demonstrating that many aspects of legal decisions are indeed quantifiable and can be studied quantitatively. As the perception of law shifts from being an art to being more of a science, the acceptance and use of AI-based decision support tools is likely to increase.

Since these biases stem from cognitive overload due to the increasing complexity of multitasking and individual tasks, reducing the cognitive load on decision-makers is likely to diminish the influence of automation bias.[78] Although it is not a simple solution, one potential approach to alleviating cognitive overload could involve an overall improvement in workplace culture, with an emphasis on fostering positive attitudes and shared social norms. These cultural factors have been shown to reduce errors in the use of decision support systems.[79]

Other measures, such as the proper design of support systems, including operational aspects like the unobtrusive placement of advice, regular updates of data and confidence levels, and the provision of supportive information,[80] are more straightforward to implement. However, while these measures are necessary, they are insufficient on their own to fully mitigate cognitive overload and its associated biases.

Therefore, any successful implementation of AI into legal decision processes has to combine them with human accountability, influence and control and – most importantly – training for digital literacy.

[73] BJ Dietvorst, JP Simmons and C Massey, 'Overcoming Algorithm Aversion: People Will Use Imperfect Algorithms If They Can (Even Slightly) Modify Them' (2018) 64 *Management Science* 1155.

[74] Burton, Stein and Jensen (n 70).

[75] S Hafenbrädl et al, 'Applied Decision Making with Fast-and-frugal Heuristics' (2016) 5 *Journal of Applied Research in Memory and Cognition* 215.

[76] Burton, Stein and Jensen (n 70).

[77] N Castelo, MW Bos and DR Lehmann, 'Task-Dependent Algorithm Aversion' (2019) 56 *Journal of Marketing Research* 809.

[78] Lyell and Coiera (n 59).

[79] M Workman, 'Expert Decision Support System Use, Disuse, and Misuse: A Study Using the Theory of Planned Behavior' (2005) 21 *Computers in Human Behavior* 211.

[80] K Goddard, A Roudsari and JC Wyatt, 'Automation Bias: A Systematic Review of Frequency, Effect Mediators, and Mitigators' (2012) 19 *Journal of the American Medical Informatics Association* 121.

V. AI in the Courtroom: From Principles to Practice

Many courts have established regulations governing the use of AI in the courtroom,[81] addressing issues such as professional ethics, specific rules of evidence, and guidance for self-represented litigants.[82] However, only a few jurisdictions, typically in innovation-friendly countries like Singapore,[83] have ventured into the official use of AI by courts and their judicial officers. Building on a rich scholarly tradition, this section explores potential rules and guidelines for the formal integration of AI systems into judicial processes.

The official use of AI in courts can be categorised into two main areas: its application in adjudication and its role in enhancing access to justice. In adjudication, AI can be utilised for tasks such as reviewing and summarising briefs and testimony, predicting outcomes, making decisions, and generating text for orders and judgments. On the other hand, in fostering access to justice, AI can assist in explaining proceedings and potential outcomes, structuring factual and legal submissions, and generally helping self-represented litigants assess their situations more effectively.

The use of AI in adjudication is often more controversial, as it directly impacts human decision-making, can easily trigger algorithm aversion, and challenges the traditional self-conception of legal professionals. Judges, clerks, and lawyers generally feel more comfortable with the use of AI in legal communication and information dissemination by the courts. These functions are perceived as institutional rather than personal, making them less likely to affect the professionals directly. However, considering the ongoing global crisis in access to justice, the application of AI in these communicative functions could have far-reaching consequences for a much larger population, many of whom currently have limited involvement in legal proceedings. Given the significant potential of AI to enhance both adjudicative and communicative functions, both areas are equally important and should be subject to the same level of scrutiny. Many jurisdictions have turned to broader principles, such as due process and specific constitutional or conventional rights, to guide the use of AI in the judiciary. The European Union, for example, has signalled a strategic interest and run experiments while relying on large-scale statutes such as the AI Act and the European Convention on Human Rights to govern its use,[84] while the Council of Europe has adopted a dedicated ethical charter.[85]

[81] The Law Society of New South Wales provides a helpful overview listing and analysing many of these protocols for individual jurisdictions: www.lawsociety.com.au/AI-hub/court-protocols-ai. For an overview of standing orders concerning the use of AI in the courtrooms in the US, see www.lexology.com/library/detail.aspx?g=cb234139-3a8a-4ff4-a4bd-ca8b3a9e8427.

[82] Evidence generated using AI tools is a highly relevant topic related more broadly to truth decay in courts as well as society at large. Readers might find the relevant section of this book useful for this topic too (see ch 3).

[83] A remarkable project is the pilot for testing AI in the Singapore Small Claims Tribunals, see L Lam, 'Generative AI being tested for use in Singapore Courts, starting with small claims tribunal' (*CNA*, 27 September 2023), available at www.channelnewsasia.com/singapore/artificial-intelligence-court-small-claims-singapore-chatgpt-3801756, which includes an interview with Justice Aidan Xu, the judge in charge of transformation and innovation at the Supreme Court of Singapore.

[84] Court of Justice of the European Union, 'Artificial Intelligence Strategy' (2023), available at curia.europa.eu/jcms/upload/docs/application/pdf/2023-11/cjeu_ai_strategy.pdf.

[85] European Commission for the Efficiency of Justice, 'European Ethical Charter On The Use Of Artificial Intelligence In Judicial Systems And Their Environment' (2018), available at rm.coe.int/ethical-charter-en-for-publication-4-december-2018/16808f699c.

The vast majority of these frameworks fortunately express a willingness to leverage AI to enhance access to justice. However, in many countries, members of the judiciary have raised concerns about various risks associated with integrating AI into the justice system.[86] While a comprehensive analysis of the specific regulations in each country exceeds the scope of this chapter, it will instead provide a condensed overview of the key philosophical and practical concerns, along with potential mitigation strategies.

The most important concern revolves around *fairness* – the absence of bias and discrimination – which goes to the heart of justice. As demonstrated with simpler machine learning and statistical evaluation tools, models tend to inherit existing biases from their training data. When coupled with users' lack of understanding, these tools can perpetuate and even exacerbate biases, potentially leading to unfair outcomes. Mitigating this risk requires a comprehensive set of safeguards, including the use of regionally and topically representative and diverse datasets, rigorous curation, and ongoing evaluation. Ultimately, biased and unfair tools do not function as intended or advertised, and vendors should not be exempt from responsibility when their software is inaccurate or malfunctioning. It is crucial that users are able to identify when something is wrong, and professional buyers must be equipped to thoroughly evaluate these systems using predefined benchmarks and test datasets to ensure that outcomes meet expectations. Regular audits, automated tests, and evaluations should be conducted to maintain system integrity. Best practices in software development also call for extensive documentation and the inclusion of open-source components to allow for independent verification. While human decisions, including court orders and judgments, are not always free from bias, courts should address technical bias with the same diligence they apply to human bias. This involves implementing clear guidelines, providing training, ensuring oversight, and maintaining constant monitoring, as well as establishing an appeal process to correct any unjust outcomes.

Many existing frameworks encourage self-represented litigants to disclose their use of AI tools in the preparation of court documents, thereby promoting *transparency*. This practice not only shifts society's perception of permissible technology use but also helps to mitigate algorithm aversion. Similar transparency should be encouraged for the use of AI by court officials. While transparency is crucial for fostering societal acceptance of AI in the legal domain, it does not necessarily require exhaustive disclosure. Although some argue for absolute technical *explainability*, it is debatable whether the majority of those seeking justice possess the technical expertise to fully benefit from such detailed explanations. In daily life, most people function effectively with a much lower level of technical understanding (for instance, using public transportation without needing to understand the intricacies of combustion engines or timetable management). However, it is essential that decision-makers within the courts have a sufficient conceptual understanding of these tools to accurately interpret their outcomes and comprehend how they reach their results. In contrast, technical staff responsible for making procurement decisions must have a detailed understanding of the AI tools to ensure they select the most appropriate technologies for implementation.

[86] Hri Kumar Nair provides a detailed and sharp analysis of both the risks and opportunities in ch 5 of this book from a procedural perspective.

While flexibility in technical transparency is important, strict *accountability* is non-negotiable. Judges and other court officials must remain fully accountable for the decisions they make, which requires the clear identification of the final decision-maker and a process design that ensures robust human oversight. However, in cases involving lower stakes and a need for expedited decisions, litigants could be given the option to choose whether their dispute is resolved without human intervention. Provided that they fully understand the process and operation of the decision-making tool and have the right to appeal in instances of gross unfairness, litigants might prefer swift justice – accurate 95 per cent of the time – over slower decisions that are accurate 98 per cent of the time.

Considering that, on a global scale, justice delayed often equates to justice denied, this option could offer a pragmatic alternative. While current error rates and the cognitive biases discussed earlier make this approach not without risk, it could potentially lead to significant efficiency gains. To assess its viability, additional data should be collected, ideally within a closely monitored, low-risk domain such as small claims tribunals, neighbourhood courts, tenancy law courts, or other courts of first instance where the impact on litigants' assets and personal well-being is limited and reversible. This controlled environment would allow for careful evaluation of the benefits and risks, contributing valuable insights into the broader application of AI in the legal system.

In summary, while dysfunctional and poorly understood statistical tools have historically sometimes resulted in undesirable outcomes and increased awareness of the associated risks,[87] the latest generation of LLMs offers the potential to overcome many of these technical and functional limitations. However, for successful deployment, it is essential that justice administrators receive proper training in using these tools and that courts employ skilled technical personnel to avoid being misled by vendors. The quality of both the models and the data they rely on is critical to achieving positive outcomes.

Use cases that prioritise transparency are likely to face less resistance from both users and litigants, with the acceptance of these tools expected to increase over time. To facilitate this process, pilot projects should be initiated in low-risk areas to gather more data and help acclimate the public to the use of machine learning-based decision support tools. During this transitional period, maintaining human oversight and ensuring individual accountability are of paramount importance. As social acceptance of these tools grows, algorithm aversion is likely to decline, particularly if users and litigants feel they have a meaningful influence on the deployment and development of these technologies. When implemented correctly, these advancements can lead to significant efficiency gains and substantially improve access to justice on a global scale.

VI. Conclusion

Courts worldwide are grappling with the simultaneous challenges of increasing legal complexity, shifting demographics, and the transformative potential of AI. As regulations grow ever more intricate, courts are finding it increasingly difficult to manage and adjudicate cases effectively, and individuals risk being overwhelmed. This has made

[87] See, eg, J Dressel and H Farid, 'The Accuracy, Fairness, and Limits of Predicting Recidivism' (2018) 4 *Science Advances* eaao5580.

the need for enhanced productivity at all levels more urgent than ever and has raised concerns about whether access to justice can be meaningfully improved in the near future.

Advancements in NLP, particularly the development of LLMs, offer a promising solution to these challenges. By augmenting human decision-making and optimising workflows, AI-driven tools have the potential to significantly boost individual productivity and institutional performance. However, successful implementation requires a nuanced understanding of both the capabilities and limitations of these technologies, as well as a keen awareness of the cognitive biases that can influence their reception and affect their effective deployment.

Automation bias and algorithmic aversion are two critical biases that underscore the necessity of carefully calibrating human-AI interaction within a socio-technical legal framework. Addressing these biases demands a multifaceted approach, including the promotion of algorithmic literacy, the establishment of robust human accountability measures, and a relentless commitment to developing high-quality, dependable applications.

As courts worldwide navigate the use and regulation of AI in legal proceedings, an analysis of existing frameworks reveals that, although comprehensive rules exist for court users, there is very little guidance provided for court officials who wish to utilise these tools. To develop more of this guidance, inspiration can be drawn from principles established for litigants and their lawyers – such as transparency, accountability, and the preservation of human oversight. While the specifics of implementation may vary across jurisdictions, the overarching goal remains consistent: to harness AI in enhancing access to justice while mitigating potential risks.

The path forward requires measured progress, guided by a commitment to rigorous evaluation and iterative refinement. By launching pilot projects in low-risk domains, gathering data, and fostering public acclimatisation, courts can gradually integrate AI-driven tools into the broader justice system. Determining the legal nature of a conflict, explaining potential outcomes, and listing and automatically checking for formal requirements to initiate and/or respond to proceedings across multiple languages seem like low-hanging fruits. Providing non-human interfaces for lay participants to verify their understanding of the law without potential embarrassment could avoid intimidating them. As social acceptance grows and algorithmic aversion diminishes, the full transformative potential of these technologies can be realised, especially when they are integrated into comprehensive software systems for an augmented administration of justice.

Ultimately, the successful deployment of AI in the administration of justice hinges on maintaining a delicate balance: harnessing AI's efficiency-enhancing capabilities while ensuring that human judgement and accountability remain central. By striking this balance, courts can move towards a future where the promise of justice is not only more accessible but also more effectively realised in an increasingly complex legal landscape.

3

Evidence Generated by Machine Learning: Opportunities and Problems

JACOB TURNER*

I. Introduction

This chapter addresses the potential for artificial intelligence (AI), and in particular a group of technologies known as machine learning (ML), to generate evidence for use in a court or tribunal.[1] After addressing briefly the legally-salient hallmarks of these technologies, the chapter considers admissibility and finally the substantive tests which might be applied in determining whether, and if so, to what extent a court should place weight on such evidence. Those issues will be analysed through the use of a case study which resembles closely the fact pattern of a dispute in which the author had acted.

In short, it will be argued that evidence generated by AI is likely to be, in principle, admissible under most legal systems (by analogy with the already widely accepted use of statistical and probabilistic evidence). There may be challenges as to the accuracy of any given system, which depend on factors including the content of the data fed into the ML system and the extent to which the court is satisfied that the system's output is sufficiently accurate and reliable. Even where those issues can be overcome, the use of AI to generate evidence also presents unique challenges in terms of its opacity – which may render it difficult for a judge to question (or explain) the results of ML systems in any judgment. These novel challenges may require the development of new rules of evidence and civil procedure, or at least case law, in order to enable these technologies to be adopted and adjudicated upon in a predictable manner, which upholds the values of justice and ultimately of the societies where they are being used.

* All views expressed in this chapter are the author's own and should not be attributed to any other party.

[1] Hereafter the chapter will refer to the decision-making body as the 'court' and the decision-maker as the 'judge', but the same points could apply equally to a tribunal and an arbitrator.

II. Artificial Intelligence and Machine Learning

In order to address the legal problems arising from the use of AI and ML to generate evidence, it is necessary first to define what is meant by those terms and to explain the underlying technology. As will be seen, without at least a cursory understanding of the manner in which the relevant systems function, it will be impossible for both litigants and judges to engage properly with the results of such technologies, and to deploy and assess them in the context of a dispute.

In this chapter, unless otherwise specified, the term AI refers to 'technology which can take decisions autonomously'.[2] This definition is technology-agnostic, meaning that it is not tied to particular types of software, algorithms or methodologies.

Autonomy, which is the hallmark of AI in the above definition, is the ability to make choices without the outcomes or methodologies which have informed those choices being explicitly pre-determined by humans.[3] It is this non-deterministic feature which distinguishes AI (as defined here) from all previous computer software and other technology, which merely has the ability to execute human commands. Typically, the human commands or instructions in traditional technology can be expressed in a series of logical propositions: for example, 'If X then Y; If Y then Z', such that with any given input there will always be the same output. Another way of putting this point is to distinguish technology which is 'autonomous' (AI) from that which is merely 'automated' (not AI).

ML is a widely used example of a technology (or family of technologies) which meets the above definition of AI.[4] ML typically falls into two broad types: 'supervised' (sometimes called 'predictive') and 'unsupervised' (sometimes called 'descriptive').

A supervised ML system operates by estimating an unknown value from a known value. This prediction feature is achieved via a process called 'training', in which the ML system is provided with a set of pre-labelled input-output pairs.[5] For example, where a supervised ML system is being taught to identify the difference between knives and forks, it will be provided with a set of labelled data – namely photographs of forks labelled as such, and the same for knives. The 'supervision' feature of supervised learning consists of the fact that the data will have been pre-labelled by a human. The training dataset of labelled photographs will enable the ML system to identify: (a) features common to most knives and forks (for example, they are often made of metal, and both have handles and elongated shapes); and (b) features unique to knives and forks, respectively (for

[2] The term 'decisions' should be understood in its widest sense, as the choice of certain outputs over others – even if the output only takes the form of a recommendation for human action.

[3] Many applications in commercial use will involve some AI systems and some non-AI systems. For the purposes of this chapter, any such combined application which involves material autonomous decisions would constitute AI.

[4] J Zerilli and A Weller, 'The Technology' in M Hervey and M Lavy (eds), *The Law of Artificial Intelligence*, 1st edn (London, Sweet & Maxwell, 2020) para 2-003.

[5] ibid para 2-012. 'Reinforcement' learning shares elements of the two types above but is typically considered a species of unsupervised ML. Reinforcement learning involves the use of 'reward' and 'penalty' functions, which shape the system's behaviour. A reinforcement learning system engages in an exercise of trial and error within a given environment, gradually learning through such feedback loops to adopt a technique which maximises reward and minimises penalties. The strategies derived by such systems may well be different from those which would have been adopted by a human.

example, the fact that knives often have a sharpened or serrated, curved edge, whereas forks typically have four or more prongs ending in points). Based on such training, the supervised system should then be able to identify the correct piece of cutlery in 'unseen' (unlabelled) new data. The features selected by the AI as being salient to its decision-making, and therefore the techniques by which it reaches an output, are generally not determined by humans.

An unsupervised ML system does not involve any labelling. Instead, when provided with a dataset, unsupervised learning systems identify commonalities of data points within that dataset, a feature sometimes referred to as 'clustering'. This technique is particularly helpful in deriving associations and trends from very large datasets.

In high-level terms, it is likely to be the case that supervised ML systems are (at least initially) the most widely used in terms of generating evidence in a disputes context, since supervised systems have a defined 'success' function (namely, making an accurate 'prediction') and involve greater degrees of human input in their training and refinement. Accordingly, the remainder of the chapter will focus on 'supervised' ML. Importantly, the types of classification ML systems have been in widespread use for around 10–12 years, and do not involve the novel types of 'generative' AI (namely AI which can create novel output of a creative nature) which have been popularised by technologies such as ChatGPT.

The use of ML in dispute resolution is reasonably well-established as a tool for identifying salient documents for the purposes of discovery and disclosure, and increasingly in terms of slightly more complicated tasks such as identifying documents which are privileged.[6]

What is less established, however, is the question of whether, and if so, to what extent, the output of ML systems can be deployed by parties in order to prove their case through evidence. The use of ML in this manner is no longer merely a hypothetical problem: in both criminal and civil proceedings there have now been instances in various jurisdictions of parties seeking to prove their cases in this manner. The present chapter focuses on one particular case study, which involves the use of ML in a civil claim. However, almost all of the issues identified could, with the necessary changes, apply equally in a criminal context.

III. Machine Learning in Dispute Resolution: A Case Study

The case study considered in this chapter is as follows: a group of claimants allege that they have been harmed as a result of a longstanding and widespread market manipulation carried out unlawfully by a group of defendants. The claimants allege harms over a ten-year period. As to the evidence available, there are multiple public sources of data on the relevant markets, which involve all of the trades made both by

[6] For an example of judicial endorsement of AI in the disclosure process, see *Pyrrho Investments Ltd v MWB Property Ltd* [2016] EWHC 256 (Ch) in which the High Court approved a form of 'technology assisted review' of documents in disclosure – the use of which is now not only commonplace but specifically required to be considered by the parties in the Business and Property Courts of England and Wales. See Practice Direction 57AD para 3.2(3).

the defendants and third parties. The market prices said to have been manipulated are publicly available for the entire period. There is evidence of the communications between the officers of the defendants said to have carried out the illegal manipulation. The claimants' basic case is that due to the manipulation, their trades were carried out at unfavourable prices.

The claimants need to prove three things: (a) that unlawful conduct occurred; (b) that the unlawful conduct caused a material change to the relevant market prices; and (c) that the change to the relevant market prices caused them loss. The traditional way of proving these elements would likely have included the following:

i. locating and isolating the relevant conversations between traders from the different defendants (part (i)): namely, the unlawful conduct in colluding to attempt market manipulation;
ii. cross-referencing those conversations against movements in the market price (part (ii));
iii. demonstrate (probably using expert evidence) a causative link between parts (i) and (ii);
iv. demonstrate (again using expert evidence) that part (ii) caused the claimants' loss, potentially (part (iii)). This task might involve a counterfactual situation showing what the claimants' position would have been but for the unlawfully-caused price movements.

Proving such a case would have been a painstaking and potentially costly exercise, depending on the volume of data to be considered and the time period of the wrongdoing. Nonetheless, it would have been essential in most legal systems for the above to be demonstrated by the claimants (at least to the relevant civil standard of proof) in order for them to be able to claim damages.

The novel aspect of this case study is that instead of relying on traditional evidence to prove their case, the claimants here have sought to use ML to prove parts (i) to (iii). In the case study, the claimants have taken 500 instances of what they described as 'known market manipulation' and used such examples as the 'Training Data' to train a ML model to 'recognise' further instances of market manipulation said to have caused the claimants loss (the Model). The Training Data has been derived from the defendants' communications, but the claimants have declined to explain precisely what information the Training Data comprises, or how it has been selected. Finally, the model is deployed on data other than the Training Data (the Unseen Data) in order to purportedly identify further alleged manipulation days. The remainder of this chapter considers the legal consequences of a claimant or group of claimants seeking to adduce such evidence in a dispute.

IV. Is ML-Generated Evidence Admissible in Principle?

The first question to be addressed is whether ML-generated evidence can be admitted at all. The answer will of course depend on the procedural rules applicable to the dispute in question. The following analysis concerns a limited number of major jurisdictions.

The English courts have broad procedural powers to admit or exclude evidence, including expert evidence. The Civil Procedure Rules (CPR) 32.1 provides:

(1) The court may control the evidence by giving directions as to –
    (a) the issues on which it requires evidence;
    (b) the nature of the evidence which it requires to decide those issues; and
    (c) the way in which the evidence is to be placed before the court.
(2) The court may use its power under this rule to exclude evidence that would otherwise be admissible.

In *Great Future International Ltd & Ors v Sealand Housing Corporation & Ors*,[7] Arden LJ held at [24] that the power in CPR 32.1(2) 'must be used with great circumspection for the purpose of achieving the overriding objective'. The overriding objective as set out in CPR 1.1 is that cases are dealt with justly and proportionately. The editors of *Cross & Tapper on Evidence* state that: '[t]he first and most important rule of the law of evidence, though one that is not always perceived or observed, is that evidence is admissible only if it is indeed relevant to an issue between the parties.'[8]

Subject to admissibility, the courts will seek to work with whatever means are available to determine whether the relevant threshold of proof has been met – a point made by Devlin J in *Biggin & Co Ltd v Permanite Ltd*: 'Where precise evidence is obtainable, the court naturally expects to have it, [but] where it is not, the court must do the best it can.'[9] Accordingly, the categories of evidence which may be admitted are not closed. In *Lucas v Williams & Sons*, Lord Esher made the following distinction: 'Primary evidence is evidence which the law requires to be given first: secondary evidence is evidence which may be given in the absence of that better evidence, when a proper explanation of its absence has been given.'[10]

Consistent with the above general principles, it is well established that statistical evidence can be used both as a means of proving a case and/or demonstrating the quantum of damages. For these purposes, statistics is defined as 'the branch of mathematics that concerns the collection, presentation and analysis of data'.[11]

As the editors of *Phipson on Evidence* observe, there is no division in principle between calculations of statistical probability and other, more traditional, types of evidential inference: 'All inferential reasoning from evidence is fundamentally probabilistic, since inference is concerned with uncertainty.'[12] That said, statistical association is not the same as legal proof, which, as those reading will be aware normally,[13] requires (in the civil context), among other things, that a case be proved on the balance of probabilities:

[7] *Great Future International Ltd & Ors v Sealand Housing Corporation & Ors* [2002] EWCA Civ 1183.

[8] R Munday, *Cross & Tapper on Evidence*, 13th edn (Oxford, Oxford University Press, 2018) 64.

[9] *Biggin & Co Ltd v Permanite Ltd* [1951] 1 KB 422, 438.

[10] *Lucas v Williams & Sons* [1892] 2 QB 113, 116.

[11] HM Malek et al (eds), *Phipson on Evidence*, 20th edn (London, Sweet & Maxwell, 2021) para 34-01.

[12] ibid para 34-24.

[13] For an exception, not relevant to this case but which proves the general rule, see *Fairchild v Glenhaven Funeral Services Ltd & Ors* [2002] UKHL 22, in which the House of Lords held that the appropriate test was again whether the defendant had materially increased the risk, rather than whether he caused the harm. This exceptional, statistical approach to causation appears to have been developed for specific policy reasons, relating to an insurmountable deficit of other evidence.

'Even at a general level, evidence of a statistically significant association between X and Y does not, of itself, demonstrate causation.'[14]

Similarly, the editors of *Clerk & Lindsell on Torts* caution as follows: 'Care has to be exercised when relying on statistics as a means of establishing causation. The court must look at the claimant's individual circumstances rather than at the general statistics … To be a figure in a statistic does not by itself give him a cause of action.'[15]

The editors of *Phipson on Evidence* devote an entire chapter to the use of statistical analysis as a means of evidence. The editors note that statistical evidence is normally admitted as the evidence of an expert witness, specifically an expert in statistics or in a field where statistical analysis is widely used. There is no restriction on the types of cases in which statistical evidence can be used, or the uses to which it can be put.

In competition (antitrust) law cases it has become relatively common for both claimants and defendants to seek to use statistical evidence.[16] That is especially so in 'follow-on damages' cases, where the effect of the operation of a cartel on other market participants is inherently a matter of uncertain counterfactual inferences.

Thus, in *Michael O'Higgins FX Class Representative Limited v Barclays Bank PLC and others*,[17] Sir Marcus Smith, the presiding judge of the UK Competition Appeal Tribunal (CAT),[18] gave the following guidance on the criteria to be applied to assessing statistical evidence in competition law cases at [234(1)(iii)]:

> … the pleadings are the critical source for identifying areas of disputed fact, so that the parties and the court can marshal the evidence that will be required to resolve them. Particularly in competition and markets cases – but more generally also – the courts are receptive to expert statistical evidence in support of a pleaded case provided it is not too abstract, theoretical, unrepresentative or uncertain. Furthermore, extrapolation based upon sampling that is not underpinned by statistical analysis may be a perfectly acceptable way of pleading a claim.

As to the type of statistical evidence which would be acceptable in a competition law claim where market effects are alleged as a result of infringing conduct, the CAT in *O'Higgins* suggested at [234(3)] two ways (though it emphasised that pleadings were ultimately a matter for the parties): (a) evidence of 'the statistical relation between the infringements … and the effects on the market … In short, such a plea would involve looking at the start point and end point of a causal chain … without necessarily articulating all of the detailed links in that chain'; and/or (b) the 'additional cost to the market of the unlawful infringements could be articulated and its transmission through the

[14] *Phipson on Evidence* (n 11) para 34-28. See also Marcus Smith J in *BritNed Development Ltd v ABB AB and another* [2018] EWHC 2616 (Ch), [299]: 'Regression can be either "simple" or "multiple". Simple regression is rather like correlation, save that correlation does not distinguish between independent and dependent variables, whereas simple regression has a designated predictor variable and a designated dependent variable. Just as with correlation, however, regression analyses do not allow analysts to claim a causal association. There is correlation, from which causation may be inferred, at most.'

[15] MA Jones, AM Dugdale and M Simpson (eds), *Clerk & Lindsell on Torts*, 23rd edn (London, Sweet & Maxwell, 2020) para 2-30.

[16] For example, the Practical Guide on Quantifying Harm in Actions for Damages based on Breaches of Article 101 or 102 of the Treaty on the Functioning of the European Union (C(2013) 3440), June 2013, a non-binding publication of the European Commission containing guidance and suggestions for Member States' courts, contains an extensive section on the use of statistical analysis to prove harm.

[17] *Michael O'Higgins FX Class Representative Limited v Barclays Bank PLC and others* [2022] CAT 16.

[18] The CAT is a specialist court which hears the most significant competition law cases.

market described. This would involve the articulation of the links in the causal chain, which the first method side-steps.'

It is clear from the above that the weaker the qualitative evidence, the more need there is for it to be supplemented by quantitative evidence. That said, in order to be accorded any weight, the statistical material must be appropriately linked to the underlying evidence. In any event, the court is not bound to accept in part or in full any statistical analysis. Courts remain free to depart from both parties' statistical evidence where neither meets the relevant threshold of proof.

There does not appear to be any discussion in English case law of ML techniques being used to generate evidence for use in a civil claim.[19] Given the relative novelty of ML technology being used commercially, and the even greater novelty of its use in court settings, the lack of precedent or theoretical discussion of the point is not surprising.[20]

In the textbook *Electronic Evidence and Electronic Signatures*, the editors (Professor Stephen Mason and Associate Professor Daniel Seng) state as regards the admissibility of electronic evidence generally: 'That evidence takes electronic form has not been an impediment to its admissibility. … The types and categories of electronic evidence are not closed.' They explain further: 'Evidence is admitted into legal proceedings if it is relevant to an issue in dispute, subject to a number of exceptions. It is a matter of law for a judge to determine whether evidence is admissible.'[21]

The editors of *Electronic Evidence* devote a section to AI and ML, in which they note: '… the range of evidence that is generated by ML devices is practically limitless. This in turn engenders a careful review of the nature of such evidence, including an examination of the authentication of such evidence … .'[22] The editors make the following observations regarding the proper approach to the interrogation of ML-generated evidence:

> Machine learning systems apply probabilistic reasoning and statistical techniques to solve problems. They therefore introduce the same types of error as in more traditional applications of statistics. For example, the data on which they are trained might not be representative of reality, and so any conclusions drawn may not be accurate, or the uncertainty present in the output of the system might not be properly interpreted.[23]

[19] There are a handful of references in the case law to (what might be) ML evidence in criminal cases. See, eg, *R v Brown (Nico)* [2019] EWCA Crim 1143, in which the output of automatic number plate recognition technology formed part of the evidence used to convict the defendant.

[20] For completeness, there is a passing reference to the use of ML technology in the justice system in the Court of Appeal judgment *R (Bridges) v Chief Constable of South Wales Police v Information Commissioner and others* [2020] EWCA Civ 1058. This was a judicial review of the legality of the South Wales Police Force's use of automated facial recognition (AFR) technology in public places (which, it would appear, incorporated ML – the first instance judgment [2019] EWHC 2341, [24]). The Court of Appeal made the following obiter comment in its concluding remarks, which appears to contemplate the wider use of AFR (and likely ML technology more generally): 'We would hope that, as AFR is a novel and controversial technology, all police forces that intend to use it in the future would wish to satisfy themselves that everything reasonable which could be done had been done in order to make sure that the software used does not have a racial or gender bias.' Though this point was not in issue in the proceedings, there was no suggestion that evidence derived from the AFR technology would have been inadmissible in court.

[21] S Mason and D Seng (eds), *Electronic Evidence and Electronic Signatures*, 5th edn (London, University of London Press, 2021) paras 2.67–2.68.

[22] ibid para 1.103.

[23] ibid para 1.107.

Within the section of *Electronic Evidence* on AI-generated evidence, the editors also discuss the admissibility of computer simulations, saying as follows:

> In addition to collecting and evaluating evidence, an important role of AI and related technologies is to help communicate complex data to the trier of facts. This can range from data visualization tools that, for instance, make channels of email communication within an alleged criminal network visible, to visual recreation of crime scenes or dynamic reconstructions of putative events.[24]

The editors of *Electronic Evidence* continue:[25]

> Computer simulations do not fall easily within any of the existing categories of evidence because they are synthetic evidence: they are not contemporaneous records of the facts but are produced after the relevant events have occurred. … Therefore, computer simulations should be seen for what they are – representations of opinions about facts. They should be treated as expert evidence and should be admitted only when reasonably required and with the judge's permission to resolve the proceedings. While computer simulations have been admitted in both criminal and civil cases, their limited use has been permitted only as mechanisms to enable the disputed issues to be refined, and only when the raw data that serve as the source of simulations are of sufficiently high quality.

In a paper published in 2021, Lord Sales considered the legal framework applicable to AI-generated evidence.[26] Lord Sales explained that electronic evidence must be 'authentic and (to some extent) reliable'.[27] Authentication occurs when evidence is identified as being what it purports to be. One has to satisfy the court: (a) that the contents of the record have remained unchanged; (b) that the information in the record does in fact originate from its purported source, whether human or machine; and (c) that extraneous information such as the apparent date of the record is accurate. The authenticity of the evidence is a condition precedent to its admissibility. In concluding, Lord Sales did not consider that 'AI-generated evidence fundamentally changes the role of courts once the evidence has been deemed admissible.' He explained: 'The task of the courts remains the same – to use the evidence before them, ascribing to it an appropriate degree of weight, in order to determine cases efficiently and fairly.'[28]

ML-generated evidence has been analysed by courts on several occasions, particularly in US litigation, albeit that the use of the technology has not been invoked as the means of proof of a cause of action. Although there are many reported examples of law enforcement agencies using AI as part of their investigations,[29] such technology does not yet appear in the reports of contested cases.

The procedural laws of the relevant forum state as regards the admissibility of evidence, as well as other relevant provisions, such as constitutional protections, can

[24] ibid para 1.104.

[25] The editors cite in support of this passage various civil cases, including, eg, *The Owners of the Ship Pelopidas v The Owners of the Ship TRSL Concord* [1999] 2 All ER 737 (Comm).

[26] Lord Sales, 'Artificial Intelligence and Evidence', Seminars in Law and Technology (SLATE III) (15 September 2021).

[27] ibid para 9.

[28] ibid para 23.

[29] See, eg, T Revell, 'AI Detective Analyses Police Data to Learn How to Crack Cases' (*New Scientist*, 10 May 2017), available at www.newscientist.com/article/mg23431254-000-ai-detective-analyses-police-data-to-learn-how-to-crack-cases.

vary significantly. For example, Professor Sabine Gless has suggested that there may be important differences between courts' treatment of ML-generated evidence between inquisitorial systems (typically found in civil law countries), and adversarial systems (typically found in common law countries).[30]

In *Houston Federation of Teachers v Houston Independent School District*,[31] a group of teachers challenged the use of a proprietary algorithm by the Houston Independent School District between 2011 and 2014 to undertake teacher appraisals. The claimants alleged that these appraisals violated their constitutional rights because, among other things, there was no way of assessing how scores were calculated or verifying their accuracy. US Magistrate Judge Stephen Smith refused a motion by the District for summary judgment, noting that the algorithms' scores would remain 'a mysterious "black box", impervious to challenge'. Following that ruling, the case settled, with the District agreeing to cease using the algorithm in question. The issue in that case was the underlying compatibility of the algorithm with constitutional rights rather than the use of the algorithm as a tool to prove some separate legal infringement. Nonetheless, it is an example (albeit from a junior court in the US, and only on a summary judgment basis) of a situation where the use of an algorithm could be deemed sufficiently unfair as to violate constitutional protections in circumstances where its reasoning is opaque and unverifiable.

By contrast, in *State v Loomis*,[32] the Wisconsin Supreme Court rejected a challenge to the use by the state of an algorithmic tool to assess a convicted criminal's (Mr Loomis') likelihood of re-offending as part of his sentencing. The technology used, which involved ML, was proprietary to its developers and therefore opaque both to the offender and the court. However, in *Loomis* the challenge was dismissed on the grounds that the ultimate decision-maker in the sentencing exercise remained the judge. The output of the algorithm was a mere recommendation, which should be assessed with caution but did not render the sentencing process unfair.

In addition to live cases, some academics have written on the possibility of AI-generated evidence. The broad consensus is that such evidence is admissible, potentially subject to constraints as to its relevance and reliability. For example, US Federal Rules of Evidence rules 401 and 402 provide for similar tests to those in the UK:

> Evidence is relevant if: (a) it has any tendency to make a fact more or less probable than it would be without the evidence; and (b) the fact is of consequence in determining the action.

In view of the above, US District Judge Paul Grimm, together with Professors Maura Grossman and Gordon Cormack, have written that, subject to satisfying the court of validity (the accuracy of its results against what is supposedly being measured) and reliability (the ability for the system to reach similar results in substantially similar

[30] S Gless, 'AI in the Courtroom: A Comparative Analysis of Machine Evidence in Criminal Trials' (2020) 51 *Georgetown Journal of International Law* 195.

[31] *Houston Federation of Teachers v Houston Independent School District* 251 F. Supp. 3d 1168 (S.D. Tex. 2017).

[32] *State v Loomis* 881 NW 2d 749, 752–53 (Wis. 2016).

circumstances), ML-generated evidence is likely to be admissible under the US procedural rules.[33]

In conclusion, it appears that there is no general bar to the admissibility of ML-generated evidence in English law. However, that overall position is subject to the caveat that any party seeking to adduce ML-generated evidence must provide sufficient explanation of the internal functioning of the AI model(s) used. If such an explanation cannot, on the facts, be given, then a party resisting such evidence would have good grounds to do so.

V. Substantive Assessment of ML Evidence

Set out below are various points of potential scrutiny and weakness in the ML model considered in the case study set out above, but the general principles are likely to be applicable to some degree wherever ML evidence is deployed.

A. Selection of Training Data – 'Garbage in, Garbage out'

The suitability of any training data is a crucial first step to the efficacy of any ML process based on supervised learning, because the system will seek to learn based solely on that data. If the data is insufficient or biased, it is likely that any system trained on it will be inaccurate or ineffective in its given task. This issue is often colloquially described by the phrase 'Garbage in, Garbage out'.

There are at least six potential problems with the Training Data in the case study:

(a) First, the claimants allege that the 500 instances of market manipulation used in the Training Data were selected from the defendants' communications. However, as noted above, no details are given of the selection criteria. Without such information it is impossible for the defendants or the court to interrogate and assess the Training Data. For example, even if the claimants can show that the defendants used certain words or phrases which the claimants say are suggestive of illegal manipulation, the claimants would still need to demonstrate that the use of that language referred to illegitimate manipulation attempts. There may have been entirely legitimate reasons for the use of the impugned phrases in everyday conversation, wholly unrelated to any illegitimate manipulation. Moreover, there might have been legitimate uses within trading of some of the techniques/labels which are impugned by the claimants.

(b) Second, even if such language was present in the defendants' communications on the relevant days, it would need to be demonstrated that it referred to attempts to manipulate the market subject to the claim, and on the same day (as opposed to another day). Indeed, given the complexity of any kind of market-fixing exercise,

[33] PW Grimm, MR Grossman and GV Cormack, 'Artificial Intelligence as Evidence' (2021) 19 *Northwestern Journal of Technology and Intellectual Property* 9. See also P Nutter, 'Machine Learning Evidence: Admissibility and Weight' (2019) 21 *University of Pennsylvania Journal of Constitutional Law* 919.

especially taking into account the large number of contingent factors involved, it seems unlikely that the planning for any manipulation would take place solely on the day of the manipulation (as opposed to happening at least partially in advance).

(c) Third, even if all the above were satisfied, the claimants would need to show that the attempts to manipulate the market actually succeeded in doing so. That exercise would necessarily involve not just a review of the defendants' communications but also the raw data in order to ascertain whether any allegedly suspicious price movements occurred. This might involve the provision of particulars as to specific market movements said to have been caused by the alleged manipulation. Statistical regression techniques[34] may then be needed to demonstrate that causation by other means was unlikely.

(d) Fourth, even if allegedly suspicious price movements *had* occurred and even if those movements apparently corresponded to the tactics discussed in the defendants' communications, the claimants would need to then exclude (at least on the balance of probabilities) any other legitimate reason for the allegedly suspicious price movements, for example, another market player unrelated to the alleged cartel undertaking a trade which moved the market. As the CAT in *O'Higgins* observed at [238(7)] (speaking in the context of losses, rather than infringement), demonstrating causation of market movements in the foreign currency exchange (FX) market may be difficult:

> Nor are we confident that the regression analysis would demonstrate the kind of correlation between the infringements found in the Decisions and the movements in the market (in particular, the widening and narrowing of spreads) so as, in and of itself, to make good the causative link between the infringements and the losses alleged. That is because of the multitude of other factors that may affect the level of spreads in the FX market, which will be hard to control for. …

(e) Fifth, the references to the selection of the Training Data must be sufficiently representative of all the types of wrongdoing (as well as the market behaviour more generally in the reference period). There may have been variations based on the time period concerned, the particular behaviours said to have been engaged in, as well as the market dynamics more generally (caused by factors unrelated to the wrongdoing). Absent sufficient homogeneity within the Training Data, its utility for training the Model will be reduced and potentially even eliminated altogether, since the Model will be reliant on being shown enough similar examples to be able to determine what has made them similar (and to apply such heuristic to the Unseen Data).

(f) Sixth, scrutiny would need to be applied to the method in which the Model predicts results of wrongdoing and any thresholds applied. That is because typically ML does not produce a definitive 'yes' or 'no' answer but rather a statistical

[34] A regression is a statistical technique that relates a dependent variable to one or more independent (explanatory) variables. A regression model is able to show whether changes observed in the dependent variable are associated with changes in one or more of the explanatory variables.

prediction. ML techniques can only ever show correlation, rather than causation. Correlation is a relative concept, usually expressed as a score from 0 to 1. As noted above, even perfect correlation does not indicate causation between two data points. In the case study, the output of the claimants' Model is not a binary determination of manipulation or no manipulation but rather an expression of relative confidence in a prediction. What is not clear is the percentage certainty that has been applied by the claimants before a result of the Model is deemed to be an instance of wrongdoing. A 51 per cent certainty threshold would presumably generate more instances of wrongdoing than a 90 per cent certainty threshold.[35]

B. The 'Black Box' Issue

In addition to the issues concerning the accuracy of ML systems set out above, a further major problem with ML systems is that their functioning is opaque, in that the internal processes are unpredictable, and not readily capable of being explained.[36] This is known as the 'black box' problem.

This problem arises from the fact that ML models function by developing their own methodologies for associations between data. These methodologies are not constructed in the form of binary or logical rules but rather arise from the calibration of connections between components called artificial neurons (together forming an artificial neural network), which process data. This is a fundamental difference between ML and other automated technologies, such as mechanical applications or standard software programs. Whereas all traditional programs, as well as statistical analyses, can be set out in a series of logical steps, each of which can be queried, the same does not apply to ML.

Though ML systems can be very effective at narrow tasks notwithstanding their opacity – and are therefore adopted in many businesses where explainability is not a key concern – in the legal context the requirements are different.

Those opposing the use of ML-generated evidence may argue that the well-known axiom of Lord Hewart CJ that 'it is of fundamental importance that justice should not only be done, but should manifestly and undoubtedly be seen to be done'[37] applies equally to cases where ML is used. The proposed use of ML-generated evidence here is doubly problematic: *first*, it does not do justice in that the Training Data set on which the model was trained appears to lack any basis or independent verification; *second*, and importantly for present purposes, *even if* the ML system was potentially accurate, it would be necessary for parties seeking to rely on it to explain precisely how the model functions, in order to avoid a breach of Lord Hewart's principle as to open justice.

[35] One common method for assessing the accuracy of a ML model is the use of a 'confusion matrix', also known as an error matrix. The matrix represents the relationship between the 'true' classification of data (ie, whether there was actually market manipulation by the defendants on a given day) and the predicted classification.

[36] For a high-level overview of this issue, see The Royal Society, 'Explainable AI: The Basics – Policy Briefing' (November 2019), available at www.royalsociety.org/-/media/policy/projects/explainable-ai/AI-and-interpretability-policy-briefing.pdf.

[37] *R v Sussex Justices, ex p McCarthy* [1924] 1 KB 256.

If a court or tribunal is to rely on the ML evidence as part of its ratio decidendi, at the minimum it should be able to explain how the model works.

Various technical methods have been developed for 'explaining' ML systems, including, for example, the use of an additional program to describe the functioning ML model by taking representative samples and then generating a simplified set of propositions based on its predicted behaviour (a technique known as 'Local Interpretable Model-agnostic Explanations').[38] In broad terms these techniques tend to involve developing interpretable proxies for the true functioning of a system since at a fundamental level ML programs do not proceed in neat, logical steps. No such technique is universally accepted, and the utility of each will depend on the particular ML model. Given the lack of precedent on the topic, it is difficult to predict with any certainty how a court might address the 'black box' issue.[39] The 'black box' issue does not map neatly onto the standard criteria for the admissibility of evidence (relevance and the minimum weight threshold).[40] That said, one way of presenting the arguments would be to say that there is no way of assessing the minimum weight of evidence where it is fundamentally opaque in nature.[41]

In order to seek to apply proper scrutiny to AI, parties seeking to use ML-generated evidence might be asked (by the court or the opposition) to produce the following:

(a) the precise criteria used by the model(s) they have trained, as well as the weighting (or importance) applied to each criterion, and how they interact with each other;
(b) any worked examples of how those criteria would be applied, on a step-by-step basis; and
(c) counterfactual explanations showing how the results might have changed depending on the alteration of particular variables.

VI. Conclusion

In conclusion, the deployment of AI- and ML-generated 'evidence' for use in disputes is likely to be admissible in many courts and tribunals, by analogy with well-established techniques such as statistical inference, especially by expert witnesses. However, ML produces certain novel difficulties for the parties seeking to deploy it, as well as the decision-makers, because of its ability to take decisions and reach inferences which had not been expressly programmed into it. This aspect calls for great scrutiny of the input to ML systems (ie, the training data) as well as the choices made in the establishment of

[38] See, eg, IBM, 'What is Explainable AI', available at www.ibm.com/uk-en/watson/explainable-ai; See also A Holzinger et al, 'Explainable AI Methods - A Brief Overview' in A Holzinger et al (eds), *xxAI - Beyond Explainable AI* (Cham, Springer, 2022).

[39] The 'black box' issue is essentially the same as the criticism made by the plaintiffs as to the opacity of the ML systems under challenge in both the *Houston Teachers* and the *Loomis* cases in the US, discussed above (with differing results in each case).

[40] As well as perhaps also 'authenticity', as defined by Lord Sales above. It is hard to see how this criterion would realistically bar the use of ML though.

[41] *Great Future* (n 7) [24].

system architecture, namely the algorithms used to process such training data and arrive at outputs. Finally, the opaque nature of AI systems (known as the 'black box' problem) could raise issues which go beyond the mere accuracy of the system and instead give rise to fundamental questions as to open justice.

The use of ML-generated evidence may be a new phenomenon, but it is likely to be an increasingly common feature in disputes, so long as such evidence remains admissible. On the positive side, such ML use may well save parties considerable time and costs, and potentially even generate more reliable results than traditional means. In order for litigants, and societies more broadly, to make full use of these new technologies and to do so in a predictable manner, it is likely to be necessary for legal systems around the world to consider the issuance of guidance for litigants and judges on best practices (and perhaps even mandatory standards) in terms of the deployment of AI. In addition to standards for litigants, training for the judiciary in the functioning, and potential pitfalls of AI – including but not limited to the issues set out in this chapter – may be a sensible next step.

4

The Chinese Practice of Empowering the Judiciary by Using Artificial Intelligence

DU WEIKE AND GAO XIAOLI

Artificial intelligence (AI) has emerged as a new frontier of human development, and the rapid advancements of related technologies have profoundly impacted economic growth, social progress, and the evolution of human civilisation. As of August 2024, China has introduced over 190 generative AI models offering public services, attracting more than 600 million registered users.[1] Between 2014 and 2023, Chinese inventors submitted more than 38,000 patent families related to generative AI.[2] The rapid advancement of AI technologies, increasingly abundant data and computing resources, and the continuous diversification of application scenarios have established a solid foundation for AI-driven innovation. These advancements have also had a significant impact on the trials, services, and management of courts.[3]

Chinese courts are committed to serving the public in their judicial functions. They fully leverage cutting-edge technologies, such as AI, to facilitate litigation for parties involved, assist judges in case management, and enhance the quality and efficiency of trials. The courts are dedicated to creating a modern litigation service system, implementing intelligent management of case workflows, and effectively improving the digital and intelligent applications within the judicial system. This ongoing transformation aims to promote the modernisation of the judicial system continually.

[1] Cyberspace Administration of China, 'China Registers and Launches over 190 Generative AI Models Providing Services' (*China Electronics News*, 14 August 2024).

[2] WIPO, 'Patent Landscape Report - Generative Artificial Intelligence (GenAI)' (2024), available at www.wipo.int/web-publications/patent-landscape-report-generative-artificial-intelligence-genai/en/index.html.

[3] Ministry of Science and Technology, Ministry of Education, Ministry of Industry and Information Technology, Ministry of Transport, Ministry of Agriculture and Rural Affairs, and National Health Commission, 'Guiding Opinions on Accelerating Scenario Innovation to Promote High-quality Economic Development through High-level Applications of Artificial Intelligence' (29 July 2022).

I. China's Ongoing Improvement of the Institutional Framework for AI Development and Application

A. Establishing Laws, Administrative Regulations, and Macro Policies for AI

China actively embraces AI and is committed to fostering innovation and development in this field. The country recognises the importance of AI safety governance and is gradually building a robust legal and regulatory framework that incorporates AI development into its broader legal governance system.[4] To address issues of data security and privacy protection, China has implemented laws and regulations, including the Personal Information Protection Law of the People's Republic of China, Cybersecurity Law of the People's Republic of China, Data Security Law of the People's Republic of China, Administrative Measures for Internet Information Services, and Regulations on Network Data Security Management.

Regarding policies, the State Council issued the Plan for Development of the New Generation of Artificial Intelligence in July 2017, the first national-level strategic plan for AI development in China. In 2021, the Ministry of Science and Technology released the Ethical Norms for New Generation Artificial Intelligence. Subsequently, in July 2022, multiple government departments, including the Ministry of Science and Technology, issued the Guiding Opinions on Accelerating Scenario Innovation to Promote High-quality Economic Development through High-level Applications of Artificial Intelligence, aimed at driving innovation in AI applications across various sectors.[5] On 3 November 2022, the Cyberspace Administration of China, the Ministry of Industry and Information Technology, and the Ministry of Public Security jointly released the Administrative Provisions on Deep Synthesis in Internet-Based Information Services. This regulation is designed to strengthen the management of deep synthesis technologies, highlight the core values of the socialist system, safeguard national security and public interests, and protect the legitimate rights and interests of citizens, legal entities, and other organisations. On 14 July 2023, the Cyberspace Administration of China and other departments issued the Interim Measures for Generative AI Service Management, which emphasises 'the encouragement of innovative applications of generative AI technology across various industries and sectors, the exploration of optimized application scenarios, and the establishment of an application ecosystem'.[6] This regulation serves as a critical guideline for fostering the healthy development and regulated use of generative AI in China at this stage. In September 2024, the Cyberspace Administration of China

[4] Prime Minister Li Qiang, speech at the opening ceremony of the 2024 World Artificial Intelligence Conference and High-level Meeting on Global AI Governance (4 July 2024), available at www.gov.cn/yaowen/liebiao/202407/content_6961222.htm.

[5] 'Six Departments, Including the Ministry of Science and Technology, Jointly Issued a Document, Aimed at Accelerating Scenario Innovation to Promote High-quality Economic Development through High-level Applications of Artificial Intelligence' (28 August 2022), available at www.gov.cn/zhengce/2022-08/28/content_5707162.htm.

[6] Interim Measures for Generative AI Service Management, Art 5, available at www.gov.cn/zhengce/zhengceku/202307/content_6891752.htm.

published the Draft Measures for Identifying AI-Generated Synthetic Content, inviting public feedback. Earlier that year, the concept of AI Plus was introduced in China's Government Work Report for the first time.[7] On 18 July 2024, the Third Plenary Session of the 20th Central Committee of the Communist Party of China adopted the Resolution on Further Deepening Reform Comprehensively to Advance Chinese Modernization. This document emphasises the need to boost institutional supply in emerging sectors, refine policies and governance systems to support the development of strategic industries, including new-generation information technology and AI, and ensure the healthy and orderly growth of emerging industries. It highlights the importance of improving mechanisms for developing and managing generative AI, enhancing cybersecurity systems, and establishing oversight systems for AI safety. This document outlines the path forward for innovation and effective governance in China's AI landscape.

B. Strengthening the Top-Level Design for the Deep Integration of AI and Judicial Trials

President Xi Jinping has stressed the importance of leveraging internet technology and information tools at work and integrating innovations such as big data and AI into judicial functions. The Plan for Development of the New Generation of Artificial Intelligence, issued by the State Council, focuses on addressing key challenges in social governance, including judicial management, by promoting the application of AI technology and advancing the modernisation of governance systems. This plan explicitly highlights the development of 'digital courts', proposing the creation of a comprehensive data platform that supports trial processes, personnel management, data utilisation, judicial transparency, and dynamic monitoring. The aim is to enhance the use of AI in evidence collection, case analysis, and the examination of legal documents, thereby transforming the court trial system and trial capabilities through intelligent technologies.

Deepening the application of AI technology in China's judicial system and further improving the legal governance framework for AI is both a necessary and inevitable response to the rapid evolution of AI technology. It is also a crucial avenue for ensuring judicial fairness, enhancing judicial efficiency, optimising judicial decision-making, and promoting reforms and innovations within the judicial system.

With the accelerated advancement of information technology in the People's courts, trial processes have shifted from offline to online platforms, and data has transitioned from physical documents to the cloud. This has profoundly transformed the case-handling mode of the People's courts, how parties participate in litigation, and the rules of litigation procedures.[8]

In 2017, the Supreme People's Court issued the Opinions on Accelerating the Construction of Smart Courts, which mandated that the People's courts ensure that all court functions and processes are transparent, interconnected, accessible online,

[7] Government Work Report, delivered on 5 March 2024, at the Second Session of the 14th National People's Congress, available at www.gov.cn/gongbao/2024/issue_11246/202403/content_6941846.html.

[8] L Shaoping, 'The Establishment and Development of Internet Justice in People's Courts' (*People's Court Daily*, 16 September 2021).

and empowered by AI.[9] Since 2021, the Supreme People's Court has introduced several key regulations, including the Online Litigation Rules of the People's Courts, Online Mediation Rules of the People's Courts, and Online Operation Rules of the People's Courts, while amending the Interpretation of the Supreme People's Court on the Application of the Civil Procedure Law of the People's Republic of China. This has led to the establishment of a comprehensive system of online litigation rules that delineates responsibilities, ensures seamless connections, and effectively covers all areas of judicial activities throughout the entire trial and enforcement process, providing a legal framework for various online judicial activities. Among these regulations, the Online Operation Rules of the People's Courts specify that

> [P]eople's courts shall utilize information technologies such as the internet, big data, cloud computing, mobile connectivity, artificial intelligence, and blockchain to enhance smart court information systems, standardize application methods, and strengthen operational management, thereby efficiently meeting the diverse judicial needs of the public and supporting trial and execution activities online.

The amendments to the Civil Procedure Law of the People's Republic of China, made at the end of 2021, extensively incorporate relevant outcomes from the People's courts' internet judicial reform. This establishes the legal validity of online litigation in law and provides solid legal support for further promoting the rule of law in cyberspace.

C. The Supreme People's Court Issued the Opinions on Regulating and Strengthening the Application of Artificial Intelligence in Judicial Fields

In 2022, the Supreme People's Court issued its Opinions on Regulating and Strengthening the Application of Artificial Intelligence in Judicial Fields (the Opinions), comprising six sections encompassing 20 provisions. The Opinions adhere to the core principles, including safety and legality, fairness and justice, transparency and credibility, and ethical standards. The document outlines the guiding ideology, overall goals, basic principles, application scope, system construction, and comprehensive support for the application of AI technology in People's courts. The document proposes a two-phase plan: the first phase aims to establish a relatively comprehensive judicial AI application system by 2025, while the second phase aims to develop a judicial AI application and theoretical system with rule-setting and demonstration effects by 2030. This system will provide whole-process high-level intelligent assistance to support people-centred justice and impartial adjudication, significantly alleviate judges' administrative workloads, effectively safeguard judicial integrity, and precisely serve social governance needs.

To ensure that technology serves a beneficial purpose, improves services for litigants, and enhances the efficiency of dispute resolution, the Opinions delineate five fundamental principles to be followed when applying AI in judicial proceedings: First, the *Security and Legality Principle*: the development and application of AI must not compromise

[9] J Yu, 'On Digital Courts' (2004) 4 *Legal Studies*.

national security or infringe upon legitimate rights and interests, ensuring that national secrets, cybersecurity, data security, and personal information are protected. Second, the *Fairness and Justice Principle*: AI products and services must guarantee non-discrimination and impartiality, ensuring that the judgment process and outcomes are not adversely affected by technological intervention, or by biases in data and models. Third, the *Supporting Judgment Principle*: AI-generated assistance can serve as a reference for judicial work or supervision, ensuring that judicial decisions are always made by judges, who ultimately bear judicial responsibility. Fourth, the *Transparency and Trustworthiness Principle*: all aspects of judicial data collection and management, as well as the logic behind AI-assisted decision-making, must be open to examination and evaluation by relevant responsible entities in a manner that is explainable, testable, and verifiable. Fifth, the *Public Order and Good Morals Principle*: the application of AI in the judicial context must not violate public order or morals, must not harm public interests or societal order, and should establish robust risk control measures to prevent and mitigate potential ethical risks arising from the application of AI in the judicial system.

II. The Supreme People's Court Advances Judicial Modernisation through Digital Courts

The Supreme People's Court regards the development of digital courts as a key pillar and defining feature of modernising judicial work. By leveraging cutting-edge technologies such as AI, blockchain, and big data, the Court aims to enhance accessibility for litigants, support judges in case management, and improve the quality and efficiency of judicial processes. This initiative seeks to build a modernised litigation service system, enabling all court services to be conducted online and case procedures to be managed intelligently. Through these efforts, the Court strives to elevate the digitalisation and smart capabilities of judicial operations.

A. Delivering Accessible and Efficient Judicial Services with a People-Centred Approach

The People's Court Online Services Platform has been established. The platform offers intelligent features like online risk assessments for pleadings, compensation calculators, litigation assistants, and automatic case information filling. It also supports the transition from in-person procedures to online and mobile services, enabling litigants to remotely handle every step of the litigation process. Using the 'Litigation Assistant' module, users can refer to system-generated lists of required materials and templates to fill out and submit case filing documents online. Even those unfamiliar with legal procedures or lacking legal knowledge can easily complete the filing process. The platform also provides risk assessment reports based on key factors such as legal risks, suggested actions, resolution options, and asset preservation, as well as time and financial costs, helping users set realistic litigation expectations. Through this platform, litigants can participate in filing, mediation, document delivery, evidence exchange, and trials entirely online. Previously, litigants had to visit the court an average of six times to complete a case. Now, the process requires only one or two visits – in some cases, even none – significantly reducing their burden. As of June 2024, the platform had over 42.611 million registered users, with 7.583 million daily visits.

The People's Court Mediation Platform has been launched. The platform was established to break down informational silos across departments, regions, and hierarchies. It integrates resources from various mediation sources, including public, administrative, industry, and professional mediators, forming a 'Court Plus' system for diversified dispute resolution. This approach promotes the early resolution of disputes at their source. By June 2024, more than 3,500 courts, 109,000 mediation organisations, and 430,000 mediators had joined the platform. Every working day, tens of thousands of disputes are mediated online, helping resolve conflicts at the grassroots level and at an early stage.

B. Enhancing Auxiliary Technologies for Improving Accessibility of Online Services

Paperless case handling has been adopted throughout all procedures. This transition has changed the traditional method of accessing physical case files in person, enabling electronic case files to be accessed online across the country. Previously, transferring appeal case files to higher courts could take days or even months; now, higher courts can access these files in real time, significantly reducing retrieval times. Judges can fully manage electronic case files throughout the review, circulation, storage, and archiving process. They can also conduct an in-depth analysis of relevant litigation information through the case management platform, generating profiles of the parties involved and case summaries, allowing for a more comprehensive analysis of related cases and the litigation situations of the parties. A unified delivery platform for all courts has been established, utilising blockchain technology to verify the authenticity of electronic documents online. This ensures that all electronic delivery documents are delivered and verified immediately, safeguarding the authority of each electronic judicial document in the digital age, greatly improving efficiency and significantly reducing costs.

In-depth application of intelligent services supports case handling. During the filing stage, the case handling platform enables automatic input of electronic case file information. The system can automatically extract and fill in all case details for online filings. Paper materials can be scanned for offline filings to create electronic files, which are then automatically categorised and indexed. The system extracts structured information from the litigation materials, automatically capturing and filling in registration details such as the parties' identities, addresses, and litigation requests, thereby reducing manual input workload. Through the 'filing assistance' feature, the system can analyse risks related to repetitive litigation, malicious litigation, and related cases, supporting pre-filing risk alerts. During the court hearing, voice recognition technology can automatically distinguish different speakers and generate real-time transcripts, improving efficiency by over 20 per cent. During the adjudication stage, judges can analyse in-depth electronic case file information through the case handling platform. The platform can generate profiles of the parties involved based on attributes such as name, age, gender, and education, as well as historical litigation records.

Additionally, case profiles are created by analysing fundamental case information, party details, litigation subject matter, information on adjudication, and court documents. This assists judges to comprehensively evaluate cases. The system can automatically suggest key issues, similar cases, and potentially the applicable law and rules based on the claim. It can also automatically extract case elements, enabling one-click generation of all procedural documents, including notices, subpoenas, announcements, and delivery receipts. The system assists in creating judgment documents by quickly generating portions of the content through related case elements, complaint summaries, defence statements, trial transcripts, and similar cases. It supports the automatic formatting and quality checking of judgment documents, identifying logical errors, omitted claims, and citation errors that may be overlooked during ordinary manual review, thereby reducing judges' procedural workload by over 30 per cent. In the closing stage, the system allows for a one-click conversion of electronic case files into electronic archives, significantly enhancing work efficiency. In the enforcement stage, relying on a nationally unified enforcement case handling system, courts nationwide can conduct cross-region enforcement and supervision.

Blockchain technology enhances judicial processes. The Supreme People's Court has issued the Opinions of the Supreme People's Court on Strengthening Blockchain Application in the Judicial Field and has established a unified blockchain platform for courts nationwide, thus facilitating the use of blockchain technology in judicial work. As of June 2024, over 4.68 billion records have been securely stored through blockchain technology. This platform allows for the online verification of electronic documents, ensuring their authenticity and enabling instant delivery and receipt validation, effectively addressing challenges such as tampering and verification difficulties. By June 2024, more than 245,000 verifications had been completed, significantly enhancing the authority of electronic judicial documents, improving delivery efficiency, and reducing costs. Furthermore, cross-chain collaborations enable coordination with other industries, including copyright, trademarks, and internet finance.

C. Driving Judicial Modernisation Through the Digital Revolution

A Big Data Management and Service Platform has been established for the People's courts. The platform automatically aggregates case data from all the courts nationwide every five minutes, ensuring the systematic and efficient transformation of various judicial information resources into vast amounts of effective data. As of June 2024, over 350 million case records had been collected, with more than 8.117 million statistical reports generated annually, thus providing a solid data foundation for the modernisation of trial management. Integrating case handling and management is essential for constructing a comprehensive judicial quality management indicator system. This involves enhancing data analysis to monitor the progress of cases across all levels of courts in real time and evaluating the situation from the perspectives of quality, efficiency, and effectiveness so as to promptly identify defects in judicial work. An integrated management platform for judicial work has also been established, along with analytical windows for judicial trends and quality assessments across various fields.

Innovative approaches are being adopted to enhance the application of judicial big data. A judicial composite index system was established in 2018 and regularly updated over the following years. The system includes six categories and 32 indicators. The six categories of indexes are as follows: law-based government, business environment, integrity-based society, safe and secure society, harmonious living, and ecological civilisation. This system analyses the systematic connections between judicial data and socio-economic development, serving as a key reference for promoting the development of the local economy and society, as well as enabling scientific and evidence-based decision-making in social governance.

D. Establishing the People's Court Case Library and Legal Q&A Network (Fa Da Wang) to Ensure Consistent Judicial Practices

The Supreme People's Court has initiated the development of a case database (the People's Court Case Library). From its launch in July 2023 to June 2024, over 4,000 cases have been added to the database. This case repository includes authoritative cases deemed by the Supreme People's Court to hold referential and demonstrative value for similar cases, encompassing guiding and reference cases. Judges are required to search the case database before adjudicating cases and to consider similar cases within the database, further unifying application of the law. The case database is accessible to the public, including litigants, lawyers, researchers, and the general public. This enhances the evaluative, guiding, and educational functions of judicial rulings and helps to prevent and reduce conflicts from the outset.

The Legal Q&A Network (Fa Da Wang) has connected all courts in China. Judges can pose questions regarding issues in the application of laws encountered in their adjudication practices, and judges from the Supreme People's Court or High People's Courts may provide answers to these queries. This platform was launched on 1 July 2023, and by June 2024, judges across the country had submitted 518,000 questions, with 422,000 answered.

III. Practices of Empowering Judicial Trials with AI

A. Strengthening the Development of Judicial Data Middle Platform and Digital Court Brain

The Information Technology Service Center of the People's Court is leveraging common technological achievements from key national research and development projects, to promote the physical and large-scale application of the Digital Court Brain. The Digital Court Brain provides service support for various judicial tasks and lays the foundation for the digital transformation and upgrading of the judicial system. The integration of the Digital Court Brain with large judicial models has been completed, enabling intelligent search, smart application, interactive communication, and smart recommendation capabilities for court users.[10] As of June 2024, an AI engine platform was established, providing services that utilise large models, including legal and regulatory queries, document generation and error correction, and transcript summarisation. The integrated management of 11 foundational AI capabilities was also completed, with tools for voice recognition, offline transcription, text translation, and image recognition incorporated into the case-handling platform and unified workspace. A unified framework and portal for the knowledge base were also developed.

The Supreme People's Court has successfully integrated its case-handling systems with those of 16 provincial-level High People's Courts, offering 23 intelligent services such as image digitisation. Through a unified integration framework for intelligent services, pilot programs have been launched at the Henan High People's Court, providing standardised sentencing assistance, AI large model services, and offline voice transcription capabilities.

As of June 2024, the Information Technology Service Center of the People's Court managed a total of 1.14 billion knowledge points, and the Digital Court Brain has rolled out 62 intelligent services, providing 9.8 billion instances of smart services across the country, including electronic file classification, case filing assistance, and similar case recommendations.[11]

B. Empowering Intellectual Property Trials with AI

On 22 April 2024, the Supreme People's Court held a launch ceremony for the pilot project Copyright AI Intelligent Trial, establishing a digital application trial in the courts of Shanghai, Jiangsu, Zhejiang, Anhui, Shandong, and Guangdong. The High People's Courts of these six provinces jointly signed the Copyright AI Intelligent Trial Digital Application Sharing Agreement. This marks a significant step in officially integrating AI into the core processes of copyright trials in China, such as identifying the source of infringing works and determining the nature of infringement, thereby transitioning judicial decision-making from being experience-based to data-driven. By way of the 'image search' function and a vast data reservoir, the initiative achieves three key functionalities: image duplication detection, originality assessment and picture comparison. This further addresses challenges related to recognising ownership and similarity comparisons in copyright cases involving images. This initiative is expected to significantly enhance the accuracy of fact-finding and judgment in copyright trials, effectively resolving disputes over copyright. It will reduce the difficulty for rights holders in obtaining evidence, avoid the abuse of copyrights and frivolous lawsuits, and ultimately reduce image copyright disputes from the outset, providing essential legal support for the flourishing development of culture and science.

[10] Institute of Law, Chinese Academy of Social Sciences, '2024 Blue Book of Rule of Law: Report on the Informatization Development Of Chinese Courts'. More details can be found at www.chinacourt.org/article/detail/2024/05/id/7942963.shtml.

[11] ibid.

The Shanghai courts have developed a feature for the unified application of law in counterfeit trademark cases, which screens and compares data from all relevant cases within their jurisdiction. It automatically extracts key elements such as actual sales revenue, the value of seised products, primary and secondary offender roles, and other related factors. Based on this information, it establishes reasonable sentencing ranges. For cases where the sentencing deviates by more than 30 per cent from the recommended range, the system automatically informs judges, providing guidance to ensure consistency in sentencing.

China has successively established the Supreme People's Court, the Intellectual Property Court,[12] four intellectual property courts,[13] three internet courts,[14] and multiple internet tribunals.[15] These courts have lawfully adjudicated landmark cases such as the first copyright infringement case involving AI-generated images and the first case concerning the validity of a Data Intellectual Property Registration Certificate. China is also establishing new rules for emerging technologies, business models, and fields, providing regulatory guidance for developing and applying cutting-edge technologies like AI. Moving forward, Chinese courts will continue to strengthen intellectual property protection in the AI domain, and foster the research, development, and commercialisation of AI innovations.

C. Enabling Criminal Adjudication with AI

The Shanghai courts have developed an intelligent criminal case-handling system. This system facilitates end-to-end online processing of cases and adopts a 'single set' approach to managing electronic case files. Employing digital and intelligent technologies – such as continuous intelligent sensing, full-process traceable operations, and dynamic monitoring – enhances judicial efficiency, quality, predictability and transparency. Leveraging big data and AI, the system refines evidence guidelines for different stages of criminal proceedings, including conviction and sentencing. Digital tools are employed to exclude illegal evidence or address reasonable doubts within the evidence chain at various stages of the process.[16] The intelligent sentencing model, built using deep learning algorithms, covers 300,000 theft cases nationwide, integrating all relevant facts and sentencing factors within a single model.[17] The system further utilises big data

[12] According to the Decision of the Standing Committee of the National People's Congress on Certain Issues Concerning Litigation Procedures for Patent and Other Intellectual Property Cases and the Provisions on Issues Concerning the Intellectual Property Court by the Supreme People's Court, the Intellectual Property Court was officially inaugurated on 1 January 2019, marking the launch of a national-level appellate mechanism for intellectual property cases.

[13] The Beijing, Shanghai, and Guangzhou Intellectual Property Courts were established in 2014, followed by the Hainan Free Trade Port Intellectual Property Court in 2020.

[14] The Hangzhou, Beijing, and Guangzhou Internet Courts were established in August 2017 and September 2018.

[15] Since 2018, courts in Tianjin, Shanghai, Hubei, Jiangsu, Sichuan, Fujian, Guizhou, and other regions have actively set up internet tribunals, panels, or teams, drawing on the experience of internet courts and tailored to local internet-related disputes and industries.

[16] J Weidong, 'Data and Algorithm-Driven Modernization of Chinese Justice' (2024) 4 *China Law Review*.

[17] M Changshan, 'The Reshaping Effects and Limitations of Judicial Artificial Intelligence' (2020) 4 *Legal Studies*.

analysis, video image recognition, and semantic analysis, ensuring the entire case-handling process is visible, traceable, and supervised, promoting judicial accountability and transparency.

Courts in various regions have actively explored and developed intelligent sentencing standardisation assistance systems. In 2017, the High People's Court of Hainan province developed an intelligent sentencing standardisation assistance system based on big data and AI technology. The system is able to intelligently extract facts concerning a criminal case and identify the sentencing factors that should be considered. Furthermore, the system automatically provides relevant legal provisions and similar cases, recommends sentences based on historical data, and automatically drafts procedural legal documents, judgment outlines, and multidimensional data statistics.[18] Since the implementation of this system across all levels of courts in Hainan province, the average time for handling criminal cases has been reduced by approximately 50 per cent, the average time for delivering judgment has been shortened by about 70 per cent, and the average time for producing procedural documents has decreased by nearly 90 per cent. This system has substantially alleviated the workload for judges, avoiding inconsistency and enhancing the precision and efficiency of case handling.[19]

D. Empowering Civil and Commercial Trials with AI

On 28 June 2024, the Shenzhen Intermediate People's Court debuted an AI-assisted trial system. This system comprehensively covers four major stages and 85 specific procedures related to litigation,[20] including case filing, case review, court hearings, and document preparation. It seamlessly flows from litigation materials to digital documents, information platforms, judge interaction, and content generation. The system has several key features.

First, it emphasises the role of AI as an auxiliary tool, ensuring that judicial decisions are always made by judges. The authority to rule remains with the judicial organisation, and the ultimate responsibility lies with the adjudicator. Each stage of the system includes options for review, confirmation, and decision-making, adhering to the principle that judges are responsible for reviewing, modifying, and deciding on AI-generated materials and documents. Additionally, the system prompts judges based on intelligent comparisons and checks, assisting in generating judgments according to the decisions made by the judges. This process allows for timely corrections and ensures all actions are traceable throughout the trial.

Second, the intelligent trial module enhances the entire trial process, ensuring that proceedings are more efficient. Before the trial, the system intelligently recommends issues for judges. During the trial, it provides real-time assistance for evidence

[18] W Zhuhua, 'To Avoid Inconsistent Rulings in Similar Cases, Hainan Introduces an AI "Judge"' (*Science and Technology* Daily, 5 April 2019), available at digitalpaper.stdaily.com/http_www.kjrb.com/kjrb/html/2019-04/15/content_419177.htm.

[19] W Jian, 'AI in Case Handling: The Digital Revolution in the Judicial Field' (2024) 27 *Democracy and Rule of Law Weekly*.

[20] For more details, see www.chinacourt.org/article/detail/2024/07/id/8012486.shtml.

verification, ensuring seamless connections at every stage and improving the quality and efficiency of the trial.

Third, the system utilises big data and intelligent algorithms to match similar cases and recommends applicable legal provisions and authoritative legal opinions, ensuring uniformity in judicial standards. With enhanced retrieval capabilities based on vertical models, the system automatically recommends relevant cases and legal references from the People's Court Case Library and Legal Q&A Network (Fa Da Wang) to judges during the analysis of case facts and dispute resolution, facilitating a transition from manual searches to automated recommendations. This system thus allows for the quick generation of case retrieval reports and case summaries.

Fourth, the system innovatively employs a hierarchical prompting mechanism for managing judicial standards. It provides a unified and transparent framework for judicial guidance, incorporating self-learning and feedback mechanisms based on a new generation of model-tuning paradigms. This allows the system to dynamically optimise according to judges' usage habits and judgment outcomes, ensuring continuous evolution and improvement to meet the complex demands of judicial practice. It can summarise various types of litigation opinions in full text or by key elements. It can also automatically generate standard sections for 29 common types of judgment documents, covering 90 per cent of civil and commercial cases. Previously, judges spent an average of one hour drafting a standard section of a typical judgment; now, this time has been reduced to under five minutes, achieving a 92 per cent reduction in time spent.

Fifth, the system aids in diagnosing case facts and facilitates mediation efforts. It can predict possible challenges in mediation for 208 kinds of typical civil and commercial disputes, intelligently providing rules and exemplary cases for mediators to achieve non-litigious resolutions of disputes.

Sixth, the system intelligently extracts 212 key data points from cases, thoroughly analysing factors such as party characteristics, dispute features, and stakeholder interests. By instantaneously comparing information from commercial authorities, grid data, and related cases, it identifies characteristics and accurately analyses the nature and causes of conflicts in specific domains, providing support and reference for government decision-making and social governance. The system boasts extensive compatibility, portability, and scalability, establishing standard data and service interface specifications for interoperability and data sharing with external systems such as public security, prosecution, judicial administration, and labour arbitration.

Since its trial run began in January 2024 and lasted until June 2024, the AI-assisted trial system has covered all common civil and commercial cases, assisting with the filing of 291,000 cases and generating 11,600 draft documents.[21] A tool that can generate all the components of a judgment has been launched for four common types of cases: design patent infringement, financial loan contract, sales contract, and labour disputes. For example, in labour disputes, the system can intelligently summarise 17 issues, matching them with unified court rules, reducing the document generation time from over two hours to under five minutes, resulting in a 96 per cent decrease in processing time. In the case of design patent infringement disputes, since its launch in

[21] 'AI Assistant On Duty: The First Trial Model is Activated' (29 June 2024), available at baijiahao.baidu.com/s?id=1803182305505211004.

January 2024, the original team of 20 persons (5 judges and 15 assistants and clerks) has been streamlined to 8 (2 judges and 6 assistants and clerks), improving judges' work efficiency by 2.5 times over a year.

IV. Vision and Outlook

AI is a transformative technology with far-reaching impacts on judicial proceedings, government management, economic security, social stability, and global governance. Driven by AI, data and knowledge have become core elements of economic growth, with human-machine collaboration emerging as a mainstream mode of production and service, while cross-sector integration evolves into a vital economic model.[22] However, there is a growing risk of widening AI and other digital gaps between and within nations, and urgent action is needed to bridge these divides. As we advance AI development, it is crucial to stay vigilant against the potential security risks it may pose, enhancing proactive prevention and regulatory guidance to minimise risks and ensuring the safe, reliable, and controllable development of AI so as to achieve inclusive, equitable, and sustainable growth.

The rule of law is the cornerstone of human civilisation. In the face of new opportunities and challenges, it is essential to emphasise the integration of AI's technological and social attributes, fostering a legal environment conducive to AI research, development, and application. Good governance can promote deep integration of AI across various industries and sectors, unlocking its potential to drive socio-economic development. Moreover, it is essential to adopt a systematic thinking approach and conduct forward-looking research to analyse and anticipate the risks and challenges posed by AI, and to accordingly reinforce institutional support and rule guidance. We must pay closer attention to foundational theoretical issues related to AI laws and ethics and continuously refine legal regulations, ethical standards, and policy frameworks. This includes clarifying the responsibilities of decision-makers, developers, and users of AI, and establishing accountability mechanisms for AI systems' safety. Legal issues concerning AI-related civil and criminal liability, privacy and property rights protection, and information security, must also be addressed.

In the AI era, courts worldwide will play an irreplaceable role in upholding fairness and justice, adhering to human-centred principles, ensuring intelligence for good, and aligning with fundamental moral values. Chinese courts will enhance international judicial cooperation and exchange in relevant fields, better safeguarding fairness and justice while promoting the establishment of equitable, reasonable, open, and inclusive international rules for AI governance.

[22] The Shanghai Declaration on Global AI Governance, issued at the 2024 World Artificial Intelligence Conference and High-Level Meeting on Global AI Governance on 4 July 2024.

5

The Role of Artificial Intelligence in the Adjudication of Disputes

HRI KUMAR NAIR*

I. Introduction

In an address on the subject of 'Legal Systems in a Digital Age: Pursuing the Next Frontier' (2023 Address), Sundaresh Menon highlighted that we stand on the cusp of radical change in our legal systems, precipitated by new and emerging technologies.[1] The transformation of legal practice and our justice systems will be accelerated dramatically by advances in artificial intelligence (AI), and there is an urgent need to examine how we may need to overhaul our justice systems and prepare for change.[2]

The legal profession, and judiciaries in particular, are no strangers to change. A recent example is how judiciaries across the world reacted in response to the challenges posed by the COVID-19 pandemic. In many jurisdictions, we witnessed a rapid shift from in-person hearings to virtual platforms that kept courts open and accessible. Where it might once have been inconceivable for the business of the court to be conducted from homes and offices, the pandemic changed that mindset and indelibly reshaped our judicial landscape. Remote hearings are now an accepted and even permanent fixture in many of our proceedings. This change did not come without its challenges, and there remain issues to be addressed. However, one of the lessons it brought home is that change – even fundamental change – may arrive dramatically and not at a time or pace of our choosing.

While the shift to remote hearings was not a change that occurred because of advances in technology, the shift would not have been possible without such advances. It is likely that absent the pandemic, the same advances would eventually have transformed our courts. However, that transformation would almost certainly have been implemented at a far slower pace and perhaps to a lesser extent.

* The author is grateful to his law clerk, Elias Khong, and his colleagues, Assistant Registrars Tan Ee Kuan and James Low, for their assistance in the research and preparation of this chapter. He is also grateful to Associate Professor Daniel Seng for his helpful comments on an earlier draft. He remains responsible for all errors.

[1] S Menon, 'Legal Systems in a Digital Age: Pursuing the Next Frontier', address at the 3rd Annual France-Singapore Symposium on Law and Business (11 May 2023) para 3.

[2] ibid.

Although changes brought by the pandemic are often cited as examples of how justice systems have adapted and changed, in truth, those changes were largely administrative or operational, and did not affect the fundamental practices and principles of open justice – that parties are entitled to present their evidence and arguments before a competent and independent assessor, who will evaluate and determine their claims transparently in accordance with the law and precedents. We are now faced with significant technological developments that promise or threaten to challenge our understanding of what justice is, and how it should be dispensed. This chapter refers, of course, to AI. While there is no universally agreed definition of AI, it suffices for present purposes to adopt the definition used in the Model Artificial Intelligence Governance Framework by Singapore's Infocomm Media Development Authority and Personal Data Protection Commission. It reflects a broad consensus on how AI should be defined, as 'a set of technologies that seek to simulate human traits such as knowledge, reasoning, problem solving, perception, learning and planning, and, depending on the AI model, produce an output or decision (such as a prediction, recommendation, and/or classification)'.[3]

AI promises to not only revolutionise the medium in which we host our hearings; it will also redefine the processes involved in the administration of justice and, perhaps, justice itself.

This chapter will focus on AI and its uses in the realm of adjudication. It will consider the challenges of using AI in adjudicating disputes and will contrast these challenges against those in relation to human judges. Following this, three key questions when considering the adoption of AI will be suggested.

Finally, as part of the process of reimagining the future of dispute resolution in an age of AI, this chapter will briefly discuss the impact of AI on access to justice and conclude by highlighting some possible ramifications for the legal profession. The topic of access to justice is explored in further detail in chapters six and seven.

II. AI in Adjudication

A distinction can be drawn between the use of AI to augment or complement human adjudication (Complementary AI) and the use of AI in place of human adjudication (Substitutive AI).[4]

Complementary AI can take various forms, some of which are already being employed by judicial systems around the world.[5] In the US, for example, the Correctional

[3] Infocomm Media Development Authority and Personal Data Protection Commission Singapore, *Model Artificial Intelligence Governance Framework*, 2nd edn (21 January 2020) para 2.15. Other definitions of AI include: 'a field of science concerned with building computers and machines that can reason, learn, and act in such a way that would normally require human intelligence or that involves data whose scale exceeds what humans can analyze' (see Google Cloud, 'What is Artificial Intelligence (AI)?', available at cloud.google.com/learn/what-is-artificial-intelligence); and 'technology that enables computers and machines to simulate human learning, comprehension, problem solving, decision making, creativity and autonomy' (see C Stryker and E Kavlakoglu, 'What is AI' (*IBM*, 9 August 2024), available at www.ibm.com/think/topics/artificial-intelligence).

[4] F Bell et al, *AI Decision-Making and the Courts: A Guide for Judges, Tribunal Members and Court Administrators* (The Australasian Institute of Judicial Administration, June 2022) (AIJA Report) 9.

[5] ibid 15–29 for a discussion of the areas AI has been used in litigation and the courts.

Offender Management Profiling for Alternative Sanctions tool (COMPAS) assesses, among other things, the risk of recidivism among criminal defendants and generates a score from one (indicating the lowest risk) to 10 (indicating the highest risk). Judges take these scores into account in deciding whether to grant bail, probation, or parole, or for the purposes of sentencing.[6] In Malaysia, courts have employed AI to generate sentencing recommendations. When the program was first rolled out in 2020, it was limited to cases involving drug possession in Sabah and sexual assault in Sarawak, due to the availability of data for these specific offences.[7] The AI program is said to consider several key factors: employment status; age; marital status; nationality; gender; and past acquittals, and offers a recommended sentence as a starting point for the judges.[8] Tan Sri David Wong, the former Chief Judge of Sabah and Sarawak, highlighted that this initiative aimed to enhance the efficiency and consistency of sentencing decisions, but stressed that it would only act as a 'guideline'.[9] A study in 2020 showed that, in practice, Malaysian judges deviated from the AI recommendation in 67 per cent of cases.[10] It has been suggested that some reasons for this deviation include the AI system's apparent lack of consideration for mitigating factors,[11] and the court's view that certain cases called for greater deterrent sentences than recommended.[12] As of July 2023, the AI program has been rolled out in respect of 20 offences.[13]

One country appears to be pushing the boundaries and starting to blur the distinction between Complementary and Substitutive AI in the extent and scope of utilising AI. In China, the courts have reportedly taken a significant step forward in integrating AI into their judicial systems. Its nationwide Smart Court System taps into AI and

[6] ibid 22.

[7] ME Liew, 'How Courts in Sabah and Sarawak are Sentencing With the Help of AI', (*GovInsider*, 24 November 2021), available at govinsider.asia/intl-en/article/how-courts-in-sabah-and-sarawak-are-sentencing-with-the-help-of-ai-abang-iskandar-malaysia.

[8] ibid; H Sanghvi et al, 'Digitalisation of Judiciary in Malaysia: Application of Artificial Intelligence in the Sentencing Process' in YC Adam and AWA Manaf (eds), *Proceedings of the International Conference on Law and Digitalization (ICLD 2022)* (Dordrecht, Atlantis Press, 2022) 92–93.

[9] S Tawie, 'Chief Judge: Sabah, Sarawak High Courts to Use AI to Propose Punishments' (*Malay Mail*, 17 January 2020), available at www.malaymail.com/news/malaysia/2020/01/17/chief-judge-sabah-sarawak-high-courts-to-use-ai-to-propose-punishments/1828985.

[10] C Lim and R Gong, 'Artificial Intelligence in the Courts: AI Sentencing in Sabah and Sarawak' (*Khazanah Research Institute*, 18 August 2020) 8, available at www.krinstitute.org/assets/contentMS/img/template/editor/210206%20AI%20in%20the%20Courts%20v4.pdf. The author is not aware of any more recent studies on the rate at which judges deviate from the AI recommendation.

[11] D Khong and CC Ho, 'Case Commentary: Artificial Intelligence in Malaysian Courts: PP v Denis P Modili' (2022) 2 *Asian Journal of Law and Policy* 127, 135.

[12] *PP v Denis P Modili* [2020] 2 SMC 381 at [24]; Khong & Ho (n 11) at 129–30.

[13] Chief Registrar of the Federal Courts of Malaysia, 'Application of Sentence Guidelines Using Artificial Intelligence Technology in Lower Courts in Peninsula Malaysia' (22 July 2021), available at www.kehakiman.gov.my/sites/default/files/documents/Kenyataan_Media/2021/Kenyataan%20Media%20%20Garis%20Panduan%20Pelaksanaan%20Penghukuman%20Menggunakan%20Teknologi%20Artificial%20Intelligence%20di%20Mahkamah%20Rendah%20Semenanjung%20Malaysia.pdf; Rina Chandran, 'As Malaysia Tests AI Court Sentencing, Some Lawyers Fear for Justice' (*Thomson Reuters Foundation*, 12 April 2022), available at www.reuters.com/article/idUSL8N2HD3V7/; Tun Tengku Maimun binti Tuan Mat, 'Opening Address by The Right Honourable Tun Tengku Maimun binti Tuan Mat, Chief Justice, Federal Court of Malaysia', International Malaysia Law Conference 2023 (10 July 2023) para 19, available at www.malaysianbar.org.my/article/news/speeches/speeches/opening-address-by-the-right-honourable-tun-tengku-maimun-binti-tuan-mat-chief-justice-federal-court-of-malaysia-at-imlc-2023-10-july-2023-shangri-la-hotel-kuala-lumpur-.

connects to 'every working judge across the country'.[14] The system automatically screens court cases for references, recommends laws and regulations, drafts legal documents, and identifies human errors.[15] China's Supreme People's Court has made it mandatory for all judges to consult this AI system for every case they handle.[16] If judges choose to diverge from the AI's recommendation, they are required to submit a written explanation. Courts in Suzhou appear to have gone further in applying an AI program which reportedly writes judgments for disputes in traffic accidents.[17] According to a spokesperson from China's Supreme People's Court, the use of AI in the Chinese courts has reduced a judge's average workload by over a third and saved more than ¥300 billion from 2019 to 2021.[18]

Given the extent to which Complementary AI is increasingly being utilised, is Substitutive AI the next logical step? It appears that technology has not (yet) reached the level necessary for Substitutive AI.[19] That has not stopped much ink from being spilt on the idea – scholars have been ruminating on the notion of automated judicial decision-making as early as the 1970s.[20] The same question has assumed greater prominence and importance today in view of the significant developments in generative AI. Generative AI is a subset of AI that can generate new content such as text, music and even videos in response to prompts from users, without being explicitly trained for these tasks.[21] The newer generation of generative AI models demonstrates such sophistication that some commentators see in them the sparks of artificial general intelligence.[22]

As the prospect of Substitutive AI shifts ever closer with each rapid technological advance, it has become increasingly important to consider the issues that Substitutive AI portends.

In the section that follows, issues concerning AI from the perspective of Substitutive AI will be explored. While Substitutive AI is presently still in the realm of hypothesis, the issues it raises are amplified versions of the issues in AI in adjudication generally. As we will see, the issues discussed can also be applied when considering some forms

[14] S Chen, 'China's Court AI Reaches Every Corner of Justice System, Advising Judges and Streamlining Punishment' (*South China Morning Post*, 13 July 2022), available at www.scmp.com/news/china/science/article/3185140/chinas-court-ai-reaches-every-corner-justice-system-advising.

[15] ibid.

[16] ibid.

[17] A Zhabina, 'How China's AI is Automating the Legal System' (*DW*, 20 January 2023), available at www.dw.com/en/how-chinas-ai-is-automating-the-legal-system/a-64465988.

[18] Chen (n 14). See also B Chen and Z Li, 'How Will Technology Change the Face of Chinese Justice' (2020) 34 *Columbia Journal of Asian Law* 1.

[19] eg, UK Courts and Tribunals Judiciary, 'Artificial Intelligence (AI): Guidance for Judicial Office Holders' (12 December 2023) 6, available at www.judiciary.uk/guidance-and-resources/artificial-intelligence-ai-judicial-guidance/, stating that current public AI chatbots do not produce convincing analysis or reasoning.

[20] A D'Amato, 'Can/Should Computers Replace Judges' (1977) 11 *Georgia Law Review* 1277.

[21] Infocomm Media Development Authority, *Generative AI: Implications for Trust and Governance* (2023) 4–5.

[22] See S Bubeck et al, 'Sparks of Artificial General Intelligence: Early Experiments With GPT-4' (*Microsoft Research*, 22 March 2023) 4, referring to Artificial General Intelligence as systems that demonstrate broad capabilities of intelligence, including reasoning, planning, and the ability to learn from experience, and with these capabilities at or above human-level. See also ibid 4. That said, commentators have pointed out that there are critical differences between generative AI and Artificial General Intelligence, and that we may still be some time away from realising Artificial General Intelligence – see, eg, McKinsey & Company, 'What is Artificial General Intelligence (AGI)?' (21 March 2024), available at www.mckinsey.com/featured-insights/mckinsey-explainers/what-is-artificial-general-intelligence-agi#/.

of the use of Complementary AI.[23] First, the three principal challenges that have been raised in relation to AI adjudication will be discussed. Next, these challenges will be considered in view of concerns that apply to human judges, but without AI's advantages. Finally, this section identifies some factors to consider that arise from the foregoing comparison between AI and human judges.

A. Challenges in the Use of AI in Adjudication

In Sundaresh Menon's 2023 Address, he highlighted three principal concerns that have been raised over the use of AI tools in criminal adjudication, namely, objections concerning opacity, bias and humanity.[24] This section adopts and elaborates on each of these three points.

i. Opacity

In discussing the problem of opacity in relation to AI,[25] or more specifically machine learning algorithms, a useful distinction has been drawn between three forms of opacity: (a) opacity as intentional corporate or institutional concealment or protection; (b) opacity stemming from technical illiteracy; and (c) opacity that arises from the characteristics of machine learning algorithms and the scale required to apply them usefully.[26] Each of these forms gives rise to inter-linked issues that affect consideration of AI in adjudication.

In relation to corporate or institutional secrecy, the source code or datasets for AI models are commonly in the hands of private technology firms that may have expended enormous resources to acquire both the computing power and top programmers and researchers required to develop cutting-edge proprietary AI systems. These private technology firms (and their financial backers) are reasonably motivated by commercial concerns to keep the systems secret and proprietary.[27] This, however, obscures the inner workings of the system and prevents access to the means to know how a decision has been reached, including what matters the system is designed to consider. Such secrecy fetters a user's ability to understand or challenge the system. When used in adjudication, it may run counter to notions of open justice, where users and the public need to be able to examine the adjudicatory process and see how justice is being done.[28] A related concern is in whose hands access and control over systems used in a public adjudicatory context should be placed. To some extent, this level of opacity can be addressed through recourse to the court's discovery powers in the event a challenge is brought against the

[23] There are likely to be forms of Complementary AI which are less objectionable because they are used in a more administrative or supportive context, such as the use of AI for summary or translation. In respect of such uses, the concerns discussed below in relation to Substitutive AI would have less force.

[24] Menon (n 1) para 47.

[25] The opacity issue is often described as the 'black box' of AI. See, eg, Y Bathaee, 'The Artificial Intelligence Black Box and the Failure of Intent and Causation' (2018) 31 *Harvard Journal of Law & Technology* 889.

[26] J Burrell, 'How the Machine 'Thinks': Understanding Opacity in Machine Learning Algorithms' (2016) 3 *Big Data & Society* 1.

[27] There could be other important reasons to keep such a system confidential, eg, to reduce the chances of users gaming the system.

[28] AIJA Report (n 4) 30.

use of the AI system,[29] or perhaps more comprehensively by implementing regulations that mandate transparency.[30] The other forms of opacity would still, however, have to be addressed.

As regards technical illiteracy, given the highly esoteric nature of these advanced AI systems, it is simply the case that even if provided with the code behind these AI systems, a large majority will not have the specialist knowledge required to interpret or understand the systems.[31] This lack of understanding may have an impact on the level of trust in these systems and is exacerbated by the third form of opacity, which is inherent in the AI systems themselves. The third form arises because, by their nature, these systems possess a degree of unavoidable complexity, operating on such a scale of information that makes it difficult or impossible for even a trained human to grasp.[32]

Opacity may have consequences for the rights of a party. The parties involved may not be able to understand, challenge, or appeal a decision by the AI system, as the basis of the AI system's output is concealed. This lack of transparency may, in turn, violate principles of due process and natural justice. This is not a new issue. In the context of executive decision-making, the US Court of Appeal dealt with a case involving the use of a software system by the Michigan Unemployment Insurance Agency to detect and recover fraudulent unemployment claims.[33] Over 40,000 individuals were flagged as fraudsters and suffered heavy penalties. The US Court of Appeal upheld the lower court's findings that the opaque system violated the claimants' due process rights.

A possible answer to the opacity concern is to develop AI that can explain its decisions or answers (ie, one that has interpretability). However, it is not clear that this would be a sufficient response for the purposes of adjudication and the law. First, it might be difficult to frame the explanation. An explanation as to how the AI system arrived at its decision can potentially be made at different levels or from different perspectives and be of varying complexity. Any explanation of the AI system's process is likely to involve over-simplification or conversely, be hard to comprehend.[34] Even if an explanation is technically feasible, it may not be an explanation of a kind the law requires.[35] Alternatively, the AI system could plausibly generate a justification or basis for its decision or answer, ostensibly premised on legal concepts or facts. However, that justification may have nothing to do with the methods by which it in fact arrived at the position.[36] Regardless of how the explanation is framed, there will be an element of subjectivity, including in its implementation arising from, for

[29] D Seng and S Mason, 'Artificial Intelligence and Evidence' (2021) 33 *Singapore Academy of Law Journal* 241, 272–76. This approach may still present barriers in terms of the significant time and effort that might be required to pursue it.

[30] ibid 276–78.

[31] This would include the public, court users and judges (eg, sitting on appeal from the decisions). There have been calls for the legal profession as a whole to secure the requisite technical knowledge and expertise to understand the issues that may arise – see, eg, Seng & Mason (n 29) 278 (in relation to electronic evidence but equally applicable to other pertinent technological matters as well).

[32] Burrell (n 26) 9.

[33] *Cahoo v SAS Analytics Inc*, 912 F 3d 887 (6th Cir, 2019) 892.

[34] J Tasioulas, 'The Rule of Algorithm and the Rule of Law', Vienna Lectures on Legal Philosophy (7 January 2023) 14; AIJA Report (n 4) 31.

[35] J Soh, 'Legal Dispositionism and Artificially-Intelligent Attributions' (2023) 43 *Legal Studies* 1, 17.

[36] Tasioulas (n 34) 15, characterising such a justification as perhaps a fool's gold version; AIJA Report (n 4) 31.

example, what the system has been designed to reveal (and not reveal) and how these design choices are made.

ii. Bias

The issue of bias is likewise one that vexes a significant proportion of commentaries on AI in adjudication. An AI decision-maker would be trained using historical data. This runs the risk of perpetuating pre-existing biases that may be reflected in the dataset. This was a highly criticised aspect of the US' COMPAS tool, which has been reported to contain internal biases against African-American defendants.[37] This aspect of AI has been highlighted as being the most difficult example of bias to overcome in current machine learning methods.[38]

Bias in the dataset may also arise from incomplete data or an attempt to apply available data to situations foreign to the circumstances in which the original data was derived.[39] Apart from this, commentators have highlighted the risks of automation bias – a tendency to trust or regard automated output as authoritative,[40] and the inequality that might arise between parties that are able to understand and have the resources to utilise AI systems, and those who are not.

For each of the above types of bias, the fact that the AI systems may learn from and use instances of bias to in turn reinforce the extant bias might result in a feedback loop that strengthens and entrenches the bias.[41] In addition, the problems of bias may be exacerbated by the opacity issue because the user might not know what data and what connections the AI system used and what weightage the AI system gave to each factor. Bias may creep in indirectly from unanticipated directions.[42] The party who owns the system might have little incentive or means to detect such biases. Even if bias was detected in the dataset, correcting for the bias (if possible) is not a straightforward exercise.[43] The nature and extent of intervention or correction may itself require human choices and value judgements.

[37] J Angwin et al, 'Machine Bias: There's Software Used Across the Country to Predict Future Criminals. And It's Biased Against Blacks' (*ProPublica*, 2016), available at www.propublica.org/article/machine-bias-risk-assessments-in-criminal-sentencing; J Dressel and H Farid, 'The Accuracy, Fairness, and Limits of Predicting Recidivism' (2018) 4 *Science Advances*, available at www.science.org/doi/10.1126/sciadv.aao5580.

[38] AIJA Report (n 4) 34.

[39] ibid 34.

[40] ibid 34.

[41] ibid 35.

[42] A recent report suggests that large language models manifest covert negative stereotypes in relation to African American English, although their overt stereotypes associated with typical users of the dialect are much more positive: see V Hofmann et al, 'Dialect Prejudice Predicts AI Decisions about People's Character, Employability, and Criminality' (1 March 2024) arxiv.org/abs/2403.00742, 1. Further, scaling the model or training with human feedback, which are strategies to mitigate overt stereotypes, did not resolve the dialect prejudice, suggesting that covert racism may be hidden behind overt positive stereotypes (9–10).

[43] S Goel et al, 'The Accuracy, Equity, and Jurisprudence of Criminal Risk Assessment' (SSRN, 9 January 2019) 9–11, available at ssrn.com/abstract=3306723, highlighting, eg, that where the bias in the dataset itself arises out of correlations in society, attempting to force equal rates to achieve parity between groups might itself introduce double standards or harm. See also K Hao and J Stray, 'Can You Make AI Fairer Than a Judge? Play Our Courtroom Algorithm Game' (*MIT Technology Review*, 17 October 2019), available at www.technologyreview.com/2019/10/17/75285/ai-fairer-than-judge-criminal-risk-assessment-algorithm.

iii. Humanity Objection

In the 2023 Sir Francis Burt Oration, James Allsop gave three powerful examples to illustrate the indefinable humanity of the law centred on a sense of justice done and of human engagement with justice.[44] Sundaresh Menon likewise described this objection to AI as a deep conviction that (criminal) adjudication should be 'entrusted to and left under the control of humans, who share our moral outlook, methods of reasoning and the gift of exercising an appropriate degree of empathy in any given case'.[45]

To the extent that the humanity objection to AI adjudication relates to a subjective human perception of the justice of the process,[46] it may appear less concrete than the concerns of opacity and bias earlier discussed. But it would be a mistake to view it as such, for it too is a fundamental concern that goes to the very role of the courts and the legitimacy of any AI adjudication. Indeed, the prior two concerns, in eroding the trust that users may have in AI adjudication, would feed into or reinforce the humanity objection.

Two other concerns with AI buttress or are relevant to the humanity objection – these are the exercise of discretion and the ability to develop the law. Unlike the perception aspects of the humanity objection, these touch upon the outcome of AI adjudication.

Judicial discretion permeates nearly every facet of decision-making and serves as the cornerstone of adjudication.[47] It often comes into play in a situation where facts do not fall neatly within a particular rule.[48] Apart from rules, the criteria for the application of a standard or concepts, such as reasonableness, are imprecise.[49] This requires judges to weigh different factors before deciding on a just and appropriate course of action. Reasonable people may disagree about the meaning of a particular standard and the factors relevant to its application, and even (or especially) the weight to give those factors.[50] There is a serious question whether it is possible for AI to replicate the assessment of factors and exercise of discretion, or to do so in a way humans would accept as legitimate.[51]

A related aspect of the above is the ability to modify existing legal concepts or categories or develop new ones. The current generation of AI systems is built upon existing data. There is a question as to whether such systems can identify the key values and social norms that underpin the practice of law or can apply the same to develop the law in a sense that we are intuitively familiar with. A reliance on existing data gives rise to the concern that the AI systems will not be able to accommodate or develop new

[44] J Allsop, 'The Legal System and the Administration of Justice in a Time of Technological Change: Machines Becoming Humans, or Humans Becoming Machines?', 2023 Sir Francis Burt Oration (21 November 2023).

[45] Menon (n 1) para 47(c).

[46] R Hollander-Blumoff and T Tyler, 'Procedural Justice and the Rule of Law: Fostering Legitimacy in Alternative Dispute Resolution' (2011) 2011 *Journal of Dispute Resolution* 1, 3.

[47] J Steiner, 'Judicial Discretion and the Concept of Law' (1976) 35 *Cambridge Law Journal* 135.

[48] A Zuckerman, 'Artificial Intelligence – Implications for the Legal Profession, Adversarial Process and Rule of Law' (2020) 136 *Law Quarterly Review* 427, 439.

[49] ibid 439.

[50] ibid 439.

[51] ibid 438–39.

principles.[52] The result is the potential freezing or ossification of law,[53] which renders AI unfit for purpose, and diminishes trust in its application.

B. The Human Judge

At this stage, it might seem that there are insuperable issues facing AI adjudication.

However, to have any meaningful discussion on the use of AI in adjudication, we must compare it with what we currently have – human judges. It might be suggested that all the foregoing discussion on bias and opacity could, without doing too much violence to the language, equally apply to human judges.

Taking opacity, much like AI systems, the human brain is inscrutable and difficult to explain. Even if available, explanations as to the actual firing of neurons or psychology are likely to be incomprehensible to a majority, and legally irrelevant. The written or oral grounds a judge issues may mask factors for the decision that are not articulated and not susceptible to verification. On this construction, there is not too much difference between the AI adjudicator and a human judge. On the contrary, because the AI system will reach its results free of any individual quirks, and can be tested, it will arguably enhance justice, or the perception of justice.

Similarly, it can hardly be said that human judges are immune from bias. Judges are fallible. In *Noise: A Flaw in Human Judgment*,[54] Daniel Kahneman and his co-authors highlight a perennial issue in human judgement – unjustified variability. For instance, a study revealed striking discrepancies in sentencing by US federal judges presented with the same set of facts.[55] Some studies have also suggested the fallibility of human judges to extrinsic factors that can influence their mood and consequently their decisions.[56] Such disparities in outcomes would strike many as the very definition of injustice. As far as fallibility is concerned, some computer scientists have suggested that machines offer 'far greater' visibility into

[52] R Re and A Solow-Niederman, 'Developing Artificially Intelligent Justice' (2019) 22 *Stanford Technology Law Review* 242, 268.

[53] C Markou and S Deakin, 'Ex Machina Lex: Exploring the Limits of Legal Computability' in S Deakin & C Markou (eds), *Is Law Computable? Critical Perspectives on Law and Artificial Intelligence* (Oxford, Hart Publishing, 2020) 151, 232.

[54] D Kahneman, O Sibony and C Sunstein, *Noise: A Flaw in Human Judgment* (New York, Little, Brown Spark, 2021).

[55] ibid 20–22, referring to a 1981 study involving 208 US federal judges whose sentencing decisions to the same 16 hypothetical cases showed striking variation. eg, in only 3 of the 16 cases was there a unanimous agreement to impose a prison term. Even where most judges agreed that a prison term was appropriate, there was a substantial variation in the lengths of prison terms recommended. In one fraud case in which the mean prison term was 8.5 years, the longest term was life in prison. In another case, the mean prison term was 1.1 years, yet the longest prison term recommended was 15 years.

[56] eg, Kahneman et al refer to a study of thousands of juvenile court decisions which found that when the local football team loses a game on the weekend, the judges make harsher decisions on the following Monday (ibid 22). Another study suggested that when judges make repeated rulings, an increased tendency to rule in favour of the status quo can be overcome by taking a break to eat a meal: see S Danziger, J Levav and L Avnaim-Pesso, 'Extraneous Factors in Judicial Decisions' (2011) 108 *Proceedings of the National Academy of Sciences of the United States of America* 6889, 6892, available at www.pnas.org/doi/full/10.1073/pnas.1018033108. See however, commentary challenging the conclusions in such studies, and cautioning against using them in haste as an argument in favour of AI adjudication: K Chatziathanasiou, 'Beware the Lure of Narratives: "Hungry Judges" Should Not Motivate the Use of "Artificial Intelligence" in Law' (2022) 23 *German Law Journal* 452.

'the ingredients and motivations of decisions, and hence far greater opportunity to ferret out discrimination'.[57]

In relation to the humanity objection, it could be said that it is not in every case before a judge that parties experience the ineffable sense of justice being done. Much would, of course, depend on the individual judge, and the individual circumstances of the case. With humanity come the variety of human judges, with their differing backgrounds, personalities, abilities, and outlooks, each of which might affect how a case before them is conducted, and the outcome of the case.[58]

To the extent the humanity objection arises from the need to feel justice being done, it can be viewed as part of the overall perception that a decision-making process is fair. Factors that have broadly been identified to contribute to this include: (a) whether the individual feels their voice has been heard; (b) whether the process is impartial and applied consistently and transparently; (c) trust in the third-party authority, as shaped by how the authorities act and their perceived motivations; and (d) whether the individual is treated with courtesy and respect.[59] In this regard, a study done in the US found a perceived fairness gap where human judges were seen as procedurally fairer than AI judges.[60] However, the gap was consistent even when the stakes involved in the decision increased, suggesting that the gap was not driven by some perceived human advantage (that would presumably become more important as the stakes increased). Moreover, the gap was more strongly driven by perceptions of factors such as accuracy and thoroughness rather than factors like the extent to which the decision-maker understood the litigant's perspective.[61] This suggests that this aspect of the humanity objection might not be an insurmountable challenge, but will undoubtedly require considered design and the increasing acceptance of and trust in AI.[62] Indeed, where the decision of a human judge may be perceived to be affected by factors such as the status or identity of the parties, or even that of their lawyer, the AI adjudicator might well be more accepted than human judges. Additionally, there are other important aspects of justice to which AI adjudication might potentially bring benefits, in particular improving access to justice, and savings of time and costs that may otherwise be spent on disputes.[63] This is discussed below.

[57] J Kleinberg et al, 'Discrimination in the Age of Algorithms' (2018) 10 *Journal of Legal Analysis* 113, 163.

[58] Zuckerman (n 48) 439–40.

[59] Hollander-Blumoff and Tyler (n 46) 5–6.

[60] B Chen et al, 'Having Your Day in Robot Court' (2022) 36 *Harvard Journal of Law & Technology* 127, 160 and 162. The gap arose consistently across three distinct scenarios: consumer refund arbitration, bail determination and sentencing (162–63). See however, C Starke et al, 'Fairness Perceptions of Algorithmic Decision-Making: A Systematic Review of the Empirical Literature' (2022) 9 *Big Data & Society* involving a literature review that concluded that the results of the perceived fairness of human decision-making versus algorithmic decision-making are inconclusive and context specific (at 11).

[61] Chen et al (n 60) 163–64.

[62] Zuckerman (n 48) 443; Chen et al (n 60) 164–65, where the authors found that a human-led process with no hearing and resulting in an uninterpretable sentence was seen as no fairer than an AI-led process with the opportunity for a hearing and an interpretable sentencing decision.

[63] Chen et al (n 60) 167.

C. Some Observations

Does that leave us to decide between 'flawed humans' and 'imperfect machines'?[64] Do courts have to choose between embracing an untested technology or eschewing its benefits?

The choice is seldom (and should not be) so stark. The use of AI in adjudication is not an all-or-nothing proposition.[65] There are three key inter-related questions to consider when contemplating the use of AI in adjudication, whether in the form of Complementary or Substitutive AI.[66]

First, why is AI being used? Does the use of AI in a particular context bring any specific benefits or come with any risks, including in relation to the court's needs and values?

If the technology works to a satisfactory extent (to which see the second and third questions below), there may be room even for AI to be designated to adjudicate on disputes where parties consent, which favour a rigid and mechanical application of the law, or where speedy, efficient and inexpensive resolution are the dominant concerns of the parties. This may include simple small-value commercial disputes, where the value and costs of adjudicating the dispute might mean that parties may not have otherwise exercised their right to seek any determination at all. Other areas where the benefits may exceed the risks are in relation to some aspects of family law disputes,[67] where there currently are frameworks with largely predictable outcomes based on the parties' financial positions and needs (for maintenance orders) and their financial and non-financial contributions to the family (for the division of matrimonial assets). In such cases, it is conceivable that AI adjudication or input may impose objectivity and distance for parties who otherwise might be incentivised to raise legally irrelevant matters in a bid to sway a human adjudicator. With time, the courts may even consider if an AI adjudicator can generate a sufficiently quick and accurate outcome that would provide speed and certainty to parties in relation to minor or administrative offences that do not involve incarceration. In each example, having an error correction mechanism in the form of an appeal (in limited circumstances)[68] may ameliorate concerns. In fact, it has been suggested that we can even leverage AI itself to develop algorithms trained to identify cases requiring the attention of human judges.[69]

On the other hand, it may not be suitable to deploy AI where the risks are not commensurate with its benefits or indeed may result in even greater harm or uncertainty. Examples of this would include where there are issues of constitutional, national or social importance, where there is a need for careful deliberation of arguments fully ventilated in the public sphere.[70]

[64] Chen et al (n 60) 165.
[65] Zuckerman (n 48) 444.
[66] See generally, AIJA Report (n 4) which sets out matters to consider and questions for the court in relation to different aspects of AI, including the questions discussed here.
[67] Zuckerman (n 48) 444.
[68] eg, for cases which raise points of law or public interest.
[69] Zuckerman (n 48) 444. This would perhaps involve a different AI system that oversees the AI adjudication system. Issues will nevertheless still have to be worked out regarding, eg, the accuracy of this adjunct system.
[70] Zuckerman (n 48) 444.

That is not to say that there is no room at all for AI even in such cases. Even if AI has not gone so far as to be able to make acceptable autonomous decisions, it can potentially facilitate the adjudicatory process through more supportive tasks, such as analysing a body of case law or even producing briefs or draft judgments that a human adjudicator can review.[71]

Second, what output is the AI providing, and what are the limits of this output?

The mechanisms of AI (in particular, generative AI) are not comprised of technology or knowledge that most would intuitively grasp. Generative AI has been programmed to allow users to interact easily with it. It is, however, important not to anthropomorphise the system without understanding the nature of what it does and, more importantly, what its output might represent. This includes an appreciation of the nature of the data that the tool may be based upon, how different inputs might affect the system and the possible issues arising out of using that data.

The approach of the Supreme Court of Wisconsin in the *Loomis* case[72] is instructive. In *Loomis*, the Court held that the use of the COMPAS tool was permissible so long as the judge made the final determination and *was notified of the tool's limitations*. These limitations included the undisclosed method by which the scores were determined, the lack of evidence regarding the validity of the method, indications from some studies of potential bias in the tool, and the necessity to monitor and adjust the tool for accuracy as population data changes.[73] *Loomis* is discussed in greater detail in chapter six.

Of course, asking the right questions would be of little use without a concomitant ability to understand and appreciate the answers. Given the nature of the technology, this underscores the need for adjudicators, counsel, and other stakeholders to continue to keep abreast of developments and to have sufficient knowledge to appreciate the pitfalls or potential issues.

Third, what are the safeguards and checks on the use of the AI system?

It may not be practical or feasible for each judge to test the AI system or interrogate or audit the safeguards and checks that may have been conducted on an AI tool or system before it is used. This is more appropriately reviewed at an institutional level. However, there remains a necessity for caution when utilising any public tool, or a tool that has yet to be approved by the judicial institution for use.

The issue of safeguards underscores that courts and judiciaries may need to regularly keep abreast with technological developments and remain engaged in the process of the development of AI. This cannot, and should not, be left entirely to the technology companies alone. This is to allow judiciaries to be able to safeguard, monitor, or otherwise shape the use and development of the technology as it relates to the legal profession or judiciaries. The scale and complexity of AI systems are likely to require courts to work with private sector companies in the field. It is in the judiciaries' interest to retain some measure of control or influence over these potentially powerful tools.

[71] The requirement for human review remains important. Even in what appear to be apparently relatively straightforward applications, there could still be risks (eg, of 'hallucinations') that will have to be assessed and managed.

[72] *State of Wisconsin v Eric L Loomis* 881 NW 2d 749 (2016).

[73] ibid [87]–[101].

In short, there is no easy answer as to when or how judiciaries should adopt AI. The technology is improving rapidly, and our assumptions about what is possible may be shown to be incorrect before we know it. Nevertheless, certain fundamental hurdles will have to be addressed before the use of AI in adjudication or in the courtroom becomes more commonplace. We will need to assess these hurdles with an eye on the limitations and benefits, both from the perspective of the AI system and human judges.

III. AI and Access to Justice

This chapter turns to briefly discuss AI and its impact on access to justice. The integration of AI into the legal landscape presents a tremendous opportunity to revolutionise access to justice, particularly for those who face barriers due to resource constraints. Indeed, a study conducted by the World Justice Project in 2023 has estimated that 1.4 billion people do not have access to appropriate help, resolution processes, and outcomes for their civil justice needs.[74] The same study found that in half of the countries surveyed, out of people with legal problems, 35 per cent or more could not find adequate information to solve them, and 50 per cent or more did not have access to appropriate assistance and representation.[75] Out of people who had a resolution to their problem, 37 per cent or more found the process unfair, and 17 per cent or more struggled to afford the costs they incurred to solve their problems.[76] These numbers underscore the urgent need for innovative solutions to address the access to justice gap.

The promise of AI is that it would go some way towards narrowing the gap. Four aspects are highlighted below.

First, AI has the potential to significantly improve a party's ability to access legal information and even legal advice. Current AI technology has already demonstrated the capability to provide a relatively accurate summary of cases and conduct documentary analysis in seconds. It can understand prompts written in natural language and respond in kind. It is conceivable that in the near future, if not already, AI will be able to assist self-represented individuals to answer legal questions, including as to rights and processes, and do so taking into account the specific facts of the case.[77] In other words, users may be able to obtain automated legal information or advice that does not require the time and costs of a lawyer. The information could be translated into the user's preferred language and obtained at a preferred time and place. With further advances in technology, AI tools would additionally be able to prepare legal documents or submissions at a fraction of the costs and time it takes a human lawyer, and at a scope and scale that no single lawyer can provide. Even if the advice or legal product requires input from a human lawyer, AI will significantly reduce the knowledge-gap between

[74] World Justice Project, 'Dissecting the Justice Gap in 104 Countries: WJP Justice Data Graphical Report I' (2023) 8, available at worldjusticeproject.org/our-work/research-and-data/wjp-justice-data-graphical-report-i.

[75] ibid 8, 21.

[76] ibid 21.

[77] See, eg, Lee LY, 'Small Claims Tribunals to Roll Out AI Program to Guide Users through Legal Processes' (*The Straits Times*, 27 September 2023), available at www.straitstimes.com/singapore/small-claims-tribunal-to-roll-out-ai-program-to-guide-users-through-legal-processes.

laypersons and lawyers and allow the former to (better) assess the quality of their legal representation.

Second, developments in AI in adjudication can also aim to generate predictive outcomes. Again, this can be done without consulting a human lawyer and conceivably with a reasonable degree of accuracy. A reasonably reliable prediction can serve as a useful starting point to facilitate the amicable settlement of disputes in civil cases or aid parties (including accused persons) in making informed decisions regarding their legal issues.

Third, as discussed above in the context of AI in adjudication, the use of AI contains the potential to ensure that justice remains blind to extraneous factors that should not influence decisions. This applies both in the context of adjudication and to a user who is seeking impartial legal advice and may go to some extent to address the inequality of arms for those who would otherwise not have been able to afford legal representation.

Finally, the time and money saved may well be a life-altering difference for those who have no choice but to engage the justice system. This benefit should not be understated.

However, it goes without saying that there are pitfalls as well in using AI to enhance access to justice. The concerns of opacity, bias and humanity remain issues to address. If the biases result in skewed or inaccurate information, there is a risk that the user ends up in a worse position than if the AI had not been consulted. A related concern is likewise that the information provided by the AI tool will need to be sufficiently explained or made clear. Suitable warnings and disclaimers will have to accompany the information to guard against automation bias and to allow a recipient to appreciate the context of the information and its limitations. As even the use of disclaimers and warnings may not be sufficient (particularly for self-represented persons), serious consideration should be given towards providing redress, including on a no-fault basis.[78]

IV. Conclusion

As we navigate the potential impact of AI on our legal systems, we must not fail to consider the broader implications it has on the profession. Three potential ramifications are highlighted.

First, the use of AI in adjudication, even as an aid to decision-making, poses the risk of progressively eroding 'human control over outcomes'.[79] This is not necessarily a bad thing – the promise of AI is precisely that it would enhance speed and consistency. We should nevertheless remain alive to the risk of becoming 'complacent, over-reliant or unduly diffident when faced with the outputs of a reliable autonomous system'.[80] Indeed,

[78] See Infocomm Media Development Authority, *Proposed Model AI Governance Framework for Generative AI* (16 January 2024) 7, available at aiverifyfoundation.sg/downloads/Proposed_MGF_Gen_AI_2024.pdf, discussing broadly the issue of ex post safety nets (ie, for issues that are subsequently discovered following the use of generative AI).

[79] Zuckerman (n 48) 447.

[80] This has been referred to as the 'control problem': see J Zerilli et al, 'Algorithmic Decision-Making and the Control Problem' (2019) 29 *Minds and Machines* 555, 556 available at doi.org/10.1007/s11023-019-09513-7. Zerilli highlights several difficulties with monitoring AI systems: the cognitive and attentional limits of human performance, the attitudes of human operators (whose role becomes less demanding as the quality of automation approves), and the decreasing currency of human skills that deteriorate without practice or use (560–61).

some commentators have observed that should the number of traditional lawyers shrink, the pool from which judicial appointments are typically drawn (in common law systems) will likewise decline, resulting in fewer lawyers and judges, and perhaps an increasing reliance on AI. Lawyers will have to be consciously trained to retain their skill sets or learn new ones. A smaller profession may also lead to reduced competition and, consequently, slower progress in the field of law.[81]

Second, it is crucial to remember that justice does not merely involve the courts and the rights of the parties involved in the dispute. The public's confidence in the legal system is an integral aspect of the rule of law. The spectacle of justice plays a pivotal role in reinforcing public belief in the enforcement of the law, the fair administration of justice, and the deterrence of unlawful behaviour.[82] The adoption of AI by public institutions, including courts and judiciaries, and any potential impact on the public's trust and confidence in the institutions, should always be considered through this lens.

Third, in adopting AI, we should be prepared that there might be unintended consequences. For example, notwithstanding any aim to use AI to increase the certainty or efficiency of litigation, the adoption of AI could, in the short- or medium-term, increase disputes or litigation as parties question, mount challenges to or explore the limits of the AI systems. Observers have also noted that the adoption of AI in the legal profession, in particular in adjudication, may lead to disillusionment in judges whose authority and prestige may be diminished to being little more than ministerial support staff for an AI tool.[83]

While AI has the potential to enhance efficiency and accessibility, it is essential to carefully consider the broader implications on procedural justice, the legal profession, and the administration of justice. Striking a balance between leveraging the benefits of AI and upholding the fundamental principles of the legal system will be crucial as we chart the future of justice in the age of technological advancement.

[81] Zuckerman (n 48) 442.
[82] ibid 448.
[83] Re and Solow-Niederman (n 52) 274.

6

Ethical Implications of the Use of Artificial Intelligence in Justice Systems

D Y CHANDRACHUD

I. Introduction

Within the realm of judicial dialogues, we find a rich tradition of cultural exchange and mutual learning. These dialogues serve as a bridge between legal systems and cultivate a deeper understanding of the diverse perspectives that enrich the global community. The 4th Judicial Roundtable on the Future of Justice in Durham (Roundtable) symbolised a significant shift in our imagination of law and justice and featured a diverse array of perspectives brought forth from every corner of the globe. From examining the role of artificial intelligence (AI) in promoting access to justice to discussing its ethical implications, each contribution provided a unique lens to view the intersection of technology and law.

From James Watt's pioneering innovation of the steam engine in the eighteenth century to the digital age, humanity's journey through the annals of history has been marked by remarkable leaps, each fuelled by the insatiable quest for progress. These first-generation inventions revolutionised transportation, manufacturing, and industry, laying the foundation for the Industrial Revolution. They created a framework for ingenuity, inspiring inventors and entrepreneurs to push the boundaries of what was possible. From the cotton gin to the spinning jenny, new technologies emerged at a staggering pace, transforming every aspect of daily life and propelling humanity forward into a future limited only by the bounds of imagination.

Fast forward to the present day, and we find ourselves immersed in another technological revolution—the digital age. The internet, born out of the collaboration of brilliant minds and fuelled by the relentless pursuit of information, has connected billions around the globe, transcending geography and fostering unprecedented levels of communication, collaboration, and creativity. What began as a network of interconnected computers has evolved into an ecosystem of digital information, where ideas flow freely. In doing so, the threshold for barriers to entry has been lowered with each incremental change rendering them illusory. Each leap forward has brought with it new challenges and unprecedented opportunities, pushing us to adapt and innovate in ways previously beyond conception. We are yet to visualise the end of this journey. What we do visualise is that technologies which are unknown to us today will refashion every aspect of our existence in the foreseeable future in ways which are yet unforeseen. Inscrutable are the paths of knowledge.

Perhaps none of the changes affecting us have been as profound as the emergence of AI—a term coined by Emeritus Professor John McCarthy of Stanford University in 1955, who defined it as 'the science and engineering of making intelligent machines'.[1] In this moment, the convergence of human creativity and machine intelligence is a harbinger of the possibilities that lie ahead. In its infancy, AI promises to redefine the way we live, work, and interact with the world around us. From self-driving cars to personalised healthcare, the potential applications of AI are as vast as they are varied, offering solutions to some of the most pressing challenges facing humanity.

In exploring the realm of AI, we are often drawn to the sphere of imagination, where science fiction meets reality. Steven Spielberg's film, 'A.I. Artificial Intelligence' (2001), is set in a future where humanoid robots known as 'mechas' coexist with humanity. The film provides a compelling narrative to ponder over the nature of consciousness, identity, and ethics. One scene, in particular, stands out—a tender moment between David, a young AI boy, and his human mother, evoking profound questions about the nature of consciousness and the boundaries of human emotion. As David yearns for the love and acceptance of his human creators, we are forced to confront our own preconceptions about what it means to be human and the ethical implications of creating sentient beings in our own image.

Having explored these philosophical questions, this chapter begins by outlining the role of AI in adjudication and enhancing access to justice. It will then consider the ethical implications of the use of AI in justice systems.

II. AI and Its Role in Adjudication

In simpler terms, AI has been defined as a 'suite of related technologies' powered by algorithms that can perform tasks otherwise requiring human intelligence.[2] In the realms of judicial and administrative decision-making, two primary types of AI are currently used: (1) trained, machine-learning algorithms or predictive analytics, and (2) explicitly coded, closed-rule algorithms in decision-making.[3]

A. Predictive Analytics

Predictive analytics is an example of machine learning algorithms analysing past data to develop rules that may be generalised going forward. For instance, researchers analysed decisions of the European Court of Human Rights, employing AI to

[1] C Manning, 'Artificial Intelligence Definitions' (*Stanford Institute for Human-Centered Artificial Intelligence*, September 2020), available at hai.stanford.edu/sites/default/files/2020-09/AI-Definitions-HAI.pdf.

[2] D Schatsky, C Muraskin and R Gurumurthy, 'Demystifying Artificial Intelligence: What Business Leaders Need to Know about Cognitive Technologies' (*Deloitte*, 2014), available at www2.deloitte.com/insights/us/en/focus/cognitive-technologies/what-is-cognitivetechnology.html.

[3] K Ashley, *Artificial Intelligence and Legal Analytics: New Tools for Law Practice in the Digital Age* (Cambridge, Cambridge University Press, 2017).

predict case outcomes. The AI analysed case text to identify patterns, enabling it to classify each case as either a 'violation' or a 'non-violation'. The program was able to predict the outcome of cases presented to it in textual form with 79 per cent accuracy on average.[4] Another compelling example comes from an algorithm developed by the Illinois Institute of Technology and the University of South Texas. This algorithm, based on data from the US Supreme Court spanning from 1791 to 2015, successfully predicted the decisions and votes of Supreme Court justices from 1815 to 2015 with remarkable accuracy. It achieved a predictive accuracy of 70.2 per cent for the decisions.[5]

Another significant point of discussion is the use of risk-assessment software in the criminal justice system. These sophisticated algorithms aim to inject objectivity into sentencing decisions, purportedly making them more transparent and rational. One of the most striking innovations in the US criminal justice system in the course of the last three decades has been the introduction of risk-assessment software, powered by sophisticated and often proprietary algorithms, to predict whether individual offenders are likely to re-offend (the so-called 'risk of recidivism').[6]

The Wisconsin Supreme Court case of *State v Loomis* (*Loomis*), which has already been referred to in the previous chapters, serves as a poignant illustration of its practical usage.[7] The defendant, Eric Loomis, a 31-year-old man, was arrested on charges related to a drive-by shooting. An automated risk-assessment system—COMPAS (Correctional Offender Management Profiling for Alternative Sanctions)—was employed to aid in determining the defendant's sentence. COMPAS assesses variables under five main areas: criminal involvement, relationships/lifestyles, personality/attitudes, family, and social exclusion.[8] The system estimates the risk of recidivism based on an interview with the defendant and information from the defendant's criminal history. In imposing the maximum sentence of six years' imprisonment and five years' extended supervision, the trial court (Circuit Court) specifically mentioned the COMPAS score. The judge ruled out probation because of the seriousness of the crime and because of the risk-assessment tools that had been utilised, which suggested that the defendant was extremely 'high risk' to the community.[9] The Supreme Court ultimately upheld the decision, highlighting the intricate interplay between AI and judicial discretion.[10] The ethical implications of this case will be explained in a later segment of this chapter.

[4] S Shead, 'This "AI Judge" is Predicting the Results of Human Rights Cases' (*World Economic Forum*, 26 October 2016), available at www.weforum.org/agenda/2016/10/this-ai-judge-is-predicting-the-results-of-human-rights-cases.

[5] L Stanila, 'Living in the Future: New Actors in the Field of Criminal Law – Artificial Intelligence' (2020), the 7th International Scientific Conference of the Faculty of Law of the University of Latvia 300–12.

[6] D Kehl, P Guo and S Kessler, 'Algorithms in the Criminal Justice System: Assessing the Use of Risk Assessments in Sentencing' (*Responsive Communities Initiative, Berkman Klein Center for Internet and Society, Harvard Law School*, 2017), available at dash.harvard.edu/bitstream/handle/1/33746041/2017-07_responsive communities_2.pdf.

[7] *State of Wisconsin v Eric L Loomis* 881 NW 2d 749 (2016).

[8] ibid 754.

[9] ibid 755.

[10] ibid 769.

B. AI in Other Decision-Making Processes

A significant aspect of AI's role in the legal domain lies in explicitly coded, closed-rule algorithms, often referred to as 'legal experts'. These algorithms are designed to analyse legal data and provide insights to support decision-making processes, ranging from boardrooms to government agencies. For instance, over 40 per cent of CEOs report using generative AI to inform their decision-making processes.[11] The Port of Rotterdam's pioneering platform—PortXchange Synchronizer—exemplifies this trend.[12] By aggregating data from multiple sources, including vessels, shipping operators, public data, and AI forecasting applications, the platform offers real-time insights to optimise decision-making in port operations and infrastructure planning.[13] Similar platforms are being adopted by seaports worldwide, underscoring the growing reliance on AI-driven solutions to enhance efficiency and productivity.

There exists a continuum in the extent to which AI is integrated into legal decision-making processes. In a Colombian case, Justice Juan Manuel Padilla utilised ChatGPT, an AI-powered chatbot, to deliver a judgment involving insurance claims for an autistic child.[14] The judge engaged in a conversation with ChatGPT to seek clarity on legal nuances. Based on this exchange, he rendered a verdict affirming that, under Colombian law, an autistic child is indeed exempt from fees for therapy. However, the judge was keen to stress that the use of AI does not supplant the role of judges as independent and reasoning individuals. Similarly, in the Punjab and Haryana High Court in India, ChatGPT was consulted to broaden the perspective on a bail petition.[15] The judge, while rejecting a bail petition due to allegations of involvement in a brutal, fatal assault, turned to ChatGPT for insights. However, it is crucial to clarify that ChatGPT's input was not considered by the High Court when assessing the case's merits. Instead, it was intended to offer a broader understanding of bail jurisprudence, particularly in cases involving cruelty as a factor.

Despite the advancements in AI technology, the question remains: to what extent does the administration of justice always require human intervention? Human judges bring unique qualities such as empathy, moral reasoning, and contextual understanding to legal proceedings, which AI algorithms may struggle to replicate fully. The following examples of cases heard by the Supreme Court of India around the time the Roundtable was held will illustrate the point. For instance, the court heard arguments on the impassioned plea of a differently abled person that a film on disability was not a comedy, as it professed to be, but a parody. Or take the case of a mother with a child suffering from a rare genetic disorder who told the

[11] P Meissner and Y Narita, 'Artificial Intelligence Will Transform Decision-Making. Here's How' (*World Economic Forum*, 27 September 2023), available at www.weforum.org/agenda/2023/09/how-artificial-intelligence-will-transform-decision-making.

[12] Example cited in M Purdy and M Williams, 'How AI Can Help Leaders Make Better Decisions Under Pressure' (*Harvard Business Review*, 26 October 2023), available at hbr.org/2023/10/how-ai-can-help-leaders-make-better-decisions-under-pressure.

[13] ibid.

[14] L Taylor, 'Colombian Judge Says He Used ChatGPT in Ruling' (*The Guardian*, 3 February 2023), available at www.theguardian.com/technology/2023/feb/03/colombia-judge-chatgpt-ruling.

[15] *Jaswinder Singh v State of Punjab*, CRM-M-22496-2022, Order dated 27 March 2023.

court that her employer, the state, did not have a childcare leave policy. Yet another case involved a nine-judge bench hearing a constitutional issue—can the redistribution of the material resources of the community encompass private property? These cases raise ethical, moral and value-based choices for the adjudicator. While AI can augment decision-making processes by providing insights and analysis, the final judgment often necessitates human interpretation and discretion. These cases demonstrate the evolving role of AI in assisting judges and legal practitioners, but they also emphasise the importance of maintaining human judgment and independence in legal proceedings.

Certain types of legal disputes may indeed lend themselves more readily to AI utilisation, depending on their characteristics and complexities. For example, in intellectual property disputes, AI-powered systems can swiftly analyse large volumes of patent filings, prior art, and legal precedents to identify relevant patterns and similarities. This enables legal professionals to build stronger cases, identify potential infringements, and formulate effective legal strategies. Similarly, in financial fraud investigations, AI algorithms can analyse vast amounts of transactional data, detect anomalies, and identify suspicious patterns indicative of fraudulent activity. By automating the analysis process, AI technologies enable investigators to uncover fraudulent schemes more efficiently and effectively. Compensation claim cases involving motor accident cases in India are resolved largely on the application of mathematical formulae involving age, multipliers and statutory additions.

Moreover, routine administrative tasks within the legal domain, such as processing land records or drafting standard legal documents, represent another area where AI can play a transformative role. For instance, in India, where land ownership records are crucial for property transactions and legal disputes, AI algorithms can streamline the process of updating, verifying, and maintaining land records. Additionally, AI-powered systems can assist legal professionals in drafting various legal documents, such as property deeds, leases, and contracts, ensuring accuracy and efficiency in transactions and litigation. AI algorithms excel at automating repetitive and time-consuming tasks, allowing human professionals to redirect their efforts toward tasks requiring higher-order cognitive skills and ethical judgment. By delegating routine administrative duties to AI systems, legal practitioners can increase efficiency, reduce errors, and allocate their expertise more effectively to tasks that demand critical thinking, creativity, and empathetic understanding.

III. AI and Access to Justice

This chapter next explores AI and its potential to improve access to justice by providing cost-effective and scalable solutions to legal challenges.

The onset of the COVID-19 pandemic prompted a rapid shift towards digitalisation in various sectors, including the legal system. Courts worldwide faced unprecedented challenges as they grappled with the need to balance the administration of justice with public health concerns. In response to these challenges, the Supreme Court of India took proactive measures to ensure the continuity of judicial proceedings while safeguarding the well-being of all stakeholders.

One of the key adaptations made by the Indian legal system during this period was the transition to remote proceedings. In lieu of traditional in-person oral arguments, the Supreme Court embraced technology, allowing lawyers to appear via video, mobile, or other electronic means. This shift towards remote proceedings not only ensured the uninterrupted operation of the judicial system but also minimised the risk of virus transmission among court personnel and litigants. Additionally, the Supreme Court of India introduced live transcription services, an initiative aimed at enhancing accessibility to legal information. Machine learning has helped in addressing linguistic diversity, translating judgments into 18 regional languages, including Hindi, ensuring that legal information is accessible to citizens across India. Moreover, the use of AI-driven translation further promotes fairness in court proceedings by providing accurate and timely translations, thereby facilitating effective communication and understanding among all parties involved. This underscores the potential of AI to enhance the efficiency of court proceedings by automating routine tasks such as document review, case management, and scheduling.

The 2023 Risk Outlook Report by the Solicitors Regulation Authority of the United Kingdom predicts that AI could automate time-consuming tasks, as well as increase speed and capacity.[16] This could benefit smaller firms with limited administrative support. This is because it has the potential to reduce costs and—potentially—increase the transparency around legal decision-making, assuming the technology is well-monitored.

In the UK, the Civil Justice Council recommended the introduction of Her Majesty's Online Court for civil disputes under the value of £25,000.[17] The proposed court would operate with a tiered system: the first tier would allow disputants to evaluate their problems by inputting information into an online system, which would categorise their issues, provide information about their rights and entitlements, and suggest options available to resolve the dispute.[18] This tier encourages parties to resolve the dispute on their own based on the information provided by the system.[19] The second tier involves online facilitators reviewing information and documents provided by the disputants and assisting with the resolution of the matter by mediating, advising, or encouraging negotiations.[20] This tier resembles court-connected alternative dispute resolution. The third and final tier would involve online adjudication by the judges of the court based on electronic submissions, online pleadings and arguments, and telephone conference facilities.

This determination could be binding and enforceable, with the same force as a decision made in a physical courtroom. Lord Justice Briggs suggested a similar model be introduced, which also called for the possibility of face-to-face hearings in the third tier

[16] Solicitors Regulation Authority, 'Risk Outlook Report: The Use of Artificial Intelligence in the Legal Market' (*SRA Website*, November 2023), available at www.sra.org.uk/sra/research-publications/artificial-intelligence-legal-market.

[17] Report of the Online Dispute Resolution Advisory Group of the Civil Justice Council, 'Online Dispute Resolution for Low Value Civil Claims' (February 2015) 6–7 (CJC Report); *see* also the policy paper by the Ministry of Justice of the Government of the United Kingdom and Her Majesty's Courts and Tribunal Service, 'Transforming our Justice System' (September 2016).

[18] CJC Report (n 17) 19.

[19] ibid 19–20.

[20] ibid 20.

as an absolute last resort, and included details about how the online court would allow litigants to appeal a decision into the mainstream court system.[21]

In such online dispute resolution systems, AI can play a crucial role in streamlining processes, categorising issues, providing personalised advice, and facilitating communication between parties. In contexts where individuals may lack access to legal representation or face barriers to legal assistance, AI-powered tools can bridge the gap by offering self-help resources, automated legal guidance, and virtual assistance. For example, chatbots equipped with AI capabilities can provide users with legal information, guidance on navigating legal procedures, and assistance in completing legal forms, thereby empowering individuals to better understand their rights and responsibilities and access essential legal services. Through innovative solutions, AI has the potential to democratise access to legal services and ensure that all individuals have equal opportunities to seek redress and uphold their rights within the legal system.

IV. Ethical Accountability—How can AI Governance be Structured to Tackle these Issues?

While discussing access to justice, it is imperative to address the ethical implications of AI.[22] To navigate this landscape effectively, we must focus on two fundamental aspects: (i) *how we build AI,* and (ii) *how we use it responsibly.*

A. How do We Build AI Systems?

When we embark on creating AI systems, we must pose two critical questions. Firstly, where does the data originate, and what biases might it harbour? Secondly, we must examine the architecture of these systems. What lies beneath the surface?

Understanding the sources of our data is paramount in building AI systems that are fair and inclusive. By identifying and mitigating biases, we can ensure that our AI systems do not inadvertently discriminate against certain groups, thereby upholding principles of equity and justice. One form of discrimination that can arise is indirect discrimination, where seemingly neutral policies or algorithms disproportionately affect specific groups, undermining their rights and protections. A notable example of indirect discrimination was highlighted by the European Court of Human Rights in the case of *DH and Others v Czech Republic*.[23] In this case, apparently neutral tests assessing the intellectual capabilities of children resulted in a disproportionate number of

[21] Lord Justice Briggs, 'Civil Courts Structure Review: Interim Report' (*Judiciary of England and Wales*, December 2015) 76; Lord Justice Briggs, 'Civil Courts Structure Review: Final Report' (*Judiciary of England and Wales*, July 2016) 58.

[22] This topic has been widely discussed in many articles. See B Hise and J Dao, 'Ethical Considerations in the Use of AI' (*Reuters*, 2 October 2023), available at www.reuters.com/legal/legalindustry/ethical-considerations-use-ai-2023-10-02; also see European Parliament, 'The Ethics of Artificial Intelligence: Issues and Initiatives' (2020), available at www.europarl.europa.eu/RegData/etudes/STUD/2020/634452/EPRS_STU(2020)634452_EN.pdf.

[23] *DH and Others v Czech Republic*, no 57325/00 (ECtHR, 7 February 2006).

minority Roma children being placed in special schools due to cultural and linguistic differences that the tests failed to consider. Indirect discrimination can manifest at two crucial stages in the AI process.[24] Firstly, during the training phase, incomplete or inaccurate data may lead to biased outcomes. Secondly, discrimination may occur during data processing, particularly within opaque 'black box' algorithms that obscure the decision-making process from human developers. A 'black box' refers to algorithms or systems where the internal workings are hidden, making it challenging to understand how decisions are made or why certain outcomes occur.[25]

The 'garbage-in, garbage-out' principle encapsulates the idea that the quality of decisions produced by AI systems is only as good as the quality of the data they are trained on.[26] In essence, if flawed or biased data is input into the system, the outcomes generated are likely to be biased and flawed as well. This principle is particularly relevant in the context of machine learning, where the quality of results is heavily dependent on the quality of the training data. Since AI systems rely on pre-existing datasets of case laws and other judicially relevant information to generate responses, any historical biases, discriminations, or flawed judgments present in the data can perpetuate within the AI's decision-making process.

The algorithms used in predictive policing systems are often black boxes, meaning that the inner workings of the algorithms are not transparent to the public or even to the developers themselves. This opacity can lead to discriminatory outcomes, particularly if the historical crime data used to train these algorithms reflects biases or systemic inequalities present in the criminal justice system. For instance, if certain neighbourhoods have historically been over-policed or subject to biased law enforcement practices, the predictive policing algorithms may inadvertently perpetuate these biases by targeting those same neighbourhoods as 'high-risk' areas for future crime.[27] This can result in disproportionate surveillance and policing of already marginalised communities, exacerbating social inequalities and perpetuating cycles of discrimination.

The Wisconsin Court in the *Loomis* case, a case about the sentencing of a 31-year-old man, which was referred to earlier, attempted to mitigate the risks associated with algorithmic assessments by mandating a 'written advisement of limitations' to accompany any pre-sentencing report containing a risk-assessment score.[28] This advisement highlighted key concerns, including the proprietary nature of the tool, its reliance on group data rather than individual characteristics, and the potential for bias against minority offenders. Despite these warnings, the court allowed judges to consider but

[24] A Basu and E Hickok, 'Artificial Intelligence in the Governance Sector in India – Working Draft' (*Centre for Law and Society*, 2018), available at cis-india.org/internet-governance/ai-and-governance-case-study-pdf; see also A Basu, 'Discrimination in the Age of Artificial Intelligence' (*OxHRH Blog*, 23 October 2018), available at ohrh.law.ox.ac.uk/discrimination-in-the-age-of-artificial-intelligence.

[25] *See* the definition given in R Awati, 'What is Black Box AI?' (*TechTarget*, October 2024), available at www.techtarget.com/whatis/definition/black-box-AI#:~:text=Black%20box%20AI%20is%20any,to%20how%20they%20were%20reached.

[26] The principle 'Garbage In, Garbage Out' was first introduced in R Wang, 'Beyond Accuracy: What Data Quality Means to Data Consumers' (1996) 12 *Journal of Management Information Systems* 5.

[27] W Heaven, 'Predictive Policing Algorithms are Racist. They Need to be Dismantled.' (*MIT Technology Review*, 17 July 2020), available at www.technologyreview.com/2020/07/17/1005396/predictive-policing-algorithms-racist-dismantled-machine-learning-bias-criminal-justice/.

[28] *Loomis* (n 7) 769–70.

not rely on these scores for sentencing decisions. The distinction is not merely semantic; while 'consideration' denotes a peripheral, non-determinative input, 'reliance' would allow the risk score to become a foundational basis for sentencing. In practice, however, cognitive effects such as anchoring and automation bias can blur this boundary, subtly influencing judicial reasoning even where formal rules prohibit dependence on the score. However, the Court's approach fell short of addressing deeper concerns about the fairness and transparency of algorithmic tools.[29] While the court acknowledged the risks, it did not provide clear guidance on how judges should interpret or use these scores in sentencing. This lack of meaningful restraint left room for judges to be unduly influenced by the risk assessments, potentially perpetuating biases and unfairness in sentencing outcomes.

Moreover, the Court's reliance on a 'warning label' approach failed to address external pressures and cognitive biases that may impact judges' decision-making processes.[30] The expectation that judges can exercise discretion without preconceived biases, especially when presented with automated risk scores, overlooks the reality of cognitive biases such as 'automation bias' and 'anchoring'. Anchoring is a cognitive bias that describes the tendency for individuals to rely heavily on the first piece of information they receive (the 'anchor') when making decisions.[31] This initial information then influences subsequent judgments, even if it is irrelevant or inaccurate. In the context of judicial decision-making, anchoring can manifest when judges are presented with automated risk scores generated by AI systems. These scores may serve as the anchor point for judges, shaping their perception of the case and influencing their subsequent decisions.

In the Indian context, similar concerns exist, particularly regarding biases against the Scheduled Caste and the Scheduled Tribe communities. Research conducted by the Centre for the Advanced Study of India at the University of Pennsylvania suggests the presence of certain in-group biases among segments of law enforcement, particularly in specific contexts involving marginalised communities.[32] Further, surveys and empirical studies indicate that caste-based discrimination persists, with some datasets suggesting that nearly one in five members of Scheduled Caste communities continue to face discriminatory treatment.[33] Given India's existing societal sensitivities and the challenges already present within the criminal justice system, the incorporation of AI-based systems fraught with biases would be detrimental to the fundamental rights of several Indian citizens.

To effectively navigate the challenges posed by AI in diverse contexts like India, the principle of 'contextualisation' becomes paramount. As articulated by Professors Urs Gasser and Viktor Mayer-Schönberger in their book 'Guardrails: Guiding

[29] H Liu, CF Lin and Y Chen. 'Beyond State v Loomis: Artificial Intelligence, Government Algorithmization and Accountability' (2019) 27 *International Journal of Law and Information Technology* 122.

[30] ibid.

[31] Harvard Law School, 'Program on Negotiation' (*Harvard Law School Blog*, November 2023), available at www.pon.harvard.edu/tag/anchoring-effect.

[32] P Novosad, 'In-Group Bias in the Indian Judiciary: Evidence from 5 Million Criminal Cases' (*Center for the Advanced Study of India, UPenn*, 4 November 2021), available at casi.sas.upenn.edu/events/paulnovosad.

[33] N Sahgal et al, 'Religion in India: Tolerance and Segregation' (*Pew Research Center*, 2022), available at www.pewresearch.org/religion/2021/06/29/attitudes-about-caste.

Human Decisions in the Age of AI',[34] contextualisation emphasises the importance of understanding and adapting to the specific social, cultural, and institutional contexts in which AI systems operate. India's rich demographic patterns, characterised by linguistic diversity, regional variations, and cultural nuances, present a unique set of challenges and opportunities for AI deployment.

Unlike homogeneous populations, the Indian landscape requires AI models to accommodate a wide array of data inputs reflecting the diverse perspectives and experiences of its people. Standardisation becomes a significant hurdle in such a diverse environment, as different regions may have varying norms, practices, and languages. Incorporating contextualisation into AI design involves more than just technical considerations; it requires a deep understanding of the social and cultural dynamics that shape human interactions and decision-making processes. Rigorous evaluation of datasets for biases must account for these contextual factors, ensuring that AI systems are inclusive and representative of the diverse population they serve. Moreover, designing algorithms with built-in fairness mechanisms becomes essential to mitigate biases that may arise from cultural or regional disparities. By promoting transparency in decision-making processes, stakeholders can foster trust and accountability in AI systems, enhancing their acceptance and effectiveness in addressing societal challenges.

We must also examine the architecture of these AI systems. What lies beneath the surface? Is the code robust, or does it leave room for errors and 'hallucinations'? Hallucinations, in this context, refer to erroneous outputs generated by flawed algorithms or data.[35] By scrutinising our architectural integrity, we can minimise the risks of misleading outcomes and enhance the reliability of our AI systems.

B. How do We Use AI Ethically and Responsibly?

We turn to the responsible use of AI. Once we have built these systems, it is paramount that we wield them ethically. This involves asking ourselves three vital questions.

Firstly, how do we mitigate the risk of hallucinations, especially in sensitive decision-making processes? While AI can assist us in making decisions, it should never be the sole determinant, particularly in critical scenarios like evidence evaluation or deepfake detection. When it comes to evidence evaluation, especially in legal contexts where the stakes are high, human judgment plays a crucial role in interpreting complex evidence, assessing credibility, and weighing the implications of various factors. While AI algorithms can analyse data and identify patterns, they may overlook subtle nuances, cultural context, or emotional cues that a human evaluator would recognise. In legal proceedings, where the consequences of erroneous judgments can be life-altering, it

[34] U Gasser and V Mayer-Schönberger, *Guardrails: Guiding Human Decisions in the Age of AI* (Princeton, Princeton University Press, 2024); *see* also S Jain, 'Contextualization: The Key To Unlocking Generative AI's Potential' (*Forbes Technology Council*, 30 August 2023), available at www.forbes.com/sites/forbestechcouncil/2023/08/30/contextualization-the-key-to-unlocking-generative-ais-potential/?sh=2e366dce2e7c.

[35] Definition explained in *The Economist*, 'AI Models Make Stuff Up. How can Hallucinations be Controlled?' (*The Economist*, 28 February 2024), available at www.economist.com/science-and-technology/2024/02/28/ai-models-make-stuff-up-how-can-hallucinations-be-controlled.

is essential to incorporate human judgment as a safeguard against potential biases or misinterpretations that AI may introduce.

The emergence of deepfake technology further complicates this issue. Deepfake technology allows for the creation of highly realistic but fabricated audio-visual content. It poses a significant threat to the integrity of evidence, as it can be used to manipulate or fabricate videos, audio recordings, and images with unprecedented realism. Relying solely on AI for evidence evaluation in scenarios involving deepfake content poses inherent risks. AI algorithms may not possess the contextual understanding or forensic expertise necessary to identify nuanced inconsistencies in digital media. Deepfake detection often requires human judgement to assess factors such as facial expressions, audio anomalies, and inconsistencies in lighting or perspective, which AI algorithms may overlook. Therefore, while AI algorithms can certainly aid in identifying anomalies or inconsistencies in media content, human expertise is indispensable in distinguishing between genuine and manipulated content, considering the intricacies of audio-visual production techniques, and assessing the broader context in which the media is disseminated.

Secondly, we must ensure that those tasked with using AI are well-versed in its limitations and potential pitfalls. Educating users and building their capacity to navigate AI's complexities can prevent misuse and promote responsible deployment. This includes legal professionals, judges, policymakers, and law enforcement personnel who interact with AI systems in various capacities. Assistant Professor Dirk Hartung's remarks at the India-Singapore Conference on Technology underscore the importance of legal education and capacity building in this regard. He emphasised the need for a 'T-shaped lawyer'—someone with deep expertise in a particular legal domain (the vertical stroke of the T) and a broad understanding of interdisciplinary subjects such as technology, data science, programming, and ethics (the horizontal stroke of the T).[36]

For law students, acquiring technology skills alongside legal knowledge can be invaluable in today's digital age. An introduction to data science, programming languages, and emerging technologies equips future legal professionals with the tools they need to engage with AI systems effectively. Moreover, an understanding of ethics is essential to ensure that AI is used responsibly and ethically within the legal domain. By integrating technology education into legal curricula and providing ongoing training and professional development opportunities for legal practitioners, we can cultivate a workforce that is equipped to leverage AI's benefits while mitigating its risks. This approach not only enhances the capabilities of individual professionals but also strengthens the overall integrity and fairness of AI-driven legal systems.

Finally, accountability is key. While AI itself cannot be held accountable, those deploying and overseeing its use must take responsibility for its outcomes. By embracing the concept of augmented intelligence, we recognise that AI should augment human decision-making, not replace it entirely. Augmented intelligence refers to the symbiotic relationship between humans and AI systems, where AI enhances human capabilities rather than supplanting them. In this model, AI serves as a tool to assist humans

[36] The concept has also been explained in Thomson Reuters, 'Arise, the T-Shaped Lawyer and How Law Firms Play a Pivotal Role' (*The Law Gazette*, September 2018), available at lawgazette.com.sg/practice/tech-talk/arise-the-t-shaped-lawyer-and-how-law-firms-play-a-pivotal-role.

in processing information, identifying patterns, and making informed decisions. Human judgment, critical thinking, and ethical reasoning remain essential components of the decision-making process, while AI provides insights and support based on data analysis and algorithmic processing.

V. Conclusion

In conclusion, as we navigate the evolving landscape of AI in decision-making, it is imperative to prioritise resources that mitigate risks and promote transparency, accountability, and access. While there is growing acceptance of AI technologies, trust remains a crucial factor in determining their adoption. Building trust requires open, transparent systems that allow for scrutiny and accountability. AI is inevitable in our increasingly digitised world, offering promising solutions to complex challenges. The question of whether AI systems will be open or closed has significant implications for access and equity. Open systems that provide universal access to AI technologies have the potential to democratise decision-making processes and empower individuals. Conversely, closed systems may perpetuate inequalities by restricting access to AI technologies, leading to a concentration of power in the hands of a few.

Ultimately, the goal of AI in decision-making should be to contribute to a just society by providing timely, cost-effective solutions that improve outcomes for all stakeholders. By embracing transparent, accountable AI practices and prioritising equity and access, we can harness the full potential of AI to create a more just and equitable world. Yet, even as technology evolves, the human judge remains the moral centre of the justice system, ensuring that constitutional values, empathy, and ethical reasoning continue to guide the future of adjudication.

7

Generative Artificial Intelligence and the Legal Endeavour

SUNDARESH MENON*

I. Introduction

It was not many years ago that ChatGPT first entered the consciousness of most of us. What was most striking about this new tool, which was described as a species of generative artificial intelligence (Gen AI), was its seeming ability to understand our prompts and inputs in plain language and to respond relevantly and helpfully. The initial euphoria did run into some dampeners quite soon. First, there was the phenomenon of hallucinations, when ChatGPT displayed a propensity at times to provide responses that were not founded in fact. That led to our gaining a better understanding of ChatGPT as a large language model (LLM) that essentially used statistical and probabilistic principles to construct its responses to our prompts. But then, just as we thought we were getting to understand this better, there was a story of a reporter who had a conversation with another Gen AI tool, Bing, and was left feeling quite disturbed when it declared its love for him.[1]

Without question, Gen AI has taken the world by storm, and it is here to stay. To illustrate this, ChatGPT became the fastest-growing consumer internet application of all time, gathering around 100 million *monthly* users in just two months (far outpacing the growth of Instagram and Facebook, which took over two years and four and a half years respectively, to reach the same number of users).[2] By October 2025, less than three years after it was launched, ChatGPT reached 800 million *weekly* users.[3] The speed and scale at which Gen AI has been adopted by the mainstream public is unsurprising, given that it has shown some remarkable abilities, including in producing art, music,

* The author is deeply grateful to his colleagues, Assistant Registrars Wee Yen Jean and Ong Kye Jing, as well as his former colleagues, Mr Tan Ee Kuan and Mr Bryan Ching, for all their assistance in the research for and preparation of this chapter.

[1] K Roose, 'A Conversation with Bing's Chatbot Left Me Deeply Unsettled' (*The New York Times*, 16 February 2023), available at www.nytimes.com/2023/02/16/technology/bing-chatbot-microsoft-chatgpt.html.

[2] J Porter, 'ChatGPT Continues to be One of the Fastest-growing Services Ever' (*The Verge*, 7 November 2023), available at www.theverge.com/2023/11/6/23948386/chatgpt-active-user-count-openai-developer-conference.

[3] R Bellan, 'Sam Altman Says ChatGPT has Hit 800M Weekly Active Users' (*TechCrunch*, 6 October 2025), available at techcrunch.com/2025/10/06/sam-altman-says-chatgpt-has-hit-800m-weekly-active-users.

recipes, itineraries for holidays and, most relevantly for present purposes, in generating, summarising and organising text. The last of these brings us directly to the law, a field that is predominantly based on text.

It is remarkable that despite the capabilities that Gen AI has already demonstrated over the past couple of years, the technology continues to advance at an exponential pace. To give just one prominent example, Gen AI models developed by Google and OpenAI achieved historic gold medals at the International Mathematical Olympiad in 2025, surpassing the silver medal performance from just a year before.[4] This dramatic improvement has led experts to predict that Gen AI may be less than a year away from resolving previously unsolved mathematical problems at the frontier of the field.[5]

Indeed, this is a field where breakthroughs occur with such regularity and momentum that even Moore's Law feels like a gentle progression by comparison. Developments that we describe as current or cutting-edge today may no longer reflect the technological reality after a few short months, and this is a challenge that any commentary in this space will invariably face. Even so, Gen AI has already matured to a stage where we can meaningfully distil some of its key features and assess its impact on the courts with reasonable confidence. Against that backdrop, the subject of this chapter is the role that Gen AI might play in advancing the legal endeavour. Its central thesis is as follows:

(a) Existing Gen AI tools do not and cannot employ the legal method, which has been central to the legal endeavour in our societies.

(b) Despite this, it seems likely that Gen AI will be able to make an immense contribution to our legal systems. In particular, Gen AI should help us to address two critical threats that are faced by our justice systems: the problems of access to justice and the complexification of legal disputes. Our main strategy for tackling these problems has hitherto been to seek to augment the lawyers and the legal resources that are devoted to addressing them. But this approach is inadequate given the sheer *scale* of the aforementioned challenges. Gen AI offers us new and previously unimaginable methods to deal with these problems, and it therefore holds the real potential to impact our legal systems in very significant ways.

(c) Hence, we should usher Gen AI into our legal systems, and to this end, there are two key strategies. First, we will need to transform both university legal education and continuing legal education to ensure that legal professionals are able to use AI effectively and responsibly. Second, as we go about incorporating Gen AI into our justice systems, we should take an incremental and measured approach to ensure the legitimate and successful adoption of Gen AI.

This chapter will develop this thesis in four main sections:

(a) Section II begins with a brief overview of the legal endeavour. It identifies the overarching function and sources of law and then endeavours to categorise the

[4] *The Business Times*, 'Google and OpenAI's AI Models Win Milestone Gold at Global Math Competition' (22 July 2025), available at www.businesstimes.com.sg/lifestyle/google-and-openais-ai-models-win-milestone-gold-global-math-competition.

[5] K Cai and J Singh, 'Google Clinches Milestone Gold at Global Math Competition, while OpenAI also Claims Win' (*Reuters*, 22 July 2025), available at www.reuters.com/world/asia-pacific/google-clinches-milestone-gold-global-math-competition-while-openai-also-claims-2025-07-22.

legal endeavour into several tasks, while noting that these tasks have historically been carried out through the use of the legal method.

(b) Section III turns to Gen AI. It first describes the nature of current Gen AI tools, before outlining an objection to the use of such tools in the legal context, which will be referred to as the 'legal method objection'. It then explains why the legal method objection should not be accepted as a basis for rejecting the endeavour to incorporate Gen AI into our legal and justice systems.

(c) Section IV turns to the problems of access to justice and the complexification of disputes. It discusses these challenges and explains how Gen AI is at present perhaps our best hope to mitigate these challenges.

(d) Finally, section V discusses the two strategies referred to above: transforming legal education and adopting a progressive approach towards incorporating Gen AI into our judicial processes.

II. The Legal Endeavour: Its Function, Sources, Tasks, and Method

The legal endeavour can be expressed in a variety of ways, but this chapter suggests that, in essence, it is to provide order and justice in the relations and dealings between a state and its subjects and between those subjects.[6] To this end, legal systems as a whole enact legislation, and generate case law that interprets legislation, fills in interstitial gaps, and creates free-standing legal norms. Such legal rules impose duties and confer powers on the state and its subjects, and they thereby order and structure relations within a community.

The legal endeavour comprises the following main tasks:

(a) creating sources of law such as legislation and judicial decisions;

(b) providing information about aspects of the law, as and when people need such information to: (i) access rights conferred by the law (for example, rights of citizenship); and (ii) conduct their affairs in compliance with the law; and

(c) where disputes arise over the law or its application in particular cases: (i) identifying the applicable laws and outcome, where this is clear; (ii) where the law or legal response is unclear, predicting the likely legal outcome; and (iii) ultimately, if disputes persist, assisting in the resolution of those disputes and enforcing the law.

Traditionally, these tasks have been discharged through the use of the legal method: the body of principles and techniques that underlie legal reasoning and the expression of legal rules.[7] This includes general methods of reasoning – such as inductive reasoning, deductive reasoning, and reasoning by analogy – as well as specific legal concepts and

[6] Prime Minister Lee KY, Speech to the University of Singapore Law Society Annual Dinner at Rosee D'Or (18 January 1962) 5.

[7] J Holland and J Webb, *Learning Legal Rules: A Students' Guide to Legal Method and Reasoning*, 7th edn (Oxford, Oxford University Press, 2010) 1; I McLeod, *Legal Method*, 9th edn (London, Palgrave Macmillan, 2013) 3.

principles such as the maxims of statutory interpretation or the rules of precedent. The legal method is used to identify the law, whether embodied in legislation or case law; to develop and make new law, in the form of statutes and judgments; and to apply the law to specific cases. In all these ways, the legal method has underlain the legal endeavour.

III. The Nature of Gen AI and the Legal Method Objection

How then can Gen AI advance the legal endeavour? To address this question, we must first appreciate the nature and capabilities of Gen AI – at least in its present form and as we understand it today.

A. The Nature and Capabilities of Gen AI

Gen AI tools are digital algorithmic systems that can generate a range of outputs, including, as has been noted, text, art, and music, in response to prompts by users. Such tools have capabilities that can seem remarkably human, in at least two aspects.

(a) Gen AI can produce output that closely resembles human creations. For example, in the legal sphere, tools like Harvey and CoCounsel can presently produce summaries, research memos, and even deposition questions,[8] which are comparable or even superior to the work of human lawyers.[9] In this way, Gen AI tools can greatly enhance both the efficiency *and* quality of legal work.

(b) Such tools can also mimic emotions and empathy in their responses to input. They can thereby appear to exhibit social intelligence, which is a fundamentally human attribute.

Given these capabilities, it is common and natural to anthropomorphise Gen AI by likening the operation of such tools to human activity. But this would be a mistaken approach because it is vital to appreciate at the outset that Gen AI systems are *not* digital analogues of humans. Most significantly, based on the current state of the art, Gen AI tools *do not comprehend what language means to humans and they cannot reason in the way we do*. Rather, they are essentially prediction engines that select the next best token (such as a word or a musical note) in a series of tokens.[10] More precisely, Gen AI tools operate by: (a) first identifying a range of tokens that are ranked according to the probability that they would follow an earlier series of tokens; (b) then selecting a token, based

[8] Harvey, 'Products', available at www.harvey.ai/products; V McConnell, 'What is CoCounsel?', available at help.casetext.com/en/articles/7040012-what-is-cocounsel.

[9] Vals AI, a US-based company that evaluates AI tools, published in 2025 the results of a study that evaluated the performance of four legal AI tools across seven discrete legal tasks. All four tools outperformed the lawyers in two areas – the summarisation of documents and the analysis of court transcripts. Harvey, the platform developed by the eponymous start-up, outperformed the lawyers in two additional areas – data extraction and document review and analysis. See Vals AI, 'Vals Legal AI Report', available at www.vals.ai/vlair.

[10] Microsoft Learn, 'How Generative AI and LLMs Work' (*Microsoft Learn*, 21 May 2024), available at learn.microsoft.com/en-us/dotnet/ai/conceptual/how-genai-and-llms-work.

on parameters including algorithmic settings that control the creativity of the tool, by determining how often and when less probable tokens may be selected; and then (c) continuing the process, one token at a time.[11]

To illustrate what this means in a legal context, suppose that a user inputs a legal query into a Gen AI tool, which responds by identifying a legal rule and suggesting how it applies to the user's situation. In producing this output, the tool does not actually apply the law to the facts in the conventional sense. Indeed, it cannot even understand the semantic meaning of the legal rule cited in its response. That response is more accurately seen as the result of a process of predictive computing that is determined by statistical and other technical factors, all of which are distinct from the legal method and do not even resemble it. Moreover, the exact manner in which this process of predictive computing is carried out remains largely unclear, and it has been observed that AI systems are 'fundamentally inscrutable'.[12]

Yet, what we do know is that Gen AI provides us with an expanding *range of capabilities* that we can use in different ways in our work. AI should not be seen as a single agglomerated concept, but ought to be disaggregated into its distinct functions and capabilities, which are themselves not static but ever evolving. Indeed, a study by the Harvard Business School and the Boston Consulting Group found that AI's current capabilities 'cover an expanding, but uneven, set of knowledge work', which they described as a 'jagged technological frontier'. *Within* the growing jagged frontier, AI can complement and even displace human work. But *outside* this frontier, its output was found to be 'inaccurate, less useful, and degrades human performance'.[13]

The challenge therefore lies in understanding where precisely this frontier lies at any given point, because it is rapidly expanding and constantly shifting. The contours of the jagged frontier are also likely to vary depending on the specific field of knowledge in question.[14] Thus, a 2025 study found that while LLMs were capable of *basic* legal analysis, they were also 'limited by brief responses lacking detail, an inability to commit to answers, false confidence, and hallucinations'.[15]

B. The Legal Method Objection

This gives rise to a threshold objection to the use of Gen AI in legal systems. As noted earlier, the legal method has underpinned the legal endeavour, but today's Gen AI tools simply do not and cannot use that method. In this light, it might be asked how Gen AI could possibly enhance our legal systems, especially given its present limitations. This

[11] Google AI for Developers, 'About Generative Models', available at ai.google.dev/gemini-api/docs/models/generative-models.

[12] D Leiser, 'The Inscrutability of AI Systems – A Constructivist Perspective' (SSRN, 2025), available at ssrn.com/abstract=5296298.

[13] F Dell'Acqua et al, 'Navigating the Jagged Technological Frontier: Field Experimental Evidence of the Effects of AI on Knowledge Worker Productivity and Quality', Harvard Business School Working Paper 24-013.

[14] S Menon, 'The Role of Technology in Justice Systems: A Vision of Accessible and Collaborative Justice', paper delivered at Sejong International Judicial Conference (29 September 2025) para 11.

[15] L Peoples, 'Artificial Intelligence and Legal Analysis: Implications for Legal Education and the Profession', forthcoming in *Law Library Journal* (2025).

may be described as the legal method objection. In a nutshell, it posits that Gen AI cannot advance the legal endeavour because it does not and cannot employ the legal method.

The legal method objection is flawed at two levels at least. First, while Gen AI may not be able to perform certain legal tasks because it does not use the legal method, it plainly is able to advance the legal endeavour by supporting the work of judges and lawyers in some areas. For instance, eDiscovery software can significantly expedite document disclosure by rapidly identifying relevant documents from copious amounts of evidence. This picks out a fallacy in the legal method objection, which is the implicit assumption that Gen AI should only be used if it can serve as a *complete substitute* for humans. But Gen AI should instead be seen as a *tool* that legal professionals can harness. And, as a tool, Gen AI can significantly advance the legal endeavour by enhancing the work of judges and lawyers even if it relies on a methodology that has nothing to do with the legal method.

Second, Gen AI is already able to perform certain legal tasks to a high standard despite the fact that it does not use the legal method. Consider two tasks that are key aspects of the work of a litigator: predicting the likely outcome of litigation and anticipating the queries that may be raised by a judge at a hearing. As to the first task, Lex Machina, a legal analytics tool, has demonstrated its ability to predict the likelihood of success in US patent litigation better than most patent litigators.[16] And as to the second task, Harvey reportedly accurately predicted several queries that were subsequently raised by a judge at a recent appellate hearing.[17] These examples demonstrate that the legal method is not the only way to achieve the outcomes that are desired from certain legal tasks. Instead, data analytics can be a powerful source of insight, especially in a field like the law, which tends to be bound in and driven by precedent.

This is a point of importance because most citizens are ambivalent as to *how* their problems are solved. Their key concern is the *outcome*, and not the process by which it is achieved – as Professor Richard Susskind and Professor Daniel Susskind have noted, people 'want trustworthy solutions, whether they rely on flesh-and-blood professionals or AI'.[18] In other words, it will not matter to most people that Gen AI does not employ the legal method. They will initially accept and later even demand the use of Gen AI if it can secure reliable results, and even more so if it reduces the cost and time needed to obtain legal solutions.

Hence, the legal method objection cannot be a basis for excluding Gen AI tools from our legal and justice systems. On the contrary, we should recognise that such tools can advance the legal endeavour, even though they do not use the legal method, and think creatively of how we can make the best use of them. This chapter will examine the contribution that Gen AI could make to two critical problems affecting the legal endeavour: access to justice and the complexification of disputes.

Before turning to these issues, it should be noted that there is a practical question, arising from the legal method objection, as to whether judges who use Gen AI for

[16] R Susskind, 'Artificial Intelligence' in *Tomorrow's Lawyers: An Introduction to Your Future*, 3rd edn (Oxford, Oxford University Press, 2023) ch 22.

[17] This was conveyed to the author by Mr Winston Weinberg, CEO of Harvey.

[18] R Susskind and D Susskind, 'Generative AI will Upend the Professions' (*Financial Times*, 18 June 2023), available at www.ft.com/content/96a1877f-0bbb-48c7-be8f-4fed437810e8.

specific tasks such as the analysis of evidence should make the relevant disclosures to the parties. Such disclosures might encompass both the fact that Gen AI is used and the actual output produced. Where the latter is concerned, there is a related question as to whether the parties are entitled to challenge the accuracy and reliability of the output.

Arguments in favour of disclosure may rest on several bases. It might be suggested that such disclosures are warranted because the use of Gen AI entails the application of a methodology which is fundamentally different in kind from the legal method. And as the authors of previous chapters in this book have discussed, this methodology has given rise to some valid concerns:[19]

(a) One such concern has been referred to above – the existing tendency of Gen AI tools to hallucinate and thereby propagate untruths. If this problem persists, it would be a matter of serious concern because, unlike legal professionals, Gen AI tools are neither bound by professional ethical obligations nor guided by values such as integrity and professionalism.

(b) Another concern is the problem of opacity. The inner workings of Gen AI tools are often not disclosed by developers and may mask hidden systemic biases, a point that will be elaborated on below. And even if the algorithms and underlying datasets are disclosed, they will often not be intelligible to most laypersons, even as work on Explainable AI is seeking to close this gap. Such forms of opacity have potential implications for trust in the judiciary, given that courts secure public trust by, among other things, enhancing transparency and accountability in the adjudicatory process.

On the other hand, it might be contended that disclosure requirements are unnecessary and possibly counterproductive. They may potentially have a chilling effect on the adoption of innovative AI tools and practices that would significantly enhance the effectiveness and efficiency of courts. It might suffice for judges to be trained on how to use Gen AI tools safely and to recognise the vital need to independently verify all AI-generated output.

While this is an issue that merits further discussion and consideration, it is suggested, provisionally, that a contextual approach may be adopted to determine when disclosures are required. A key consideration should be the extent to which AI-generated output influences judicial decision-making. For instance, returning to the earlier example, if a Gen AI tool produces an analysis of the parties' evidence that the judge then relies on in reaching a decision, natural justice would seem to require that the parties be given the opportunity to challenge or at least comment on the output. But if the Gen AI tool is used to produce a summary of the parties' pleadings solely to provide the judge with a quick initial overview of the matter, this may not invite disclosure if there is an understanding and expectation that the judge will ultimately review and directly refer to the parties' pleadings when making her decision.

[19] S Menon, 'Judicial Responsibility in the Age of Artificial Intelligence', keynote speech at the Inaugural Singapore-India Conference on Technology (13 April 2024) paras 12–18.

IV. The Promise of Gen AI: Access to Justice and Complexification

A. Access to Justice

i. The Problem of Access to Justice and What it Requires

This chapter now turns to examine how Gen AI might contribute to addressing two critical challenges facing legal and justice systems: access to justice and the complexification of disputes.

In gist, the problem of access to justice refers to the inability of people to obtain justice for their legal problems. This is a worldwide predicament: a study by the World Justice Project (WJP) found that *two-thirds of the global population (an estimated 5.1 billion people)* lack access to justice because they have unmet justice needs, are excluded from legal protections, or live in extreme conditions of injustice.[20] Furthermore, the COVID-19 pandemic has worsened and intensified the problem of access to justice.[21] At its core, the problem is fundamentally one of *size*: around one *billion* legal issues arise each year[22] and the task of providing fair solutions to all of these issues is a monumental challenge. In this regard, a WJP report based on data from over 100 countries noted that in *seven out of ten countries*, at least *62* per cent of people who needed access to a dispute resolution mechanism could not obtain such access.[23] And in recent years, this state of affairs has worsened as many justice systems have deteriorated – from 2022 to 2023, the quality of civil justice fell in two out of three countries.[24] These stark findings underscore the magnitude of the access to justice problem: it is nothing less than a *global crisis*.

It is important to appreciate the nature of the justice gap. The problem of access to justice primarily manifests itself at the bottom end of the legal market, in that: (a) it disproportionately affects low-income citizens; and (b) it mainly relates to relatively simple or routine legal problems.

(a) The problem of access to justice predominantly affects *low-income citizens*, for at least two reasons. First, impecuniosity generally gives rise to more legal problems: the WJP found that in at least 70 per cent of countries, people living in poverty face more legal problems than others.[25] Further, low-income individuals

[20] World Justice Project, *Measuring the Justice Gap: A People-Centered Assessment of Unmet Justice Needs Around the World* (2019) 7–8, available at worldjusticeproject.org/our-work/research-and-data/access-justice/measuring-justice-gap.

[21] World Justice Project, *Grasping the Justice Gap: Opportunities and Challenges for People-Centered Justice Data* (2021) 5, available at worldjusticeproject.org/sites/default/files/documents/Grasping-the-Justice-Gap_Challenge-Paper_final.pdf.

[22] Hague Institute for Innovation of Law, 'Understanding Justice Needs: The Elephant in the Courtroom' (2018) 14.

[23] World Justice Project, *Dissecting the Justice Gap in 104 Countries: WJP Justice Data Graphical Report I* (2023) 7–8, available at worldjusticeproject.org/our-work/research-and-data/access-justice/measuring-justice-gap.

[24] World Justice Project, *Disparities, Vulnerability, and Harnessing Data for People-Centered Justice: WJP Justice Data Graphical Report II* (2023) 37–38, available at worldjusticeproject.org/our-work/research-and-data/wjp-justice-data-graphical-report-ii.

[25] ibid 5, 20–21.

face greater barriers to justice.[26] To illustrate this, a recent study found that low-income Americans do not receive sufficient legal help for 92 per cent of their civil legal problems.[27]

(b) Next, many legal problems which are not adequately addressed are of a recurrent nature and are relatively straightforward both factually and legally. The Hague Institute for Innovation of Law has estimated that 60 per cent of legal problems fall into just five categories – family, employment, land, crime and neighbour disputes. Moreover, many of these problems largely involve similar or recurrent fact patterns.[28] For example, most employment disputes relate to wages, dismissal or harassment, while neighbour disputes often tend to involve noise, smell, and boundary issues.

What then does access to *justice* require? Historically, justice has been equated with adjudication: that is, the exhaustive determination of the parties' legal rights, through the application of the law to the evidence. But in the context of access to justice, we should abandon this process-based conception of justice.

(a) First, even if adjudication reflected the ideal of justice, it would be impossible to achieve that ideal in respect of every legal problem. As noted above, around one *billion* legal problems arise each year, and our societies simply do not have the physical, financial, and human resources to resolve all of these through adjudication. Yet we can significantly enhance access to justice using mediation and other alternative dispute resolution (ADR) methods that can offer practical and meaningful remedies, even if these do not accord with traditional notions of 'perfect' justice. It follows that in our quest to enhance access to justice, we should frame our goal in a way that does not confine us to improving access to *adjudication* but would instead open up other pathways to justice.

(b) Second, the ordinary citizen does not primarily see justice in procedural terms. Most people have an *outcome-based* conception of justice: they take justice to be a fair result of what one is due.[29] And with this view, many would doubt that justice demands the adjudication of *all* disputes. Adjudication is often costly and protracted, and these features can undercut the practical value of remedies obtained through the process. It can also heighten tensions and entrench conflict, thereby worsening the parties' relationships and aggravating their disputes. Further, adjudication focuses on the parties' legal *rights* instead of their *interests* and can therefore produce outcomes that do not meet the parties' needs. For these reasons, adjudication can and not infrequently does fail to deliver justice.

Hence, in line with the common understanding of justice that has been noted above, we should adopt a *practical and outcome-centred conception of justice* when thinking about how to promote access to justice: in other words, justice as the *just resolution* of legal

[26] ibid 22.
[27] Legal Services Corporation, 'The Justice Gap – Section 5: Comparing Income Groups' (April 2022), available at justicegap.lsc.gov/resource/section-5-comparing-income-groups.
[28] Hague Institute for Innovation of Law (n 22) 15.
[29] LM Friedman, 'Access to Justice: Some Historical Comments' (2010) 37 *Fordham Urban Law Journal* 3, 3–4.

problems[30] as long as the process used is fair, proportionate and accessible. On this view, justice is ultimately about *providing fair and acceptable solutions to legal issues.*

ii. The Impediments to Justice and the Traditional Approach to Them

What are the main sources of the problem of access to justice? Broadly, there are three types of impediments to justice:[31]

1. *The literacy impediment*: This has at least two elements. First, people who face problems often do not realise that those problems have a *legal* dimension, and that the law can help to resolve them. Hence, many laypersons do not even seek legal recourse for their difficulties because they do not perceive that this is an option. Second, even if some appreciate that they face a legal problem and contemplate seeking legal remedies, many do not understand the law and are unfamiliar with legal procedure and processes. They therefore often struggle to navigate the justice system.
2. *The resources impediment*: Traditionally, lawyers have been the gatekeepers of our legal systems. Yet many people cannot afford a lawyer and therefore struggle to obtain justice. To illustrate this, a 2022 study found that low-income Americans sought legal help for just 19 per cent of their civil legal problems; and one in two of those who did not seek legal help cited cost as a reason.[32] This underscores that a lack of financial resources, coupled with the escalating costs of legal representation, can hinder many people from even attempting to obtain justice.
3. *The physical impediment*: Physical distance from lawyers and the courts also impedes access to justice. This is a major problem even in developed countries. For example, a 2020 report found that 40 per cent of counties in the US are 'legal deserts' (a term that describes geographical regions with less than one lawyer per 1,000 residents).[33] Citizens living in such areas face significant challenges in obtaining legal solutions for family, housing, and other common legal problems, simply because it is difficult to reach a lawyer.[34]

Historically, we have used one principal strategy to mitigate these barriers to justice: providing legal aid and pro bono services. Yet although this is and must remain a key plank of efforts to enhance access to justice, we cannot rely on this alone and urgently need to develop other approaches. This is so for a number of reasons.

First, legal aid and pro bono services are highly resource-intensive and realistically cannot be expanded sufficiently to resolve the problem of access to justice. As noted

[30] RL Sandefur, 'Access to What?' (2019) 48 *Daedalus* 49, 49.

[31] S Menon, 'Technology and the Changing Face of Justice', lecture delivered at the Negotiation and Conflict Management Group ADR Conference 2019 (14 November 2019) paras 11–27.

[32] Legal Services Corporation, 'The Justice Gap – Section 4: Seeking and Receiving Legal Help' (April 2022), available at justicegap.lsc.gov/resource/section-4-seeking-and-receiving-legal-help.

[33] American Bar Association, *ABA Profile of the Legal Profession 2020* (July 2020) 2.

[34] H Hamacher, 'Legal Deserts: Scarcity of Lawyers Threatens Justice in Many Rural Areas' (*Daily Record*, 22 November 2023), available at thedailyrecord.com/2023/11/22/legal-deserts-scarcity-of-lawyers-threatens-justice-in-many-rural-areas.

above,[35] access to justice is a *global crisis*, and traditional approaches simply cannot measure up to the sheer scale and magnitude of the challenge. To illustrate this, in 2022, there was an average of just 2.8 paid civil legal aid lawyers for every 10,000 US residents in poverty.[36] Indeed, in recent years, funding for legal aid has fallen in several countries as demands on the public purse increase. For example, public spending on legal aid in the UK fell by 28 per cent in real terms from 2012–13 to 2022–23.[37] In addition to this, it has to be acknowledged that there are finite limits to our ability to undertake pro bono work given the economic constraints on the time and the resources that can be devoted to this endeavour. Hence, it is imperative to identify and promote other strategies that can be scaled up readily to enhance access to justice.

More fundamentally, legal aid and pro bono work may not even be needed for many simple or routine problems. For example, a landmark study found that applications for no-fault divorce filed by laypersons using templates were comparable to – and even contained fewer errors in some respects than – applications filed by lawyers.[38] Separately, not-for-profit agencies that were not staffed by lawyers were found to have performed better than solicitors in handling debt, welfare, housing, and other simple civil matters that were referred to administrative tribunals.[39] These studies suggest that it may not be necessary or even useful to deploy lawyers to help resolve certain straightforward or standard legal problems. And this is a key insight because, as noted above, the access to justice crisis primarily stems from the lack of adequate solutions to these kinds of legal problems.[40] This too points us towards looking for new and innovative methods to enhance access to justice.

iii. How Gen AI can Advance Access to Justice

This is where Gen AI can play a significant role. It ought to be seen not only as a viable tool to enhance access to justice, but as a *necessary* one given the reality of the global justice gap. The adoption of Gen AI must also be seen in context – in jurisdictions which face an extremely large caseload, the alternative to the use of Gen AI would be to effectively shut out many would-be litigants from the justice system.

Seen in this light, Gen AI can advance access to justice by mitigating the *literacy* and *resources* impediments. Gen AI is perhaps less suited to addressing the *physical* impediment, which can instead be alleviated using other forms of technology such as legal kiosks, online filing, and video conferencing.[41] In Singapore, we have brought court services such as the filing of applications to enforce maintenance orders to community

[35] See section IV.A.i. above.

[36] American Bar Association, 'ABA Profile of the Legal Profession 2023 – Civil Legal Aid', available at www.abalegalprofile.com/legalaid.html.

[37] A Gray, 'Legal Aid Cuts Risk Shifting Costs to Other Public Services, Says UK Watchdog' (*Financial Times*, 9 February 2024), available at www.ft.com/content/31bebd57-51bd-4097-a749-e9862fda3bf6.

[38] RC Cavanagh and DL Rhode, 'Project: The Unauthorized Practice of Law and Pro Se Divorce: An Empirical Analysis' (1976) 86 *Yale Law Journal* 104, 123–29.

[39] R Moorhead et al, 'Contesting Professionalism: Legal Aid and Nonlawyers in England and Wales' (2003) 37 *Law & Society Review* 765, 777, 784–89.

[40] See section IV.A.i. above.

[41] S Chisham, 'Legal Deserts: How Scarce Representation is Affecting Immigrants' (*The Globe*, 14 November 2023), available at dglobe.com/news/local/legal-deserts-how-scarce-representation-is-affecting-immigrants.

centres in the heartlands,[42] and have also introduced online filing for divorce and probate applications made by laypersons.[43] Further, our courts routinely conduct certain kinds of hearings through remote video conferencing, such as case management conferences. Such non-AI innovations can significantly reduce the physical gap between the justice system and citizens.

However, the real value of Gen AI lies in its huge potential to ameliorate the literacy and resources impediments, by transforming our processes and creating novel solutions that were previously unimaginable. First, Gen AI can enhance legal literacy in the following ways:

(a) At the most basic level, Gen AI products can help people understand that many common problems often have legal dimensions and potential legal solutions. For example, Justice Connect, an Australian not-for-profit body, is developing an AI tool that is specifically designed to parse everyday language used by laypersons, especially those from vulnerable communities, to identify and diagnose potential legal issues.[44] Such products are invaluable because, as noted earlier, one major barrier to justice is that many people do not even realise that the law governs and can help to resolve some of their problems.

(b) Further, Gen AI tools can explain the specific legal rules and procedures that may be relevant to a user. Existing Gen AI tools can already perform this function to some extent, and Professor Richard Susskind has suggested that such products will soon be able to offer highly user-friendly explanations of the law. He predicts that, within the next five years, Gen AI will be able to 'simplify, summarise and explain legislation, customised for different categories of readers, complete with flow charts', as well as convert legal rules into question-and-answer systems that can help users understand their legal positions.[45] These features could greatly help laypersons to understand legal jargon, how legal rules interact with each other, and how the law may apply to them.

In addition to this, Gen AI can also mitigate the *resources* impediment. As mentioned earlier, this obstacle arises because many people cannot afford to pay for lawyers, who have traditionally been the gatekeepers of the justice system. Gen AI can help to overcome this hurdle by aiding people to obtain justice without engaging a lawyer. For instance, in Singapore, we have developed Pair Search in collaboration with the Government Technology Agency of Singapore. Pair Search is a freely available AI-powered tool that allows users to quickly and easily conduct research on court judgments and legislation. Apart from helping users identify the most relevant cases that are responsive to their keyword searches, it can help extract key principles from cases, categorise the search results thematically or chronologically, and provide case summaries that can be easily understood.[46]

[42] SG Courts, *Annual Report 2022*, 'Access to Justice – Filing Maintenance Enforcement Applications in the Heartlands', available at judiciary.gov.sg/AnnualReport2022/ATJ-Filing-Maintenance-Enforcement.html.

[43] SG Courts, 'eServices' available at services.judiciary.gov.sg.

[44] Justice Connect, 'Our Artificial Intelligence (AI) Project', available at justiceconnect.org.au/about/innovation/legal-help-experience/ai-project.

[45] R Susskind, 'I Asked ChatGPT to Write Some Laws — This is What Happened' (*The Times*, 4 April 2024).

[46] Menon (n 14) para 16. See search.pair.gov.sg/?source=judiciary.

In certain types of settings, Gen AI has the potential to help the ordinary citizen to secure justice through adjudication by assisting her to represent herself in litigation. To explore and hopefully to realise this, the Singapore courts have embarked on a ground-breaking project with Harvey.AI, the start-up behind the eponymous tool, to use Gen AI to assist users in the Small Claims Tribunals (SCT).[47] By way of background, the SCT's jurisdiction is limited to certain types of lower-value civil claims, such as those relating to contracts for the sale of goods or provision of services, and contracts for residential leases not exceeding two years. The SCT hears claims of up to SGD20,000, which may be increased to SGD30,000 if the parties consent.

Our initial deployment of Gen AI in the SCT was to provide the on-demand *translation* of court documents into Chinese, Malay and Tamil, these being the other official languages of Singapore apart from English. In September 2025, we launched a Gen AI tool that would *summarise* the parties' documents, so that they may better understand the other side's position and hopefully reach an amicable resolution of the dispute. In time to come, we hope that this tool will be able to help self-represented persons draft documents such as claims and responses, understand the evidence they should produce, organise their materials, and prepare their submissions.[48] In these ways, Gen AI can come to the aid of laypersons as they embark on the often unfamiliar and daunting tasks of litigation, and thus ease their path to justice through adjudication.

More radically, Gen AI might even come to be used in the *adjudication* of certain simple civil disputes. Gen AI systems could potentially be used as first-deciders for certain routine civil matters that do not require significant normative judgment but involve issues that can generally be resolved by applying common patterns (for example, maintenance applications in family proceedings).[49] As highlighted above, the problem of access to justice primarily manifests itself in these types of disputes.[50] A Gen AI tool could identify an outcome for such disputes, which would, upon application by a party, be subject to review by a judge but which would otherwise bind the parties unless and until it is overturned. Such tools could significantly reduce the time and cost needed to secure an outcome from the courts, and thereby further alleviate the resources impediment.

And, beyond adjudication, Gen AI has enormous potential to enable citizens to obtain justice through ADR mechanisms cheaply, simply and quickly. ADR is often the most appropriate means for resolving simple or routine civil disputes as well as cases that arise from the breakdown in the relationships between parties, such as family or neighbour disputes. But laypersons are often not aware of ADR options or of their value. Hence, a key role of lawyers has been to inform clients of the availability of ADR tools, advise them to consider ADR and, if ADR proceeds, devise creative and mutually acceptable solutions that can advance the parties' interests.

[47] Lee LY, 'Small Claims Tribunals to Roll out AI Program to Guide Users through Legal Processes' (*The Straits Times*, 26 September 2023), available at straitstimes.com/singapore/small-claims-tribunal-to-roll-out-ai-program-to-guide-users-through-legal-processes.

[48] Menon (n 14) para 19.

[49] S Menon, 'Legal Systems in a Digital Age: Pursuing the Next Frontier', Opening Address at the 3rd Annual France-Singapore Symposium on Law and Business (11 May 2023) paras 48–49.

[50] See section IV.A.i. above.

Gen AI tools will likely soon be able to perform some of these functions, at little or no cost to users. For instance, it is hoped that the Gen AI tool for users of the SCT in Singapore may in time be able to prompt litigants to consider mediation and perhaps even suggest how a dispute might be settled. Similarly, in the UK, AI-driven ADR systems are being integrated into online court platforms, and these will encourage users to engage in pre-action ADR such as mediation or early neutral evaluation.[51] In such ways, Gen AI can mitigate the resources impediment by expanding access to cost-effective, speedy, and practical solutions to legal problems that citizens can obtain without the need to hire lawyers.

And critically, Gen AI can make substantial headway on these fronts due to one vital feature that differentiates it from legal aid and pro bono services. Once AI systems are developed, the marginal cost of using them is relatively low.[52] Hence, AI tools can be applied at scale without appreciable increases in cost. This is fundamental because, as noted above,[53] the access to justice crisis is, at its core, a problem of *size* arising from the plethora of justice issues, which calls for strategies that can scale up significantly.[54] Gen AI tools can meet this demand and will therefore bring a step change in the quest to advance access to justice.

B. Complexification

i. *The Problem of Complexification*

A second key problem for our legal systems is the complexification (that is, the increasing complexity) of legal disputes.[55] This has at least three main facets.

(a) *Evidential* complexity refers to the massive quantities of data, documents and other sources of information that are increasingly being adduced as evidence. To illustrate this using reported examples, in the *Bell Group* litigation, over *86,000* documents were tendered;[56] and in a single power plant dispute, the claimant raised more than *120,000* events of disruption.[57] The growth of evidential complexity can be traced to advances in digital technology, which have fuelled an exponential increase in the generation, sharing and storage of information.

(b) *Technical* complexity relates to the arcane and sophisticated nature of many disputes, which often involve abstruse scientific methods and procedures. For example, a recent patent dispute before the Singapore courts raised highly specialised issues regarding the production of synthetic diamonds using

[51] G Vos, 'The Future for Dispute Resolution: Horizon Scanning' (17 March 2022) paras 3, 6, 42.

[52] I Bremmer and M Suleyman, 'Building Blocks for AI Governance' *Finance and Development* (December 2023) 11.

[53] See section IV.A.i. above.

[54] Hague Institute for Innovation of Law, 'Use of Digital Technologies in Justice Reform and Access to Justice Cooperation' (2021) 62.

[55] S Menon, 'The Complexification of Disputes in the Digital Age', Goff Lecture 2021 (9 November 2021).

[56] *Bell Group Ltd (in liq) v Westpac Banking Corporation (No 9)* [2008] WASC 239.

[57] J Risse, 'An Inconvenient Truth: The Complexity Problem and Limits to Justice' (2019) 35 *Arbitration International* 291, 293.

chemical vapour deposition.[58] The rise in technical complexity flows from the rapid and continuing advances in science. These have not only made the subject matter of disputes more esoteric but have also driven the 'scientisation of factual inquiry', which is the growing use of scientific methods to determine the truth in many areas.[59] Consequently, fact-finding in many cases now turns on scientific analysis and interpretation.

(c) *Legal* complexity refers to the involved and voluminous nature of the law. This is reflected in the increasing amount of law as well as the growing cross-references and connections between legal rules. To illustrate this, the text of and cross-references in the federal legislation of Germany and the US grew by more than 50 per cent from 1994 to 2018.[60] And in Singapore, between the late 1980s and 2017, both the number of reported judgments per year and the length of those judgments grew by more than four times.[61] The increase in legal complexity can be traced to external causes such as the proliferation of rules and regulations,[62] as well as factors internal to the law such as the inherent tendency of the common law to develop distinctions and nuances as it is applied in case after case.[63]

The phenomenon of complexification presents a serious challenge to legal systems at two levels.[64] First, it undermines the ability of individual lawyers and adjudicators to apply the legal method because there are limits to the amount and difficulty of material that any human can process. Second, at a systemic level, complex cases take up considerable legal resources that could otherwise be used to resolve other disputes and therefore place a huge strain on legal systems.

Historically, legal professionals have dealt with complexity by harnessing large teams of lawyers to gather, process, and summarise information. In recent years, some of this work has been delegated to technology, such as eDiscovery software, which can substantially expedite document review and production. However, much of the legal work which is done to manage and reduce complexity – such as the preparation of chronologies, Scott Schedules, and summaries of the law – is still largely performed by human lawyers, applying the legal method.

Yet this strategy is not sustainable because it simply cannot measure up to the sheer extent and pace of complexification. As explained above, this trend derives from sources such as advances in science and technology as well as the steady accretion of legal rules, and there are no signs that any of these drivers will diminish. We must therefore expect ever more complex disputes, and the reality is that only a finite supply of legal talent is available to cope with this ever-increasing load. Hence, there is an urgent need for new and creative methods to address complexification. These can include innovative court

[58] *IIa Technologies Pte Ltd v Element Six Technologies Ltd* [2023] 1 SLR 987.

[59] MR Damaška, *Evidence Law Adrift* (New Haven, Yale University Press, 1997) 143.

[60] DM Katz et al, 'Complex Societies and the Growth of the Law' (2020) 10 *Scientific Reports* 18737, 3.

[61] A Phang et al, 'The Development of Singapore Law: A Bicentennial Retrospective' (2020) 32 *SAcLJ* 891, para 56 Figure 1, para 57, para 60 Figure 3, para 61.

[62] Katz et al (n 60); Lord Justice Haddon-Cave, 'English Law and Descent into Complexity', Gray's Inn Reading 2021 (17 June 2021) para 23.

[63] GK Hadfield, 'More Markets, More Justice' (2019) 48 *Daedalus* 37, 39.

[64] Menon (n 55) paras 23–38.

protocols and mechanisms to contain and downsize disputes.[65] But beyond this, Gen AI can also play an invaluable role in supporting the effective and efficient disposal of cases.

ii. How Gen AI can Mitigate the Problem of Complexification

One significant way in which Gen AI tools can mitigate evidential and legal complexity is by producing reasonably accurate summaries that can help legal professionals digest large amounts of factual or legal information.

(a) In relation to *evidential* complexity, Gen AI tools can produce summaries that can help judges and lawyers to identify and marshal the key pieces of evidence in a dispute. For example, CoCounsel's Timeline feature can create, from a set of documents, a chronology of events that is cross-referenced to the documents.[66] This can potentially eliminate many hours of painstaking work that would have been spent by juniors in manually preparing case chronologies.

(b) Gen AI can also assist judges and lawyers to deal with *legal* complexity. Take GPT-Legal, a tool developed by the Singapore Academy of Law and the Infocomm Media Development Authority of Singapore, which has been integrated into LawNet, the leading legal research portal in Singapore.[67] This can provide quick summaries of the facts and holdings of Singapore judgments, that will help legal professionals quickly assess whether a judgment is relevant to the case at hand.

That said, there are at present limits to how far Gen AI can help legal professionals to manage complexity. In particular, it is unlikely that existing Gen AI tools will be able to help with complex legal disputes whose resolution will turn to a very large extent on *novel* issues and arguments. Take, for instance, the ruling of the Supreme Court of the US in *Brown v Board of Education*[68] that racial segregation in public schools violated the equal protection clause in the 14th Amendment to the US Constitution. This was based on an analysis of the impact of racial segregation on African American students coupled with a fresh interpretation of the equal protection clause. It is unlikely that Gen AI will be able to develop legal arguments of this nature – that is, legal reasoning that is both fundamentally creative and normatively compelling – at least in the near future. Or consider the formulation of the neighbour principle by the House of Lords in *Donoghue v Stevenson*,[69] which rationalised the English case law up to that point on the duty of care in tort. Again, it is improbable that Gen AI will be able at this time to identify and articulate such overarching or unifying legal principles. Ultimately, it is likely that innovative reasoning of this nature can only be carried out through the legal method. As noted earlier, existing Gen AI tools do not and cannot employ the legal method, and

[65] ibid paras 53–62.

[66] Casetext, 'CoCounsel Adds Another Skill' (*Casetext Blog*, 14 December 2023), available at casetext.com/blog/cocounsel-new-skill-timeline.

[67] M Elangovan, 'Faster, More Efficient Legal Research from September' (*SAL Blog*, 31 May 2024), available at sal.org.sg/blog/2024-GPT-Legal-ATxSG-IMDA-AISG.

[68] *Brown v Board of Education* 347 US 483 (1954).

[69] *Donoghue v Stevenson* [1932] AC 562.

absent developments in the way these tools operate, they may struggle to cope with problems of this sort.

But the reality is that such novel legal reasoning only features in a small number of cases. Competent legal professionals will be able to use Gen AI tools to reduce and manage complexity in relation to the vast majority of legal problems, which do not require the articulation or development of new legal principles. And as with access to justice, Gen AI can potentially make a very significant contribution to this because such tools can be scaled up without significant cost. This suggests an important insight: *it is precisely because Gen AI tools do not hinge on human lawyers applying the legal method that they promise to bring significant value to the legal endeavour.* What on first sight was a weakness – the fact that Gen AI does not involve legal reasoning by humans – can instead be seen as a strength, because it means that Gen AI can be applied at scale. This is a benefit which we can and should exploit to advance the legal endeavour.

V. Two Key Strategies to Usher Gen AI into our Legal Systems

How then should we usher Gen AI into our legal systems? This section will focus on two key strategies: transforming legal education and adopting an incremental and measured approach in incorporating Gen AI into justice systems.

A. Transforming Legal Education

Legal education will be critical because, if Gen AI is to play an even greater role in the legal domain, legal professionals must have the knowledge and skills to use Gen AI tools effectively and responsibly. Hence, we must revamp both university and continuing legal education to ensure that they equip budding and current legal professionals with AI-related competencies. There are at least four key areas.

First, legal education must impart at least a basic awareness of the nature and limitations of Gen AI. Critically, legal professionals must appreciate that Gen AI products cannot think like humans, but instead they produce output purely through a process of computing determined by statistical and other factors. Hence, such tools are currently prone to hallucinations (producing incorrect answers). Indeed, a 2024 study found that two leading AI legal research tools offered by LexisNexis and Thomson Reuters, respectively, which were coded and trained to reduce hallucinations, still produced erroneous answers in at least one out of six responses.[70] This is a major issue because accuracy is essential to legal work. Legal education must imbue a keen awareness of this limitation and of other core aspects of Gen AI tools. This could be part of an introductory course on computer science and digital thinking, which could help develop 'digital intuition'[71] as to how Gen AI and other digital tools operate.

[70] V Magesh et al, 'AI on Trial: Legal Models Hallucinate in 1 out of 6 (or More) Benchmarking Queries', (*Stanford University Human-Centred Artificial Intelligence Blog*, 23 May 2024), available at hai.stanford.edu/news/ai-trial-legal-models-hallucinate-1-out-6-or-more-benchmarking-queries.

[71] A term used by Assistant Professor Dirk Hartung during a discussion at the 4th Roundtable.

Second, legal professionals must become adept at using Gen AI. In this regard, it has been suggested that legal education providers should provide structured first-hand exposure to Gen AI tools. This could comprise a brief introduction to the relevant tools, practical tips (such as to 'converse' with the tool instead of treating it as a search engine, and to reframe prompts in an iterative way to improve answers), and guided assignments (in which students could be asked to use Gen AI in different phases such as preparing outlines, drafting, and revising drafts, and to submit all of the prompts used and responses generated along with the final work product).[72] Such methods could impart skills in prompt engineering and other techniques that could enhance one's ability to leverage Gen AI.

The third area is professional ethics. Legal professionals need to be familiar with what their professional conduct obligations require in relation to the use of Gen AI. For example, the duty of competence and diligence calls on lawyers to verify the accuracy of *all* AI-generated output, while the duty to maintain client confidentiality requires lawyers to ensure that client information is not included in prompts that are entered into public AI tools.[73] It would be useful to flesh out such standards for the use of Gen AI in our legal systems. In this regard, a possible initiative is for judiciaries to collaborate and to explore the development of a model governance framework for the use of AI in court, building on frameworks that have already been introduced by national courts.[74] In Singapore, the Ministry of Law released a Guide for Using Generative AI in the Legal Sector in March 2026, which explains how key principles such as professional ethics, confidentiality and transparency should inform the use of Gen AI in legal work.[75]

Fourth, legal education should impart knowledge of emerging legal and normative issues arising from the use of AI. For example, one overarching legal issue concerns how AI should be conceptualised: should AI systems be treated as agents with legal rights, or as entities whose conduct is largely determined by human actors through programming?[76] This may be relevant to issues of liability arising from the use of Gen AI tools that cause harm or loss, which legal professionals will need to be familiar with if such tools are used regularly in the course of our daily work. The use of Gen AI might also raise normative issues, such as whether its use in adjudication would infringe what has been called 'the right to a human decision'.[77] This debate has a direct bearing on, among other things, how we might use Gen AI tools in adjudication to advance access to justice and to contain or downsize disputes. It will therefore be important for lawyers to be apprised of these philosophical issues, in order to weigh in on them.

[72] J Bliss, 'Teaching Law in the Age of Generative AI' (2024) 64 *Jurimetrics* 111.

[73] S Menon, 'Answering the Call in the Age of Artificial Intelligence', Mass Call Address 2023 (21 August 2023) paras 21–22.

[74] The Singapore Judiciary has published the *Guide on the Use of Generative Artificial Intelligence Tools by Court Users*, available at judiciary.gov.sg/docs/default-source/news-and-resources-docs/guide-on-the-use-of-generative-ai-tools-by-court-users.pdf.

[75] The Ministry of Law of Singapore, *Guide for Using Generative AI in the Legal Sector* (6 March 2026), available at mlaw.gov.sg/files/Guide_for_using_Generative_AI_in_the_Legal_Sector__Published_on_6_Mar_2026_.pdf.

[76] J Soh, 'Legal Dispositionism and Artificially-intelligent Attributions' (2023) 43 *Legal Studies* 583.

[77] See, eg, J Tasioulas, 'Ethics of Artificial Intelligence: What It Is and Why We Need It', The 2023 Elson Ethics Lecture (4 October 2023).

Apart from these AI-related competencies, there are also second-order concerns that we should be actively thinking about and addressing through legal education and other solutions.

The first relates to skills degradation. We must ensure that our legal professionals continue to develop and enhance their critical thinking and problem-solving skills, so as to guard against the risk of automation bias, a problem which has already been discussed in the previous chapters of this book. Indeed, recent studies have revealed the potential adverse consequences that AI may have on our cognitive abilities.[78] For instance, in the medical field, a study found that AI helped clinicians to better detect pre-cancerous growths in the colon. However, when the AI assistance was removed, it was revealed that their ability to detect tumours decreased by about 20 per cent compared with the rates before the AI tool was introduced.[79] In a similar vein, researchers from the Massachusetts Institute of Technology have reported the 'cognitive cost' of LLM-assisted essay writing. The team assigned research participants to three groups – the first and second relied on an LLM (ChatGPT) and search engine (Google), respectively, to write essays, while the third did not rely on any tools. The results of the study revealed that those in the first group 'consistently underperformed at neural, linguistic, and behavioral levels' and were less inclined to 'critically evaluate the LLM's output or "opinions"'.[80] Studies such as these show that the problem of skills degradation has become a real and urgent issue that needs to be addressed by universities as well as providers of continuing legal education.

Another second-order concern that we must address is the loss of on-the-job training opportunities arising from the increasing adoption of Gen AI tools.[81] Traditionally, junior legal professionals developed their technical competencies and lawyering skills through the repeated performance of basic legal tasks such as document review and drafting. Such training opportunities will become more scarce because these are precisely the areas that Gen AI tools excel in. We must therefore proactively enhance existing training opportunities and even create new ones in order to ensure that young legal professionals continue to develop the relevant competencies and skills. For instance, in Singapore, we have introduced training programmes such as the Junior Lawyers Professional Certification Programme, an industry-wide initiative that aims to help our young lawyers develop the practical skills that are necessary for modern legal practice, including critical problem-solving abilities.[82]

Finally, in a world where Gen AI is becoming increasingly sophisticated and hence able to replace legal professionals in many basic legal tasks, we must ensure that our lawyers develop completely new skills to ensure that 'humans' remain in control of the 'machine'. As James Allsop has said, '[t]o mistake the machine for the Master will lead to the end of

[78] See, eg, N Kosmyna et al, 'Your Brain on ChatGPT: Accumulation of Cognitive Debt when Using an AI Assistant for Essay Writing Task' (2025) arXiv:2506.08872 [cs.AI].

[79] K Budzyń et al, 'Endoscopist Deskilling Risk After Exposure to Artificial Intelligence in Colonoscopy: A Multicentre, Observational Study' (2025) 10 *The Lancet Gastroenterology & Hepatology* 896.

[80] Kosmyna et al (n 78) 142–43.

[81] S Menon, 'The Future of the Legal Profession: A Shared Vision', opening address at the Legal Profession Symposium 2025 (29 July 2025) para 54.

[82] Singapore Academy of Law, 'Junior Lawyers Professional Certification Programme', available at sal.org.sg/learn/junior-lawyers-professional-certification-programme.

the spirit of the law as human and free. The danger is not the machine becoming human; it is the human becoming machine'.[83] One such skill may be the ability to seamlessly integrate interdisciplinary knowledge with legal knowledge, and the former may extend to areas such as data science, digital thinking, and digital ethics and regulation.

B. An Incremental and Measured Approach in Incorporating Gen AI into Justice Systems

Apart from legal education, the second key strategy relates to the approach that we should take to incorporate Gen AI into justice systems. It is suggested that a measured and thoughtful approach should be adopted with *three* main prongs: (a) setting guardrails to define permissible uses of Gen AI; (b) proceeding incrementally with extensive testing of Gen AI tools before implementation; and (c) obtaining objective measurable data to assess the reliability and accuracy of the output generated by AI.

To begin with, judiciaries will have to delineate the legitimate use cases of Gen AI within our justice systems, to ensure that the permitted uses are consistent with core legal values. We should harness the immense potential of Gen AI by using it in the areas where it can deliver the most impact to our users and staff, while being sensitive to the type of cases in which it is being used. For instance, the use of existing AI tools in criminal adjudication is likely to be problematic because we share a deep conviction that criminal justice, which involves the imposition of severe sanctions, should be left under the control of humans, 'who share our moral outlook, methods of reasoning and the gift of exercising an appropriate degree of empathy in any given case'.[84] Further, given that the judiciary must remain impartial, it would be inappropriate for Gen AI tools provided by the courts to offer legal advice – as distinct from legal information and assistance – to litigants. These examples illustrate the importance of setting guardrails on the use of Gen AI to ensure that such use in our justice systems does not trespass into impermissible areas or functions.

Next, it would be prudent to proceed incrementally and to test Gen AI tools extensively before adopting them. This has been our methodology in Singapore. By way of examples:

(a) In exploring the development of a Gen AI tool for court users, we have chosen to focus at the outset on one setting: the SCT. As has been explained above, we chose this testing ground because: (i) disputes before the SCT are generally simple and low-value and feature some recurrent fact patterns and, hence, are more amenable to assistance by AI; and (ii) the launch of a Gen AI tool in the SCT would not directly affect lawyers, because legal representation is not permitted before the SCT. If the tool performs well, we may consider extending it to other types of simple civil cases.

[83] J Allsop, 'The Legal System and the Administration of Justice in a Time of Technological Change: Machines Becoming Humans, or Humans Becoming Machines?', the 2023 Sir Francis Burt Oration (21 November 2023) 26.

[84] Menon (n 49) para 47(c).

(b) We had also experimented with chatbots, in the hope that these could provide legal information to the public on family, probate, and other routine cases. However, after comprehensive testing, these were found to deliver inaccurate information on occasion. Therefore, at the time of writing, that project has been shelved for the foreseeable future.

Finally, to guard against over-reliance on Gen AI, we must obtain objective measurable data to assess the reliability and accuracy of the output generated by Gen AI tools. This should take place both before and after the relevant tools are introduced by our judiciaries. There ought to be clear rules and practices to obtain empirical validation as well as user feedback. As will be elaborated below, this is especially important for external-facing tools, given the potential for public trust to be significantly diminished if such tools are found to be highly unreliable or inaccurate.

Drawing these three strands together, judiciaries may wish to consider thinking of the incorporation of Gen AI through a matrix framework that systematically maps the capabilities of Gen AI against different types of cases. Such a matrix would recognise the following fundamental principles that have already been set out in this chapter:

(a) Gen AI should not be used or seen as a complete substitute for judges. It ought not to be relied upon to provide definitive answers or be treated as the end point of the judicial process. This would be fundamentally inconsistent with the constitutional role of the courts to oversee the administration of justice and to safeguard the rule of law.

(b) Instead, we should work with Gen AI and identify where it can deliver maximum benefit whilst remaining sensitive to the nature of the cases and the degree of human intervention required. Thus, while Gen AI may excel at summarising documents and generating chronologies across most case types, its potential application in providing analytical insights may vary significantly depending on the complexity and nature of the issues to be resolved.

As far as it concerns the work of judges, we might categorise the distinct capabilities of Gen AI into at least three broad areas:

(a) The first is the *processing and organisation of information*. This would include the generation of summaries, chronologies, comparative tables, and other forms of useful information that can help reduce the complexity of disputes.

(b) The second area concerns Gen AI's *investigative and research* capabilities. This would include legal research as well as the ability of Gen AI to help judges 'interrogate' the evidence (for instance, to set out all the instances in which Party A wrote to Party B regarding Agreement C).

(c) The final area relates to Gen AI's *evaluative and analytical capabilities*. This may include evaluating the parties' submissions, reviewing draft judgments to flag potential errors, omissions and ambiguities, and even extend to predicting or suggesting the outcomes of cases.

The following matrix is an illustrative example of what has been outlined above, which has been prepared for the purposes of this chapter only and on the basis of the current state of the art. The cells in light grey indicate that Gen AI is likely to be of significant assistance; the cells in dark grey reflect the need for continued testing and experimentation to discern the potential utility of Gen AI; and the cells in black represent areas where Gen AI should not be used.

Capabilities of Gen AI	Simple civil cases involving similar or recurrent fact patterns	Complex civil cases	Criminal cases
Information processing and organisation			
Investigation and research			
Evaluation and analysis			

In the final analysis, it is suggested that an incremental and measured approach, with a willingness to step back from unpromising ventures, is warranted, because the hurried adoption of Gen AI is likely to lead to the deployment of tools that may have significant drawbacks. This would be calamitous for at least two reasons. First, such tools may conflict with key legal norms or values. For instance, a common critique of AI systems is that they may reflect and perpetuate racial, ethnic, and other biases in the data on which they are trained. Indeed, the COMPAS tool, which is used in several jurisdictions in the US to assess one's risk of recidivism, was found to be almost twice as likely to incorrectly flag black persons as being at risk of reoffending than it was to make the same mistake for white offenders.[85] The use of biased AI could not only yield incorrect conclusions, but might also offend fundamental legal principles of equality. Hence, it is imperative that we review and test Gen AI tools thoroughly to eliminate biases and other serious flaws as far as possible.

Further, the deployment of flawed AI tools would likely diminish public trust in the use of Gen AI by the courts. This would be a major setback for the project to exploit AI to advance the legal endeavour. Studies have found that many people exhibit 'algorithm aversion' (that is, they prefer to rely on human judgement instead of algorithms);[86] and one key reason underlying this is that people reject algorithms as soon as they see them making mistakes, even if these algorithms *generally* outperform humans.[87]

The cautionary tale of the Robodebt scheme demonstrates this. Robodebt was a debt recovery system that was introduced in Australia in 2016, and which sought to identify and recover purported overpayments to recipients of welfare benefits using automated processes. Due to critical flaws, a sum in excess of AU$740 million was wrongfully recovered from more than 380,000 persons.[88] In 2019, the Federal Court

[85] J Larson et al, 'How We Analyzed the COMPAS Recidivism Algorithm' (*ProPublica*, 23 May 2016), available at propublica.org/article/how-we-analyzed-the-compas-recidivism-algorithm.

[86] CR Sunstein and JH Gaffe, 'An Anatomy of Algorithm Aversion' (2024) 26 *The Columbia Science & Technology Law Review* 290.

[87] BJ Dietvorst et al, 'Algorithm Aversion: People Erroneously Avoid Algorithms After Seeing Them Err' (2015) 144 *Journal of Experimental Psychology: General* 114.

[88] Commonwealth of Australia, *Report of the Royal Commission into the Robodebt Scheme* (7 July 2023) (Robodebt Report) xxix (Royal Commissioner: Catherine Holmes AC SC).

of Australia held that the Robodebt methodology was unlawful,[89] and the scheme was then scrapped. A Royal Commission was convened to conduct a public inquiry into the Robodebt program, and one of its key findings was that the scheme had been rushed in its design and its implementation.[90] Significantly, the Robodebt scandal was reported to have left deep distrust in AI and technology more generally in Australia.[91]

It would plainly be counterproductive for judiciaries to adopt Gen AI in haste, since this will likely engender the use of flawed AI tools that undermine the broader mission of incorporating AI into our justice systems. Rather, we should be 'crossing the river by feeling the stones' because this is the best strategy to secure the successful adoption of Gen AI.

VI. Conclusion

Advances in AI are occurring rapidly, and these will likely bring radical change to the law. For instance, Professor Richard Susskind postulates that AI will enable the translation of the law into code, which will be embedded in physical systems to implement the law – speed limits, for example, might be implanted into the software of cars so that breaking of such rules becomes impossible.[92] Such innovations might lead to a new paradigm of 'preventive justice' and transform our concept of the rule of law. AI will also interact with other innovations to bring about developments that we cannot yet conceive. History has shown that new technologies 'collid[e] and combin[e] with other technologies … forming new building blocks for future technologies',[93] resulting in new products and tools that could not have been predicted. Consider the telephone: when this was invented by Bell in 1876, no one could have predicted that it would morph into the smartphone, a device that can be used to take photographs, play games, book flights, conduct banking and trading, and do much else – apart from also making calls.

It is therefore unclear what transformations AI will ultimately bring to the legal domain. But what is evident is that Gen AI, as it already exists, has huge potential to advance our legal systems, including by helping us to address the key problems of access to justice and complexification. Legal stakeholders must therefore urgently explore the use of Gen AI and create the conditions for its successful implementation, so that we may realise its tremendous promise to advance the legal endeavour.

[89] Robodebt Report xxix; *Amato v the Commonwealth of Australia* (2019, Federal Court of Australia).

[90] Robodebt Report 29–30, 136, 655.

[91] T Flew, 'The Other Cost of Robodebt: Distrust in Technology, Media & Government' (*Australian Academy of the Humanities – Newsroom*, July 2023), available at humanities.org.au/power-of-the-humanities/the-other-cost-of-robodebt-trust-in-technology-media-and-government.

[92] Susskind (n 45).

[93] M Suleyman and M Bhaskar, 'A Cambrian Explosion' in *The Coming Wave* (New York, Crown, 2023) ch 4.

PART II

Data Protection and Privacy

8

Introduction to Data Protection and Privacy

MATTHEW S R PALMER*

E ngā mana, e ngā waka, e ngā reo, tēnā koutou, tēnā koutou, tēnā koutou katoa.[1]

I. Culture and Privacy

This chapter begins with a greeting in another language, *te reo Māori*, the language of the indigenous people of Aotearoa New Zealand. It is a reminder that we all approach issues with our own perspective, shaped by our own experiences, values, and cultures. The fourth Judicial Roundtable saw discussions on how cultural perspectives are inherent in languages, and the issues that may pose for the application of artificial intelligence (AI) developed in one language to issues framed in another language. Similar issues can arise in relation to data protection and privacy.

The principles underlying laws of data protection and privacy can look very different depending on the values of the society, culture and jurisdiction in which they are developed. In late 2023, the New Zealand Privacy Commissioner released guidance for all New Zealanders on AI and the New Zealand information privacy principles (IPPs).[2] The IPPs are encapsulated in the Privacy Act 2020 and apply to both public and private sector organisations. The Office of the Privacy Commissioner has expressed 'expectations' for agencies using AI tools, which include the expectations that organisations will:[3]

- have senior leadership approve the use of AI tools based on full consideration of the risks and mitigations;
- review whether a generative AI tool is necessary and proportionate given potential privacy impacts and consider whether a different approach may be taken;
- conduct a privacy impact assessment before using these tools;

* The views expressed in this chapter do not represent the views of the New Zealand judiciary. The author acknowledges with thanks the assistance of his clerks Toni Wharehoka and Sarah Burton.

[1] To all authorities, canoes and voices, I greet you all.

[2] Privacy Commissioner | Te Mana Mātāpono Matatapu, 'Artificial Intelligence and the Information Privacy Principles' (September 2023), available at www.privacy.org.nz/assets/New-order/Resources-/Publications/Guidance-resources/AI-Guidance-Resources-/AI-and-the-Information-Privacy-Principles.pdf.

[3] ibid.

- be transparent, including telling people how, when, and why the tool is being used;
- engage with Māori about potential risks and impacts to the taonga (treasure) of their information;
- develop procedures about accuracy and access by individuals to their information;
- ensure human review prior to acting on AI outputs to reduce risks of inaccuracy and bias; and
- ensure that personal information is not retained or disclosed by the AI tool.

The New Zealand approach to these issues reflects a unique path-dependent evolution of its privacy and data protection laws.[4] Each jurisdiction has its own approach. But crosscurrents of fashion and conceptual thinking from one jurisdiction can influence others. Internationally, American and European conceptions of data protection and privacy can be very different. It is possible to identify six key differences:

- the European Union (EU) views privacy as a fundamental human right, while the United States (US) treats it more as a consumer protection issue;
- the EU takes an omnibus approach with the General Data Protection Regulation (GDPR) as a comprehensive protection law, whereas the US has a sectoral approach;
- the GDPR has an opt-in consent model, while US laws generally deploy an opt-out model;
- the GDPR prohibits the processing of personal data by default without a *legal basis*, whereas US laws tend to allow such processing unless specifically restricted;
- the GDPR grants broad rights to individuals over their personal data, which are more limited under US laws; and
- the GDPR has strict data transfer rules, while US laws are more permissive of cross-border transfers.

At least, those six points of difference were what Perplexity, an AI-powered 'answer' engine, gave when the question was posed. Comfortingly, those themes also came through in the papers presented by participants during the session at the Roundtable on data protection and privacy. This introductory chapter will, in brief terms, outline the two chapters that follow, by Justice of Appeal Godfrey Lam and Mr Yeong Zee Kin, respectively.

II. Outline of Chapters Nine and Ten

Justice of Appeal Godfrey Lam from the Court of Appeal of Hong Kong focuses on the profound implications of big data and AI for privacy and data protection. He presents the right to privacy as a human right which should be treated as a fundamental value and not easily overridden. Against that backdrop, his chapter explores some of the legal issues relating to the processing of personal data. The chapter begins with a comprehensive overview of a typical legal framework for data protection, followed by a careful

[4] See generally G Gunasekara, 'Data Sovereignty and Privacy: A Chimera or Realistic Prospect in Aotearoa/ New Zealand?' (2024) 31 *New Zealand Universities Law Review* 57.

examination of the meaning and scope of *personal* data, which is to be contrasted with data that is *anonymised*. Justice Lam then considers the legal issues in connection with both the *data collection* and *deployment* phases in AI technologies. In respect of the former, he introduces the three primary means of data collection commonly used by AI developers – data trading,[5] secondary use[6] and web scraping[7] – and then considers the principal legal bases that may be relied on to justify processing data through those means. He concludes with a brief discussion of the principles applicable to the tort of misuse of private information, which serves as a common law mechanism for data protection claims.

Mr Yeong Zee Kin is the Chief Executive of the Singapore Academy of Law and a former Deputy Commissioner of the Personal Data Protection Commission of Singapore. His chapter explores the regulatory and legal issues relating to the processing of data in the *development and deployment of AI systems*. In particular, the focus of the chapter is on issues relating to *copyright* and *data privacy*. He divides his analysis into two sections. The first relates to regulatory and legal issues that arise during *model development*, when data is processed for the training of AI systems. Such issues include, for instance, whether web scraping for the purpose of pre-training foundational models for generative AI systems constitutes 'fair use' under copyright law. The second section of the chapter focuses on issues that arise *post-deployment*, after the trained model is operationalised in products or services. These issues include the attribution of authorship of AI-generated content.

III. Overarching Issues

The discussion of the issues raised by these chapters relates broadly to two areas: the global reach of the issues and the global uncertainty as to the legal responsibilities of online platforms.

In the first area, global data flows and supply chains depend on the transfer of data across borders. Data can be accessed in one jurisdiction and used in breach of the law in another. Data protection obligations often derive from standardised contractual clauses. How are they to be interpreted? In addition, the location of storage and use of data can be difficult to identify. What power does a national court have to order a party to produce documents stored in a multi-region bucket spanning data centres in two or more countries? How should a court approach the need for an injunction to have worldwide effect? The *Google* case in Canada provides an example of a worldwide injunction to delist search results based on copyright infringement.[8]

[5] This refers to the purchase of datasets from third parties.

[6] This refers to the use of data collected by the business or connected entities for purposes other than that for which it was originally collected.

[7] This refers to the collection of data from public sources.

[8] *Google Inc. v Equustek Solutions Inc.*, 2017 SCC 34. The Supreme Court of Canada upheld a worldwide interlocutory injunction against Google, stating that it was necessary to prevent 'the irreparable harm that flows from Datalink carrying on business on the Internet' and that Google's argument that a global injunction would violate international comity or result in Google violating the laws of a foreign jurisdiction was theoretical: see [42]–[44].

These are standard issues of extraterritoriality. The question of the extra-territorial reach of courts of a national jurisdiction arises in many, if not most, areas of law. But it is heightened in relation to data protection and privacy by several key factors. First, information technology now is such that there are few effective technical barriers, and low marginal costs, to the transmission and use of data across jurisdictional boundaries. Second, the size, influence and multi-jurisdictional basis of the largest technology companies, the so-called 'tech giants', mean that their power rivals or exceeds that of many nation states. Third, as noted above, there are significant fissures in the fundamental approaches of different legal regimes in relation to data protection and privacy. Data protection was deliberately left out of the Hague Judgments Convention[9] because of the likely conflicts over positive obligations to disclose data.

Therefore, reliance is based primarily on reciprocity between specific legal regimes and their enforcement mechanisms. In an age of increased international tension, that is more difficult. Singapore's use of a voluntary statutory undertaking, as opposed to investigations and fines, is one mechanism that may increase compliance by multi-national corporations.

Turning to the public and private responsibilities of online platforms, these are uncertain in most jurisdictions, and agreement on them is internationally rare. The basis on which online platforms acquire data is important. Are there property rights in data or personal information, and who is the owner? Is the owner the person whom the information concerns or the person who generated and collected it? Is the basis for the acquisition of data a transaction over property or the waiver of a human right of a person to access and control their own personal information? What if the value of the information only arises when it is aggregated with the information of others in large datasets?

The discussion could become more personal when focusing on the use of AI to profile the views of individual judges. France has banned this, to protect judicial independence and anonymity.[10] More than 20 years ago, the Delhi High Court issued a contempt notice for an article ranking judges on various parameters.[11] But it is perhaps fair to say that such profiling inevitably happens anyway, and judges cannot avoid public scrutiny. These issues reveal tensions between defending institutional legitimacy, the right to freedom of expression and the right to receive and impart information and opinions.

IV. Conclusion

Discussions between judges do not usually explicitly involve competing jurisprudential theories. Yet, the fundamental distinction between information as property and as a human right pervaded our discussions at the Roundtable. The set of assumptions on

[9] Convention on the Recognition and Enforcement of Foreign Judgments in Civil or Commercial Matters (The Hague, 2 July 2019).

[10] *loi* n° 2019-222 du 23 mars 2019 de programmation 2018-2022 et de réforme pour la justice (1) [French Law No. 2019-222 from March 23 2019], art 33.

[11] *Shri Surya Prakash Khatri & Anor. v Smt. Madhu Trehan and Ors* (2001) CRI LJ 3476.

which a legal regime is based can set up very different ways of regulating data protection and privacy.[12] It can significantly affect the valence of a legal argument if a human right is recognised to be at stake. In addition, differences between jurisdictions make international agreement difficult.

The market power, size and cross-jurisdictional basis of the tech giants raise a conceptual question about whether their decisions should be governed by public law as much as private law. If the purpose of judicial review of administrative action is to constrain the arbitrary use of coercive power, why should it not apply to the tech giants as much as it does to the decisions of the executives of nation states? This could become a significant issue in both public administrative law and in contractual and equitable law contexts. But it deserves a future chapter all to itself.[13] No doubt there will be further twists and turns in the path-dependent evolution of the legal cultures in our jurisdictions.

Nō reira, tēnā koutou, tēnā koutou, tēnā tātou katoa.[14]

[12] This is illustrated by the decisions of the Indian Supreme Court and the Supreme Court of Singapore in *Justice K.S. Puttaswamy (Retd.) & Anor v Union of India and Anors* AIR 2017 SC 4161 (2018) and *Bellingham, Alex v Reed, Michael* [2021] SGHC 125, respectively.

[13] See, eg, C Harlow, 'Public and Private Law: A Redundant Divide' in JNE Varuhas and SW Stark (eds), *The Frontiers of Public Law* (Oxford, Hart Publishing, 2019); and S Thomson, 'Into the Quagmire: Social Media as Regulators and the Limits of Judicial Review' [2024] *Public Law* 695.

[14] And so I greet you all once again, thank you.

9

Data Protection and Privacy in the Big Data and Artificial Intelligence Era

GODFREY LAM*

I. Introduction

Big data, machine learning and artificial intelligence (AI) are fuelled by data, and a great deal of data concerns individuals and is commonly regarded as personal data. They therefore clearly raise enormous implications for data protection and privacy. Moreover, each of us leaves a good deal of digital footprints on a daily basis, leading to the creation of data at an unprecedented speed. Some studies put the growth rate of digital data in the world at 100 per cent every two years. It has been estimated that by 2025 the data generated annually will reach 175 Zettabytes.[1] Issues relating to data protection and privacy are of increasing prevalence and significance, especially with the advent of generative AI such as ChatGPT, which depend for their functioning on access to the massive datasets they have been trained on, and the IoT (Internet of Things) which is based on web- and inter-connected devices embedded with sensors and software that collect, use, store, analyse and transmit data.

The aggregation of data collected through various channels and their coordination and analysis can reveal intrusive details. Quite apart from the invasion of privacy, unless proper safeguards are in place, personal data can be misused for various purposes such as targeted cyberattacks, phishing, impersonation fraud, surveillance or intelligence purposes, and unsolicited marketing communications.

In this context, it is right to recall that privacy is a fundamental human right. Article 17 of the United Nations (UN) International Covenants on Civil and Political Rights, which is reproduced as Article 14 of the Hong Kong Bill of Rights,[2] provides:

* The author wishes to acknowledge the invaluable assistance given to him by Ms Cherry Xu, barrister-at-law of Hong Kong, in the preparation of this chapter.

[1] One Zettabyte is 1 followed by 21 zeros bytes. D Reinsel et al, 'The Digitization of the World: From Edge to Core' (*Seagate White Paper*, 2018), available at www.seagate.com/files/www-content/our-story/trends/files/idc-seagate-dataage-whitepaper.pdf.

[2] Enacted by s 8 of the Hong Kong Bill of Rights Ordinance (Chapter 383 of the Laws of Hong Kong). See also Art 8 of the Convention for the Protection of Human Rights and Fundamental Freedoms (Rome, 4 November 1950).

1. No one shall be subjected to arbitrary or unlawful interference with his privacy, family, home or correspondence, nor to unlawful attacks on his honour and reputation.
2. Everyone has the right to the protection of the law against such interference or attacks.

Since 2013, the UN General Assembly has adopted a number of Resolutions on the right to privacy in the digital age. The recent Resolution 77/211, adopted on 15 December 2022, affirms that the same rights that people have offline must also be protected online, including the right to privacy.

More recently, on 12 October 2023, the UN Human Rights Council also adopted Resolution 54/21, drawing attention to a wide range of concerns, including those arising from the use of digital technologies and AI systems that require the processing of large amounts of data, and in particular concerns regarding biometric identification and recognition technologies.

As Lord Hoffmann put it in *Campbell v MGN Ltd*: 'What human rights law has done is to identify private information as something worth protecting as an aspect of human autonomy and dignity.'[3] The right to privacy – sometimes referred to as the 'right to be let alone'[4] – is fundamental to the preservation of an individual's freedom. Privacy allows individuals to explore their interests without other people's knowledge and thus be free from external manipulation and unwanted attention. In this day and age, the fundamental human right to privacy is closely linked to and indeed depends on the effective protection of an individual's personal data.

This chapter seeks to explore, through a survey of the principles and relevant cases, some of the legal issues relating to the processing of personal data in the context of big data and AI technologies, from the perspective of the law on data protection and privacy. The chapter is organised as follows:

(1) Section II gives an overview of a typical legal framework for data protection, primarily with reference to the EU's regime, which has had significant impact in other regions.
(2) Section III discusses the meaning and scope of personal data and the concept of anonymisation of data.
(3) Section IV discusses the legal issues relating to the data collection phase in AI technologies.
    (a) Section IV.A introduces the three means of data collection commonly used by AI developers: data trading, secondary use of data and web scraping.
    (b) Section IV.B explores the principal legal bases that may be relied on to justify data trading, namely: (i) consent; and (ii) legitimate interest.
    (c) Section IV.C explores the availability or applicability of: (i) consent; (ii) performance of contract; and (iii) legitimate interest as legal bases for secondary use of data.

[3] *Campbell v MGN Ltd* [2004] UKHL 22, [50].
[4] S Warren and L Brandeis, 'The Right to Privacy' (1890) 4 *Harvard Law Review* 193.

(d) Section IV.D explores issues regarding web scraping. The *Clearview AI* line of cases, which concern the scraping of the Internet for facial images, will be discussed.

(4) Section V deals with legal issues in connection with data processing in the deployment stage in AI technologies.

(5) Section VI briefly discusses the principles applicable to the tort of misuse of private information as a common law basis for data protection claims.

(6) Section VII concludes the chapter.

II. Overview of Data Protection Legal Framework

A. International Patchwork

Different jurisdictions have adopted different regimes for the legal protection of data privacy. Among them, the EU's legal regime for data protection, primarily embodied in Regulation 2016/679 (the General Data Protection Regulation or GDPR), which came into effect on 25 May 2018, and its predecessor, Directive 95/46/EC (EU 1995 Directive), has influenced the data protection legislation in many other countries and regions. For example, when the relevant legislation in Hong Kong, the Personal Data (Privacy) Ordinance (PDPO)[5] was drafted, reference was made to the relevant requirements under the OECD Privacy Guidelines 1980[6] and the EU 1995 Directive. Reference was also made to the GDPR when the PDPO was reviewed more recently.

Similarly, Japan has sought to amend and supplement its Act on the Protection of Personal Information to make it compatible with the GDPR, which eventually led to Japan receiving an adequacy decision from the European Commission in 2019.[7] In 2020, Singapore introduced substantial amendments to its Personal Data Protection Act to align its regime more closely with the GDPR.[8] In 2018, the California Consumer Privacy Act[9] became the first comprehensive privacy law to be enacted in the US, incorporating privacy principles akin to the GDPR (though with notable differences). Since then, many US states have also passed comprehensive privacy laws.[10] Australia has had a Privacy Act since 1988, which has been updated from time to time, with the latest amendments in 2024 influenced in part by the GDPR. In Mainland China, the Personal

[5] Chapter 486 of the Laws of Hong Kong.

[6] The first internationally-agreed privacy principles: OECD, 'Recommendation of the Council Concerning Guidelines Governing the Protection of Privacy and Transborder flows of Personal Data', OECD/LEGAL/0188, available at legalinstruments.oecd.org/en/instruments/OECD-LEGAL-0188.

[7] Commission Implementing Decision (EU) 2019/419 of 23 January 2019.

[8] Personal Data Protection Commission, 'EU GDPR', available at www.pdpc.gov.sg/help-and-resources/2017/10/eu-gdpr; 'Broad Comparison of the PDPA's Consent and Exceptions to Consent Provisions with the EU GDPR's Six Legal Bases for Processing Personal Data', available at www.pdpc.gov.sg/-/media/Files/PDPC/PDF-Files/EU-GDPR/Broad-Comparison-of-the-PDPAs-Consent-Exceptions-with-EU-GDPRs-Legal-Bases-for-Processing-Personal-Data-1-Apr-2021.pdf.

[9] Cal. Civ. Code § 1798.100 et seq.

[10] See K Nahra et al, 'Big Data Analytics Privacy Law Considerations, A Practical Guidance® Practice Note' (*LexisNexis Practical Guidance*, May 2023), available at www.wilmerhale.com/-/media/files/shared_content/editorial/publications/documents/20230515-big-data-analytics-privacy-law-considerations.pdf.

Information Protection Law (PIPL) – the first piece of legislation in Mainland China dedicated to the protection of personal information – came into effect on 1 November 2021. It has similarities to the GDPR, although the two do not fully overlap. India also enacted a Digital Personal Data Protection Act on 11 August 2023, providing protection broadly similar to the GDPR.

These legislative developments in numerous jurisdictions reflect not only a growing recognition by governments of the importance of data privacy, due no doubt in part to the growing demand of their populations for privacy rights in the digital era, but also a notable trend of convergence of the ethical and legal principles applicable in data protection. Given the borderless nature of cyberspace and the ease with which data can be transported across jurisdictions, the emergence of a set of robust data privacy norms, if not specific rules, is surely to be welcomed.

B. Main Elements of the Legal Framework

This chapter uses the GDPR as a reference framework, not only because it stands out as being one of the more sophisticated, comprehensive and influential legal regimes, but also because with a relatively long history of operation (including its predecessor), there has been a substantial amount of case law from courts and data protection authorities (DPA) as well as guidelines and opinions issued by authoritative sources. These include, in particular, the European Data Protection Board (EDPB), which is a body composed of the heads of the national data protection authorities of the European Economic Area (EEA), and its predecessor, the Article 29 Working Party (Article 29 WP).[11]

The principal elements of the legal framework in the GDPR can, so far as relevant, be very broadly identified as follows. The GDPR applies in relation to 'personal data' of natural persons. It defines 'personal data' to mean any information relating to an identified or identifiable natural person, which in turn means a person

> who can be identified, directly or indirectly, in particular by reference to an identifier such as a name, an identification number, location data, an online identifier or to one or more factors specific to the physical, physiological, genetic, mental, economic, cultural or social identity of that natural person.

The 'processing' of personal data is regulated. 'Processing' is widely defined to mean

> any operation or set of operations which is performed on personal data or on sets of personal data, whether or not by automated means, such as collection, recording, organisation, structuring, storage, adaptation or alteration, retrieval, consultation, use, disclosure by transmission, dissemination or otherwise making available, alignment or combination, restriction, erasure or destruction.

The GDPR requires compliance with six specified 'principles', including, first and foremost, that the processing of personal data must be lawful. In short, those principles

[11] Working Party on the Protection of Individuals with regard to the Processing of Personal Data, set up under Art 29 of the EU 1995 Directive. It was replaced by the EDPB on 25 May 2018.

are: (1) lawfulness, fairness and transparency;[12] (2) purpose limitation;[13] (3) data minimisation;[14] (4) accuracy;[15] (5) storage limitation;[16] and (6) integrity and confidentiality.[17] They are similar to the six Data Protection Principles found in the PDPO of Hong Kong.[18] 'Accountability' is also required, in the sense that the burden rests on the controller (ie, the person who determines the purposes and means of the processing of personal data) to demonstrate compliance with the core principles, including the legal basis for processing (required under the lawfulness principle).[19]

The GDPR goes on to provide that the processing of personal data (other than the special categories of personal data referred to below) is lawful only if one or more of six specified bases apply, namely: (1) consent of the data subject;[20] (2) performance

[12] GDPR, art 5(1)(a): Personal data shall be 'processed lawfully, fairly and in a transparent manner in relation to the data subject'.

[13] GDPR, art 5(1)(b): Personal data shall be 'collected for specified, explicit and legitimate purposes and not further processed in a manner that is incompatible with those purposes; further processing for archiving purposes in the public interest, scientific or historical research purposes or statistical purposes shall, in accordance with Article 89(1), not be considered to be incompatible with the initial purposes'.

[14] GDPR, art 5(1)(c): Personal data shall be 'adequate, relevant and limited to what is necessary in relation to the purposes for which they are processed'.

[15] GDPR, art 5(1)(d): Personal data shall be 'accurate and, where necessary, kept up to date; every reasonable step must be taken to ensure that personal data that are inaccurate, having regard to the purposes for which they are processed, are erased or rectified without delay'.

[16] GDPR, art 5(1)(e): Personal data shall be 'kept in a form which permits identification of data subjects for no longer than is necessary for the purposes for which the personal data are processed; personal data may be stored for longer periods insofar as the personal data will be processed solely for archiving purposes in the public interest, scientific or historical research purposes or statistical purposes in accordance with Article 89(1) subject to implementation of the appropriate technical and organisational measures required by this Regulation in order to safeguard the rights and freedoms of the data subject'.

[17] GDPR, art 5(1)(f): Personal data shall be 'processed in a manner that ensures appropriate security of the personal data, including protection against unauthorised or unlawful processing and against accidental loss, destruction or damage, using appropriate technical or organisational measures'.

[18] PDPO, Principle 1: Data must be collected for a lawful purpose, by lawful and fair means, and where appropriate, with the knowledge or consent of the data subject. This is similar to the GDPR principle on lawfulness, fairness and transparency.

> Principle 2: Personal data should be accurate, up-to-date, and kept no longer than necessary. This is similar to the GDPR principles on accuracy and storage limitation.
>
> Principle 3: Unless the data subject gives consent otherwise, personal data must not be used for any purpose other than the one for which it was collected. This is similar to purpose limitation under the GDPR.
>
> Principle 4: Reasonable steps must be taken to protect personal data from unauthorised or accidental access, processing, erasure, loss or use. This is similar to the integrity and confidentiality principle under the GDPR.
>
> Principle 5: Data users should take practical steps to make information about their data policies and practices readily available. This is similar to the lawfulness, fairness and transparency principle under the GDPR.
>
> Principle 6: Individuals have the right to access their personal data and make corrections if necessary. This is similar to the right to be forgotten, to restrict processing and to data portability under the GDPR.

[19] These principles found in the EU's GDPR and Hong Kong's PDPO are also similar to the 'Personal Data Protection Principles' set out in the ASEAN 2016 Framework on Personal Data Protection. By that framework, the ASEAN Member States agree to endeavour to implement those principles in their domestic laws and regulations, although the implementation may differ in timing depending on the level of development of a member state.

[20] GDPR, art 6(1)(a): 'the data subject has given consent to the processing of his or her personal data for one or more specific purposes'.

of contract;[21] (3) compliance with legal obligation;[22] (4) protection of vital interests;[23] (5) public interest;[24] and (6) legitimate interests.[25]

The GDPR treats certain 'special categories' of personal data (eg, racial origin and religious belief)[26] more stringently by specifically prohibiting the processing of such data except where certain specified and narrower bases apply. They include, among other situations, where the data subject has given explicit consent to the processing, where processing is necessary to protect the vital interests of the data subject, where the personal data has been manifestly made public by the data subject, where processing is necessary for reasons of substantial public interest, and where processing is necessary for archiving purposes, scientific or historical research purposes or statistical purposes.[27]

The GDPR confers specified rights on the data subject, such as the right to information about the data controller, the right of access to the personal data, and the right to erasure of personal data (the right to be forgotten). It requires data controllers to implement technical and organisational measures to ensure that processing is performed in accordance with the GDPR and to protect the rights of data subjects.[28]

Under this framework, every data subject shall have the right to lodge a complaint with a supervisory authority against an infringement of the regulations which may result in an administrative fine, as well as the right to judicial remedy for infringement of his or her rights under the GDPR. Any person who has suffered damage as a result of an infringement of the regulations shall be entitled to compensation from the data controller or processor.

III. Scope of Personal Data

A. Definition of 'Personal Data'

Personal data protection laws are concerned not with any data, such as data about the physical world or even about human beings generally, but *personal* data. This is a threshold issue which determines whether the fundamental right to privacy is engaged in the

[21] GDPR, art 6(1)(b): 'processing is necessary for the performance of a contract to which the data subject is party or in order to take steps at the request of the data subject prior to entering into a contract'.

[22] GDPR, art 6(1)(c): 'processing is necessary for compliance with a legal obligation to which the controller is subject'.

[23] GDPR, art 6(1)(d): 'processing is necessary in order to protect the vital interests of the data subject or of another natural person'.

[24] GDPR, art 6(1)(e): 'processing is necessary for the performance of a task carried out in the public interest or in the exercise of official authority vested in the controller'.

[25] GDPR, art 6(1)(f): 'processing is necessary for the purposes of the legitimate interests pursued by the controller or by a third party, except where such interests are overridden by the interests or fundamental rights and freedoms of the data subject which require protection of personal data, in particular where the data subject is a child'.

[26] GDPR, art 9(1): 'personal data revealing racial or ethnic origin, political opinions, religious or philosophical beliefs, or trade union membership, and the processing of genetic data, biometric data for the purpose of uniquely identifying a natural person, data concerning health or data concerning a natural person's sex life or sexual orientation'.

[27] GDPR, art 9(2)(a)–(j).

[28] GDPR, arts 24 and 25.

first place. Under the GDPR, 'personal data' is defined as any information relating to an identified or identifiable natural person (the data subject). The general consensus is that the concept of 'personal data' should be given a broad interpretation, so as to include all information which may be linked to an individual.[29] Hong Kong's PDPO is more explicit in defining personal data as, among other things, data 'from which it is practicable for the identity of the individual to be directly or indirectly ascertained'.

Three features may be noted in the approach in determining whether a person is identifiable. First, the test is an objective one, focusing on whether a natural person can be singled out or distinguished from other individuals, taking into account 'all the means reasonably likely to be used … either by the controller or by another person to identify the natural person directly or indirectly'.[30] On the other hand, identification does not mean an educated guess. In *Information Commissioner v Miller*, the Upper Tribunal cited with apparent approval the following passage from the UK Information Commissioner's Code of Practice on 'Anonymisation: managing data protection risk':[31]

> [Identification] implies a degree of certainty that information is about one person and not another. Identification involves more than making an educated guess that information is about someone; the guess could be wrong. The possibility of making an educated guess about an individual's identity may present a privacy risk but not a data protection one because no personal data has been disclosed to the guesser. Even where a guess based on anonymised data turns out to be correct, this does not mean that a disclosure of personal data has taken place.

Second, as observed by the European Court of Justice in *Breyer v Germany*, if identification is prohibited by law or practically impossible because it requires a disproportionate effort in terms of time, cost and manpower, so that the risk of identification is in reality insignificant, then the person would not be identifiable.[32] A similar approach has been adopted in Australia.[33]

Third, the circumstances are important. In assessing the 'means reasonably likely to be used' for identifying a person, account should be taken of all objective factors.[34] The following observations of the Article 29 WP are of note:[35]

[29] Art 29 WP's *Opinion 4/2007 on the concept of personal data* (adopted on 20 June 2007) (WP 136) 4. The Opinion concerned the definition of personal data under the EU 1995 Directive, which adopted a definition largely similar to that under the GDPR. Some earlier UK authorities adopted a narrow approach to the meaning of personal data which involved asking where the data falls 'in a continuum of relevance or proximity to the data subject' and examining whether the information is biographical in a significant sense and has the putative data subject as its focus: *Durant v Financial Services Authority* [2003] EWCA Civ 1746, [27]–[28]. That suggestion in *Durant* was distinguished in later cases and eventually put to rest by the subsequent decision in *Efifiom Edem v Information Commissioner* [2014] EWCA Civ 92.

[30] GDPR, recital 26; see also Art 29 WP, WP 136, 13–14.

[31] *Information Commissioner v Miller* [2018] UKUT 229 (AAC) [16].

[32] *Breyer v Germany* (C-582/14) [46].

[33] Under Australia's Privacy Act 1988 (Cth), 'personal information' includes information or opinion about an individual 'whose identity … can reasonably be ascertained, from the information or opinion'. It has been held that an organisation is not required to 'scour the public domain to ascertain whether there is information that can be married with the information or opinion it holds in order to ascertain the identity of the individual. What it means is that the organisation must keep in mind what might be matters of general knowledge': *Telstra Corporation Ltd v Privacy Commissioner* [2015] AATA 991 [107]; *GMW v Victoria Legal Aid (Human Rights)* [2022] VCAT 922 [35]–[39].

[34] GDPR, recital 26.

[35] Art 29 WP, WP 136, 15.

> The cost of conducting identification is one factor, but not the only one. The intended purpose, the way the processing is structured, the advantage expected by the controller, the interests at stake for the individuals, as well as the risk of organisational dysfunctions (eg breaches of confidentiality duties) and technical failures should all be taken into account. On the other hand, this test is a dynamic one and should consider the state of the art in technology at the time of the processing and the possibilities for development during the period for which the data will be processed.

B. Anonymisation of Data

Personal data can be anonymised so that it ceases to be personal data. Sometimes, big data analytics do not require the use of data that identifies individuals, resulting in a win-win solution, as data can be made available for the intended use without privacy concerns.

'Anonymisation' is to be distinguished from 'pseudonymisation'. The latter means that the identity of the specific data subject is hidden but may be ascertainable with the use of additional information kept by the data processor and is thus often reversible. The common techniques of pseudonymisation include encryption, hashing and tokenisation, whereas the common methods of anonymisation include randomisation and generalisation.[36] At least in the EU, the general view is that pseudonymised data remains personal data, given the possibility of re-identification, and only true anonymous data falls outside the definition of personal data.[37]

Properly anonymised data does not raise privacy concerns. As stated in GDPR Recital 26, the principles of data protection should not apply to 'anonymous data', namely 'information which does not relate to an identified or identifiable natural person or to personal data rendered anonymous in such a manner that the data subject is not or no longer identifiable'. Likewise, China's PIPL (Article 4) expressly provides that personal information does not include anonymised information.

The focal question is the effectiveness of anonymisation as a means to irreversibly prevent identification of the data subject, so as to justify the conclusion that the dataset falls outside the scope of personal data protection law. Because of the rapid development of technology, anonymisation techniques may change in response to changing means of re-identification. It is generally recognised that the law should not insist on absolute impossibility of identification. A key concept that imports notions of proportionality is that account has to be taken of all the means 'likely reasonably' to be used for identification by the controller and third parties. As stated by Article 29 WP in its Opinion 05/2014 on Anonymisation Techniques on 10 April 2014 (WP 216),[38] in order to anonymise any data, it must be 'processed in such a way that it can no longer be used

[36] For an explanation of these methods, reference may be made to Art 29 WP, *Opinion 05/2014 on Anonymisation Techniques* (adopted on 10 April 2014) (WP 216), 12–23 and its Annex 'A primer on anonymisation techniques'.

[37] See, eg, Art 29 WP, WP 136, 18; WP 216, 3, 20; Binding Decision 1/2021 of the EDPB dated 28 July 2021 [94], [101], [112], [156].

[38] Although the Opinion was rendered on the basis of the EU 1995 Directive, it continues to be relevant given the similar concepts and definitions thereunder and under the GDPR.

to identify a natural person by using "all the means likely reasonably to be used" by either the controller or a third party'.[39] An assessment of the risk of re-identification is necessary, taking account of the cost of and the availability of the know-how needed for re-identification, as well as the cost and effort required for the anonymisation process. It must also be borne in mind that while certain data may seem anonymous to third parties, the data controller may have other records in combination with which re-identification of the data subject is possible (such as where the data collector has retained the original raw data or part of it). The risk must therefore be assessed having regard to the context and purposes of the processing for which the anonymised data is intended.

The legal issues arising in relation to anonymisation are illustrated and highlighted in several cases. In the decision of the European Data Protection Supervisor (EDPS) in complaint case 2020-1013 submitted against the European Parliament by its members,[40] the complainants questioned the European Parliament's website setup for COVID-19 PCR testing since it was discovered that, during a certain period, the website used, among other things, Google Analytics and Stripe cookies which collected information about visitors to the website and transferred such information to the US, where both Google and Stripe were located. The EDPS confirmed that[41]

> natural persons may be associated with online identifiers provided by their devices, applications and protocols, such as internet protocol addresses (IP addresses), cookie identifiers or other identifiers. This information can lead to the identification of the natural persons, in particular when combined with unique identifiers and other information received by the servers.

The EDPS found that the tracking cookies of Stripe and Google Analytics were personal data[42]

> even if the traditional identity parameters of the tracked users are unknown or have been deleted by the tracker after collection. All records containing identifiers that can be used to single out users, are considered as personal data under the Regulation and must be treated and protected as such.

In *Common Services Agency v Scottish Information Commissioner*,[43] the UK House of Lords considered the effectiveness of perturbation – a technique for generating synthetic data by adding 'noise' to raw data[44] – as a means to anonymise personal data, in deciding whether a request for statistical information should be complied with. The request was for details of all incidents of childhood leukaemia by year from 1990 to 2003, by census ward, for the Dumfries and Galloway postal area. A census ward had a minimum of 50 residents or 20 households. The request was refused by the agency on

[39] Art 29 WP, WP 216, 5.

[40] The decision was made in the context of Regulation EU 2018/1725 which dealt specifically with the processing of personal data by EU institutions etc.

[41] European Data Protection Supervisor, Decision in complaint case 2020-1013 submitted by Members of the Parliament against the European Parliament (5 January 2022) 12–13.

[42] ibid 13.

[43] *Common Services Agency v Scottish Information Commissioner* [2008] 1 WLR 1550.

[44] X Shen, X Bi and R Shen, 'Data Flush' (*Harvard Data Science Review*, 9 May 2022), available at hdsr.mitpress.mit.edu/pub/x1ozqj10/release/3. On the technique of noise addition, see WP 216, 12. In *Common Services Agency*, the perturbation technique involved is *barnardisation*, which is described at [23], [26] and [50] of the decision.

the ground that, given the combination of low numbers, the specified age group and the small geographic area, the request was for personal data within the meaning of the Data Protection Act 1998. The regulator commissioner agreed but ordered that the data be 'perturbed' so as to stop it being personal data and that the perturbed data be released. The agency appealed to the court.

The majority considered that data would not be personal data if they have been put into a form from which the individual or individuals to whom they relate cannot be identified at all, even with the assistance of the other information from which they were derived. In that case, the barnardisation used a modification rule which involved modifying each internal cell of every table by +1, 0 or −1.[45]

As it was a question of fact as to whether the process of barnardisation would enable the data to be sufficiently anonymised for it not to be personal data, the case was remitted to the commissioner so that he could re-examine the facts and make a determination. Subsequently, the commissioner came to the view that the barnardised data by itself could still lead to identification and that the effect of barnardisation on the actual figures did not have the effect of concealing or disguising the data. The barnardised statistics therefore constituted personal data (and, in particular, sensitive personal data).[46]

In *R (Department of Health) v Information Commissioner*,[47] Cranston J explained that the House of Lords' decision in *Common Services Agency* should be understood as recognising that, even though the data controller holds the key to identifying individuals to which the data relates, whether the data is personal information when disclosed depends on the question of fact of 'whether any living individuals can be identified by the public following disclosure of the information'. In that case, ProLife Alliance had asked for statistics of late-term abortions. The Department of Health refused on the ground (among others) that the data was personal data. Although there was some expert evidence that there was a real possibility of identification from the requested statistics, the Information Tribunal concluded that, on the evidence, the risk of identification by a third party was 'extremely remote'. Cranston J considered that the assessment of likelihood of identification was only 'partly a question of statistical expertise, as regards matters such as the sensitivity of the data', but also partly 'a matter of assessing a range of every day factors, such as the likelihood that particular groups, such as campaigners, and the press, will seek out information of identity and the types of other information, already in the public domain, which could inform the search'. He concluded there was no basis to impugn the assessment of the Tribunal and, on this footing, held that the requested statistics were 'fully anonymised' and their disclosure to the public would not constitute the processing of personal data.

Much depends, therefore, on the means of anonymisation employed and the ways in which they can potentially be reversed, including the lengths to which the person attempting the reversal is prepared to go. In that connection, the UK authorities have referred to a 'motivated intruder' test. This is 'a person who starts without any prior knowledge but who wishes to identify the individual or individuals referred to in the

[45] It randomly added 0, +1, or −1 to the values where the true value lay in the range of 2–4 and added 0 or +1 to cells where the value was 1. 0s were always kept at 0.

[46] Scottish Information Commissioner's Decision 021/2005 (26 May 2010) [14]–[21].

[47] *R (Department of Health) v Information Commissioner* [2011] EWHC 1430 (Admin).

purportedly anonymised information and will take all reasonable steps to do so'. The question is 'whether, taking account of the nature of the information, there would be likely to be a motivated intruder within the public at large who would be able to identify the individuals to whom the disclosed information relates'.[48] While the motivated intruder is not assumed to have any specialist knowledge, it is assumed that he is[49]

> reasonably competent, has access to resources such as the Internet, libraries, and all public documents, and would employ investigative techniques such as making enquiries of people who may have additional knowledge of the identity of the data subject or advertising for anyone with information to come forward.

IV. Legal Issues in Data Collection

Data is the cornerstone of AI model training. To achieve adequate performance, deep learning models need to be trained on very large volumes of data. Typically, the generalisation error rate tends to decrease more or less linearly with the size of the training data. As a result, AI developers are incentivised to push the training process towards the furthest end of the learning curve.[50] This requires data to be harvested for use in training and subsequent deployment of the AI technology. There are various ways in which data may be collected, which may involve personal data. This chapter shall focus on the legal issues associated with the following means of collection: (1) data trading: purchasing datasets from third parties;[51] (2) secondary use of data: using data collected by the business or connected entities for purposes other than that for which it was originally collected; and (3) web scraping: collecting data from public sources.

A. Data Trading

With the rise of big data and AI, data broking, or data trading, has become a business. In fact, it has been suggested that the data trading industry is worth multiple billions.[52] The performance of a contract of sale by the transmission of data to the purchaser will constitute processing of data. Insofar as the data traded involves personal data, a legal basis is required for the processing. As mentioned above, for personal data, the legal bases are listed in GDPR Article 6. For sensitive data, stricter requirements have to

[48] *Information Commissioner v Magherafelt District Council* [2013] AACR 14 [37].
[49] Information Commissioner's Office, 'Anonymisation: Managing Data Protection Risk Code of Practice' (November 2012) 22–23.
[50] J Bellegarda, 'Synthetic Data Generation in Service of Privacy-Preserving Deep Learning: Three Practical Case Studies' in H Matsumi et al (eds), *Computers, Privacy and Data Protection Vol 15: Data Protection and Privacy in Transitional Times* (London, Bloomsbury Publishing, 2024) 28–29.
[51] Some refer to this as 'data sharing', but that term has also been used to refer to sharing between (1) connected entities or (2) law enforcement entities, which more properly fall within the category of secondary use. The term used in this chapter is data trading, which is how this is referred to in some literature: eg, H Ruschemeier, 'Data Brokers and European Digital Legislation' EDPL 1/2023; V Janecek and G Malgieri, 'Data Extra Commercium' in S Lohsse et al (eds), *Data as Counter-Performance – Contract Law 2.0?* (London, Bloomsbury Publishing, 2020).
[52] H Ruschemeier, 'Data Brokers and European Digital Legislation' EDPL 1/2023, 28.

be complied with under Article 9. The discussion below shall focus on the bases of (1) consent and (2) legitimate interest.

i. Consent

Consent can serve as a legal basis for collecting data for monetisation purposes.[53] Under the GDPR, to come within its definition in Article 4(11), consent must be: (1) freely given; (2) specific; (3) informed; and (4) unambiguous. These elements, which overlap to some extent, together with further conditions for consent set out in Article 7, will be discussed below.[54]

First, consent has to be freely given. The concept of consent under the GDPR is arguably narrower compared to that required for the formation of a contract at common law. In particular, the GDPR contains principles that guard against bundling or tying. Data controllers sometimes try to make the provision of a service conditional on the customer's consent to the processing of personal data, which is said to be necessary for the performance of the contract between them. The conditionality raises questions in relation to both bases of 'consent' and 'performance of contract'. A data subject who does not wish to make his or her personal data available for processing by the controller runs the risk of being denied the services sought. In assessing whether consent is freely given, Article 7.4 of the GDPR requires 'utmost account' to be taken of whether the performance of a contract, including provision of a service, is conditional on consent to the processing of personal data that is not necessary for the performance of that contract. On the other hand, there may be a genuine choice if the data subject is able to choose between a service that includes consenting to the use of personal data for additional purposes, and a genuinely equivalent service offered by the same controller that does not involve such consent.[55] The exercise requires an assessment of the scope of the contract and what data is clearly and objectively necessary for its performance in the case of each individual data subject.[56]

The rationale is that in the protection of fundamental rights, an individual's control over their personal data is essential, which in turn justifies a strong presumption that consent to the processing of personal data that is *unnecessary* cannot be seen as a mandatory consideration in exchange for the performance of a contract or the provision of a service.[57]

In addition, for there to be real freedom of consent, the principle of *granularity* requires that, where the data processing is done for more than one purpose, there has to be granularity, 'ie the separation of these purposes and obtaining consent for each purpose'. The data subjects should be free to choose which purpose they accept, rather

[53] Art 29 WP, *Opinion 06/2014 on the notion of legitimate interests of the data controller under Article 7 of Directive 95/46/EC* (adopted on 9 April 2014) (WP 217) 18, 47.

[54] As an important source for reference, it should be noted that the Art 29 WP has in 2018 issued its *Guidelines on consent under Regulation 2016/679* (revised and adopted on 10 April 2018) (WP 259 rev.01) and the EDPB has also issued *Guideline 05/2020 on consent under Regulation 2016/679* (adopted on 4 May 2020) (EDPB Guideline 05/2020).

[55] Art 29 WP, WP 259 rev.01, 9; EDPB Guideline 05/2020, para 37.

[56] Art 29 WP, WP 259 rev.01, 8; see also GDPR, recital 43.

[57] Art 29 WP, WP 259 rev.01, 8.

than having to consent to a bundle of processing purposes.[58] In the context of data trading, for example, in addition to the consent for collection of the personal data for monetising purposes, it is arguably necessary to obtain a separate consent for the transfer of the data to a third-party purchaser.[59]

Second, consent has to be specific. In other words, the consent must be given in relation to one or more specific purposes. This requirement is closely related to the requirement of 'informed' consent as well as the principle of granularity – in order for consent to be specific, the relevant purposes must be specified, and there must be freedom of choice in relation to each of them.[60] This requirement should also be seen in combination with the principle of purpose limitation (Article 5(1)(b) GDPR), which requires that personal data shall be collected for specific, explicit and legitimate purposes and not further processed in a manner that is incompatible with those purposes, in order to guard against the widening of use of the data after initial consent for its collection – a phenomenon known as 'function creep'.

Third, consent should be informed. The principle of transparency and fairness (GDPR Article 5(1)(a)) is closely related to the requirement of informed consent. Clear and intelligible information has to be provided to data subjects prior to obtaining their consent, such that they are able to understand what they are agreeing to and can exercise their right to withdraw their consent. GDPR Article 7(2) requires that the request for consent be presented in a manner which is clearly distinguishable from other matters, in an intelligible and easily accessible form, using clear and plain language.

The Article 29 WP has suggested the following 'minimum content requirements' for consent to be informed:[61] (1) the controller's identity; (2) the purpose of each of the processing operations for which consent is sought; (3) what (type of) data will be collected and used; (4) the existence of the right to withdraw consent;[62] (5) information about the use of the data for automated decision-making[63] where relevant; and (6) information on the possible risks of data transfers to a third country or an international organisation.[64]

Where the data is to be transferred to other controllers who wish to rely on the original consent, the names of these other controllers should be named in the original request for consent. Articles 13 and 14 of the GDPR also require controllers to provide a list of the recipients or categories of recipients of the personal data, upon collection from the data subjects and upon further transfer to another controller.[65]

[58] Art 29 WP, WP 259 rev.01, 10.

[59] V Janecek and G Malgieri, 'Data Extra Commercium' in S Lohsse et al (eds), *Data as Counter-Performance – Contract Law 2.0?* (London, Bloomsbury Publishing, 2020).

[60] Art 29 WP, WP 259 rev.01, 9, 11.

[61] Art 29 WP, WP 259 rev.01, 13.

[62] GDPR, art 7(3) requires that prior to giving consent, the data subject shall be informed of the right to withdraw his or her consent at any time and that it shall be as easy to withdraw as to give consent.

[63] This refers to decisions based solely on automated processing, including profiling, which produce legal effects concerning the data subject or similarly significantly affect him or her. GDPR, art 22 provides that the data subject has the right not to be subject to such a decision unless, inter alia, the data subject has given 'explicit consent'.

[64] This refers to the risks due to the absence of an 'adequacy decision' under GDPR art 45 and of appropriate safeguards as described in GDPR art 46.

[65] EDPB Guideline 05/2020, para 65.

Fourth, consent must be unambiguous. Unambiguous consent requires 'a statement' or 'a clear affirmative action' which 'signifies agreement to the processing'.[66] A clear affirmative action means that the data subject must have taken a deliberate positive action or other active behaviour to consent to the particular processing. According to GDPR Recital 32, this can include ticking a box when visiting a website, but not '[s]ilence, pre-ticked boxes or inactivity'. The requirements of specificity and affirmative action mean that, under the GDPR, consent is not regarded as being given through an act accepting the general terms and conditions of a service. Specifically, the GDPR 'does not allow controllers to offer pre-ticked boxes or opt-out constructions that require an intervention from the data subject to prevent agreement (for example 'opt-out boxes')'.[67]

In relation to the use of cookies, the Article 29 WP has stated that active behaviour on the part of the user is required 'such that the website operator can be confident that the user has actively requested to engage with the website and (assuming the user is fully informed) does therefore indeed consent to cookies and that the action is an active indicator of such consent'. A click to a 'more information on cookies' link cannot, however, be deemed consent, since by clicking on it the user merely explicitly requests more information. 'The user action must be such that, taken in conjunction with the provided information on the use of cookies, it can reasonably be interpreted as indication of his/her wishes.'[68]

The following cases shed light on the requirements for consent in the context of data trading. In *Bundesverband v Planet 49 GmbH*, a German online gaming company hosted a promotional lottery on its website.[69] Internet users wishing to take part in the lottery were directed to a web page which contained a *pre-ticked* checkbox accompanied by text explaining that by ticking the checkbox, the user was consenting to cookies being stored on his computer which would enable the company to evaluate the user's internet behaviour so that advertising could be targeted towards his interests.[70] The German Federation of Consumer Organisations brought an action for an injunction requiring the company to cease using the checkbox, contending that it did not satisfy the requirements of national law transposing the EU's ePrivacy Directive,[71] which required that the storing of information, or gaining of access to information already stored, on a user's terminal equipment should only be allowed where the user had given his 'consent', as defined under the EU 1995 Directive. The German court referred to the Court of Justice of the European Union (CJEU) questions concerning whether the checkbox complied with those two Directives.

[66] GDPR, art 4(11).

[67] Art 29 WP, WP 259 rev.01, 16; see also 30.

[68] Art 29 WP, *Working Document 02/2013 on obtaining consent for cookies* (WP 208) 4–5.

[69] *Bundesverband v Planet 49 GmbH* (Case C-673/17).

[70] The text for the checkbox (which was pre-ticked) read: 'I agree to the web analytics service Remintrex being used for me. This has the consequence that, following registration for the lottery, the lottery organiser, Planet49 GmbH, sets cookies, which enables Planet49 to evaluate my surfing and use behaviour on websites of advertising partners and thus enables advertising by Remintrex that is based on a user's interests. I can delete the cookies again at any time. You can read more about this here.'

[71] Dir 2002/58/EC.

The CJEU confirmed that *active* consent is required both under the EU 1995 Directive and the GDPR.[72] Consent given in the form of a pre-ticked checkbox 'does not imply active behaviour on the part of a website user', because[73]

> it would appear impossible in practice to ascertain objectively whether a website user had actually given his or her consent to the processing of his or her personal data by not deselecting a pre-ticked checkbox nor, in any event, whether that consent had been informed. It is not inconceivable that a user would not have read the information accompanying the preselected checkbox, or even would not have noticed that checkbox, before continuing with his or her activity on the website visited.

The CJEU stated that the requirement for 'clear and comprehensive information' to be given about the purposes of the processing means that a user must be

> in a position to be able to determine easily the consequences of any consent he or she might give and ensure that the consent given is well informed. It must be clearly comprehensible and sufficiently detailed so as to enable the user to comprehend the functioning of the cookies employed.

In relation to the cookies in that case, which aimed to collect information for advertising purposes, the duration of the operation of the cookies and whether or not third parties could have access to them were part of the clear and comprehensive information which must be provided to the user. Thus, the information which the controller must provide to a data subject prior to the collection of personal data includes also 'any further information such as the recipients or categories of recipients of the data in so far as such further information is necessary, having regard to the specific circumstances in which the data are processed, to guarantee fair processing in respect of the data subject'.[74]

In the UK, the Information Commissioner's Office (ICO) has, in October 2020, published a report on its 'Investigation into data protection compliance in the direct marketing data broking sector.' The report focused on the ICO's investigation into the offline marketing services[75] of the data broking industry and, in particular, the activities of the UK's three largest credit reference agencies, which also operate in the data broking industry: Experian, Equifax and TransUnion. Data broking involves collecting data about individuals from a variety of sources (such as the open electoral register, publicly available data and third-party suppliers), then combining it and selling or licensing it to other organisations such as businesses, political parties, or charities for their fundraising campaigns. The services data brokers provide include selling lists of contact details; adding data to the profile the recipient already holds on people; data matching (eg, providing phone numbers for people already in the recipient's database); and audience segmenting (eg, identifying sub-groups within an audience for tailored messaging).

The ICO focused on the grounds of consent and legitimate interests. In the case of Equifax, it claimed that personal data was supplied to it by third-party data brokers on

[72] The GDPR had replaced the EU 1995 Directive by the time of the decision.

[73] *Bundesverband* (n 69) [52], [55].

[74] ibid [74]–[81].

[75] ie, services providing marketing to individuals through methods other than the Internet, eg, postal, telephone and SMS marketing.

the basis of consent, and it subsequently relied on this consent to process it for data broking purposes. The ICO found that none of the consents reviewed by the auditors met the standard required by the GDPR. For example, the consents were neither informed nor specific.

Experian likewise relied on consent as the basis for collecting data from third parties (who had collected information from the relevant data subjects) and also on legitimate interests for its own processing activities after obtaining the data. The ICO rejected this, opining that '[s]witching from consent to legitimate interests meant that the original consent was no longer specific or informed, the degree of control and the nature of the relationship with the individual was misrepresented, and the right to withdraw consent was also undermined'. An enforcement notice was issued to Experian requiring it to delete data supplied on the basis of consent, which was processed by Experian purportedly on the basis of its legitimate interests.

ii. Legitimate Interest

Another legal basis for processing personal data is legitimate interests. In terms of GDPR Article 6(1)(f), processing is lawful where it 'is necessary for the purposes of the legitimate interests pursued by the controller or by a third party, except where such interests are overridden by the interests or fundamental rights and freedoms of the data subject which require protection of personal data'. GDPR Recital 47 suggests that central to this basis are the reasonable expectations of data subjects based on their relationship with the controller.

Three cumulative conditions have to be satisfied: (1) the pursuit of a legitimate interest by the data controller or by a third party; (2) the need to process personal data for the purposes of the legitimate interests pursued; and (3) the interests or fundamental rights and freedoms of the data subject do not take precedence over the legitimate interest of the controller or the third party.[76]

First, the pursuit of a legitimate interest:

(1) Pursuant to GDPR Article 13(1)(d), it is the responsibility of the controller, at the time when personal data relating to a data subject is collected from that person, to inform him or her of the legitimate interests pursued where that processing is based on the legitimate interest ground.[77]

(2) The interest must be sufficiently clearly articulated to allow the balancing test to be carried out.[78]

(3) The interest at stake must be 'pursued' by the controller, which requires a 'real and present interest, something that corresponds with current activities or benefits that are expected in the very near future'. Interests that are too vague or speculative will not be sufficient.[79]

[76] *Meta Platforms Inc v Bundeskartellamt* (Case C-252/21) [106].

[77] ibid [107].

[78] Art 29 WP, *Opinion 06/2014 on the notion of legitimate interests of the data controller under Article 7 of directive 95/46/EC* (adopted on 9 April 2014) (WP 217) 24.

[79] Art 29 WP, WP 217, 24.

Second, the necessity requirement:

(1) The legitimate interest pursued cannot reasonably be achieved just as effectively by other means less restrictive of the fundamental rights and freedoms of data subjects (in particular the rights to respect for private life and to the protection of personal data).[80]

(2) The condition must be examined in conjunction with the 'data minimisation' principle under Article 5(1)(c) in accordance with which personal data must be 'adequate, relevant and limited to what is necessary in relation to the purposes for which they are processed'.[81]

(3) The CJEU has adopted a strict interpretation and held that the data processing must be *strictly necessary* for the purposes of the legitimate interest pursued.[82]

Third, the balancing test:

(1) The reference to the interests and rights of data subjects should be given a broad interpretation. All the relevant interests of the data subject should be taken into account.[83]

(2) The interests and fundamental rights of the data subject may in particular override the interest of the data controller where personal data is processed in circumstances where data subjects do not reasonably expect such processing.[84]

(3) The balancing test has to be carried out in the circumstances of a specific case. 'Legitimate interests of the controller, when minor and not very compelling may, in general, only override the interests and rights of data subjects in cases where the impact on these rights and interests are even more trivial. On the other hand, important and compelling legitimate interests may in some cases and subject to safeguards and measures justify even significant intrusion into privacy or other significant impact on the interests or rights of the data subjects.'[85]

(4) The Article 29 WP has identified the following key factors to be considered when applying the balancing test: '(a) assessing the controller's legitimate interest, (b) impact on the data subjects, (c) provisional balance, and (d) additional safeguards applied by the controller to prevent any undue impact on the data subjects'.[86]

(5) The impact on the data subjects should be assessed in a broad way. Relevant factors may include: (a) the nature of the data; (b) the way data is being processed; (c) the reasonable expectation of the data subject; and (d) the status of (or power balance/imbalance between) the controller and data subject.[87] 'Seemingly innocuous data, when processed on a large scale and combined with other data may lead to inferences about more sensitive data ….'[88]

[80] *Meta* (n 76) [108].
[81] ibid [109].
[82] ibid [126].
[83] Art 29 WP, WP 217, 29–30.
[84] *Meta* (n 76) [112], citing GDPR, recital 47.
[85] Art 29 WP, WP 217, 30.
[86] ibid 33.
[87] ibid 37–41.
[88] ibid 39.

(6) On the other hand, the presence of additional safeguards may alleviate the impact on the data subject. Various means may be used to reduce and/or limit the impact of data processing, such as functional separation (ie, measures to ensure that the data cannot be used to take decisions or other actions with respect to individuals), pseudonymisation, increased transparency and data portability.[89]

Article 29 WP has suggested that, where the processing involves extensive profiling, data sharing, online direct marketing or behavioural advertisement, consent would be a more appropriate ground.[90] It is unlikely that a commercial controller can rely on the legitimate interest ground to justify extensive profiling and trading in such profiles in the absence of informed consent and a workable mechanism to object.[91] It is also likely to be difficult for data brokering businesses to rely on legitimate interest as the legal basis of processing.

In *Fashion ID GmbH & Co KG v Verbraucherzentrale NRW eV* (Case C-40/17), Fashion ID was a German clothing retailer that embedded on its website a social plug-in, namely the Facebook 'like' button.[92] As a consequence, whenever a person visited Fashion ID's website, the visitor's web browser would transmit the computer's IP address, as well as the browser's technical data, to Facebook's server. Such transmission of data would occur regardless of whether the visitor was a member of Facebook and regardless of whether they clicked on the like button. A German consumer protection association sought an injunction to restrain Fashion ID from embedding the like button on its website. The German appeal court referred to the CJEU various questions, including whether one should consider the legitimate interests of Fashion ID or Facebook.

The CJEU found that Fashion ID, as the website operator, was a 'controller' jointly with Facebook, in respect of the operations involving the collection and disclosure by transmission of the personal data of visitors to its website. Given that both Fashion ID and Facebook were controllers, it was necessary that each of them should pursue a legitimate interest through those processing operations in order for those operations to be justified in respect of each of them.[93]

In the UK ICO's report on 'Investigation into data protection compliance in the direct marketing data broking sector', referred to in IV.A.i. above, the credit reference agencies which acted as data brokers also relied on the legitimate interest ground to justify their data processing. The ICO rejected that defence because the 'legitimate interest assessments' (LIAs) conducted by the agencies for their marketing services were not 'properly weighted' in the sense that they gave little weight to the fact that they were processing a large amount of personal data in highly targeted ways, profiling individuals, along with significant issues of non-transparency. LIAs must be conducted objectively, taking into account all factors. The agencies were required to revise their LIAs to reconsider the balance of their own interests against the rights and freedoms of individuals in the context of their marketing services.

[89] ibid 42.
[90] ibid 18.
[91] ibid 26.
[92] *Fashion ID GmbH & Co KG v Verbraucherzentrale NRW eV* (Case C-40/17).
[93] ibid [95]–[97].

B. Secondary Use

Apart from data trading, personal data may also come to be processed through secondary use. Secondary use refers to the use of data that businesses have already collected (eg, from other operations or by connected entities in the same group). The grounds that are commonly invoked by data controllers to justify secondary use of data include consent, performance of contract and legitimate interest.

i. Consent

The general principles pertaining to consent as a legal basis have been discussed above. The discussion here shall focus on the application of the relevant principles to specific cases involving the secondary use of personal data.

An important recent case is *Meta Platforms Inc v Bundeskartellamt*, with the judgment issued on 4 July 2023, where the CJEU examined the Meta group's operation of Facebook. The business model of Facebook was based on financing through online advertising, which was made possible by detailed user profiles arising from the data collected from users.[94]

For the processing of this data, Meta relied on the user agreement which Facebook users accepted when they clicked on the 'sign up' button, together with the general terms of Meta. Acceptance of those terms was necessary in order to use Facebook. The general terms referred to the company's data and cookies policies, which stated that Meta collected 'user- and device-related data about user activities on and off the social network and links the data with the Facebook accounts of the users concerned'. The off-Facebook data referred to data concerning visits to third-party webpages and apps, which are linked to Facebook through programming interfaces – 'Facebook Business Tools' – as well as data concerning the use of other online services belonging to the Meta group, including Instagram and WhatsApp.

The proceedings were originally brought by the German Federal Cartel Office (FCO) with respect to Meta's abuse of its dominant position. The FCO required Meta to adapt its general terms to make clear that the off-Facebook data would neither be collected nor linked with Facebook user accounts nor used without the consent of the user concerned. Meta appealed the decision and, in the meantime, introduced new general terms expressly stating that the user, instead of paying to use Facebook products, agrees to being shown advertisements.

In dealing with Facebook's appeal, the German court referred various questions to the CJEU, including whether consent by a user can effectively be given to an operator with a dominant position on the national market for online social networks. The CJEU answered that a social network's dominance in the market does not, as such, prevent the users of that social network from validly giving their consent to the processing of their personal data by the operator of the network. Such a circumstance must, however, be taken into consideration in assessing whether the user of that network has validly and freely given consent, 'since that circumstance is liable to affect the freedom of choice of that user, who

[94] *Meta* (n 76) [27].

might be unable to refuse or withdraw consent without detriment'. The dominant position of the operator may create a clear imbalance within the meaning of GDPR Recital 43 between the data subject and the controller, that imbalance favouring, among other things, the imposition of conditions that are not strictly necessary for the performance of the contract, which must be taken into account under GDPR Article 7(4).[95]

The CJEU considered that the users must be free to refuse consent for particular data processing operations not necessary for the performance of the contract, without having to refrain entirely from using the online social network, 'which means that those users are to be offered, if necessary for an appropriate fee, an equivalent alternative not accompanied by such data processing operations'. The court considered that it was appropriate to have the possibility of giving separate consent for the processing of the on-Facebook and off-Facebook data, respectively. In the absence of such a possibility, the users' consent to the processing of the off-Facebook data must be presumed not to be freely given.[96]

Following the CJEU's decision in the *Meta* case and the EDPB's urgent binding decision regarding Meta (see section IV.B.iii. below), Meta has recently offered people in the EU (and EEA and Switzerland) the option to pay a monthly subscription to use Facebook and Instagram without any ads – a model colloquially dubbed 'consent-or-pay' or 'pay-or-okay'.[97] In doing so, Meta appears to be relying on the CJEU's observation in the *Meta* case that, to promote free choice, 'users are to be offered, *if necessary for an appropriate fee*, an equivalent alternative not accompanied by such data processing operations' [emphasis added].

Whether this will pass muster with the supervisory authorities and the courts remains to be seen. The DPAs from the Netherlands, Norway and Germany had requested the EDPB to take a formal position on the 'pay-or-okay' model'.[98] The EDPB issued an opinion on 17 April 2024 relating to large online platforms, concluding that 'in most cases', the requirements of valid consent will not be met if users are only given a binary choice between consenting to processing of personal data for behavioural advertising purposes and paying a fee.[99] The non-profit organisation, the NOYB – European Centre for Digital Rights, also filed a complaint against Meta's 'pay-or-okay' model with the Austrian DPA in November 2023, arguing that consent given to avoid a high price (Meta proposes to charge €12.99 per month for Facebook and €8 for Instagram) is not freely given.[100] NOYB cited research suggesting that 99.9 per cent of visitors agreed to tracking when faced with a €1.99 fee, whereas only 3 to 10 per cent of users actually wanted their personal data to be used for targeted advertising. The European Consumer Organisation and some of its members also filed a joint complaint against Meta in

[95] ibid [147]–[149].

[96] ibid [150]–[151].

[97] A Folks, 'Meta's New Digs: A Deep Dive into Practical Considerations of Consent' (*IAPP*, 9 January 2024), available at iapp.org/news/a/metas-new-digs-a-deep-dive-into-practical-considerations-of-consent.

[98] 'DPAs seek EDPB position on "pay or OK" advertising model' (*IAPP*, 26 January 2024), available at iapp.org/news/a/several-eu-data-protection-authorities-seek-edpb-position-on-pay-or-ok-advertising-model.

[99] EDPB, *Opinion 08/2024 on Valid Consent in the Context of Consent or Pay Models Implemented by Large Online Platforms* (adopted on 17 April 2024).

[100] NOYB, 'NOYB Files GDPR Complaint Against Meta of "Pay or Okay"' (28 November 2023), available at noyb.eu/en/noyb-files-gdpr-complaint-against-meta-over-pay-or-okay.

December 2023, alleging that the subscription model violates EU consumer laws by using unfair, deceptive, and aggressive practices to pressure users into subscribing.

While there is not yet any CJEU decision on this point, decisions from national authorities seem to suggest that the 'pay-or-okay' model is in principle acceptable.[101] There can, however, be objections in principle to the practice which commoditises fundamental rights to privacy and potentially exacerbates social inequalities. Assuming the model is acceptable in principle, difficult questions will nevertheless arise on what level of fees may be charged before they become so exorbitant as to leave the user with no real option.

ii. Performance of contract

The basic idea of the 'performance of contract' basis (GDPR Article 6(1)(b)) is that processing of personal data may be lawful if it is *necessary* for the performance of a contract to which the data subject is party. As pointed out by the Article 29 WP, the provision 'must be interpreted strictly and does not cover situations where the processing is not genuinely necessary for the performance of a contract, but rather unilaterally imposed on the data subject by the controller'.[102]

The recent decision of the CJEU in *Meta* (discussed above) also discussed performance of contract as a ground for the secondary use of data. In particular, the CJEU considered whether Meta could rely on the ground of necessity for performance of contract to justify collecting off-Facebook data, linking them with the user's Facebook account and using them for targeted advertising. The CJEU said that this ground must be interpreted restrictively in circumstances where there was no valid consent for the processing in question. The fact that the processing may be referred to in the contract or may be *useful* for the performance of the contract is not sufficient. The processing has to be 'objectively indispensable for a purpose that is integral to the contractual obligation intended for the data subject' and 'essential for the proper performance of the contract', and 'there [must be] no workable, less intrusive alternatives'. In other words, it must be demonstrated that 'the main subject matter of the contract cannot be achieved if that processing does not occur'.[103] Furthermore, where the contract consists of several separate services or elements of a service that can be performed independently of one another, the necessity should be assessed for each of those services separately.[104]

Meta argued that off-Facebook data of the users was processed in order to ensure personalised content and the consistent and seamless use of the Meta group's own services, which was necessary to ensure proper performance of the contract. The CJEU

[101] See, eg, the decision of the Norwegian Privacy Appeals Board in *Grindr* (PVN-2022-22) (which seemed to suggest that the requirement for voluntary consent would likely have been met had the user been given the choice between using the free version of the application and the advertising-free paid versions before the registration process was completed); and the decisions of the Austrian DPA in the *Der Standard* case (2023-0.174.027) and the German DPA in the *Heise.de* case (4.2 05475-02-0301/21) (which took the view that the alternative of a paid subscription was in principle permissible, but that the consent obtained in both cases was not validly obtained).

[102] Art 29 WP, *Opinion 06/2014 on the notion of legitimate interests of the data controller under Article 7 of Directive 95/46/EC* (WP 217) 16.

[103] *Meta* (n 76) [93]–[99].

[104] ibid [100].

rejected the argument. First, although it was useful to the user to view content corresponding to his or her interests, personalised content did not appear to be necessary in order to offer that user the services of the online social network. Personalisation was not objectively indispensable for a purpose that was integral to the social network services. Second, as to the consistent and seamless use of the Meta group's own services, a user did not have to subscribe to the various services offered by the Meta group in order to use Facebook. The various products and services offered by the group could be used independently of each other. Accordingly, the Court concluded that the processing of personal data from services offered by the Meta group, other than the online social network service, did not appear to be necessary for the latter service to be provided.[105]

Complaints about Facebook made to the Irish DPA have also led to two decisions by the EDPB: (1) Binding Decision 3/2022 relating to Facebook, and (2) Binding Decision 4/2022 relating to Instagram. In these decisions, both made in December 2022, the EDPB found that Meta was not entitled to rely on the performance of contract ground to process personal data for the purposes of behavioural advertising.[106] As opposed to off-Facebook data (which was the focus in the *Meta* case in the CJEU), these two EDPB decisions were concerned with the collection of personal data on Meta platforms. As with off-Facebook data, Meta links the on-Meta data to the user's Facebook account[107]

> to enable advertisers to tailor their advertising to Facebook's individual users based on their consumer behaviour, interests, purchasing power and personal situation. … Meta IE offers its services to its users free of charge and generates revenue through this personalised advertising that targets them, in addition to static advertising that is displayed to every user in the same way.

Interestingly, there was an argument about whether there was a valid contract in the first place. Relying on a Gallup Institute poll which showed that only 1.6 to 2.5 per cent of the 1,000 respondents understood the request to accept Facebook's Terms and Conditions to be a 'contract' that provided them with a contractual right to personalised advertisements, the complainants contended that there was no genuine contract relevant to the use of the data in question. The EDPB considered that the validity of the contract was 'questionable given the strong indications that the Complainant was unaware of entering into a contract, and … serious transparency issues in relation to the legal basis relied on' but did not reject the defence on this ground and instead went on to consider whether behavioural advertising was necessary for Meta to provide its Facebook/Instagram service to the user.[108]

On that question, the EDPB noted that 'it is important to determine the exact rationale of the contract, i.e. its substance and fundamental objective, as it is against this that it will be tested whether the data processing is necessary for its performance', and that regard should be given to the 'particular aim, purpose, or objective of the service'

[105] ibid [101]–[104].
[106] EDPB Binding Decision 3/2022 on the dispute submitted by the Irish SA on Meta Platforms Ireland Limited and its Facebook service (Art 65 GDPR) (adopted on 5 December 2022), [133], [484]; EDPB Binding Decision 4/2022 on the dispute submitted by the Irish SA on Meta Platforms Ireland Limited and its Instagram service (Art 65 GDPR) (adopted on 5 December 2022) [137], [451].
[107] Binding Decision 3/2022 [95]. Given the two decisions are largely identical, the reference to paragraph numbers below will be to those in Binding Decision 3/2022.
[108] ibid [97]–[111].

and that the processing has to be objectively necessary and 'integral to the delivery of that contractual service to the data subject'. Significantly, it was pointed out that necessity is examined 'by reference to the fundamental and mutually understood contractual purpose', which depends 'not only on the controller's perspective, but also on a reasonable data subject's perspective when entering into the contract'.[109]

The EDPB considered that 'as a general rule, processing of personal data for behavioural advertising is not necessary for the performance of a contract for online services', which is supported by the absolute right of data subjects (under GDPR Article 21(2)(3)) to object to the processing of their data (including profiling) for direct marketing purposes. Although there were references in Meta's Terms and Conditions to the provision of personalised service under the headings 'Provide a personalised experience for you' and 'Help you discover content, products and services that may interest you', Meta had principally promoted Facebook and Instagram as a social network that allowed users to communicate with others. Meta had described Facebook and Instagram's mission as 'to give people the power to build community and bring the world closer together'. The EDPB found it telling that the Facebook/Instagram terms did not provide for any contractual obligation binding Meta to offer personalised advertising to users or any contractual penalty if Meta failed to do so. At least from the perspective of the users, this processing was not necessary for the performance of the contract.

Nor did Meta's business model of offering services at no monetary cost for the user and relying on behavioural advertisement to support its Facebook service make the data processing necessary to perform the contract. Under the GDPR, it is the business model which must adapt itself and comply with the requirements of the GDPR and not the reverse. In the EDPB's view, there were realistic, less intrusive alternatives to behavioural advertising that made Meta's processing not necessary, such as contextual advertising based on geography, language and content, which did not involve intrusive measures such as profiling and tracking of users.

Given that behavioural advertising is a set of data processing operations 'of great technical complexity, which has a particularly massive and intrusive nature', coupled with the 'very brief and insufficient' information provided about it by Meta in its terms, the EDPB found it extremely difficult to accept that an average user could be fully aware of its consequences and impact on their rights to privacy and data protection. As such, the EDPB found that the main purpose for which users use Facebook/Instagram and accept their terms was to communicate with others, not to receive personalised advertisements.

The EDPB also highlighted the importance of transparency. In particular, it considered that the conditions of the 'performance of contract' basis cannot be met where the data subject is 'not provided with sufficient information to know that they are signing a contract, the processing of personal data that it involves, for which specific purposes and on which legal basis, and how this processing is necessary to perform the services delivered'. These transparency requirements are 'an indispensable and constitutive part of the legal basis' and are especially important where the users face a 'take it or leave it'

[109] ibid [112]–[113].

situation resulting from the standard contract pre-formulated by Meta IE and the lack of few alternative services in the market.[110]

The EDPB concluded that Meta could not rely on the performance of contract ground and lacked a legal basis to process the users' personal data for the purpose of behavioural advertising. Pursuant to the EDPB's decisions, on 31 December 2022, Ireland's DPA imposed on Meta a fine of €210 million (in the case of Facebook) and €180 million (in the case of Instagram).

iii. Legitimate Interests

Another basis for processing personal data, ie, legitimate interests under GDPR Article 6(1)(f), was also considered in the *Meta* line of cases.

In the CJEU case of *Meta*, one of the questions referred to the CJEU was whether Meta could rely on the legitimate interests ground to justify the processing of off-Facebook data. In particular, a number of purposes were raised by Meta as justifications potentially capable of falling within the scope of legitimate interests, including personalised advertising, product improvement, the sharing of information with law enforcement agencies, and the offer of services for commercial communication intended for the user and of analytics tools intended for advertisers and other business partners, enabling them to evaluate their performance.

With regard to personalised advertising, the CJEU noted that direct marketing purposes may be considered a legitimate interest of the controller. However, the user of an online social network such as Facebook cannot reasonably expect that the operator will process his or her personal data, without consent, for the purposes of personalised advertising. Further, the processing in question was particularly extensive since it related to potentially unlimited data and had a significant impact on the user whose online activities were monitored by Meta. In those circumstances, it was held that the interests and fundamental rights of the user overrode the interest of that operator in personalised advertising, so that the processing of data for such purposes did not fall within GDPR Article 6(1)(f).[111]

With respect to product improvement, the CJEU did not rule it out as a potential legitimate interest. However, in the circumstances of the case, the CJEU doubted whether this objective could override the interests and fundamental rights of data subjects, given the scale of the processing and its significant impact on users, as well as the fact that the user could not reasonably expect this data to be processed by Meta.[112]

In principle, the CJEU said that sharing information with law enforcement agencies in order to prevent, detect and prosecute criminal offences cannot constitute a legitimate interest pursued by the controller. 'A private operator such as Meta Platforms Ireland cannot rely on such a legitimate interest, which is unrelated to its economic and commercial activity.' The position may be different if the processing is objectively necessary for the operator to comply with its legal obligation.[113]

[110] ibid [126]–[127].
[111] ibid [115]–[118].
[112] ibid [122]–[123].
[113] ibid [124].

Separately, following the EDPB's two Binding Decisions in 2022 relating to Meta, which rejected the performance of contract ground (see section IV.B.ii. above), Meta later raised and relied on the legitimate interests ground instead as justification for processing data for behavioural advertising. In July 2023, the Norwegian DPA imposed a temporary ban on Meta regarding the processing of personal data of data subjects in Norway for behavioural advertising, and in October 2023 the EDPB issued its Urgent Binding Decision 01/2023 at the request of the Norwegian DPA.[114]

In this case, Meta identified four legitimate interests that were pursued either by itself or third parties (businesses that use Facebook/Instagram and other users of Meta's products): (1) Meta's and other users' interests in providing a positive user experience which is tailored to users; (2) Meta's and other users' interests to enable Meta to generate revenue and continue to innovate, improve and develop the Meta Products and new technologies; (3) Meta's interest and third parties' (eg, advertisers) interest in providing businesses the opportunity to connect with the users who are most likely to be interested in their products and services; and (4) Meta's interest and third parties' and other users' interests for businesses to be able to promote their products and services to users.

There was no dispute that these could be legitimate interests within the meaning of GDPR Article 6(1)(f). The EDPB, however, found that Meta did not satisfy the necessity test, particularly because it was not satisfied that there were no other less intrusive alternatives (as found in the two Binding Decisions of 2022 – see section IV.B.ii. above) or that the principle of data minimisation (ie, that personal data must be 'adequate, relevant and limited to what is necessary in relation to the purposes for which they are processed') had been complied with.[115]

With regard to the balancing test, the EDPB took into account Meta's failure to facilitate the users' right to object and, in particular, that the objection tools did not enable the users to turn off processing of data collected directly by Meta for advertising purposes. The EDPB also took into account the lack of any consideration by Meta of the right to private life or data minimisation, and the insufficient consideration by Meta of the impact of the processing on the purpose limitation principle. The EDPB accepted that the CJEU decision in *Meta* concerned off-Facebook data, whereas the present inquiry concerned on-Meta data, but considered that the way the balancing exercise might be carried out for the purpose of behavioural advertising, as outlined by the CJEU, was also relevant for personal data collected on Meta's products. The EDPB reiterated its previous guidelines[116] where it highlighted that 'it would be difficult for controllers to justify using legitimate interests as a lawful basis for intrusive profiling and tracking practices for marketing or advertising purposes, for example those that involve tracking individuals across multiple websites, locations, devices, services or data-brokering'. This guidance was relevant since the processing by Meta was intrusive given its scale and the extensive amounts of data processed. Overall, the EDPB concluded that Meta had

[114] EDPB Urgent Binding Decision 01/2023 requested by the Norwegian SA for the ordering of final measures regarding Meta Platforms Ireland Ltd (Art 66(2) GDPR) (adopted on 27 October 2023).

[115] ibid [121]–[131].

[116] Art 29 WP, *Guidelines on Automated individual decision-making and Profiling for the purposes of Regulation 2016/679* (WP 251 rev.01), 15.

not demonstrated that its legitimate interests in processing for behavioural advertising outweighed the fundamental rights and freedoms of data subjects.[117]

C. Web Scraping

Web scraping refers to the practice of trawling through the Internet for data that is publicly accessible. It is generally done in an automated manner using software tools such as Python. Bots (sometimes called a 'spider' or 'spider bot') are employed to crawl around websites to collect the information for which they were designed. Data may be scraped from social media networks and online forums that contain people's opinions, preferences, biodata or identities. Although the personal data has been placed on the Internet in the first place, probably by the data subjects or with their consent, and in that sense has entered into the public domain, web scraping still raises controversies. In particular, the extracted data may be combined with other data and used for purposes never intended or envisaged by the data subjects, raising data protection concerns.

The issue has attracted attention from various authorities. On 24 August 2023, the DPAs of 12 countries/regions[118] issued a Joint Statement on Data Scraping and the Protection of Privacy, which states by way of background that:

> In most jurisdictions, personal information that is 'publicly available', 'publicly accessible' or 'of a public nature' on the internet, is subject to data protection and privacy laws. Individuals and companies that scrape such personal information are therefore responsible for ensuring that they comply with these and other applicable laws. However, social media companies and the operators of other websites that host publicly accessible personal information (SMCs and other websites) also have data protection obligations with respect to third-party scraping from their sites. These obligations will generally apply to personal information whether that information is publicly accessible or not. Mass data scraping of personal information can constitute a reportable data breach in many jurisdictions.

The Joint Statement calls on social media companies and other websites to implement 'multi-layered technical and procedural controls' to mitigate privacy risks from unlawful data scraping, including 'rate limiting' the number of visits per hour or day by one account to others and limiting access if unusual activity is detected, taking steps to detect scrapers by identifying patterns in bot activity, taking steps to detect bots such as by using CAPTCHAs,[119] blocking the IP address where data scraping activity is identified, and taking appropriate legal action where data scraping is suspected or confirmed. The Joint Statement also encourages individuals to consider limiting the information they post online and to understand and manage the privacy settings of the websites they use in order to limit the information made publicly accessible.

Consent and necessity for performance of contract, as lawful bases for data processing, are usually not relevant to web scraping cases, as it is unlikely that the scraper would have obtained consent from or entered into a contract with the data subjects. Where

[117] Binding Decision 01/2023 (n 114) [135]–[146].
[118] Including Australia, Hong Kong and the UK.
[119] Completely Automated Public Turing test to tell Computers and Humans Apart – a program that tests whether a user is a human or a bot.

the web scraping is carried out by a commercial entity, it is arguable, depending on the circumstances, that the legitimate interests of the web scraper do not outweigh the rights and freedoms of the data subjects, given the massive volume of data processed, the usually intrusive nature of the scraping operations, and the possibility of aggregating data to profile and make inferences about individuals.

i. The Clearview AI line of cases

Clearview AI is a US company that provides a service to law enforcement agencies which assists them to identify and locate victims and suspects in criminal investigations. The key to its service is its facial recognition software. Clearview AI has used a web crawler to build a database of facial images drawn from the Internet. When the web crawler collects images, it also collects the meta-data associated with those images (in particular the website address the image was found on). Law enforcement agencies which have a relationship with Clearview AI can upload photos of suspects or victims and receive images from the database if the Clearview AI software identifies a matching image on its database. The inquiring agency is also provided with the meta-data associated with each of the matching images.[120] As of October 2022, it was estimated that Clearview AI's database included over 20 billion images with a growth rate of 75 million images per day.[121]

The UK, EU and Australian authorities recently considered whether the activities of a web crawler operated by Clearview AI were in compliance with data protection laws. One of the issues in the Australian case (*Clearview AI Inc v Australian Information Commissioner*) was whether Clearview AI's data processing violated the Australian Privacy Principles APP 3.3, which provided that sensitive information about an individual can only be collected with the individual's consent in circumstances where no other exceptions applied.[122] In October 2021, the Australia DPA found that Clearview AI was in breach of privacy laws. On appeal, on 8 May 2023, the Australian Administrative Appeals Tribunal found that the images collected by Clearview AI's web crawler were 'biometric information' and hence 'sensitive information' under the statutory definitions. Whilst an image of a person's face would not in every context constitute biometric information, in the context of Clearview AI's business, which involved the automated recognition of individuals by analysis of their face, any image of a face it sought to acquire was biometric information.[123] It was held that there was a breach of APP 3.3 so long as Clearview AI collected images from servers located in Australia.

The DPAs of Italy (February 2022), Greece (July 2022), France (October 2022) and Austria (May 2023) also found Clearview AI's collection and use of personal data to

[120] *Clearview AI Inc v Australian Information Commissioner* [2023] AATA 1069 (8 May 2023) [1].
[121] *Clearview AI Inc v The Information Commissioner* [2023] UKFTT 00819 (GRC) [40].
[122] Australia's Privacy Act 1988 (Cth), sch 1.
[123] *Clearview AI Inc v Australian Information Commissioner* (n 120) [126]–[129].

be unlawful under the GDPR.[124] There was no dispute that the individuals whose images were collected never consented to such collection. The French DPA also found that Clearview AI could not rely on the legitimate interest ground, particularly given the intrusive and massive nature of the processing, which made it possible to retrieve the images present on the Internet of millions of users. These people (even those who uploaded photos to social media voluntarily) do not reasonably expect their images to be processed by the company to supply a facial recognition system that could be used by states for law enforcement purposes.[125] The Italian DPA also rejected Clearview's reliance on the legitimate interest ground.[126]

In the UK, the ICO also found Clearview AI's data processing unlawful and issued an enforcement notice and a monetary penalty notice against it in May 2022. On Clearview AI's appeal, the First-tier Tribunal held in October 2023 that there was processing of personal data by Clearview AI that was related to its clients' monitoring of data subjects' behaviour in the UK. Thus, even though Clearview AI was not established in the UK, it was subject to UK data protection law applicable to the monitoring of people living in the UK. However, it was held that the processing in question fell outside the material scope of the GDPR because of Brexit implementation provisions, particularly since the services were provided to foreign law enforcement agencies, and the Commissioner therefore did not have jurisdiction to enforce the law against Clearview AI.[127] As at the time of writing (in April 2024), the ICO is currently seeking permission to appeal.[128]

V. Legal Issues at Deployment Stage

Assuming that one or more legal bases can be identified for the collection of personal data, it is still necessary for data processors to ensure that the use of data in the subsequent deployment of AI technologies complies with the various principles laid down for data protection. Given the special features of big data analytics, such as the opacity of the processing and the use of algorithms, the following principles are particularly pertinent: (1) fairness; (2) accuracy; (3) storage limitation; (4) security/integrity; (5) data protection obligation; (6) transparency; and (7) safeguards against automated decision-making and profiling.

[124] NOYB, 'Clearview AI Data Use Deemed Illegal in Austria, However No Fine Issued' (10 May 2023), available at noyb.eu/en/clearview-ai-data-use-deemed-illegal-austria-however-no-fine-issued; EDPB, 'Facial Recognition: Italian SA Fines Clearview AI EUR 20 million' (10 March 2022), available at edpb.europa.eu/news/national-news/2022/facial-recognition-italian-sa-fines-clearview-ai-eur-20-million_en; GDPR Hub, 'HDPA (Greece) 35/2022', available at gdprhub.eu/index.php?title=HDPA_(Greece)_-_35/2022; and CNIL, 'Facial Recognition; 20 Million Euros Penalty Against CLEARVIEW AI' (20 October 2022), available at www.cnil.fr/en/facial-recognition-20-million-euros-penalty-against-clearview-ai.

[125] CNIL, 'Facial Recognition; 20 Million Euros Penalty Against CLEARVIEW AI' (20 October 2022), available at www.cnil.fr/en/facial-recognition-20-million-euros-penalty-against-clearview-ai.

[126] EDPB, 'Facial Recognition: Italian SA Fines Clearview AI EUR 20 million' (10 March 2022), available at edpb.europa.eu/news/national-news/2022/facial-recognition-italian-sa-fines-clearview-ai-eur-20-million_en.

[127] *Clearview AI Inc v The Information Commissioner* (n 121) [3], [154]–[157].

[128] On 6 October 2025, the Upper Tribunal allowing the appeal held that the ICO had jurisdiction to enforce UK data protection law against Clearview AI and remitted the case to the First-Tier Tribunal to determine the substantive issue of whether Clearview AI actually breached the GDPR. See *The Information Commissioner v Clearview AI Inc* [2025] UKUT 319 (AAC).

A. Relevant Principles

First, with regard to fairness, GDPR Article 5(1)(a) provides that personal data shall be processed lawfully, *fairly*, and in a transparent manner in relation to the data subject. To this end, Recital 71 states that

> the controller should use appropriate mathematical or statistical procedures for the profiling, implement technical and organisational measures appropriate to ensure, in particular, that factors which result in inaccuracies in personal data are corrected and the risk of errors is minimised, secure personal data in a manner that takes account of the potential risks involved for the interests and rights of the data subject and that prevents, inter alia, discriminatory effects on natural persons on the basis of racial or ethnic origin, political opinion, religion or beliefs, trade union membership, genetic or health status or sexual orientation, or that result in measures having such an effect. Automated decision-making and profiling based on special categories of personal data should be allowed only under specific conditions.

The requirement of fairness should be assessed objectively. It is irrelevant that the controller did not intend to be unfair,[129] and it is implicit in this requirement that the data processing should not result in discrimination.[130]

Fairness involves a balancing of competing interests, weighing any possible unfairness to the individual against the advantages gained by others, and the public welfare.[131] Fairness is to be judged primarily by reference to the data subjects, but account should also be taken of the interest of the controller and other third parties.[132] The UK ICO's Guide to the GDPR (14 October 2022) put it in this way (at 52):

> In general, fairness means that you should only handle personal data in ways that people would reasonably expect and not use it in ways that have unjustified adverse effects on them.

Second, with regard to accuracy, Article 5(1)(d) of GDPR provides that personal data shall be 'accurate and, where necessary, kept up to date; every reasonable step must be taken to ensure that personal data that are inaccurate, having regard to the purposes for which they are processed, are erased or rectified without delay'.

Third, storage limitation is concerned with the duration of retention of personal data. Article 5(1)(e) of GDPR provides that personal data shall be 'kept in a form which permits identification of data subjects for no longer than is necessary for the purposes for which the personal data are processed'. Recital 39 states that 'time limits should be established by the controller for erasure or for a periodic review'. There will be temptations to keep as much data for as long as possible since big data analytics thrives on massive quantities of data. This must be countered by a data retention policy that upholds the principle that personal data is not to be retained for longer than is necessary for and proportionate to the purposes for which the data are processed. Retaining personal data indefinitely would go against the storage limitation principle.[133]

[129] R Jay, *Data Protection Law and Practice*, 5th edn (London, Sweet & Maxwell, 2020) para 6-009.

[130] As the Art 29 WP recognised WP 251 rev.01 at 10, 'Profiling may be unfair and create discrimination, for example by denying people access to employment opportunities, credit or insurance, or targeting them with excessively risky or costly financial products.'

[131] *Infolink Ltd v Data Protection Registrar* [1992] UKIT DA90_25496 [62].

[132] ibid [64].

[133] See also WP 251 rev.01, 12.

Fourth, with regard to data security/integrity, Article 5(1)(f) of GDPR provides that personal data shall be 'processed in a manner that ensures appropriate security of the personal data, including protection against unauthorised or unlawful processing and against accidental loss, destruction or damage, using appropriate technical or organisational measures'. Recital 39 provides: 'Personal data should be processed in a manner that ensures appropriate security and confidentiality of the personal data, including for preventing unauthorised access to or use of personal data and the equipment used for the processing.' Article 32 further requires the controller and the processor to implement appropriate technical and organisational measures to ensure a level of security appropriate to the risk.[134]

Fifth, with regard to data protection, Article 25 of GDPR provides for data protection by design and by default. The EDPB Guidelines on Article 25 Data Protection by Design and by Default explained that the requirement in Article 25 is for controllers to have data protection designed into the processing of personal data and as a default setting, and this applies throughout the processing lifecycle.[135]

Sixth, with regard to the principle of transparency, Article 5(1)(a) of GDPR provides that personal data shall be processed in a transparent manner in relation to the data subject. The principle concerns information given to the data subject on the identity of the controller and the purposes of the processing as well as the risks, rules, safeguards and rights in relation to the processing of personal data. Data subjects should be informed of the existence of profiling and the consequences of such profiling and should also be provided with any further information necessary to ensure fair and transparent processing. In terms of presentation, the principle requires that any information addressed to the public or to the data subject be concise, easily accessible and easy to understand, and that clear and plain language and, additionally, where appropriate, visualisation be used. The EDPB has adopted the Article 29 WP's opinion on transparency, in which the elements of transparency under the GDPR are summarised as follows: (1) concise, transparent, intelligible and easily accessible; (2) clear and plain language; (3) in writing or by other means; and (4) free of charge.[136]

Seventh, automated decision-making and profiling need to be ring-fenced. These automated techniques may, in certain circumstances, lead to erroneous and/or biased decisions with negative impacts on individuals, perpetuating stereotypes and resulting in discrimination. The processes are often opaque, and people may not even know of their existence. Where significant consequences can ensue, automated decision-making risks eliminating human judgement and moral autonomy and debasing the data subject.

To provide protection against automated decisions, including profiling, Article 22(1) of GDPR provides:

[134] Including, as appropriate: (a) the pseudonymisation and encryption of personal data; (b) the ability to ensure the ongoing confidentiality, integrity, availability and resilience of processing systems and services; (c) the ability to restore the availability and access to personal data in a timely manner in the event of a physical or technical incident; and (d) a process for regularly testing, assessing and evaluating the effectiveness of technical and organisational measures for ensuring the security of the processing.

[135] EDPB, *Guidelines 4/2019 on Article 25 Data Protection by Design and Default* (adopted on 20 October 2020).

[136] Art 29 WP, *Guidelines on transparency under Regulation 2016/679* (adopted on 11 April 2018) (WP 260 rev.01) 6–13.

> The data subject shall have the right not to be subject to a decision based solely on automated processing, including profiling, which produces legal effects concerning him or her or similarly significantly affects him or her.

This does not apply if the decision is necessary for a contract, authorised by law or based on the data subject's explicit consent.

The EDPB has adopted the Article 29 WP's Guidelines on Automated Individual Decision-making and Profiling.[137] The Guidelines propose that controllers should

> carry out frequent assessments on the data sets they process to check for any bias, and develop ways to address any prejudicial elements, including any over-reliance on correlations. Systems that audit algorithms and regular reviews of the accuracy and relevance of automated decision-making including profiling are other useful measures.

Controllers should also

> introduce appropriate procedures and measures to prevent errors, inaccuracies or discrimination on the basis of special category data. These measures should be used on a cyclical basis; not only at the design stage, but also continuously, as the profiling is applied to individuals. The outcome of such testing should feed back into the system design.

B. Relevant cases/examples

The following cases, which concern data processing after the relevant model and/or algorithm has been put into operation, illustrate how the above principles apply in this context.

In the *Deliveroo Italy* case,[138] the Italian DPA examined data processing by Deliveroo on its rider app and found that it violated a multitude of data protection principles. Deliveroo had envisaged the retention for six years of different types of rider data collected for a plurality of purposes, after the termination of the employment relationship. Until July 2019, it also retained, for one year, external data and the content of the telephone calls made with the riders. Deliveroo argued that a general six-year retention period was the 'best tool' to provide interested parties with information in the face of 'complexity and changeability … of the provisions on data retention'. The DPA rejected the argument, noting that personal data should be stored for a period of time not exceeding the achievement of the purposes for which they are processed, and the data controller has the obligation to ensure that the retention period is limited to the minimum necessary. Deliveroo, having failed to carry out an assessment of the adequacy of its retention policy in relation to the various purposes pursued, was found to have breached the retention principle under GDPR Article 5.

The design of Deliveroo's system was also found to be in violation of the protection obligation under Article 25 of the GDPR. The system was configured in such a way as to collect and store all data relating to the order, and to allow authorised operators to pass simple functions from one system to another, with consequent sharing of the data

[137] WP 251 rev.01.

[138] Italian DPA, Case Number 9685994 (decided on 22 July 2021).

collected across the various systems. Deliveroo did not provide any specific reasons why all this data collection and data sharing was necessary for the provision of its services. The DPA found that, taking into account the quantity and variety of the data collected and the methods of processing, in relation to the purpose of managing the food or other goods delivery service, there was a violation of the protection obligation under Article 25.

It was also found that Deliveroo failed to take adequate technical and organisational measures to guarantee adequate security of the processing, in violation of Article 32 of GDPR. In particular, the company previously did not adopt adequate technical measures to prevent access to the data of Italian riders, processed through the platform, by the operators of the other companies in the group.

The DPA also found that under the transparency principle, given the invasiveness of the processing in question, Deliveroo was obliged to provide information on the specific methods of processing and on the frequency of detection of geographical position. Further, the DPA found that Deliveroo's algorithm for the assignment of orders and shifts involved automated processing, including profiling, using personal data to evaluate the reliability and availability of riders, but that contrary to GDPR Article 22(3), the company had not adopted technical and organisational measures aimed at periodically verifying the accuracy of the results of the algorithmic systems, the accuracy, relevance and adequacy of the data used by the system, and to reduce as much as possible the risk of distorted or discriminatory effects.

In the *Foodinho Italy* case,[139] the Italian DPA made similar findings against Foodinho, another food delivery platform in Italy. It was found that Foodinho violated the retention principle by adopting a 'precautionary retention period of 4 years' for various types of rider data and external data. For certain types of data, no retention period was specified, but instead it was stated that data would be retained for 'the duration of the limitation period established by the law'. Data for marketing and study purposes would be retained for 24 months, whereas voice recordings would be retained for 12 months. Information about the routes taken by the riders would be kept for 10 months. The DPA found that Foodinho had failed to identify the retention periods for different types of rider data. It was noted that, in light of the need to identify retention periods deemed appropriate in relation to each of the processing purposes, the owner must not limit himself to identifying 'blocks' of homogeneous time bands. Given the absence of measures to segregate and limit access to various types of rider data, Foodinho was also found to have violated the protection obligation under Article 25.

Likewise, it was found that Foodinho had employed automated processing, including profiling. Its systems involved using personal data of riders to evaluate riders, who would in turn be penalised or favoured depending on their actions. The DPA found that the automated decision-making was not prohibited because Foodinho could rely on the exceptions, particularly that the processing was necessary for the execution of the contract between Foodinho and the riders. Nevertheless, contrary to GDPR Article 22(3), Foodinho had failed to adopt technical and organisational measures aimed at verifying the accuracy of the results of the algorithmic systems, the accuracy, relevance and adequacy of the data used by the system, and to reduce as much as possible the risk of distorted or discriminatory effects.

[139] Italian DPA, Case Number 9675440 (decided on 10 June 2021).

VI. Tort of Misuse of Private Information

In addition to data protection legislation, the common law also offers remedies where personal data has been misused. At common law there is no tort of invasion of privacy.[140] Out of the claim for breach of confidence, however, there has been developed a separate and distinct cause of action of misuse of private information.[141] This cause of action has been classified as a tort.[142]

The principles on the tort of misuse of private information were summarised in *Prismall v Google UK Ltd*:[143]

(1) Liability for misuse of private information is determined by applying a two-stage test. Stage one is whether the claimant objectively has a reasonable expectation of privacy in the relevant information. This is an objective test. The expectation is that of a reasonable person of ordinary sensibilities placed in the same position as the claimant and faced with the same publicity. The question is a broad one which takes into account all of the circumstances of the case, including: (1) the attributes of the claimant; (2) the nature of the activity in which the claimant was engaged; (3) the place at which it was happening; (4) the nature and purpose of the intrusion; (5) the absence of consent and whether it was known or could be inferred; (6) the effect on the claimant; and (7) the circumstances in which and the purposes for which the information came into the hands of the publisher.

(2) If this is shown, then stage two is whether that expectation is outweighed by a countervailing interest of the defendant, which involves carrying out a balancing exercise that involves an intense focus on the comparative importance of the specific rights being claimed in the individual case, the justifications for interfering with or restricting each right and the proportionality of the respective interference or restriction.

Despite the breadth of the data protection legislation under the GDPR model, the tortious claim may be useful in certain scenarios, for example: (1) where personal data/private information was processed 'by a natural person in the course of a purely personal or household activity', such that the data protection principles have no application: GDPR, Article 2(2)(c); and (2) where it is more advantageous for the claimant to seek 'user damages' – an award of damages to compensate the claimant for interference with a right to control the use of property, although there has been no financial loss or physical damage to the property. User damages are available in a claim for the tort of misuse of private information, but not available for a claim under, for example, the UK Data Protection Act 1998.[144]

However, while the common law may provide a cause of action for the misuse of private information, in an ordinary case the amount of damages that can be recovered by a data subject may not justify the costs and efforts required for bringing the action. Class actions

[140] *Wainwright v Home Office* [2004] 2 AC 406.
[141] *Campbell v MGN Ltd* [2004] UKHL 22; *OBG Ltd v Allan* [2008] 1 AC 1 [255].
[142] *Vidal-Hall v Google Inc* [2015] EWCA Civ 311.
[143] *Prismall v Google UK Ltd* [2023] EWHC 1169 (KB) [66]–[70].
[144] *Lloyd v Google LLC* [2021] UKSC 50 [139], [143].

may provide an answer, but the strictures of representative actions in many jurisdictions may prove difficult to surmount. The possibility of a private lawsuit, whilst useful in appropriate circumstances, is therefore no substitute for a comprehensive legislative and regulatory system enforced by a publicly funded authority with effective sanctions and remedies.

VII. Conclusion

The rapid growth of big data and AI has transformed the landscape of data protection and privacy, demanding legal frameworks that are comprehensive and yet dynamic enough to balance innovation with the protection of privacy in a vast and developing field with novel challenges posed by the new ways in which data is collected and used. Many jurisdictions have legislated in response, a notable forerunner being the GDPR. It requires compliance with principles such as lawfulness, fairness and transparency, purpose limitation, and data minimisation, while restricting the processing of personal data to specific bases such as consent, performance of contract, and protection of interests.

The *Meta* cases underscore the challenges of obtaining valid consent in digital environments occupied by dominant platforms and highlight the need for ensuring that consent is freely given, specific, and informed – principles often undermined by asymmetrical power dynamics. Requiring users to choose between monetising their data and paying a fee raises profound ethical questions about the commodification of privacy and the exacerbation of socioeconomic inequalities. The courts and enforcement agencies have generally insisted on transparency and proportionality and that business models adapt to legal standards, not vice versa. Web scraping cases like *Clearview AI* illustrate how the aggregation of biometric data, even when sourced from public domains, risks enabling pervasive surveillance and eroding individual autonomy. A line needs to be drawn to ensure that the scale and intrusiveness of data processing align with societal expectations and fundamental rights. The deployment of AI in processing personal data introduces additional challenges, particularly regarding fairness, accuracy, and accountability. Opaque algorithms that profile people can perpetuate bias and undermine legal rights. Effective safeguards hinge on rigorous enforcement and corporate accountability.

The recent proliferation of legislation across the world reflects a common awareness of the need for protecting privacy by law in the era of big data and AI. The efficacy of regulatory mechanisms depends on their adaptability to technological evolution and capability of addressing emerging threats, on each jurisdiction's commitment to data protection, and on cross-border cooperation. Ongoing vigilance is needed to counteract intrusive profiling, algorithmic bias, and the commodification of personal data. The law and the courts have an important role to play in ensuring that the digital age upholds privacy rights and human autonomy without stifling the transformative potential of big data and AI. In this delicate balance, the law must remain both a shield for individual rights and an enabler, perhaps even a catalyst, in promoting ethical innovation.

10

Processing Data in the Development and Deployment of Artificial Intelligence Systems

YEONG ZEE KIN*

I. Introduction

Since the term artificial intelligence (AI) was coined at Dartmouth College in 1956, AI has been through several winters. The current generation of AI is driven by machine learning, which relies on access to data. Machine learning has, in turn, been supported by advances in storage capacity and computing power over the past decade. Advances in big data gave access to the volumes and variety of data that machine learning needed access to. Advances in computing power enabled machine learning to analyse data, even as these were generated at unprecedented velocities with the popularity of social media and the ubiquity of mobile devices that are so integral to our modern digital lifestyles. Advances in graphics processing unit (GPU) technology made the computing technology necessary for model development more accessible, while the commoditisation of cloud computing democratised access to machine learning models that are accessible as on-demand services on major cloud platforms.

As more businesses deploy AI systems, legal issues relating to the access to and use of data can be expected to multiply. This is only natural as new services and business models develop. The challenge of policymakers and regulators is the calibration of regulations that enable the digital economy to use this technology, while safeguarding the interests of individuals and society. Enabling access to data supports the deployment of AI systems. Guardrails that guide the responsible use of data during model development and pre-launch testing of AI systems provide greater assurance that end users are safeguarded. As machine learning models extend beyond the earlier generation of discriminative AI – which essentially recognised patterns in order to classify or predict – the current wave of generative AI throws focus on the role of end users in ensuring a safe online environment. There is an urgent need to increase awareness and to educate end users about their role in the responsible use and dissemination of user-generated content.

This chapter examines copyright and data privacy issues relating to the processing of data in the development and deployment of AI systems. The analysis will be divided

* I wish to thank Trina Ha and Chua Ying Hong for their helpful and insightful comments on an earlier draft of this chapter.

into two sections. First, regulatory and legal issues that arise during *model development*, when data is processed to train machine learning models that form the core of many AI systems in use today. Second, issues that arise from the business-to-customer (B2C) relationship *post-deployment*, after the trained model is deployed into products or services.

II. Model Development

In model development, machine learning techniques are used to develop AI models using training datasets. Issues relating to model training are largely related to the ability to access and use data for training. Model training begins with the selection of a base or pre-trained model that may be integrated and deployed as-is, or after further training or fine-tuning. One of the concerns that deployers may have – in light of the publicity over copyright infringement claims between rights holders and developers of foundational models – is whether the model that they have selected exposes them to claims of copyright infringement. The fear is that pre-trained models are infringing copies per se and anyone dealing with them (eg, modifying or adapting a copy during model training or integrating a copy into the AI system during deployment) will therefore be liable for secondary infringement. The uncertainty and doubt arising from this fear has (for now) been put to bed. Comfort may be found in the recent decision of the UK High Court in the case of *Getty Images v Stability AI* where it was held that since machine learning models only contain learnt patterns and features from the training data (eg, weights and biases of neural networks) – and do not contain copies of the training data[1] – the models are not per se infringing copies. Accordingly, dealings with models would not amount to secondary infringement.[2]

Model training leads to the selection of a model whose performance is acceptable, and which will be integrated and deployed in a product or service. The quality of the training dataset affects model performance. When personal data is used during model development, data protection principles should be observed. The *accuracy principle* safeguards individuals when decisions affecting them are made in reliance on personal data. When applying this principle to datasets, it translates into ensuring that personal data selected as training data should be current and representative of the target customer segment, so as to ensure that model output is fair and unbiased. To meet the *protection obligation*, adequate technical and process safeguards should be implemented, such as using pseudonymised data for model training (especially when this does not affect model performance) and using synthetic data (artificial data that is generated that is statistically representative of the target population) for the conduct of pre-deployment tests.[3]

This section discusses the legal and regulatory issues concerning model development, ie, training and testing of the selected model. The key data-related issue during

[1] For a discussion of how large language models learn patterns from training data and store them as weights and biases of the neural network, see Y Zee Kin, 'Nature of Data in Pre-Trained Large Language Models' (6 July 2025), available at https://fpf.org/blog/nature-of-data-in-pre-trained-large-language-models/.

[2] *Getty Images (US) Inc & Ors v Stability AI Ltd (Rev1)* [2025] WLR(D) 571, [2025] EWHC 2863 (Ch), [597]–[601]; although there is a contrary decision from the Munich Regional Court holding that models that memorise training data are not covered by the text and data mining exception and hence infringing: see n 55.

[3] For a more detailed discussion, see Yeong Z K, 'Clear and Present Harm of AI - How Data Protection Principles may Help' (*DataGuidance*, February 2024), available at www.dataguidance.com/opinion/international-clear-and-present-harm-ai-how-data; see also the references at n 119.

model development is the ability to access and process data. The ability to access data is primarily a business challenge. The various ways in which data may be collected were outlined in the previous chapter. To recapitulate, businesses may use data that they have collected and control as training data (ie, secondary use). Training data may also be acquired from other businesses (ie, data sharing between business partners or data trading through data brokers or exchanges). For businesses with the technical wherewithal, they may also collect data from public sources to use as training data (eg, web scraping).

A. Secondary Use of Data for Model Training

Businesses may choose to use data that they have already collected as training data. This is referred to as secondary use of data. For example, an e-commerce merchant may seek to use sales data and user activity data from its e-commerce portal as training data to develop recommendation systems, and a logistics company providing last-mile delivery services may wish to use information about its drivers, their driving patterns and driving routes to develop machine learning models that offer better route predictions and planning to improve efficiency.

i. Text and Data Mining Exceptions Under Copyright Laws

Copyright law does not protect data per se but its selection and arrangement into a compilation, such as a table or electronic database.[4] Advances in storage technology have enabled the compilation of electronic databases and repositories of copyrighted material, such as document or knowledge management systems that organise a law practice's past work products, eg, contracts, pleadings and advice. Copyright may exist for individual documents even though there are (not insurmountable) challenges in satisfying the requirement of creativity in the selection and arrangement of content stored in an electronic database or repository such that the database or repository qualifies as a work of authorial creation.[5] Be that as it may, the preponderance of data that businesses own are stored in electronic databases and repositories, and these are common sources of training data.

A common scenario that arises is where a business is in possession of data that is subject to third-party copyright but wishes to use that data as part of its training dataset. Very often, third-party copyright is commingled with data that the business may own, as is the case in the legal sector. Legal publishers use data from their publications to

[4] '… in order for any copyright to subsist in the compilation, the selection or arrangement of its contents must be the product of intellectual creation': per VK Rajah JA in *Asia Pacific Publishing Pte Ltd v Pioneers & Leaders (Publishers) Pte Ltd* [2011] 4 SLR 381 [32]; and '… the compiler must exercise *sufficient creativity* in *selecting or arranging* the material within the compilation': per Sundaresh Menon CJ in *Global Yellow Pages Ltd v Promedia Directories Pte Ltd and another matter* [2017] 2 SLR 185 [24].

[5] Some of the challenges are that data is collected through sensors (eg, GPS, accelerometers) with minimal selection and their storage within an electronic database is usually chronological, based on the entry of the relevant record. However, the application of filters in the selection of data for inclusion in the database and the design and arrangement of the tables in a relational database may meet the creativity threshold. The challenges are discussed in detail in a law reform paper by the Singapore Academy of Law, *Rethinking Database Rights and Data Ownership in an AI World* (July 2020), [2.13]–[2.29].

provide legal research, contract analysis and document generation solutions that make use of large language models (LLMs). For example, legal research tools like Harvey and CoCounsel have started to provide a question-and-answer approach to legal research and can also generate drafts of documents (eg, contract analysis, document reviews and summaries). They rely on LLMs that are trained using their publications' data, while employing techniques like Retrieval-Augmented Generation to ensure that generated content is grounded in information found in their extensive publication repositories. It is safe to assume that these repositories will contain a mixture of publications that they own (eg, textbooks), publications that are licensed (eg, law reports) and information that had been obtained from public sources (eg, raw texts of judgments and legislation).

Data mining analyses datasets and individual documents to identify patterns and relationships. These may be presented visually in charts and graphs, or they may be embedded in statistical models. Models consist of algorithms and parameters; they are probabilistic in nature and may be used to classify, predict or generate. Since what is analysed and extracted is not an expression of ideas that copyright laws protect, it can be argued that there is no copying of expression and hence no copyright infringement.[6] Even if there is copying of expression, it can further be argued that such use is sufficiently transformative as to be fair use (in those copyright regimes where this exception is available).[7]

Nevertheless, in order to provide greater certainty, a number of jurisdictions have recently introduced data mining exceptions in their copyright laws to make it clear that the secondary use of data is permissible if it is for the purpose of analysing the data. Indeed, the implementation of the text and data mining exception in Singapore's Copyright Act – ie, computational data analysis – specifically supports machine learning.[8] Data mining exceptions can be especially helpful where businesses need to contend with commingled data that may include third-party copyright. A couple of features have emerged to safeguard the interests of rights holders: first, the requirement that the user has lawful access to the material in the first place (eg, through subscriptions or content freely available online);[9] and second, providing rights holders with some ability to opt out of the statutory exception.

The European Union (EU) has introduced a text and data mining exception in its Directive on Copyright in the Digital Single Market (EU Copyright Directive).[10] The EU Copyright Directive's text and data mining exception makes a distinction between use for the purposes of research and use for other purposes (eg, product development). Article 3 tips the scale in favour of scientific research by research organisations and cultural heritage institutions, by preventing rights holders from opting out of the text

[6] J Ginsburg, 'Fair Use in the United States: Transformed, Deformed, Reformed?' [2020] *Singapore Journal of Legal Studies* 265, 277.

[7] For a more detailed discussion of whether model development is fair use, see n 43 and the discussion in the accompanying main text.

[8] 'An example of computational data analysis under paragraph (b) is the use of images to train a computer program to recognise images': Copyright Act 2021 (2020 Rev Ed), illustration to the definition of 'computational data analysis' in s 243.

[9] Directive (EU) 2019/790 of the European Parliament and of the Council of 17 April 2019 on copyright and related rights in the Digital Single Market and amending Directives 96/9/EC and 2001/29/EC, Recital (14).

[10] ibid; the EU text and data mining exception also extends beyond copyright to cover its *sui generis* database rights.

and data mining exception in these cases.[11] For commercial organisations, Article 4 allows rights holders to exclude the application of the text and data mining exception through contractual terms or by making express reservations.[12] This empowers rights holders to renegotiate licensing arrangements that were made before machine learning technology became commercially viable as a technology, and also empowers owners of content that is made publicly available to prevent web scraping without authorisation. However, this also makes rights clearance significantly more difficult for aggregators, such as the legal publishers that are now in a race to introduce features that rely on LLMs. It is therefore unsurprising that – at the time of writing – the legal publishers have prioritised the introduction of these features for the US market.

In the UK, the computational data analysis exception is currently available for non-commercial research under section 29A of the UK Copyright, Designs and Patents Act 1988. Initial lawful access to the material is a prerequisite; any contract term that attempts to prevent or restrict the exception is unenforceable. To support AI adoption and broader innovation, there are plans to extend the text and data mining exception to include commercial R&D, with an EU-style opt-out.[13] However, responses to the public consultation were overwhelmingly unfavourable, with the preponderance of respondents preferring the option of requiring a licence in all cases.[14]

In Singapore, the raison d'être for supporting text and data mining is to provide regulatory certainty so as to encourage the secondary use of copyrighted works as part of the technical process of computational data analysis techniques.[15] This policy objective is of such significance that rights holders may not opt out – any contract term that purports to exclude or restrict the application of the computational data analysis exception is void.[16] Thus, the computational data analysis exception provides ample support for machine learning and model development that involves both secondary use as well as the scraping of publicly available material from the public internet. It is particularly helpful when dealing with commingled data, as it provides the regulatory clarity that businesses require to embark on innovation projects, and it tips the scale in favour of supporting innovation. While rights holders may feel short-changed, the reality is that volume and variety matter for training data, and that the compensation for inclusion of individual works in the *training dataset* is likely to be low.

The way individual works are used for training is also different from how they may be used as input data for inference. During model training, individual works are analysed *programmatically* to extract features and identify patterns and relationships that

[11] ibid Art 3 and Recital 18.

[12] ibid Art 4(3) and Recital 18.

[13] UK Intellectual Property Office (IPO), 'Copyright and AI: Consultation' (December 2024): see Section C.1 Exception with rights reservation.

[14] Department for Science, Innovation and Technology, and Department for Culture, Media and Sport, 'Copyright and Artificial Intelligence: Statement of Progress under Section 137 Data (Use and Access) Act, (December 2025): 88% of respondents preferred the option of requiring a licence in all cases while only 3% of respondents were in favour of a broad text and data mining exception with rights reservation.

[15] Copyright Act 2021 (2020 Rev Ed) Division 8 – Computational data analysis; see also, Ministry of Law and the Intellectual Property Office of Singapore, 'Public Consultation on the Proposed Copyright Bill' (5 February 2021) 12 and 13.

[16] Copyright Act 2021 (2020 Rev Ed) s 187(1)(*c*); it is one of only four categories of permitted use that are thus protected, the others being permitted use relating to public collections, computer programs, and for the purposes of judicial proceedings or seeking legal advice: ss 187(1)(*a*), 187(1)(*b*), 187(1)(*d*).

are transformed into parameters embedded in the probabilistic models. Human input is limited to specific stages: viz, before training, such as setting meta parameters, or afterwards, such as validating model output for supervised training.[17] The Japanese implementation of the text and data mining exception captures this aspect well by focusing on the fact that data mining does not involve human perception of the expression that copyright protects.[18] By contrast, including individual works in user prompts for LLMs or using AI tools that alter individual works can be infringing. Consider, for example, the inclusion of a contract template in a prompt for the generation of a new draft; or using an image enhancement tool that uses AI to sharpen a photograph that is out of focus. In these scenarios, the value is in the contract template or photograph as a standalone work, and the intention is to adapt the work. Such use is not covered by the computational data analysis exception.

ii. Managing Data Privacy Concerns when Using Personal Data

Training data are often compiled from personal data. For example, an online retailer might utilise their sales figures and customer behaviour data from their online store to train their recommendation engine for a more personalised shopping experience. Similarly, a delivery service company that handles last-mile deliveries might use data about their drivers, including their driving habits and routes, to create machine learning models for more efficient route planning. This section will use the example of a specialist ophthalmology centre that plans to use retina scans collated from its patients to develop machine learning models that assist the diagnosis by physicians.

When using personal data for model development, the first thing to consider is whether it is necessary to rely on personally identifiable information in the training dataset. If model development can be effectively achieved without the use of personal data, different techniques of *anonymisation* can be used.[19] The anonymisation of personal data is a foundational technique when it comes to the use of personal data. The objective of anonymisation is to convert personal data into a form in which individuals cannot be identified. Once anonymised, the dataset is no longer subject to data protection regulation.[20] Anonymisation is not without cost, both in terms of the resources needed to perform such processing and in the potential degradation of utility of the anonymised

[17] Model training is iterative, as the validation of model output will become the input for the next round of training.

[18] Copyright Act (Act No 48-1970), Art 30-4, available at www.japaneselawtranslation.go.jp/en/laws/view/4207#je_ch2sc3sb5at4.

[19] Personal Data Protection Commission Singapore (PDPC), 'Advisory Guidelines on Use of Personal Data in AI Recommendation and Decision Systems' (1 March 2024) (PDPC Advisory Guidelines on Use of Personal Data in AI Recommendation and Decision Systems) paras 7.8–7.12.

[20] See, eg, General Data Protection Regulation, Recital 26: 'The principles of data protection should therefore not apply to anonymous information, namely information which does not relate to an identified or identifiable natural person or to personal data rendered anonymous in such a manner that the data subject is not or no longer identifiable.' See also, Article 29 Data Protection Working Party, Opinion 05/2014 on Anonymisation Techniques (adopted on 10 April 2014) (WP216) 5: 'Once a dataset is truly anonymised and individuals are no longer identifiable, European data protection law no longer applies'; similarly, see PDPC, 'Advisory Guidelines on the Personal Data Protection Act (PDPA) for Selected Topics' (issued 24 September 2013, revised 23 May 2024), para 3.5: 'Data that has been anonymised is no longer considered personal data for the purposes of the PDPA.'

dataset. But this is nevertheless a worthwhile compromise since the anonymised data is not subject to data protection laws.

Where the training requires identifiable personal data, secondary use is permissible if a legal basis for processing can be identified.[21] As discussed in the previous chapter, one such legal basis could be data subject *consent*, in which case the terms of the consent must clearly allow for computational data analysis. This is a practical challenge, as machine learning has become commercially viable only fairly recently. It is therefore unsurprising that many of the older consent clauses were not drafted with this in mind. It may be open to interpreting consent clauses that contemplate some form of statistical analysis as permitting the use of personal data for machine learning, but it very much depends on how the consent clause has been crafted. Onboarding existing customers onto a newer version of the consent clause that expressly permits statistical analysis and machine learning is not a trivial effort. It is also one that is fraught with operational difficulties, eg, contact details may be outdated. One key challenge is keeping track of customers who have responded and are thus onboarded onto the new version of the consent clause and ensuring that the training dataset does not include those customers who have not. The time taken for a sufficiently significant segment of the customer database to respond may also be a factor, as this could delay implementation of the project. Even if most do, it is almost certain that not everyone will respond.

Because of these operational difficulties, businesses usually prefer to rely on other legal bases for processing. Returning to the example of the ophthalmology centre, its purpose for using retina images is to improve its service by introducing AI systems that augment its physicians. One possible legal basis for data processing is *legitimate interest*. This is an increasingly common legal basis for processing that is present in a number of data protection laws, including the General Data Protection Regulation (GDPR), and which was also discussed in the previous chapter. Reliance on legitimate interest as a legal basis for model training is supported by a number of data protection authorities, such as the European Data Protection Board (EDPB)[22] and the UK Information Commissioner's Office (UK ICO).[23] Indeed, the proposed EU Digital

[21] See generally, CNIL, 'Artificial Intelligence: CNIL Unveils its First Answers for Innovative and Privacy-friendly AI' (15 October 2023), available at www.cnil.fr/en/artificial-intelligence-cnil-unveils-its-first-answers-innovative-and-privacy-friendly-ai, and 'AI How-to Sheets', available at www.cnil.fr/en/ai-how-sheets; Office of the Privacy Commissioner of Canada, 'Principles for Responsible, Trustworthy and Privacy-Protective Generative AI Technologies' (7 December 2023), available at priv.gc.ca/en/privacy-topics/technology/artificial-intelligence/gd_principles_ai; and PDPC Advisory Guidelines on Use of Personal Data in AI Recommendation and Decision Systems (n 19).

[22] EDPB, *Opinion 28/2024 on certain data protection aspects related to the processing of personal data in the context of AI models* (adopted on 17 December 2024) section 3.3.2.

[23] UK ICO, *Guidance on AI and data protection* (updated 15 March 2023) available at ico.org.uk/for-organisations/uk-gdpr-guidance-and-resources/artificial-intelligence/guidance-on-ai-and-data-protection/how-do-we-ensure-lawfulness-in-ai/#legitimate-interests: see especially the section 'Can we rely on legitimate interests?' in the chapter 'How do we ensure lawfulness in AI?' (updated 28 October 2024).

Omnibus Regulation looks set to amend the GDPR and entrench legitimate interest as the default legal basis for such processing.[24]

In Singapore, legitimate interest is also available as a legal basis for processing under the Personal Data Protection Act 2012 (PDPA), which recognises two categories of legitimate interests: *specific legitimate interests* which cater for identified business purposes,[25] and a more flexible *general legitimate interest*. The Personal Data Protection Commission (PDPC) recognises general legitimate interest as a possible legal basis for processing data for model development.[26] To do so, a legitimate interest of either the data controller, data subject or third party must first be identified. In articulating the legitimate interest, the focus should be on who the intended processing will benefit and how they will benefit. Second, a risk assessment must be conducted, and measures taken to reduce identified risks. Third, a balancing test must be conducted to ascertain that the legitimate interest outweighs any residual risks to affected data subjects. Finally, reliance on general legitimate interest as the basis for processing personal data must be disclosed through publicly accessible policies.[27] Transparency only extends to the disclosure of reliance; data controllers are not required to provide copies of their risk assessments to data subjects.[28]

Hence, the ophthalmology centre in the example should not have difficulties articulating a legitimate interest to the benefit of its patients if retina scans can be used to develop AI systems that augment its diagnosis capabilities and reduce errors in diagnosis. The development of classification models to aid physicians is also unlikely to give rise to adverse effects on specific data subjects whose scans were used as part of the training dataset. Under the GDPR, what may need to be addressed is whether such use can be said to be within the expectation of patients in the context of their relationship with the ophthalmology centre.[29] Given that physicians have always shared case studies to improve their collective knowledge and abilities, the use of retina scans to develop AI systems that help them provide better diagnosis and treatment should not be so surprising. This additional consideration is not required under the PDPA.

Another basis for data processing is *business improvement*, which is unique to Singapore's PDPA. Business improvement is a lawful basis for processing personal data where there is an immediate application to the development of products or

[24] European Commission, 'Proposal for a Regulation of the European Parliament and of the Council amending Regulations (EU) 2016/679, (EU) 2018/1724, (EU) 2018/1725, (EU) 2023/2854 and Directives 2002/58/EC, (EU) 2022/2555 and (EU) 2022/2557 as regards the simplification of the digital legislative framework, and repealing Regulations (EU) 2018/1807, (EU) 2019/1150, (EU) 2022/868, and Directive (EU) 2019/1024 (Digital Omnibus)' (COM/2025/837 final): see Recitals (30) & (31) and Art 88c of the proposed Digital Omnibus Regulation (for model development).

[25] Such as, debt recovery, obtaining legal services, managing employment relationships, etc: PDPA, First Schedule, Pt 3, paras 2–10.

[26] PDPC Advisory Guidelines on Use of Personal Data in AI Recommendation and Decision Systems (n 19) paras 9.9–9.11.

[27] See *Re: RedMart Ltd* [2023] SGPDPC 1 for an illustration of how a legitimate interest analysis was applied.

[28] PDPA, First Schedule, Pt 3, para 1; see Personal Data Protection Regulations 2021 (Singapore), reg 15, which prescribes the content of the risk assessment, and the obligation to retain a copy of the risk assessment; see also, PDPC, 'Advisory Guidelines on Key Concepts in the Personal Data Protection Act' (issued 23 September 2013, revised 16 May 2022) (PDPC Advisory Guidelines on Key Concepts in the PDPA) 61, 62, 66–69, Annex C (for the Assessment Checklist for Legitimate Interests Exception).

[29] EDPB, *Opinion 28/2024 on certain data protection aspects related to the processing of personal data in the context of AI models* (adopted on 17 December 2024) paras 91–95.

enhancement of services.[30] This can be explained through the example of the e-commerce marketplace using customer purchasing information and user activity data to develop a recommendation system. The introduction of a recommendation system will qualify as an enhancement of the e-commerce marketplace. In order to rely on this legal basis, the e-commerce platform operator must first consider using anonymised data. Reliance on business improvement as a basis for processing may only be made if the intended purpose cannot reasonably be achieved without the use of personal data in an individually identifiable form.[31] Second, the purpose must be objectively appropriate, and the extent to which personal data is used must be reasonable. With the use of recommendation systems commonplace in e-commerce marketplaces these days, it is likely that adding a recommendation feature to enhance the online shopping experience will be viewed as reasonable. The conditions for business improvement as a basis for processing implement two aspects of data minimisation. First, the requirement to consider anonymisation (including pseudonymisation), and second, the requirement of proportionality when selecting both records and attributes for the training dataset.

As explained above, the e-commerce marketplace must consider anonymising its training dataset. If model performance is unsatisfactory, it may then use personally identifiable information in its training dataset. Of course, if the use of personally identifiable information makes little difference to model performance, then it cannot be said that the intended purpose cannot be achieved without using personal data in an individually identifiable form. Should the e-commerce marketplace use personally identifiable information in its training dataset, the extent of personal data that is used must be reasonable with reference to achieving its objectives. In this case, the objective is to offer recommendations to enhance the online shopping experience. A relevant consideration is the period for which past data will be selected for incorporation into the training dataset. Since consumer shopping behaviour changes with time, it may not be necessary to go too far back into history. Consumer preferences in different markets may also differ. Thus, it may well be the case that different models may be developed for different geographies, and that this may require selection of the customer records representative of the target market. Finally, consideration must also be given to which of the attributes in the customer records are reasonably required for model development. It is difficult to establish bright line rules, as the ultimate goal is a model that performs well for the intended market. The process must necessarily be iterative. With each sprint of the model development process, it should be possible to progressively identify and de-prioritise or eliminate attributes that have very low impact on model behaviour or performance.

B. Enlarging Training Datasets through Data Sharing

For most businesses, model development will largely rely on the secondary use of data. But where a business does not have adequate data, it may consider different ways of acquiring additional data. One option is to acquire data through commercial partnerships, such as

[30] PDPA, First Schedule, Pt 5 and Second Schedule, Pt 2, Div 2; see also, PDPC Advisory Guidelines on Use of Personal Data in AI Recommendation and Decision Systems (n 19), 6–8; and PDPC Advisory Guidelines on Key Concepts in the PDPA (n 28), Annex A, Table 2.

[31] See PDPA, First Schedule, Pt 5, para 1(3)(*a*) and Second Schedule, Pt 2, Div 2, para 1(2)(*a*).

retailers joining a common membership rewards programme to gain access to additional data attributes of members. Another option is to purchase data, such as by licensing mapping or directory information. Oftentimes, there will be concerns over the quality of the acquired data and the attendant technical challenges in integrating the acquired data with existing customer data. But data quality and integration issues are not insurmountable, and there are technical tools and techniques that can be used to overcome them.

The key challenges for data sharing – whether through commercial partnerships or by purchase – are often not technical but legal. For example, when purchasing contact information for marketing purposes, it is necessary to conduct due diligence to ascertain that the dataset can be disclosed and used for the intended purpose.[32] Anecdotally, three times more time is spent on clearing legal and compliance hurdles than on the actual analysis of the data once it is in hand. There are, unsurprisingly, policy initiatives to reduce the friction for data sharing in order to support innovation. In the EU, there are both policy and infrastructural interventions. The creation of Common European Data Spaces is a major infrastructural initiative.[33] Equally significant, if not more so, are the policy and regulatory initiatives to increase movement of data (GDPR for personal data and the regulation on the free flow of non-personal data), access to public sector data and to regulate data intermediation service providers (Data Governance Act), access to Internet of Things data (Data Act) and access to platform data (Digital Markets Act).

In Singapore, efforts have also been made to introduce data-sharing infrastructure (eg, SG Findex and SG Tradex). The policy interventions have, however, been far more modest and have mainly focused on two areas. First, facilitating efforts for interested collaborators to decide whether it is worthwhile to expend further resources in negotiations for their commercial collaboration. This is largely done by clarifying the application and interpretation of the PDPA through regulatory sandboxes. Second, reducing friction in negotiating data sharing agreements through efforts to standardise both the data sharing models as well as their attendant data sharing agreements.

i. Providing Regulatory Clarity through Data Privacy Regulatory Sandboxes

The PDPC, in collaboration with the Infocomm Media Development Authority (IMDA), has – and continues to – run regulatory sandboxes in Singapore to support innovation: ie, the Data Regulatory Sandbox[34] and the Privacy Enhancing Technologies (PETs) Sandbox.[35] The regulatory sandboxes provide a three-stage process for businesses to engage with the PDPC on data use in innovative technologies. Businesses first discuss their plans confidentially, potentially receiving clarification on existing policies. If extant policies are inadequate, the PDPC may issue practical guidance documents setting out how it intends to interpret the PDPA. Practical guidance, once issued, is effectively bind-

[32] See *Re Lee Chee Meng* [2023] SGPDPC 14 and *Re Amicus Solutions & Ivan Chua* [2019] SGPDPC 33.

[33] European Commission, 'Common European Data Spaces' (last updated 23 January 2025), available at digital-strategy.ec.europa.eu/en/policies/data-spaces.

[34] IMDA, 'About the Data Regulatory Sandbox' (last updated 3 August 2023), available at www.imda.gov.sg/how-we-can-help/data-innovation/data-regulatory-sandbox.

[35] IMDA, 'Privacy Enhancing Technology Sandboxes' (last updated 4 September 2024), available at www.imda.gov.sg/how-we-can-help/data-innovation/privacy-enhancing-technology-sandboxes.

ing on the PDPC under section 49(1) of the PDPA, as it indicates 'the manner in which the Commission will interpret the provisions of this Act'. While a third stage involving exemptions under section 62 of the PDPA exists, it has thus far not been used.

The regulatory sandboxes cover a range of innovative commercial use cases. Some deal with PETs applied to enable the sharing of data, such as using secure multi-party computing to allow personalisation of advertisements without reliance on third-party cookies, and using trusted execution environments to analyse consumer preferences and sales performance of pharmaceutical products.[36] The experience from the regulatory sandboxes that is relevant to the present discussion is a set of practical guidance on a common and frequent commercial problem in data sharing: how can we enable potential collaborators to quickly decide whether there are sufficient common customers in their customer records so that it is worthwhile to proceed with further negotiations for the collaboration? There are potential data privacy compliance issues that need to be overcome. What is required is the identification of the size of the intersection of their respective customer datasets, rather than who the individual customers are. This is relevant to model development, as having a sufficiently large common intersect enables the collaborators to expand the number of attributes through data sharing. This increases the variety of data in their training dataset.

There are different techniques to achieve this using a combination of pseudonymisation (or tokenisation) and a trusted third party who carries out the processing. By working with industry players through regulatory sandboxes, the PDPC has issued practical guidance opinions on how they will interpret and apply the PDPA in such situations. In gist, these lay out: (a) conditions and standards in order to ensure that each participant in this collaboration is unable to identify individuals; (b) safeguards to prevent processing by the trusted intermediary beyond the authorised purpose; and (c) restrictions on how data should be disclosed to the participants, eg, aggregated, anonymised or profile information.[37] By clarifying how it intends to interpret the PDPA, the PDPC has provided regulatory certainty and clarity on how this initial hurdle of establishing the size of the intersection between collaborators may be carried out in compliance with data protection laws.

ii. Reducing Friction through Standardised Data Sharing Models and Agreements

The other hurdle to data sharing is defining and organising the legal relationships in data-sharing arrangements. Providing examples can be helpful for the industry in a new and developing area such as this. The obvious model for data sharing is bilateral sharing,

[36] ibid, see the case studies 'Meta: Digital Advertising in a Paradigm Without 3rd Party Cookies' and 'Healthcare Services Provider: Accessing More Data through Trusted Execution Environment to Generate New Insights' respectively.

[37] See PDPC, 'Practical Guidance in Relation to Data Collaboration Arrangement Involving Common Data Intermediary', available at www.pdpc.gov.sg/-/media/files/pdpc/pdf-files/practical-guidance-provided-by-pdpc/guidance-to-data-collaboration-arrangement-involving-common-data-intermediary.pdf and 'Practical Guidance Sought by Organisations Involved in a Data Collaboration Arrangement', available at www.pdpc.gov.sg/-/media/files/pdpc/pdf-files/practical-guidance-provided-by-pdpc/guidance-to-organisations-involved-in-a-data-collaboration-agreement.pdf.

but there can also be more complex models involving multiple collaborators. The IMDA's Trusted Data Sharing Framework attempts to address the commercial, compliance and technical hurdles to data sharing by providing a framework within which common issues can be discussed in a systematic way.[38] It also provides three models for data sharing: bilateral, multilateral and multilateral (with lead). Template data sharing agreements are provided for these data sharing models, along with template consent clauses and confidentiality agreements. The provision of these template agreements is intended to help reduce the time taken for negotiating legal documentation by offering a neutral standard to facilitate negotiations.

An important aspect of legal and regulatory compliance is the conduct of due diligence for the data-sharing arrangement. The legal and regulatory issues relevant to data sharing include intellectual property rights and data privacy. Where the data-sharing arrangement is for the purpose of collaborative research, there are exceptions under both copyright and personal data protection laws. The computational data analysis exception supports sharing of copyrighted material between research collaborators to jointly or separately conduct computational analysis or to verify the results of such analysis.[39] The sharing of identifiable personal data for the purpose of research and development is also permitted under the PDPA in a couple of scenarios. First, the business improvement exception supports centralisation of R&D functions in specific entities within a group of company. Second, commercial and non-commercial collaborative research between two organisations is also permitted. The research exception permits sharing of identifiable personal data provided that it is necessary for the research and there is a clear public benefit in conducting the research. Before sharing, data controllers must assess the cost of seeking consent from data subjects against the impact on the research project. Consent need not be obtained if the assessment is that doing so will affect the viability of the research project (eg, inordinate costs or delays, skewing results or introducing bias). Finally, results of the research cannot be used to make decisions about individuals or be published in a form that identifies individuals.[40]

In the absence of an exception to copyright that can be relied on, the data provider needs to prove that it has the requisite rights over the dataset to be shared. Datasets are protected by copyright laws as compilations, and in certain jurisdictions like the EU, databases are also protected as a sui generis intangible property right. If the data-sharing arrangements involve the disclosure of personal data, the data provider also needs to show that it has the rights to do so. Consent is probably the only viable legal basis for business-to-business disclosure of personal data outside the context of collaborative research and development discussed in the preceding paragraph. This will require an examination of the scope of data subject consent. Here, IMDA's Trusted Data Sharing Framework provides a template consent clause that can be helpful. While it may not help with disclosures based on past consent, it can provide an independent benchmark against which the adequacy of such consent clauses can be measured. Importantly, it

[38] Such as, commercial issues (eg, identifying intended benefits and data valuation), legal and regulatory compliance (eg, data privacy laws) and technical and operational measures (eg, anonymisation, access controls and data destruction).

[39] Copyright Act 2021, s 244(2)(c).

[40] PDPA, Second Schedule, Division 2; see also PDPC Advisory Guidelines on Key Concepts (n 28) para 12.82 for guidance on impracticability in the context of the research exception.

provides a model that allows collaborators to migrate their customers and converge on a common consent clause as they embark on their collaboration.

C. Accessing Publicly Available Data through Web Scraping

Accompanying the frisson fomented by the potential of generative AI is the issue of web scraping. This refers to the practice of trawling publicly available information for training data. The pre-training of generative AI foundational models required access to high-capacity computing power and enormous training datasets. Only the best-funded companies could afford access to the GPU computing capacity necessary and have the technical wherewithal to harness the largest training dataset available: the public Internet. Allegations by claimants in lawsuits against the providers of these foundational models provide an idea of the volume of data involved: in *Andersen v Stability AI Ltd*,[41] the plaintiff alleged that Stability AI scraped five billion images from the Internet for training Stable Diffusion; while in *Getty Images (US) Inc & Others v Stability AI Ltd*,[42] the allegation was that Stability AI scraped millions of images from the plaintiff's websites.

Web scraping raises new dimensions to age-old issues in both copyright and data protection laws. The fundamental question is the extent to which access to, and use of, publicly available information may be circumscribed. Through the copyright lens, the threshold question is whether model training copies expressions that copyright law protects; assuming that there is copying of expression, the next question is whether making a copy of publicly available information is permitted by any exception. In some jurisdictions, this raises issues relating to whether machine learning is transformative such that it qualifies as fair use; while in others, whether access to publicly available information is authorised such that the text and data mining exception applies. Through the data privacy lens, the challenge lies in identifying an appropriate legal basis for processing publicly available information.

i. Establishing the Boundaries of Fair Use

When works are used for machine learning, there is a fundamental question concerning whether there is copying of expression, since the analysis that is performed is directed at extracting features from the training data to identify patterns and relationships. Further, this is performed by machine learning algorithms without human perception of the expression that copyright protects. Additionally, the output of machine learning is a model that consists of an algorithm and parameters (eg, vectors, connections and weights). Since what is analysed and extracted is not expression, it can be argued that there is no copying of expression and therefore no copyright infringement.[43]

Be that as it may, defendants in a number of copyright infringement cases in the US are trying to establish that web scraping for the purpose of pre-training foundational models for generative AI systems qualifies as fair use, an exception that is also available

[41] *Andersen v Stability AI Ltd* (23-cv-00201-WHO) (N.D. Cal. 2023).
[42] *Getty Images (US) Inc & Others v Stability AI Ltd* [2023] EWHC 3090 (Ch).
[43] Ginsburg (n 6) 277.

in other jurisdictions such as Singapore, Israel and South Korea. The considerations for qualifying as fair use are: (a) the purpose and character of the intended use; (b) the nature of the work that will be used; (c) how much – both qualitative and quantitative – of the work will be used in relation to the whole; and (d) how the intended use will affect the market or value of the work.

One way to establish fair use is to show that the purpose and character of the use is transformative, that is, the intended use supersedes the objects of the original creation by adding a new purpose or different character, thereby altering the original purpose with a new expression, meaning or message. The more transformative the intended use, the less significant the other considerations become.[44] However, as the US Supreme Court observed in *Andy Warhol Foundation for Visual Arts, Inc. v Goldsmith*,[45] this is a question of degree. The more distinctive the intended (or secondary) use is from the original object, the more likely that will be weighed in favour of transformative use. This should be balanced against considerations such as whether the secondary use shares the same commercial space. If the secondary use shares the same commercial space and is not sufficiently distinctive from the original object, then it is less likely to be transformative. Thus, it was held in *Thomson Reuters & West Publishing v Ross Intelligence*[46] that the defendant could not avail itself of the fair use defence for its use of the plaintiff's headnotes for model development for a number of reasons. First, using the plaintiff's headnotes to develop a legal research tool that competes with the plaintiff's Westlaw product was not transformative because the legal research tool did not have a different purpose or character. Second, the defendant's tool existed in the same commercial space as the plaintiff's product and was intended to be a market substitute.

Transformative use vs market substitution. Crawling the Internet for data to be analysed and indexed is not new and has been found to be transformative in past cases. For example, the indexing of copyrighted material and creation of thumbnail images for a better online search experience have been held to be transformative.[47] Likewise, digitising books submitted by libraries in order to allow the public to perform textual searches of the digitised books and to view snippets of text from them has also been found to be transformative.[48] One key point to note from these cases is that the benefits of search results augmented by thumbnail images and snippets from digitised books provided by online searches to end users were not provided by rights holders, and the scale of reach could not be provided by individual rights holders. Another important point is that in both examples, the transformative use increased the value of the individual works by making them more accessible.

The tensions between transformative use and market harm have emerged in the first decisions on whether making copies for the purpose of model training qualifies as fair use. Both are decisions from the US District Court of the Northern District of California on motions for summary judgment; and both were decisions in favour of transformative use. In *Bartz v Anthropic*, District Judge Alsup held that making legitimate digitised

[44] *Campbell v Acuff-Rose Music, Inc.* 510 U.S. 569 (1994) 579.
[45] 598 U. S. 508 (2023).
[46] *Thomson Reuters Enterprise & West Publishing Corp v Ross Intelligence Inc* (20-cv-613-SB) (11 February 2025) US District Court (Delaware).
[47] *Perfect 10, Inc v Amazon.com, Inc.* 487 F 3d 701 (9th Cir. 2007).
[48] *Authors Guild v Google, Inc* 804 F.3d 202, 116 U.S.P.Q.2d (BNA) 1423 (2d Cir. 2015).

copies of copyrighted material to form the corpus for the training of LLMs is transformative use. The defendant had purchased hard copies of books, including some authored by the plaintiffs, and destructively digitised them, effectively replacing the hard copies they had purchased with digitised versions.[49] These were eventually used as data for training the defendant's LLM. District Judge Alsup likened model training to reading, memorising and internalising, in order to emulate the best writing style. This has been permissible for centuries. The use of copyrighted material to train LLMs that could generate new text is quintessentially transformative. Such use is orthogonal to what copyright owners could expect to control.[50]

In *Kadrey v Meta*,[51] District Judge Chhabria also found that making copies of copyrighted material for model training was transformative.[52] This is despite the fact that these copies were downloaded from shadow libraries of pirated material. While this showed a lack of good faith, the use was nevertheless transformative, and the want of probity did not affect the outcome of the case. (By contrast, the defendant in *Bartz v Anthropic* had initially built a central library of pirated electronic books from which datasets were extracted for model training: this practice was not condoned as fair use.)

The more significant point that emerges from *Kadrey v Meta* is the *obiter dicta* relating to the market dilution argument that may subtract from the transformative nature of model training. Expert evidence from both parties was aligned in that the Llama LLM did not regurgitate a significant percentage of the plaintiffs' books: hence, there was no direct market substitution. District Judge Chhabria opined that the plaintiffs could have made a case to the effect that LLMs can produce similar works that, while not infringing, could nevertheless compete with the original works. These could be produced in large volumes fairly quickly such that while they are not direct market substitutes, they may nevertheless diminish the market for the original works through indirect substitution.[53] Unfortunately, the case for market dilution was not put forward by the plaintiffs.[54]

Direct copying vs substantial similarity. For plaintiffs to succeed at trial, it will be necessary to prove either *direct copying* of their works as input for model training or *substantial similarity* of the model output with their works. Direct copying is relevant to prove infringement during model development in circumstances where exceptions such as fair use or text and data mining are inapplicable. Substantial similarity is relevant for establishing that the model or its output infringes the copyrighted work.[55]

[49] In gist, the spines of the books were cut so that it was easier to scan the pages of the books.

[50] *Andrea Bartz and others v Anthropic* (24-cv-05417-WHA) (23 June 2025) (N.D. Cal.) 12, 13 and 16–18.

[51] *Richard Kadrey and others v Meta Platform* (23-cv-03417-VC) (25 June 2025) (N.D. Cal.).

[52] ibid 16.

[53] ibid 28 ff.

[54] The plaintiffs' main theory of harm was that they were deprived of the option of licensing their books for model training. However, there was judicial precedent that this was not a recognised market harm.

[55] There are two contradictory decisions concerning whether trained models are themselves infringing. The UK High Court's decision in *Getty Images v Stability AI* held that trained models do not contain copies of training data and are therefore not themselves infringing copies. In contrast, the Munich Regional Court in *GEMA v OpenAI* held that memorisation of training data (ie, the phenomenon whereby generative AI models regurgitate fragments of training data) rendered the trained model infringing since the text and data mining exception only permits copying for the compilation of the training corpus. In this author's view, the decision in *Getty Images* is technically sound and forms the better view. By contrast, the decision in *GEMA* adopted a more dogmatic application of copyright principles without giving adequate appreciation to what and how data is stored in foundational models.

Where the plaintiff alleges direct copying, the claim is that the developer of the foundational model made copies (eg, web scraping) and used them for model development. In *Bartz v Anthropic*, direct copying took place when the defendant bought hard copies of books – including copies authored by the plaintiffs – and digitised them to create the training corpus for developing successive versions of LLMs used to provide the Claude service.[56] Plaintiffs are required to show that copies were made (a) by the defendants in question and (b) within the jurisdiction. On the first point, interlocutory decisions have made it clear that claims cannot be maintained against defendants who were not involved in making the allegedly infringing copies. In *Andersen v Stability AI Ltd*, the US District Court for the Northern District of California dismissed the plaintiff's case against two defendants – DeviantArt and Midjourney – on the basis that they were not involved in making copies. The claim against DeviantArt was that it was a source of training data for Stability AI for their Stable Diffusion service. Midjourney was alleged to have used Stable Diffusion in its product. As the claims against DeviantArt and Midjourney did not allege that they made copies, only that they used Stable Diffusion, the claims against them were dismissed. The claim against Stability AI was maintained, as the allegation was that Stability AI used the LAION training dataset that contained copies of the plaintiff's copyrighted works. This decision is instructive, in that it highlights that where companies deploy models licensed from a third party, any direct copying by the model developer is unlikely to taint the company deploying the model, unless it was somehow involved in the model development. As for the second point, the UK case of *Getty Images v Stability AI* is illustrative: the plaintiff abandoned claims of copyright infringement during the training and development of the defendant's AI models as there was no evidence that these activities took place in the UK.[57]

When it comes to claims of infringement based on substantial similarity of output to the plaintiff's copyrighted works, it will be necessary to show how an identified model output is similar to an identified copyrighted work.[58] In *GEMA v OpenAI*, the plaintiffs succeeded in establishing infringement by comparing the original works (ie, song lyrics) with the generated output.[59] Likewise, the plaintiffs in *New York Times v Microsoft & OpenAI, et al*, demonstrated substantial similarity in their complaint by juxtaposing the original article and the generated output.[60]

However, the necessity of showing substantial similarity between the output from the model and the copyrighted work is likely to be challenging.[61] For instance, the plaintiff in *Andersen v Stability AI* conceded (at least at the hearing of the dismissal application) that none of the output images was likely to be a close match for any specific image in

[56] *Bartz v Anthropic* (n 50) 4–7; the defendant had initially obtained pirated books for their training corpus but eventually switched to destructive scanning of hardcopy books that they purchased.

[57] *Getty Images (US) Inc & Ors v Stability AI Ltd (Rev1)* [2025] WLR(D) 571, [2025] EWHC 2863 (Ch), at [9].

[58] It is insufficient to allege that every output of the model is an infringing derivative work; the plaintiff must explain how a particular output is substantially similar to a copyrighted work: *Tremblay v OpenAI, Inc.* (23-cv-03223-AMO, 23-cv-03416-AMO) (N.D. Cal. Feb. 12, 2024).

[59] *GEMA v OpenAI* (Munich Regional Court, 11 November 2025) (Ref 42 O 14139/24) at [193], available at www.gesetze-bayern.de/Content/Document/Y-300-Z-GRURRS-B-2025-N-30204.

[60] See the complaint in *New York Times v Microsoft & OpenAI, et al* (Case 1:23-cv-11195), paras 99–101.

[61] It is not technically feasible to prove memorisation except through model output. Hence, comparison of model output with copyrighted works is necessary to prove either model infringement or output infringement.

the training data.[62] It was possible that the output images were not substantially similar to the plaintiff's works that were used to train the model, as a result of substantial transformation.[63] As safeguards against copyright infringement are implemented by model developers, producing output with substantial similarity to training data will be increasingly difficult. Technical measures such as post-training, input and output filters can be effective in extinguishing output claims. The plaintiffs in *Bartz v Anthropic* conceded, for the purpose of summary judgment, that the defendant's Claude service did not output infringing responses. This was attributable to the defendant's implementation of technical measures such as output filters that prevent the verbatim regurgitation of copyrighted content to end users.[64] Post-training to reduce the risk of verbatim regurgitation is another technique. It appears to have been relatively effective in *Kadrey v Meta* in withstanding adversarial prompts that were designed to cause the Llama model to regurgitate.[65] In the UK case of *Getty Images v Stability AI*, input filters were effective in blocking prompts that were designed to elicit output that are substantially similar to the plaintiff's works such that claims of substantive similarity in generated output were abandoned.[66]

ii. Applying the Text and Data Mining Exception

The text and data mining exception was discussed earlier, in the context of the secondary use of data. It is also relevant to web scraping. When it comes to web scraping, it is safe to say that text and data mining exceptions have been formulated to condone this practice.[67] In Singapore, the computational data analysis exception applies to web scraping for model development. It makes no distinction between either the nature of the analysis (ie, commercial or non-commercial) or the source of the data (so long as the prerequisites are met, eg, lawful access). The UK's text and data mining exception applies when the development of foundational models is for non-commercial research. The EU's implementation of this exception does not contemplate any restrictions for non-commercial research but allows for reservations to be made for commercial research.

But this is not to say that everything that is accessible through the Internet can be scraped. As mentioned above, the exception is premised on users having lawful access in the first place. Restrictions exist in a couple of forms. First, hard barriers such as walled gardens and paywalls.[68] These are hard barriers, as the web crawler cannot reach the files within the walled garden or behind the paywall without authentication. Access

[62] *Andersen v Stability AI Ltd* (n 41) 11, 13, 20, 22.

[63] On this point, one of the plaintiffs' theories of infringement was that copies of their copyrighted works were stored as compressed images in the model. The court commented that if it was possible to reference the plaintiffs' works by name when creating new products, this could strengthen their claim that their protected content remained in the model.

[64] See *Bartz v Anthropic* (n 50) 11–12.

[65] *Kadrey v Meta* (n 51) 12–13.

[66] *Getty Images (US) Inc & Ors v Stability AI Ltd (Rev1)* [2025] WLR(D) 571, [2025] EWHC 2863 (Ch), at [9].

[67] eg, Directive (EU) 2019/790 of the European Parliament and of the Council of 17 April 2019 on copyright and related rights in the Digital Single Market and amending Directives 96/9/EC and 2001/29/EC, Recital (18).

[68] Walled gardens refer to closed systems that control access through authentication, and where content in walled gardens require a subscription for access, that is referred to as a paywall.

control is implemented through technical measures (eg, requiring a username/password combination or access from authorised IP addresses). Singapore's implementation of the computational data analysis exception recognises hard barriers – circumvention of paywalls renders access unlawful.[69] Thus, while Singapore's computational data analysis cannot be contracted out of,[70] it does not mean that breaching of paywalls is condoned. It follows that if a subscription is maintained, the use of data behind the paywall for text and data mining is permitted.

Second, soft barriers such as terms of use that define the boundaries of permitted access and use. Given the sheer number of websites the web crawler will scrape, it is impracticable to review the terms of use for each website. Resort to technical solutions is thus necessary. The Robots Exclusion Protocol (REP), which allows instructions to web crawlers to be set out in a robots.txt file, is an example of a technical solution. The EU's implementation of the text and data exception supports technical solutions. Where the information is publicly available online, reservations of rights should be made – and indeed, 'should only be considered appropriate' to be made – through machine-readable means.[71] Singapore's computational data analysis exception also contemplates the possibility that lawful access to a database may be circumscribed by its terms of use, except that any term that purports to exclude or restrict the exception is void.[72] This means that restrictions that prevent crawling of sub-domains or folders may potentially be void since they prevent the copying of files in these locations for analysis. But restrictions as to when crawling may take place or restrictions on the frequency of requests to protect server load may be permissible, as these terms do not prevent copying and analysis of the files. Within these parameters, breaches of contractual terms may render access unlawful and copies that were made would not be able to benefit from the computational data analysis exception.[73] While Singapore's implementation of the exception does not refer to technical solutions explicitly, there is nothing to say that restrictions cannot be implemented in both legible and machine-readable forms.

The robots.txt file gives instructions concerning who can crawl the site, which pages may be crawled, when the site may be crawled, and how intensively the web crawler can access the server. However, there are practical limits in relying on the REP as a way of circumscribing reliance on the text and data mining exception.

First, such instructions may be ignored by the web crawler.[74] Robot.txt is essentially a text file placed by the rights holder. It probably does not qualify as a technological measure for access control or rights management since it merely contains instructions *about* access but does not actually *control* access to the files and folders on the web server.

[69] Copyright Act 2021, s 244(2)(*d*) and accompanying illustrations. While the illustration specifically refers to paywalls, the same principle ought to apply to walled gardens.

[70] Copyright Act 2021, s 187(1)(*c*).

[71] Directive (EU) 2019/790 of the European Parliament and of the Council of 17 April 2019 on copyright and related rights in the Digital Single Market, Art 4(3) & Recital (18); quotation is from Recital (18).

[72] Copyright Act 2021, s 244(2)(*d*), illustration (b) read with s 187(1)(*c*).

[73] However, there appears to be judicial authority to the effect that breaches of contract are not necessarily unlawful per se: *Tan Ng Kuang and another v Jai Swarup Pathak* [2021] SGHC 232, at [87]; see also, Singapore Academy of Law, 'Reform of the Computational Data Analysis Exception' for a discussion of the extent to which breach of contractual terms may (or may not) render access unlawful: 27–30.

[74] See D Pierce, 'The test file that runs the internet' (*The Verge*, 14 February 2024), available at www.theverge.com/24067997/robots-txt-ai-text-file-web-crawlers-spiders.

It is the web crawler that interprets the robot.txt file and respects its restrictions, if it is configured to do so. Hence, the robot.txt file is unlikely to be a 'technology, device or component' that controls access or manages rights and therefore cannot benefit from the statutory provisions that prohibit circumvention of access control measures.[75] Second, the REP was initially defined for search engine indexing and will need to be extended to cater for scenarios pertinent to the text and data mining exception. For example, distinguishing between commercial and non-commercial web crawling, which is a necessary distinction for some jurisdictions (eg, the EU and the UK, where the text and data mining exceptions are more permissive for non-commercial analysis).

That said, these are not insurmountable challenges. Standards are often revised and extended, and so too can the REP. The robot.txt file may not be an access control measure, but it should nevertheless be effective in establishing restrictions in a machine-readable form. Further, an argument may be made that the robot.txt file together with the web crawling algorithm *collectively* form a system for controlling access and managing rights, such that circumventing the instructions contained in the file amounts to circumvention of an access control measure. Thus, while the REP is not the perfect solution, it is as good a place to start as any.

iii. Legal Bases for Web Crawling under Data Protection Law

Where personal data is scraped from the Internet, there will also be data privacy concerns. Web scraping is essentially the collection of personal data, which is a form of data processing. Thereafter, using personal data for model development is also processing. Web scraping is permissible under data protection laws, provided a legal basis can be identified for such processing activity. Publicly available personal data may be subjected to lighter regulatory requirements in some countries, such as India and Singapore. In India, personal data that has been made available publicly by the data subject is exempted from data protection legislation.[76] In Singapore, the collection, use and disclosure of *publicly available* personal data without the data subjects' consent is permissible under the PDPA.[77] Publicly available personal data may be collected and used without limitation as to purposes, so long as the purpose is reasonably appropriate under section 18(a) of the PDPA. One may justifiably query whether an individual who uploads, for example, photographs onto social media intended for them to be used for all purposes. *In extremis*, using photographs of politicians to create fake obscene photographs is likely to be considered inappropriate by most measures.[78] But what about using photographs uploaded onto social media for pre-training of foundational models? Indeed, most of what is available on the Internet is for consumption, and it may be persuasively argued that pre-training of foundational models is not very much different

[75] Copyright Act 2021, Pt 7, Division 4 deals with rights management systems generally; the prohibition of circumventing access control measures is found in s 425; and the definitions of access control and protection measures are found in s 423.

[76] Indian Digital Personal Data Protection Act, 2023, s 3(c)(ii).

[77] PDPA, First Schedule, Pt 2, para 1.

[78] See C M Lee, 'Vivian Balakrishnan, Tan Wu Meng among MPs who Received Extortion Letters with Fake Obscene Photos' (*ChannelNewsAsia*, 20 April 2024); and F Koh, 'MPs' Extortion Plot: Deepfakes in Letters were Low-quality and Black-and-white, says Lawmaker' (*ChannelNewsAsia*, 24 April 2024).

from online search engine crawling and indexing, especially when the pre-trained LLM is deployed in a service that promotes discoverability and access to the source material. It is difficult to balance too finely what is appropriate when dealing with personal data that has been placed in publicly available platforms. It is probably more pragmatic to identify those purposes that are clearly inappropriate, such as fake celebrity pornography. In the final analysis, it is more likely than not that pre-training is *not* so clearly an inappropriate purpose, such that it should be prohibited.

There are other practical issues. Personal data that is publicly available may not remain so indefinitely. For example, end users may change their social media profile from 'public' to 'friends only'. This poses a challenge to web scraping. Once personal data has been used for model development, it is impracticable to trace and remove the contribution of specific training data without re-training the model. Reverting to an earlier model will result in loss of learning for an entire period, which is also undesirable. To address situations where personal data was publicly available at the point in time when it was collected or used but changes status thereafter, the PDPC takes the position that it is the point in time when collection takes place that determines whether the personal data is publicly available. Once collected, personal data may thereafter be used in reliance on the public availability or other exceptions regardless of changes in the status of the source.[79]

Under the GDPR, public availability is not a legal basis for processing. This means that model developers must identify one of the extant legal bases for processing. The necessity of a legal basis for processing is illustrated by the *Clearview AI Inc* decision from the UK ICO, which was discussed in the previous chapter. Clearview operates an algorithmic image search engine that matches an image provided by the user against its database of images. Clearview collected facial images and associated metadata to create facial vectors using machine learning facial recognition algorithm. The UK ICO found that Clearview had failed to identify a legal basis for processing, thereby putting them in breach of the GDPR and the UK GDPR.[80] The UK ICO imposed a penalty of £7.5 million and directed Clearview to erase images and associated biometric data of UK residents.[81] On appeal,[82] the First-tier Tribunal (General Regulatory Chamber) (FTT) agreed with the UK ICO that there was processing of personal data. However, the FTT held that since Clearview had no presence within the UK, the basis of the UK ICO's extraterritorial jurisdiction had to be established through one of the two limbs of Article 3(2) of the UK GDPR. The relevant limb was the monitoring of the online behaviour of UK data subjects, ie, Article 3(2)(b). However, Clearview's processing was limited to indexing, which in and of itself did not amount to monitoring of online behaviour. Indexing is an automated, mathematical process. Clearview did not itself monitor the UK data subjects' online behaviour, although its processing of personal data facilitated efficient searches which were used by its clients to monitor the online behaviour of UK data subjects – search results allowed them to ascertain a person's behaviour at a

[79] PDPC Advisory Guidelines on Key Concepts in the PDPA (n 28) para 12.88.

[80] Clearview AI Inc Enforcement Notice, paras 66–67; Clearview AI Inc Monetary Penalty Notice, paras 71–72.

[81] Clearview AI Inc Enforcement Notice, Annex 1; Clearview AI Inc Monetary Penalty Notice, paras 69, 70, 73–74.

[82] *Clearview AI Inc v The Information Commissioner* [2023] UKFTT 819 (GRC).

particular point in time or over an extended period of time. Further, Clearview's clients were non-UK/EU law enforcement or national security bodies and their contractors. The activities of foreign governments fell beyond the remit of the UK GDPR, as one government cannot seek to bind or control the activities of another sovereign state. Hence, the processing activities fell outside the scope of UK GDPR, and the UK ICO had no jurisdiction to issue the enforcement notices.

What might a legal basis for web scraping and model development be? The GDPR contemplates that further processing for scientific research purposes or statistical purposes should be considered to be compatible lawful processing operations.[83] The data protection authority in France has also expressed the view that re-using publicly available data from the Internet for model development is also possible where such re-use is for *a purpose compatible to the initial collection, such as research and innovation*.[84] The UK ICO has stated that legitimate interest is the *only available legal basis* for web scraping for pre-training of generative AI. However, it opined that this is a high-risk and invisible activity and exhorted model developers to enhance transparency.[85] The EDPB likewise endorses reliance on legitimate interest as a legal basis for web scraping and reminds model developers of their transparency obligation.[86] It has recommended a number of mitigatory measures specific to web scraping: viz, respecting robot.txt restrictions and excluding content that is intrusive or that relates to vulnerable individuals.[87]

In the EU, data privacy concerns over web scraping have led to a ban. Under the EU AI Act,[88] AI systems that can be used for the untargeted scraping of facial images from the Internet are classified as posing unacceptable risks and will be banned from the EU.[89] However, as both the *Clearview AI* and *Stability AI* cases have shown, this may not prevent the use of web scraping to support model development. These activities may just be relocated to other jurisdictions, ie, regulatory arbitrage, enabling them to capture the economic value of such processing activities.

D. Model Testing

Testing of systems before deployment is an age-old practice for the IT industry and is absolutely necessary. Industry practices around testing for deterministic, rule-based systems are much more mature: eg, system integration tests (SIT), user acceptance tests

[83] GDPR, Art 5(1)(b), Recital (50).

[84] CNIL, 'Artificial Intelligence' (n 21).

[85] UK ICO, 'The lawful basis for web scraping to train generative AI models', available at ico.org.uk/about-the-ico/what-we-do/our-work-on-artificial-intelligence/response-to-the-consultation-series-on-generative-ai/the-lawful-basis-for-web-scraping-to-train-generative-ai-models.

[86] EDPB, *Opinion 28/2024 on certain data protection aspects related to the processing of personal data in the context of AI models* (adopted on 17 December 2024) para 63.

[87] ibid para 105.

[88] Regulation (EU) 2024/1689 of the European Parliament and of the Council of 13 June 2024 laying down harmonised rules on artificial intelligence and amending Regulations (EC) No 300/2008, (EU) No 167/2013, (EU) No 168/2013, (EU) 2018/858, (EU) 2018/1139 and (EU) 2019/2144 and Directives 2014/90/EU, (EU) 2016/797 and (EU) 2020/1828.

[89] EU AI Act, Art 5(1)(e).

(UAT), vulnerability assessments and penetration tests (VAPT). With the deployment of probabilistic models to provide specific functions or features in AI systems, new forms of tests are also being developed. Pre-deployment tests for machine learning models are important, as these ensure that the model performs consistently, and that the model output is within an acceptable range. Models are probabilistic in nature, and there will invariably be outliers. Pre-deployment tests are intended to reduce these outliers. The output of models is also dependent on the training data. Such data can contain historical bias for various reasons, a key reason being that it reflects the gender or age distribution of the customer base. The discernible trend is that new AI regulations tend to introduce mandatory obligations for pre-deployment tests. However, data protection laws may also be interpreted to support, if not require, some of these tests.[90]

i. AI Regulations are Starting to Require Pre-Deployment Tests

What emerges from a survey of the recent AI regulations from the EU and China – both global front runners who have introduced AI regulations – is a common set of practices that deal with *data management, transparency and pre-deployment tests*. The EU AI Act regulates AI systems by prescribing requirements on how they are developed and deployed, according to a tiering system based on the risks they pose. AI systems that pose unacceptable risks are prohibited or severely restricted. For high-risk AI systems, companies are required to implement quality assurance systems and conduct *conformity assessments* before deployment, and they are further subject to registration requirements. They will also have to notify post-deployment conformity lapses. Conformity assessments are directed at providing assurance that high-risk AI systems adhere to a set of ethical principles for responsible AI, such as *accuracy and data quality*, transparency, human oversight and robustness in cybersecurity. Lastly, the EU AI Act also establishes baseline *transparency* requirements for low-risk AI systems.

China regulates providers of Internet information services that offer algorithmic recommendation services by imposing requirements similar to the EU AI Act, for example mandating *pre-deployment tests* (including for information security), post-deployment monitoring, and *transparency* of the main operational mechanisms of the recommendation service. One key feature is the requirement to conduct and file an algorithm self-assessment report with the authorities. AI systems that are used for deep synthesis[91] (ie, deep fakes) and generative AI[92] are also subject to their respective

[90] This section is adapted from an opinion piece by the author that was first published on DataGuidance: 'Clear and Present Harm of AI - How Data Protection Principles may Help' (*DataGuidance,* 16 February 2024), available at www.dataguidance.com/opinion/international-clear-and-present-harm-ai-how-data.

[91] Provisions on the Administration of Deep Synthesis Internet Information Services, available at www.chinalawtranslate.com/en/deep-synthesis.

[92] Interim Measures for the Management of Generative Artificial Intelligence Services, available at www.chinalawtranslate.com/en/generative-ai-interim.

sectoral regulations in China that build on the same principles, including protection of personal data, management of training data and pre-deployment assessments.

ii. Data Protection Laws Support Pre-Deployment Tests Without Mandating Them

While some countries have or will soon be introducing AI regulations, they are a small (albeit influential) minority. However, many countries do have data protection laws. There is no need to wait for new AI regulations in respect of pre-deployment tests, because data protection authorities are already starting to issue guidance concerning the relevance and necessity of pre-deployment tests for AI systems that process personal data. Data management and transparency are areas that data protection laws have traditionally regulated. When AI systems use personal data for training or inference, data privacy principles on data quality and openness will apply.[93] Additionally, the principle that there should be reasonable security safeguards under data protection law extends to conducting adequate pre-deployment tests for any AI system that processes personal data.[94] There are many cases where, in the context of deterministic systems, organisations were found in breach of their protection obligation for failing to conduct adequate pre-deployment tests, thus resulting in unauthorised disclosure of personal data. This included the insufficient planning of UAT scenarios or the omission to conduct any vulnerability assessments.[95]

The security safeguards principle does not specify the nature or extent of pre-deployment tests. It is therefore sufficiently flexible to encompass new types of pre-deployment tests that are relevant and necessary for probabilistic systems. Where the AI system is deployed to make predictions, recommendations or decisions using personal data as input, it may be necessary to conduct pre-deployment tests for assurance of model performance, such as tests for explainability, repeatability and reproducibility. This is akin to SIT or UAT, as it provides assurance that users' input data – which could be personal data – is processed by the model in a manner that is expected, consistent and explainable. Likewise, tests for robustness are akin to cybersecurity testing of the trained model. This may be a necessary addition to complement system-level cybersecurity tests, such as VAPT.

Synthetic data can be used – and should be encouraged – for pre-deployment tests. However, there may be occasions where using personal data for this is necessary or desirable. Bias testing – or more accurately, de-biasing – is often cited as one such example. De-biasing helps to prevent unintended discrimination of segments of customers or end users. There may be situations where the use of identifiable information promotes the objectives of bias testing. In the field of responsible AI, bias testing is fast becoming de rigueur.

[93] For example, the OECD, 'Recommendation of the Council Concerning Guidelines Governing the Protection of Privacy and Transborder Flows of Personal Data' (11 July 2013).

[94] ibid.

[95] For example, *Re: SAP Asia Pte Ltd* [2021] SGPDPC 6 where the data controller did not properly scope the pre-launch UAT scenarios; and *Re: Jigyasa* [2020] SGPDPC 9 where the data controller did not conduct any form of security assessment.

Therefore, one may rightfully conclude that while the security safeguards principle does not expressly make such tests necessary, the fact that they are starting to become industry best practices could soon make it unreasonable to omit conducting some or all of them. As these practices develop, they can be expected to form the baseline standard of practice required to meet mandatory regulatory requirements, whether these be in the form of data protection law or AI regulations.

III. Post-Deployment

Models that have been trained and tested can be deployed to enable products and services to make recommendations, provide predictions or automate decision-making. Generative AI systems are also opening up new possibilities in content creation and in the analysis and retrieval of information. When deployed, models operate on input data from both the model deployer (eg, enterprise repository) and end users. For example, an e-commerce marketplace that uses recommendation systems to infer what customers may be interested in will depend on analysing each customer's purchase history and identifying closely related items from a list of products that its merchants are promoting to make the recommendations. Another example is an online image search service that allows its users to upload a probe image which is matched against its repository of scanned facial images to identify individuals that are either exact matches or whose biometric signatures are close matches. These illustrations highlight the necessity for two data sources: new user input data for the deployed machine learning models to function, and an enterprise repository that the model can access in order to provide an output.

A. Issues Arising in the Business-to-Customer Relationship

In the context of the B2C relationship, data privacy laws require that data controllers identify a legal basis for collecting and processing personal data. This applies no differently to situations where the product or service collects and processes personal data using machine learning models. Input data may be collected directly from end users, such as their preferences and biographical data provided through their account profile, or behavioural data collected indirectly through their interactions with the web page, such as when they click on an advertisement or provide a response to something they have viewed on social media pages, or whether they completed viewing a video. With generative AI systems, the prompts provided by end users may contain more than just context and instructions but could contain personal data and copyrighted material as well. There is also a question over whether there is copyright in the output that is generated, and if so, who authored it.

i. Processing personal data for inference

Automating business decisions and offering recommendations to customers are perhaps the most common archetypes of B2C deployments of AI. In respect of the former, platforms that support the gig economy have automated tasks such as profiling of individuals for the purpose of personalised rates for car-sharing, and assignment of jobs to gig-workers.[96] Some data protection laws, such as the GDPR, govern automated decision-making.[97] Recommendation systems have become de rigueur for behavioural advertising, social media feeds, song and movie streaming services and e-commerce marketplaces. In the context of behavioural advertisements, a series of litigation between Meta and the Irish Data Protection Commission has shown that consent is probably the safest legal basis to rely on.[98] Contract necessity is a possible legal basis provided that a less intrusive means does not exist; and the service provider's conduct and contract documentation are consistent with its intention to rely on this legal basis.[99] Legitimate interest is also a possible basis. However, where the interests can be met with a less intrusive means, then the balance is likely to be struck in favour of individuals' interests and fundamental rights. Further, users are unlikely to expect that a more intrusive means would be adopted.[100] Thus, insofar as digital advertising is concerned, the availability of *contextual* advertising as the less intrusive means makes it almost impossible to rely on contractual necessity or legitimate interests as legal bases for processing personal data for *behavioural* advertising.

These topics have been covered in detail in the preceding chapter. For this section, the following observations are made. First, although it is difficult to rely on either contractual necessity or legitimate interest as legal bases for behavioural advertising, it remains to be seen whether the bar is set equally high when personal data is used for recommendation systems in other contexts, such as song and movie streaming services and e-commerce marketplaces, where users may have higher expectations for the service to provide recommendations. Second, the upshot of this series of *Meta Ireland* decisions is that a tiered strategy for the processing of personal data for AI systems may be necessary. The bar for necessity – whether in the context of contractual necessity or the balancing test of legitimate interest – is set quite high. Thus, reliance on these legal bases should be reserved for AI systems that are less intrusive. Users' expectations are also relevant in this assessment, eg, whether the recommendation is an integral part of the user experience expected by end users. Where the processing allows the provision of a higher level of personalisation, it will be prudent to rely on consent. Third, with the entry into force

[96] *Automated Decision-Making under the GDPR: Practical Cases from Courts and Data Protection Authorities* (*Future of Privacy Forum*, May 2022) 9, 15.

[97] Changes have been introduced in the UK's Data (Access and Use) Act 2025 to further reduce the hurdles for automated decision-making – which is already restricted to automatic processing of sensitive personal data – by introducing substantial public interest as an additional ground: Art 22B(3)(b); likewise, the proposed EU Digital Omnibus Regulation will likely remove the right not to be subjected to automated decision-making and replace it with a white list of situations where this is permitted, ie, contractual necessity, safeguarding rights and freedoms, legitimate interests and explicit consent: proposed amendments to Art 22(1).

[98] Having tried unsuccessfully to rely on contractual necessity and legitimate interest, Meta has switched to relying on consent. It has also proposed a subscription service for users who do not want to receive advertisements, which is now facing challenges from consumer rights groups: S Bodoni, 'Meta Hit with E.U. Complaints Over 'Pay-or-Consent' Data Collection for Targeted Ads' (*Time*, 29 February 2024); S Bodoni, 'Meta Hit with Wave of Complaints that its 'Pay-or-Consent' Facebook and Instagram Deals are a 'Smokescreen' that Violates European Data Laws' (*Fortune*, 29 February 2024).

[99] Data Protection Commission (Ireland), *In the matter of LB, a complainant, concerning a complaint directed against Meta Platforms Ireland Limited in respect of the Facebook Service* (DPC Inquiry Reference IN-18-5-5, 31 December 2022) para 3.6.

[100] EDPB, *Urgent Binding Decision 01/2023 requested by the Norwegian SA for the ordering of final measures regarding Meta Platforms Ireland Ltd (Art. 66(2) GDPR)* (adopted on 27 October 2023).

of the Digital Services Act, there are additional constraints on the use of recommendation systems and the processing of personal data for recommendations. Very large online platforms and very large online search engines must provide options for their recommendation systems that are not based on profiling of individuals.[101] For other online platforms that deploy recommendation systems, there are new requirements for transparency of the main parameters that influence the recommendations that are proffered, and to provide means for end users to modify them.[102] The same requirements apply to recommendation systems deployed for serving personalised advertisements.[103]

ii. Authorship of Generated Content

Machine learning models have been deployed to enable specific functions, such as sharpening and applying different artistic or photographic effect filters to images. With the emergence of generative AI, end users have access to services that provide access to natural language queries in a question-and-answer format (eg, ChatGPT, Gemini and Copilot) and online services that enable the generation of images (eg, Dall-E, Midjourney and Stable Diffusion). To use these solutions, users provide input data, such as an image or (in the case of generative AI) their instructions through prompts. Users are responsible for the input data that they provide. For example, not using a copyrighted image or document without permission or giving instructions in their prompts that may lead to infringement of copyright (eg, generating images in the style of an artist).[104]

Ownership of intellectual property rights in the generated content and who the author or inventor ought to be is hotly debated. It is trite law that authorship and inventorship are tied to natural persons. In respect of Singapore's Copyright Act, the Court of Appeal in *Asia Pacific Publishing Pte Ltd v Pioneers & Leaders (Publishers) Pte Ltd* unequivocally stated that 'without the identification of a human author from whom the work originates, there can be no "original work" capable of copyright protection'.[105] Again in *Global Yellow Pages Ltd v Promedia Directories Pte Ltd*, the Court of Appeal reiterated that 'for copyright to subsist in any literary work, there must be an *authorial* creation that is *causally connected* with the *engagement of the human intellect*'. (emphasis added)[106] Likewise, the US Court of Appeal for the District of Columbia has similarly held that humanity is a necessary condition for authorship, explaining that provisions such as copyright ownership and duration, and inheritance of termination interest, are premised on human authorship.[107]

Can authorship of generated content be attributed to the person providing the prompts? There are interesting and divergent decisions on this question. The US Copyright Office's Copyright Review Board refused to register an artwork, *Théâtre D'opéra Spatial*, that was

[101] Regulation (EU) 2022/2065 of the European Parliament and of the Council of 19 October 2022 on a Single Market for Digital Services and amending Directive 2000/31/EC (Digital Services Act), Art 38.

[102] ibid Art 27.

[103] ibid Art 26(1)(d).

[104] MM Kircher, 'People Love Studio Ghibli. But Should They Be Able to Recreate It?' (*The New York Times*, 27 March 2025).

[105] *Asia Pacific Publishing Pte Ltd v Pioneers & Leaders (Publishers) Pte Ltd* [2011] 4 SLR 381 [82].

[106] *Global Yellow Pages Ltd v Promedia Directories Pte Ltd* [2017] 2 SLR 185 [24].

[107] *Stephen Thaler v US Copyright Office* (18 March 2025) (1:22-cv-01564) Court of Appeals for the District of Columbia 11–13.

generated by Jason Allen using Midjourney, a text-to-picture generative AI service.[108] Allen had provided numerous revisions and text prompts – at least 624 times – to arrive at the initial version of the image; thereafter, he used Adobe Photoshop to remove flaws and Gigapixel AI to upscale the image. The Copyright Office stated that the artwork could be registered if it contained sufficient human authorship after excluding AI-generated content. The Review Board concluded that the initial version of the image that was produced by Midjourney was not a product of human authorship because Allen's prompts merely influenced how the AI system generated the image. They did not operate as instructions for the creation of a specific result because Midjourney does not treat prompts as instructions. This accounted for why Allen had to experiment with over 600 prompts. As the initial image remained in substantial form in the final image, the Board refused to register the artwork.

This approach echoes an earlier decision in the *Zarya of the Dawn* application,[109] where in respect of a comic book, the US Copyright Office found that the text and the selection and arrangements of the images and text (ie, compilation) were original works of human authorship that could be registered. However, the individual images that were produced using Midjourney were not registrable. Even though the applicant had provided 'hundreds or thousands of descriptive prompts', these merely guided Midjourney. The process could not be controlled by the applicant because it was impossible to predict what Midjourney would create. By reason of this, the Copyright Office felt that the traditional elements of authorship in the images originated from Midjourney and not from the applicant. A similar approach was again taken by the US Copyright Office concerning an AI-generated book, allowing registration for the selection, coordination and arrangement of generated text but not for the text that was generated by AI.[110]

By contrast, the Beijing Internet Court reached the opposite conclusion in *Li Yunkai v Liu Yuanchun*.[111] Li had generated an image using Stable Diffusion, and Liu had used it as an illustration for a poem on his blog without permission. Li demonstrated to the Court his process for creating the image. He started by providing prompts (including negative prompts) to generate an initial image and subsequently made sequential changes to specific parameters to create different sequential versions, before arriving at the final version. The Court found that Li's choice of prompt words and adjustments of parameters reflected his choice and arrangement. Hence, there was sufficient originality for the image to be protected as a work of fine art. Further, the Court opined that Stable Diffusion was used by Li as a tool and that there was no question that Li was the creator of the image.[112]

[108] Copyright Review Board's letter dated 5 September 2023 re: Second Request for Reconsideration for Refusal to Register Théâtre D'opéra Spatial (SR # 1-11743923581; Correspondence ID: 1-5T5320R), available at www.copyright.gov/rulings-filings/review-board/docs/Theatre-Dopera-Spatial.pdf.

[109] US Copyright Office's letter dated 21 February 2023 re: Zarya of the Dawn (Registration # Vau001480196), available at copyright.gov/docs/zarya-of-the-dawn.pdf.

[110] K Knibbs, 'How One Author Pushed the Limit of AI Copyright' (*Wired*, 17 April 2024).

[111] Beijing Internet Court Civil Judgment (2023) Jing 0491 Min Chu No 11279, available at english.bjinternetcourt.gov.cn/pdf/BeijingInternetCourtCivilJudgment112792023.pdf.

[112] There are other Chinese decisions that have followed the reasoning in *Li v Liu* in recognising subsistence of copyright when using generative AI as a tool: see Xu Yuanxiao, 'China's Controversial Court Rulings on AI Output—and How It May Affect People in the US' (3 April 2025) available at www.authorsalliance.org/2025/04/03/chinas-controversial-court-rulings-on-ai-output-and-how-it-may-affect-people-in-the-us/.

The key difference between these cases appears to be the extent to which the applicant was able to demonstrate the relationship between his prompts (and changes to parameters) and how they progressively altered successive versions as they built up to form the final version of the generated image. The first challenge lies in documenting the input at each step of the process in creating the image and in assessing whether there was sufficient creativity in the series of prompts. The second challenge is attributing this creativity to the author of the prompts. If the policy for copyright systems is to encourage and reward creativity,[113] there is much to recommend provisions like section 9(3) of the UK Copyright, Designs and Patents Act 1988, which provides clear rules for the *attribution of authorship* when computers are used to generate works: 'the author shall be taken to be the person by whom the arrangements necessary for the creation of the work are undertaken'. This approach helps focus the inquiry on where creativity may be found: ie, the instructions contained in the prompts.[114] However, a rule of attribution does not obviate the requirement of creativity: the prompts must still be intellectual creations, and the AI-generated work must still be original.[115]

B. Responsibilities of Model Deployers

When machine learning models are deployed in AI systems, they not only need end-user input data to function, but they are also often integrated with an enterprise repository. For example, in the case of the biometric search that was offered in the *Clearview AI* case, the probe image uploaded by a user was matched against a database of facial images. Many enterprise deployments of LLMs use Retrieval-Augmented Generation, where the natural language query is processed and relevant information retrieved from an enterprise repository is used to provide grounding for the prompt that is sent to the LLM, which then generates a response.[116]

The necessity of identifying a legal basis for collecting and using end-user personal data as input applies equally to personal data that may be contained in the enterprise repository. However, as the cases have taught us, there are other aspects of data protection laws that also demand attention.

i. Providing for Data Subject Rights

When an AI system integrates with an enterprise repository that contains personal data, data protection issues may arise. Take the *Clearview AI* case as an example. The UK ICO found – specific to the database – that the inclusion of images scraped from the

[113] *Li v Liu*, ibid [13]: 'The core purpose of the copyright system is to encourage creation. And creation and AI technology can only prosper by properly applying the copyright system and using the legal means to encourage more people to use the latest tools to create.'

[114] For a contrary view that statutory recognition of compute-generated works is unnecessary, see Singapore Academy of Law, 'Reform of Copyright Subsistence in Light of Generative AI', at 5–17.

[115] The UK IPO is reviewing the protection of computer-generated works (CGW). The stated policy preference is to remove this provision if there is insufficient evidence that s 9(3) has had positive effect on the production and protection of CGW: UK IPO, *Copyright and AI: Consultation*, Section D.2.

[116] AWS, 'What is RAG (Retrieval-Augmented Generation)?', available at aws.amazon.com/what-is/retrieval-augmented-generation; IBM, 'What is Retrieval-Augmented Generation?' (22 August 2023), available at research.ibm.com/blog/retrieval-augmented-generation-RAG.

internet breached the fairness principle because end users would not have expected that their online images would be scraped, stored and indexed for image matching. Clearview also did not have processes to remove images from their database when end users changed their privacy settings.[117] Additionally, there was a lack of transparency over how personal data was processed, there was no retention policy, and data subjects were not provided with adequate rights of access and erasure.[118] Hence, the need to provide effective data subject rights cannot be overlooked.

A number of data protection authorities have recently issued guidance documents on compliance with data protection principles when deploying AI systems.[119] Thus, model deployers should provide information about how personal data is processed and secured during the model development and deployment life cycle (eg, what data was used in the training dataset and whether input data is used for federated learning) and measures taken to achieve fairness and reasonableness for recommendations, predictions and decisions. For higher-impact AI systems, information should also be provided about how human agency and oversight are implemented. Where an enterprise repository is used at the deployment stage, personal data in the repository must be accurate. Processes must also be in place to enable data subjects to access their data and to request corrections. For deployments in or targeting the EU, processes should also be in place to allow EU residents to opt out of automated decision-making that has a legal effect on them and to request erasure of personal data.

ii. Minimising risk of contributory liability for copyright infringement by end users

Model deployers ought to be familiar with the risks that may arise from the use of their AI systems. End users may use the AI system in ways that infringe copyright. The balance of providing a service that enables creativity while preventing abuse is not an easy one to strike. It is advisable to implement technical measures as a matter of due diligence. In this regard, the effectiveness of post-training, input and output filters as technical measures to avoid – and possibly defeat – claims of copyright infringement have been discussed.[120]

[117] Clearview AI Inc Enforcement Notice, paras 61–62; Clearview AI Inc Monetary Penalty Notice, paras 66–67.

[118] Clearview AI Inc Enforcement Notice, paras 64, 65, 68–69; Clearview AI Inc Monetary Penalty Notice, paras 69, 70, 73–74.

[119] Office of the Privacy Commissioner of Personal Data, Hong Kong, 'Artificial Intelligence: Model Personal Data Protection Framework' (June 2024); PDPC Advisory Guidelines on Use of Personal Data in AI Recommendation and Decision Systems (n 19); Office of the Privacy Commissioner of Canada, 'Principles for Responsible, Trustworthy and Privacy-Protective Generative AI Technologies' (7 December 2023), available at /priv.gc.ca/en/privacy-topics/technology/artificial-intelligence/gd_principles_ai; Global Privacy Assembly, 'Resolution on Generative Artificial Intelligence Systems' (45th Closed Session, 20 October 2023); CNIL, 'Artificial Intelligence: CNIL Unveils its First Answers for Innovative and Privacy-friendly AI' (15 October 2023), available at www.cnil.fr/en/artificial-intelligence-cnil-unveils-its-first-answers-innovative-and-privacy-friendly-ai and 'AI how-to sheets', available at www.cnil.fr/en/ai-how-sheets; UK ICO, 'Guidance on AI and Data Protection' (updated 15 March 2023), available at ico.org.uk/for-organisations/uk-gdpr-guidance-and-resources/artificial-intelligence/guidance-on-ai-and-data-protection.

[120] See nn 63–65 and the discussion in the accompanying main text.

Taking a leaf from copyright safe-harbour provisions,[121] the implementation of a notice-and-takedown system should be considered a baseline practice. Omission to implement such measures may result in findings of copyright infringement. In the Hangzhou *Ultraman* case, the generative AI service in question enabled users to upload their own training data to create Low-Rank Adaptation (LoRA) models that can be published for access by other users of the platform. Users uploaded images of the Ultraman character, created and published LoRA models that enabled generation of Ultraman images. The generative AI service provider had stated in its terms of use that it does not review user uploaded or generated content and it also did not implement system for handling complaints. The service provider was held to have failed to take reasonable measures to prevent infringement and was found to be liable for contributory infringement. It was ordered to pay a fine and to take steps to remove the infringing images uploaded by users and LoRA models created by users.[122] This case illustrates how notice-and-takedown systems remain relevant to shield online intermediaries from contributory liability, at least for hosting of user generated content that may be infringing.

iii. Labelling and watermarking of Generated Content

An area of growing concern which has drawn the attention of policy makers is the watermarking and labelling of content created using generative AI. These terms are sometimes used interchangeably. For the purpose of this section, labels are notifications associated with the generated content that are easily perceived by end users, while watermarks are machine-readable information embedded in the metadata of the file. The main driver for labelling and watermarking is the deleterious effect of deep fakes, and how these can promote misinformation. The proliferation of generative AI services makes it easier for the creation of deep fakes. Labelling and watermarking are mentioned in a number of generative AI policy documents. The White House's Executive Order on the Safe, Secure and Trustworthy Development and Use of Artificial Intelligence calls for the development of standards and techniques for watermarking or labelling synthetic content.[123] Californian state law has picked this up and made it a requirement for large online platforms to detect and display standards-compliant provenance data, including those labelling generative AI content.[124] There are similar developments on either side of the North American continent. Across the Atlantic, the EU AI Act also requires developers of generative AI models to support watermarking of generated

[121] eg, Singapore's Copyright Act 2021, Division 2 – Remedies against network service providers, Subdivision 2 Restrictions of remedies against rights infringements in course of providing network services, and US Digital Millennium Copyright Act, section 512.

[122] (2024) Zhe0192 Minchu No. 1587, available at www.ciplawyer.cn/articles/155988.html; and (2024) Zhe01 Civil Final Appeal No. 10332, available at www.ciplawyer.cn/articles/155989.html.

[123] White House Executive Order on the Safe, Secure and Trustworthy Development and Use of Artificial Intelligence (30 October 2023), available at www.whitehouse.gov/briefing-room/presidential-actions/2023/10/30/executive-order-on-the-safe-secure-and-trustworthy-development-and-use-of-artificial-intelligence.

[124] AB-853 California AI Transparency Act amending section 22757 of the Business and Professions Code (approved 13 October 2025).

content to enable detection and tracing.[125] The UK IPO is also consulting on whether generative AI output should be labelled.[126] Across the Pacific, South Korea's newly enacted AI Basic Act requires deployers to label generated content and to display such information clearly to users.[127] Likewise, Singapore's proposed Model AI Governance Framework for Generative AI also identifies watermarking as a key technical solution for content provenance.

In this area, the Chinese regulators have taken the lead. The Provisions on the Administration of Deep Synthesis Internet Information Services[128] that regulate deep fakes impose an obligation on service providers to include a conspicuous label on the generated content.[129] This is complemented by a provision that prohibits the deletion, alteration or concealment of the labels.[130] Further, the Interim Measures for the Management of Generative Artificial Intelligence Services reinforces this by mandating that generative AI providers label generated content to the same standards.[131] It should be highlighted that the Interim Measures cast the net wider, as it does not appear to distinguish whether the content generated from generative AI services qualifies as deep fakes when imposing the labelling requirement. China has also issued technical standards specifying that generated content must be explicitly labelled so as to be clearly perceived by end users (eg, common symbols or text and voice notifications) and that watermarks must be embedded in the metadata of the file.[132]

Watermarks need to be embedded at the point of creation and retained throughout its distribution so that the generated content can be appropriately labelled when displayed to end users. Hence, the development and adoption of technical standards for watermarking is key to success. There are currently multiple standards under development: eg, the C2PA standard[133] and the IPTC standard.[134] The embedding of watermarks at the creation of the generated content enables not only the recording of content provenance but also enables the platforms that are used for distribution to label the generated content when it is displayed to end users. The developments that focus on either encouraging or mandating adoption of watermarking standards will ensure that developers and platforms – direct messaging, online search and social media inclusive – respect watermarking standards and label generated content when

[125] A Beiten, 'The AI Act - The Agreement and What It Means' (*Lexology*, 9 January 2024), available at www.lexology.com/library/detail.aspx?g=4db2cd50-a035-489a-8013-81a39e262f23; Burges Salmon LLP, 'How do you Know if Content is AI-Created? Generative AI and Watermarking' (*Lexology*, 8 January 2024), available at www.lexology.com/library/detail.aspx?g=8e996bd8-19c0-402b-af4a-283ec152d201.

[126] UK IPO, *Copyright and AI: Consultation*, Section D.5.

[127] Basic Act on the Development of Artificial Intelligence and the Establishment of a Foundation for Trustworthiness (Law No 20676), Art 31.

[128] Original text available at www.cac.gov.cn/2022-12/11/c_1672221949354811.htm; English translation available at www.chinalawtranslate.com/en/deep-synthesis/.

[129] Art 17.

[130] Art 18.

[131] Art 12; Original text available at www.cac.gov.cn/2023-07/13/c_1690898327029107.htm; English translation available at www.chinalawtranslate.com/en/generative-ai-interim/.

[132] Cyberspace Administration of China, 'Measures for Labelling of AI-Generated Synthetic Content' (7 March 2025): original text available at www.cac.gov.cn/2025-03/14/c_1743654684782215.htm; English translation available at www.chinalawtranslate.com/en/ai-labeling/.

[133] For more information on the C2PA standard, see c2pa.org/specifications/specifications/1.2/explainer/Explainer.html.

[134] For more information on the IPTC standard, see iptc.org/standards/photo-metadata/iptc-standard.

displaying them. There is also work to be done in establishing a baseline standard of practice over what information ought to be provided and how accessible they are to end users. An ecosystem approach is therefore necessary, starting with digital watermarking standards, embedding and preserving digital watermarks throughout the distribution pathway and developing industry practices on labelling. In this area, it is encouraging to note that there are voluntary initiatives in developing such practices.[135]

While the preceding measures can be effective for well-meaning developers and platforms, the risk that malicious actors may remove or alter watermarks must also be borne in mind. This is where a leaf can be taken from copyright law on the protection of rights management information (RMI) – the removal or alteration of RMI is an offence.[136] The Chinese deep fake regulation has taken a step in this direction by prohibiting the deletion, alteration or concealment of the labels for both deep fakes and content created using generative AI services.

IV. Concluding Remarks

If there is anything the foregoing survey has highlighted, it is that extant policies and laws support the access and use of data for the development and deployment of AI systems. This should not be surprising given that AI did not emerge out of nowhere. The machine learning models that are driving the present wave of development and innovation are built on data analytics. Data protection and copyright laws have been tuned to enable data analytics. Machine learning pivots the retrospective abilities of data analytics to recommendations, predictions and generation. Unsurprisingly, it stands to benefit from the policies and regulations that have been crafted to support data analytics. Hence, copyright and data privacy laws support the secondary use of data for model development and provide guardrails for collecting input data and the implementation of enterprise repositories that support deployment of machine learning models. As discussed above, even the re-use of publicly available data through web scraping was anticipated. However, the extent of collection and the fact that pre-training of foundational generative AI models is exclusive to a small number of the best-funded companies with access to high-power computing infrastructure have given rise to a sense of unease and helplessness. This in turn has given cause for rights holders to raise copyright challenges over fair use and for data protection authorities to raise the level of scrutiny over data privacy concerns.

Machine learning models present opportunities for innovation as they are deployed to provide product features and functionalities that were hitherto unavailable. Regulatory sandboxes provide an avenue for regulators and businesses to engage in constructive co-creation of policies that can support innovation and provide policy clarity. The probabilistic nature of machine learning models requires the development of different ways to test them before they are deployed, and different methods to achieve transparency.

[135] M Bickert, 'Our Approach to Labelling AI-Generated Content and Manipulated Media' (*Meta*, 5 April 2024), available at about.fb.com/news/2024/04/metas-approach-to-labeling-ai-generated-content-and-manipulated-media.

[136] For example, Singapore's Copyright Act 2021, s 411.

This is an area where data protection laws can provide interim regulatory coverage when personal data is processed, either as training data or input data. Comprehensive AI regulations will eventually arrive and can build on these governance and transparency practices.

Generative AI introduces a new front in the pursuit of responsible AI. Generative AI – as the name suggests – enables the creation of content. As more end users get their hands on generative AI tools, there is good reason to be concerned about what they are generating and how user-generated content is distributed. Authorship of user-generated content will test copyright policies as the courts are asked to decide whether generative AI solutions are authors' tools or are themselves the authors. While users should be primarily responsible for how they generate content and what they do with it, it is almost certain that developers of the tools that they use, as well as the platforms that distribute user-generated content, will be expected to step up efforts to provide a safe online environment for end users. Developments in digital watermarking and labelling can be expected to lead to greater responsibilities for online intermediaries to moderate their platforms.

PART III

Truth Decay

11

Introduction to Truth Decay

DAVID NEUBERGER AND PHILIP JEYARETNAM

Disinformation is something more than just wrong or inaccurate information. Where something that is not true is shared without malice, often in the positive belief that it is in fact true, it is more properly described as misinformation. The European Commission in its 2018 Communication defined disinformation as 'verifiably false or misleading information that is created, presented and disseminated for economic gain or to intentionally deceive the public and may cause public harm'.[1]

The recent wave of disinformation and misinformation has been described as the phenomenon of 'truth decay' in a 2018 RAND study.[2] In it, the authors describe four related trends:

(1) increasing disagreement about facts and analytical interpretation of facts and data;

(2) a blurring of the line between opinion and fact;

(3) the increasing relative volume, and resulting influence, of opinion and personal experience over fact;

(4) declining trust in formerly respected sources of factual information.

A useful framework for organising thoughts about disinformation is the 'ABC' framework describing the key vectors that characterise the transmission of disinformation, namely manipulative *actors*, deceptive *behaviour* and harmful *content*.[3]

While this topic appears distinct from the topics of previous chapters concerning the implications of artificial intelligence (AI), it in fact relates to them because AI powers the chatbots that have been used to amplify disinformation over the past decade or more. The spread of disinformation piggybacks on the algorithmic amplification that

[1] European Commission, 'Communication from the Commission to the European Parliament, the Council, the European Economic and Social Committee and the Committee of the Regions, Tackling Online Disinformation: A European Approach' COM(2018) 236 final, para 2.1.

[2] J Kavanagh and MD Rich, *Truth Decay: An Initial Exploration of the Diminishing Role of Facts and Analysis in American Public Life* (Santa Monica, RAND Corporation, 2018) (*Truth Decay*) 8.

[3] C Francois, 'Actors, Behaviors, Content: A Disinformation ABC, Highlighting Three Vectors of Viral Deception to Guide Industry & Regulatory Responses' (Transatlantic High Level Working Group on Content Moderation Online and Freedom of Expression, 20 September 2019).

social media companies have adopted as part of their business models. Moreover, AI is already in use to create harmful content, such as deepfakes. Dr Shashi Jayakumar, in his address at the 4th Judicial Roundtable, identified that what is new today is that falsehoods may be propagated cheaply, quickly and at scale. The velocity of information flow to numerous recipients at the same time enables the proliferation of falsehoods at speed, including through social media.

The first of these vectors identified in the 'ABC' framework calls for elaboration. Some bad actors create or disseminate disinformation for financial motives. For example, companies may misinform to protect the profitability of their businesses. Other actors may have political or geopolitical ends. A special class of bad actors would be some foreign governments, seeking to weaken the societies of their geopolitical rivals or even overthrow other governments. Disinformation achieves success by preying on prejudice and bias, driving hatred of others and bolstering tribal loyalties such that a group may take as a badge of identity something they actually know to be untrue. The bad actor typically exploits human psychological weaknesses to magnify or multiply the message.

In his paper submitted for the 4th Judicial Roundtable, Dr Lee McIntyre argued that it is critical to appreciate that the root of disinformation is not ignorance or faulty reasoning. These are only potential contributors to its spread. Rather, disinformation always begins with a lie, and as he notes 'for a lie, there has to be a liar'. He went on to argue that the liar will be 'someone who had an interest at stake', illustrating his point by referring to how tobacco companies confused the public about the link between lung cancer and smoking:

> If we look at where modern science denial started it's easy to see that the interests can be economic. When the big tobacco companies decided to 'fight the science' which showed that there was a link between cigarette smoking and lung cancer, they engaged in a campaign of strategic denialism. Their weapon of choice at that point was 'public relations', which allowed them to manufacture doubt where there wasn't any. And it worked. The public became confused. They suddenly thought that the scientific consensus was controversial or open for debate. 'The scientific link between smoking and lung cancer has never been conclusively proven', the tobacco companies said. And they were right. But that's only because the scientific link between ANY two things has never been 'proven'. No matter how good the evidence, scientific consensus always falls short of certainty. That's just how inductive reasoning works. So the tobacco executives said that we 'needed more study', which allowed them to buy enough time to sell more cigarettes. In their brilliant book Merchants of Doubt, Naomi Oreskes and Erik Conway tell the story of how this success created a blueprint that was later followed by the fossil fuel companies when they decided to deny global warming. And that worked too.
>
> So now it's beginning to make some sense right? Liars lie because it benefits them. The rewards don't always have to be economic -- they can also be ideological or political -- but the point is that the people who create the lies behind a disinformation campaign do so because they want something, and their route to getting it is to create an army of deniers, who are duped by their disinformation.

Dr McIntyre continued with the point that campaigns of disinformation often go beyond getting one side to believe a falsehood. They seek to engender hatred of people who do not believe the same falsehood. Another objective is to foster cynicism: 'In fact, maybe you'll become so cynical as to believe that there is no such thing as truth, or that if truth CAN be known it's only available from the leader of the team you're on.'

Former Australian Prime Minister Malcolm Turnbull has identified the profitability of what he terms anger-tainment – news coverage that draws viewers and readers by appealing to their outrage and anger – as driving polarisation, corrosion of trust in institutions and dividing society. Specifically, he has charged that Rupert Murdoch's media empire, including Fox and News Corp, has 'sought to enrage Americans, divide Americans, and divide them against each other, and it has knowingly spread lies, most consequentially the one … where Donald Trump claimed to have won the 2020 election'.[4]

Dr McIntyre had stressed the need to focus on the link in the chain that is amplification, given how hard it is to stop disinformation at source or to reduce people's desire to believe disinformation that fits with their own predilections or identity.

The discussion thus far proceeds on the premise that at the least some statements are demonstrably false, even if not conclusively so. With this premise in mind, it may be possible to design responses that are targeted at false statements and so do not impede or hinder efforts to determine the truth, efforts that are themselves of critical importance to human flourishing. Indeed, sieving out falsehoods protects reasoned discourse, which is foundational to democracy.

In his presentation, Dr Jayakumar spoke about the Singapore experience of addressing falsehoods. He prefaced his exposition by referring to the social purpose underlying Singapore's legislative attempts to counter disinformation. It is to protect the realm of public discourse and, in turn, to fortify democracy. Facts – both agreements on what the facts are and on the methods for establishing the facts – are necessary for rational discussion to proceed. In the words of Singapore's Minister for Law K Shanmugam:[5]

> A key foundation of a democracy is public discourse. Ideally, public discourse will help citizens understand complex policy issues, it will guide policy-makers to make optimal decisions, it will shape differing viewpoints, and expand common ground. … A critical piece of infrastructure in these conversations is fact, and the infrastructure of fact. Like public infrastructure, society depends on it. It provides society with a shared reality. This is necessary so that we can have diversity without conflict, and public participation, while still getting decisions made. Without it, our political system will malfunction.

Dr Jayakumar described two key pieces of legislation. The first is the Protection from Online Falsehoods and Manipulation Act (POFMA), which was enacted in 2019. Among other things, POFMA empowers ministers of the government of the day to direct the issue of a correction notice requiring websites and other online platforms to publish fact-checking links next to the false statement of fact. The minister must first conclude that it is in the public interest to issue the direction. The person against whom the notice is issued has a right to appeal to court. The principal grounds of appeal would be where the statement is not one of fact but an opinion, or the person notified shows that it is a true statement of fact.[6]

[4] P Karp, 'Former Australian PM Malcolm Turnbull Says Rupert Murdoch's "Anger-tainment" Damaged the Democratic World' (*The Guardian*, 22 September 2023), available at www.theguardian.com/media/2023/sep/22/former-australian-pm-malcolm-turnbull-comments-rupert-murdoch.

[5] K Shanmugam, Second Reading Speech on the Protection from Online Falsehoods and Manipulation Bill (7 May 2019) (Singapore), paras 102 and 105.

[6] Protection from Online Falsehoods and Manipulation Act 2019 (Singapore), s 17(5).

The second piece of legislation is the Foreign Interference (Countermeasures) Act (FICA), which was enacted in 2021. FICA empowers the Minister for Home Affairs to investigate hostile information campaigns conducted by foreign actors, including by issuing directions to social media platforms for the disclosure of information or requiring them to carry warnings about hostile information campaigns. Persons falling into various categories, such as political office holders, members of Parliament and members of the central executive committees of political parties, are defined as politically significant persons, and they are thereby subject to disclosure requirements concerning potential foreign influence over them. In addition, others may be designated as politically significant persons so that the same requirements apply to them as well.

Legal remedies, such as correction notices, address individual instances of disinformation. But there are broader systemic issues as well. Some societies are easier prey to campaigns of disinformation. It is important to consider how societies may be strengthened to better resist disinformation. There are other strategies for countering disinformation that attack the root of the problem. One key measure would be raising general levels of education and promoting critical thinking. After all, the opposite of, and indeed the antidote to, disinformation is reasoned discourse. Reasoned discourse depends on social ground rules for working out the facts and what those facts are. Broadening acceptance of such ground rules is one of the aims of education.

Another measure could be the way in which constitutional systems are designed and operate. Societies that have constitutional arrangements that promote political compromise and the middle ground as well as actively include those at the margins of the community are better inoculated against disinformation. Political polarisation, social fragmentation and personal disillusionment are not inevitable conditions of the modern world. One example of a constitutional arrangement that promotes the middle ground and fosters engagement is compulsory voting in national elections. This is a feature of both the Australian and Singaporean political systems. A recent study[7] shows how compulsory voting pushes party platforms toward the median voter's preferences, thus directly decreasing party polarisation, defined as the distance between party platforms. Other studies have suggested that compulsory voting promotes participation in the political process even beyond the act of voting.[8]

The preceding discussion of the broader policy challenges posed by the spectre of disinformation frames the specific challenges faced by the courts and judges, which are discussed in the next two chapters of this book. These challenges may be organised under three heads. First, in terms of the judicial role and function, one might ask how the legitimacy of judicial decisions may be preserved if court decisions are perceived to be nothing more than a disputable source of information, as well as how the court's forensic role of determining the facts will be impacted by the ever-growing sophistication of fakery in terms of documents, images and video.

Second, questions arise in relation to the conduct of parties, their experts and counsel within the courtroom. How do guidelines and codes of conduct need to be updated

[7] A Oprea, L Martin and G Brennan, 'Moving toward the Median: Compulsory Voting and Political Polarization' [2024] *American Political Science Review* 1951.

[8] E Chapman, 'The Distinctive Value of Elections and the Case for Compulsory Voting' (2019) 63 *American Journal of Political Science* 101.

in an age of disinformation? What other measures should be taken to reinforce the credibility and integrity of counsel and, more broadly, the ethos of the legal profession? A particular concern has been the increased use of social media by lawyers for business promotion. Some lawyers describing the decision of the court on social media to attract prospective clients may do so inaccurately or in ways that bring the court into disrepute. There should be urgent consideration of how such social media posts should be addressed where they do not amount to contempt of court under traditional doctrines of law but nonetheless have an insidious effect on public trust in courts.

Third, given the connection between disinformation and the corrosion and erosion of trust in institutions, questions arise concerning how courts can preserve institutional legitimacy and how they can enhance communications and outreach to address criticisms and renew public trust.

In chapter twelve, David Goddard examines the role of the courts in the face of disinformation, misinformation and truth decay. He notes that courts are accustomed to dealing with contested facts and evaluating the testimony offered by parties and witnesses. The courts have developed processes to make reliable factual findings notwithstanding intentional falsehoods or self-serving narratives. The concept of factual inquiry, based on evidence, originated in courts before spreading to other fields. However, he recognises that the common law system does not claim absolute authority in determining facts. Courts make findings based on the evidence presented, reaching conclusions to a specified degree of confidence. Leaving aside the laying down of legal principle, the specific findings of fact bind only the parties involved in that case. Judgments in one case generally have no influence on subsequent cases involving different parties. The court's primary function is not to establish authoritative facts for society. Instead, the trial process offers a model for evidence-based inquiry and scepticism, demonstrating how to reach provisional conclusions in an uncertain world. By doing so, they encourage robust processes for evaluating claims and promote scepticism toward less reliable sources of information.

In his chapter focused on the Australian experience (chapter thirteen),[9] Andrew Bell first discusses the general phenomenon of truth decay, before examining how this trend may be exacerbated by generative AI (as was also observed earlier in this chapter). In respect of the former, he includes an illustration of 'truth decay' from criminal justice and sentencing, where the public both mistakenly believes crime rates to be on the rise and wrongly views judges as too lenient in sentencing. He highlights how public perception diverges from reality because of the public's emotional responses, the media's sensationalist approach and human fallibility in focusing on anecdotal examples, which may in fact be outliers.

Bell also notes that courts are increasingly called upon to deal with finding facts outside the traditional context with commissions of inquiry or judicial review of executive actions. This is testament to the regard in which courts and judges are held when it comes to determining the facts and getting to the bottom of complex issues. Nonetheless, this raises the question of whether this is an apt response to a world where truth is ever more contested in that the legal forensic process affords a better way to establish the

[9] *Truth Decay* (see n 2 above).

foundation of truth for reasoned discourse and social and political debate. An alternative view might be that ready recourse to judges as factfinders for controversial matters risks damaging the judicial institution as a whole by drawing it into contested areas of policy and even the political fray.

The discussion in this chapter, and in those that follow, suggests to the authors that while there is no magic bullet to defeat lies and ensure the triumph of truth, there are important safeguards that can be put in place to safeguard public discourse and trust in public institutions.

In broad terms, our collective challenge is to improve the culture. People should be educated and encouraged to approach sources of information in an informed and critical, rather than a prejudiced and credulous, state of mind. And they should be prepared to engage with and discuss evidence as well as beliefs. More specifically, there is a heavy burden on judges, lawyers, and all those responsible for the rule of law, to lead by example in maintaining a high standard when relaying, finding, or recording facts and, where appropriate, in exposing disinformation.

12

Ascertaining Facts in an Uncertain World: The Role of the Courts

DAVID GODDARD

I. Overview

What challenges do disinformation and misinformation pose for:

(a) the courts' forensic role of determining the facts?
(b) the legitimacy of judicial decisions (if court decisions are perceived to be nothing more than a disputable source of information)?

The authors of an influential study on 'truth decay' published by the RAND Corporation in 2018 defined disinformation as '[f]alse or misleading information spread intentionally, usually to achieve some political or economic objective, influence public attitudes, or hide the truth'.[1] They defined misinformation as false or misleading information that is spread unintentionally, by error or mistake.[2] In the world of social media, disinformation is all too common, and misinformation is rife.

Disinformation and misinformation contribute to the phenomenon of 'truth decay' that is the subject of the RAND study, which the authors describe as a set of four related trends (as highlighted in chapter eleven):

(a) increasing disagreement about facts and analytical interpretation of facts and data;
(b) a blurring of the line between opinion and fact;
(c) the increasing relative volume, and resulting influence, of opinion and personal experience over fact; and
(d) declining trust in formerly respected sources of factual information.

Sundaresh Menon has described 'truth decay' as the devaluation of truth in our societies, and the fracturing of our communities into factions that increasingly fail to recognise

[1] J Kavanagh and M D Rich, *Truth Decay: An Initial Exploration of the Diminishing Role of Facts and Analysis in American Public Life* (Santa Monica, RAND Corporation, 2018) 8.
[2] ibid 10.

the same truths.[3] The rise of disconcerting terms such as 'truthiness'[4] and 'alternative facts'[5] is just one sobering symptom of this trend.

This is not a wholly new phenomenon – parallels can be drawn with other periods of rapid social change and breakdown of epistemological authority, as for example during the Reformation in Europe and England in the sixteenth and seventeenth centuries. But it has been convincingly argued by Professor Robert Post of Yale University that the internet and social media differ from all earlier forms of mass media in at least three ways: zero marginal cost, integration with life tasks, and interactivity. These factors combine to pose a number of significant challenges to the functioning of democracies, and to the public sphere more generally.[6] They strongly engage human tendencies to believe statements based on repetition, and to adopt and espouse beliefs held by a group with which one identifies, without reference to – or in spite of – evidence to the contrary.[7]

What are the implications of these challenges for courts? What do courts have to offer their communities by way of response?

The (tentative) answer proffered in this chapter has three parts.

First, courts are very familiar with contested facts, and with accounts given by parties and witnesses with a strong interest in the outcome of the dispute. Litigation for high stakes provides fertile ground for intentional falsehoods, and for honest but self-serving reconstructions of events. Courts are also very familiar with opinions proffered as if they were fact. Common law courts have developed processes that enable them to make sufficiently reliable factual findings to determine proceedings in the face of disinformation and misinformation. Indeed, as explained below, the very concept of a 'fact' ascertained by means of an evidence-based inquiry is one that appears to have first emerged in the courts before spreading to the natural sciences and other fields in the seventeenth and early eighteenth centuries.

Second, the common law makes very modest claims to epistemological authority for the findings made by a court in relation to a particular factual controversy. A court engaged in fact-finding must determine whether it is satisfied of certain matters to a specified level of confidence (generally the balance of probabilities in civil proceedings, or beyond reasonable doubt in criminal proceedings) on the basis of the evidence that the parties have chosen to place before the court. The answer may be that the evidence the parties adduce is not sufficient to satisfy the court – with the result that no finding at all is made.[8] Where a finding is made, the court need not and should not make any

[3] S Menon, 'After the Fall of Babel: The Courts in a Post-truth World', speech at the Supreme and Federal Courts' Judges Conference 2023 (23 January 2023).

[4] The quality of seeming or being felt to be true, even if not necessarily true: for an account of the origins of the term, see www.nytimes.com/2010/10/17/magazine/17FOB-onlanguage-t.html.

[5] For the origins of this phrase, see en.wikipedia.org/wiki/Alternative_facts.

[6] R Post, 'The Internet, Democracy and Misinformation' in R J Krotoszynski Jr, A Koltay and C Garden (eds), *Disinformation, Misinformation and Democracy: Legal Approaches in Comparative Context* (Cambridge, Cambridge University Press, 2025).

[7] See T Sharot and C R Sunstein, *Look Again: The Power of Noticing What Was Always There* (London, The Bridge Street Press, 2024) ch 7; and J Rauch, *The Constitution of Knowledge: A Defense of Truth* (Washington DC, Brookings Institution Press, 2021) ch 2.

[8] For an entertaining example, see S Gageler, 'Truth and Justice, and Sheep' (2018) 46 *Australian Bar Review* 205, 206–207.

claim to certainty in respect of that finding. Importantly, the judge's finding of fact binds only the parties to the proceeding in which that finding was made – others are free to litigate that same issue in other proceedings. Prior judgments in proceedings involving others generally carry no weight in subsequent proceedings – indeed, they are generally not even admissible in subsequent proceedings involving other parties as evidence of facts found. We should not be worried about court decisions being seen as a disputable source of information: for anyone except the parties to that decision, that is all they are.

Third, courts play an important role in responding to disinformation and misinformation, and to truth decay more generally. But that role is not to make authoritative findings of fact about particular issues to settle those issues for the relevant society. Rather, the claim to epistemological authority that courts can properly make is that the approach they bring to fact-finding – an open-minded, evidence-based inquiry that leads to appropriately limited claims about the truth – provides a model for fact-finding in an uncertain world. Today, as in the past, the greatest contribution courts can make by way of response to the challenges posed by disinformation and misinformation is to model robust processes for reaching explicitly provisional views about facts, and to model scepticism in the face of claims that are the product of less robust processes or that are made with greater confidence than can be justified.

This chapter begins by outlining some important features of the common law approach to fact-finding. It then examines the epistemological claims made by common law courts about the findings of fact they make, and what the modest nature of those claims means for the role of courts in the face of disinformation, misinformation and truth decay more generally.

II. Fact-finding by Common Law Courts

The starting point for a modern common law court is that the relevant fact-finder (which, depending on the jurisdiction and context, may be a judge or a jury) does not have, and cannot obtain, direct knowledge of the relevant facts. In a murder trial, the members of the jury were not at the scene of the crime to see who was present, who was holding the weapon, and how events unfolded. In a commercial case, the judge was not present when the chief executive of A Ltd made the statements that B Ltd claims amounted to an assurance that contractual rights would not be relied on, if B Ltd acted in a particular way. Nor does the court have privileged access to the truth through supernatural intervention, as was once thought to be available using techniques such as trial by ordeal.[9]

How then is the court to make findings about the factual elements of a proceeding?[10]

First, and very importantly, the fact-finder is required to be neutral and open-minded. The rules about who can serve as a judge in a particular matter are designed to exclude any person who may have an interest, direct or indirect, in the outcome – or who may be perceived as having such an interest. They are also designed to exclude anyone whose

[9] See F Pirie, *The Rule of Laws: A 4,000-Year Quest to Order the World* (London, Profile Books, 2021) 294–97.

[10] Courts distinguish between factual elements and legal (or normative) elements of a proceeding, looking to different sources and adopting different techniques of reasoning in each sphere.

mind may already be made up on factual questions that the court will be called on to determine. Similarly, individuals who are associated with parties or witnesses, or who have any interest in the outcome of a trial, are disqualified from serving as jurors in proceedings tried before a jury.

Second, in most proceedings, if parties agree on certain facts, those can be taken as given. This makes good practical sense for the parties and for the court. But it is worth noting that this is one reason why findings made by courts in particular proceedings cannot be treated as generally authoritative: they may be founded on pragmatic admissions by one or more parties that others might wish to contest.

Third, the hearing proceeds on the basis that the fact-finder should make findings about disputed facts solely on the basis of the evidence before the court. The evidential foundation for making a finding is identified and circumscribed. This is fundamental to concepts of natural justice – a fact-finder should not rely on any evidence that other parties have not had an opportunity to test and respond to. It is also an essential pre-requisite for a workable system of appeals based on the trial court record.[11]

Fourth, courts have developed rules about what evidence is admissible in particular contexts. (In most jurisdictions these common law rules have been supplemented or codified in legislation.) Evidence that is inherently unreliable is excluded. Over time the common law developed detailed rules about who could give evidence that would be sufficiently reliable to be acted on by a court, and about the process by which that evidence could be given and tested.

The rule against hearsay, seen in this light, reflects a strong preference for evidence to be given by those who have directly perceived the events or matters in relation to which findings must be made. The exceptions to the rule against hearsay recognise the difficulty of applying that standard in all circumstances, and the need to relax that rule (with appropriate safeguards) if practical justice is to be done.

The common law's concern for rational decision-making based on reliable evidence can also be seen at work in the rules found in most jurisdictions that exclude evidence that, albeit of some probative value, has an unfairly prejudicial effect. This concern is especially acute in the context of criminal proceedings tried before a jury. So, for example, evidence tending to show a defendant has a general propensity to commit criminal offences is never admissible. More difficult issues arise as the propensity sought to be demonstrated becomes more specific (say, burglary of particular types of premises using a skeleton key to effect entry): different jurisdictions draw the line in different ways.[12] But the common underlying concern is that factual findings should not be based on evidence that invites illegitimate inferences, for example because it evokes strong emotional responses. This is an important respect in which fact-finding by courts differs from the online realm: the court process is designed to support slow, deliberate thinking and to minimise the risk of swift responses driven by emotions and flawed

[11] As distinct from appeals de novo, where the entire matter is reheard before an appellate court. In most common law systems, appeals heard de novo are rare.

[12] Where and how that line should be drawn is much contested: for a recent example of divided appellate reasoning in a high-profile case see the decision of the New York Court of Appeals in *People v Weinstein* 2024 NY Slip Op 02222 (Ct App Apr 25, 2024). The evidence that the majority held should have been excluded, resulting in the conviction being set aside and a new trial ordered, would almost certainly have been admitted as propensity evidence before a New Zealand court under s 43 of the Evidence Act 2006 (NZ).

assumptions.[13] Online forums, by contrast, enable and encourage immediate reactions driven by emotional responses to the material presented – material that is often selected for its emotional salience.

In the common law tradition oral evidence is at the forefront. But there is an increasing emphasis – especially in commercial cases – on documentary evidence as the most reliable source of contemporaneous evidence about relevant actions and mental states. With the rise of electronic communications, an increasing proportion of interpersonal communication is recorded (in emails, text messages and through social media) and can be reviewed by a court. But disputes about the genuineness of such material can and do arise, and oral evidence from those involved (and from experts in digital forensics) is then needed. Similarly, the rapidly increasing volume of surveillance camera footage and bystander videos means that video recordings are often put in evidence in criminal trials; but questions of provenance and genuineness may need to be addressed through oral evidence, if disputed.

Courts also receive real evidence – be it a murder weapon or an allegedly copyright-infringing toy. But this also often requires a person with relevant knowledge of background facts to give oral evidence about the item and its provenance.

Fifth, common law courts draw a clear distinction between fact evidence – evidence a person can give of matters they perceived or of which they otherwise have direct knowledge – and opinion evidence. The common law takes a cautious approach to opinion evidence. There are some matters on which opinion evidence from non-experts may assist in communicating facts those persons perceived (for example, 'I thought the car was travelling very fast – much faster than the other cars'). But generally, opinion evidence will only be capable of providing substantial assistance to a fact-finder if it is given by a person who has specialised expertise developed through relevant training, study and experience. The expert's independence from the parties is also a material factor that may be a criterion for admissibility or may go to weight.

Another very important difference between online forums and courts is that a court will not generally receive, or give any weight to, opinion evidence from a non-expert who was not directly involved in the events in issue. A case cannot be bolstered by 'likes' from non-experts with no direct knowledge of the matters in dispute.[14]

Sixth, common law courts proceed on the basis that no witness is so authoritative that their evidence must be accepted at face value. All systems prescribe formalities for the giving of evidence that are designed to impress on witnesses the importance of telling the truth: typically, an oath or affirmation is required. Most systems prescribe penalties (potentially severe) for knowingly giving false evidence. Witnesses before common law courts must generally submit to being cross-examined.[15] Cross-examination performs

[13] That is, the process is designed to ensure decisions are made using slower 'system 2' thinking rather than faster 'system 1' heuristics: see D Kahneman, *Thinking, Fast and Slow* (New York, Farrar, Straus and Giroux, 2011).

[14] This was not always the case. Many legal systems, including English common law, allowed for trial by compurgation until surprisingly recently: see S Gageler, above n 8, summarising different trial techniques in the early common law system of justice. Trial by compurgation for certain matters was abolished by statute in England in 1833, and in New South Wales only in 1841. Many different legal systems have attempted to solve the problem of proof through some form of trial by compurgation: see F Pirie, above n 9, 290–93.

[15] Although in some types of proceeding, cross-examination may be the exception rather than the rule, often for pragmatic reasons.

the important role of confronting a witness with inconsistent evidence and with any inherent implausibilities or contradictions in their own evidence. This ensures that if an explanation is available, the witness has an opportunity to provide it. It also assists the fact-finder to assess the reliability and credibility of the account given by that witness.

Seventh, each party is able to test the evidence of other parties by calling their own evidence with a view to supporting their claims about relevant events.

Eighth, a common law court is generally confined to the evidence placed before the court by the parties to the proceeding. The court cannot summon witnesses on its own initiative, and third parties whose rights are not affected by the proceedings cannot call evidence in an attempt to influence the outcome.[16]

In most common law systems a judge or jury may take notice of certain facts which (in the language of section 128(1) of New Zealand's Evidence Act 2006) are 'so known and accepted either generally or in the locality in which the proceeding is being held that they cannot reasonably be questioned'. Judges can also generally take notice of facts capable of accurate and ready determination by reference to sources whose accuracy cannot reasonably be questioned and can receive as evidence reliable published works on matters such as public history, literature, science and the arts. But where a matter or a source is reasonably capable of being questioned, and in particular where it *is* reasonably questioned, it would be inconsistent with the role of a court and the requirements of natural justice to take notice of such matters, rather than requiring that they be the subject of evidence which can be tested and responded to by affected parties.

Ninth, the law allocates the burden of proof and specifies the standard of proof for different categories of proceedings. It follows that the court may ultimately find that it is not satisfied that X happened to the required standard, with the result that a prosecution fails or a civil claim is not made out. A positive finding that X did not happen is not required: the court has the option of saying 'on the basis of the evidence adduced by the parties, it is not possible to reach a conclusion to the required standard' and leave it at that.

In criminal proceedings, a prosecutor must generally establish each factual element of the relevant offence beyond reasonable doubt. In civil proceedings, a plaintiff seeking relief on a particular cause of action must generally establish, on the balance of probabilities, each factual element of that cause of action. Critically, a guilty verdict in criminal proceedings does not purport to be an authoritative announcement that cannot be questioned that it is certain that the defendant committed the relevant offence.[17] The

[16] A person whose rights are affected by a proceeding may seek to be joined as a party to some types of proceeding. Many jurisdictions also provide for the possibility of joinder as an intervener, though this is more common in appellate hearings: in most common law jurisdictions it would be exceptional for an intervener who is not joined as a full party to be permitted to call fact evidence at a trial.

[17] Proof that a person was convicted of an offence is, in New Zealand and some other jurisdictions, treated as proof for most purposes that the person committed the offence: Evidence Act 2006 (NZ), ss 47–49. This statutory departure from the common law rule in *Hollington v F Hewthorn and Co Ltd* [1943] KB 587 (CA) prevents relitigation of the facts that underpinned a conviction on the basis that the earlier finding reached to the criminal standard of 'beyond reasonable doubt' provides sufficient proof of those matters. But it does not elevate the conviction to a claim of absolute certainty – as illustrated by provision of rights of appeal from convictions, the establishment of agencies charged with investigating wrongful convictions such as the Criminal Cases Review Commission in England and Wales and (more recently) its counterpart in New Zealand, and the growing number of non-governmental organisations that investigate and pursue challenges to wrongful convictions (such as the Innocence Project in the US and Inside Justice in the UK).

fact-finder must be satisfied to the relevant standard that they did so. But certainty is acknowledged not to be possible and is not sought. (This is usually made explicit in directions to juries on the standard of proof: in New Zealand, for example, juries are directed that it is virtually impossible to prove anything to an absolute certainty, and the prosecution does not have to do so). A not guilty verdict is not a finding that the defendant did not commit the offence with which they were charged – indeed, it remains open to a victim to bring civil proceedings and seek to establish precisely the same facts to the civil standard, as occurred in the notorious OJ Simpson proceedings in the US.[18]

In civil proceedings, the limits of the claim to authority made by a finding of liability are greater still. The fact-finder must be satisfied on the balance of probabilities that the relevant facts are made out. The possibility that the finding may be wrong is explicitly acknowledged in the framing of the test.

Tenth, if the fact-finder is a judge, they are generally required to give reasons explaining the basis for the findings they have made.

Eleventh, and very importantly, all of this happens in public. With very limited exceptions in most common law countries, any member of the public can attend a trial and see the fact-finding process unfold. They can see and hear the evidence and see and hear it being tested. The process is open and transparent.

This is not a comprehensive account of the fact-finding methodology of common law courts. Most legal systems include many other rules that reflect a nuanced and context-dependent approach to arriving at sufficiently reliable findings of fact for the purpose in hand. But these are the key features of the system that enable claims based on disinformation and misinformation to be tested and weighed against other evidence in order to reach a (sufficiently) reliable conclusion.

The common law evidence-based approach to fact-finding has played an important part in the emergence of a fact-based public sphere over the last 500 or so years. Professor Barbara Shapiro, an eminent American historian, argues that the concept of 'fact' as a part of English and European culture had its origins in the law, and in the legal concept of the 'factum', or thing done by a person that would found a particular claim against that person, or lead to some other legal consequence. She traces the ways in which the public process of finding facts in courts, and familiarity with those processes on the part of leading scholars from the world of science (including Francis Bacon) contributed to the concept of 'matters of fact' being adopted by other disciplines and intellectual projects, and becoming part and parcel of the generally held habits of thought characteristic of late seventeenth- and early eighteenth-century culture.[19] Professor Shapiro explains how over time 'fact' as human deeds and actions was transformed into the best knowledge available to fallible human beings of a very broad spectrum of human and natural phenomena.[20]

In Professor Shapiro's words:

> Legal systems that treat fact finding as a rational rather than ritualistic process or invocation of divine intervention require methods of fact determination comprehensible to litigants and

[18] Mr Simpson was acquitted of murder at a criminal trial held in 1995, but civil claims by the victims' families in 1996–97 succeeded, resulting in an award of damages of USD33.5 million: Encyclopaedia Britannica online, www.britannica.com/event/O-J-Simpson-trial.

[19] BJ Shapiro, *A Culture of Fact – England, 1550-1720* (Ithaca and London, Cornell University Press, 2000).

[20] ibid 218.

> to the culture as a whole. They possess, whether clearly articulated or not, an underlying epistemology, that is, a set of beliefs as to human ability to arrive at 'true' and 'just' decisions. Fact finding in the legal context requires making decisions about events that are no longer present to either the disputants or the judges. It requires faith in the possibility of reaching adequate and reasonable belief about such events and a mode of thinking about what is knowable, who can know it, and under what conditions it is knowable, as well as institutional arrangements and processes for knowing.
>
> …
>
> As the concept of fact spread from the law courts, it carried with it the legal concern with witnesses, evidence and impartial judgment. All the fact-orientated disciplines exhibited a preference for personal observation and a belief that the testimony of credible witnesses under optimum conditions could yield believable, even morally certain 'facts'. It favoured first-person accounts that made vivid the experience of the 'facts' described.

The fact-finding methodologies deployed in common law courts cannot provide certain knowledge of matters that the fact-finder did not experience directly. But they can provide a sufficient level of confidence to make practical decisions about matters of significance to the parties.

Importantly for present purposes, these methodologies have for many centuries been used to evaluate claims made before courts based on disinformation or misinformation. Indeed, it is precisely the effectiveness of these methodologies in arriving at practically workable, though necessarily provisional, views about the truth that contributed to the adoption of evidence-based methodologies by scientists and others in fields that had previously been the domain of beliefs founded on superstition, religion, folk knowledge, imagination, and anecdotal accounts. Over the last few hundred years, understandings of the natural world founded on widespread misinformation have gradually been displaced by understandings based on evidence-based investigations. From a practical perspective, the method has the great advantage that it works: so, for example, evidence-based medicine is more reliably effective than other approaches to treating disease, and evidence-based science has produced many technologies that enhance the quality of our daily lives and prolong those lives far beyond the spans enjoyed by our ancestors. Scientific understandings are necessarily provisional: it is inherent in the nature of any evidence-based endeavour that understandings of facts held at any given time may evolve or be superseded as further evidence is obtained and analysed.

This is a point that deserves emphasis: the antithesis of disinformation and misinformation is not certainty about the truth. Rather, it is a commitment to open-minded, evidence-based inquiry, which we can expect to provide us with information that it is reasonable to accept as correct, while recognising that if further evidence becomes available we may need to update our understandings.

The expressly qualified and provisional nature of the factual findings that courts make is not always sufficiently appreciated. This point is addressed in more detail below.

Before leaving the topic of how common law courts make factual findings, it should be emphasised that this chapter does not suggest that the current approach adopted in the courts of New Zealand (and other similar jurisdictions) is in all respects satisfactory and could not be improved. To the contrary, if we subject the way in which courts undertake fact-finding to an evidence-based evaluation (turning the methodology on itself, in effect), we can identify a number of areas in which our approach to fact-finding could be improved in light of research on human perception and memory, and on the limits of our ability to discern whether others are telling the truth. More work needs to be done on issues such as reliance on witness demeanour to assess credibility, the reliability of oral evidence based on memory alone (especially after providing multiple accounts of the events in issue to police, lawyers and others), the reliability of identification evidence, the reliability of confessions as compared with the weight they carry even where a fact-finder is warned about reliability concerns, and the impact of popular misconceptions about how memory works on fact-finding by judges and juries alike. It is now well established that there is no perception without cognition.[21] There is also a growing body of research on the circumstances in which memories exclude events, are partial, or are 'remembered' even though they did not actually occur. Police interrogations that are intended to tap memories can instead shape and create them. And there are cases where people have come to believe, falsely, that they themselves have committed crimes even if there is clear evidence that they are innocent:[22]

> We don't simply absorb sensory data from the world; we don't simply store what we perceived. Rather, our perception and memory are shaped and informed by intelligent guesses of how the world should be – what patterns of colour and light typically correspond to a single object, what people typically do in a restaurant. Because our interpretations are based on what's probable, we sometimes get it wrong, and our mistakes reveal themselves when we encounter visual illusions and tell false stories about our pasts. But in a world of limited and fragmentary information, there might be no better way for the system to work.

In the commercial litigation context there is an increasing recognition that the contemporaneous documentary record provides a much more reliable source of information than participants' memories.[23] The implications of this approach for other fields need to be carefully worked through.

Further work is also needed on the adequacy of our current fact-finding tools to detect ever more sophisticated disinformation – for example, fake images and audio and video recordings generated using AI tools that are increasingly difficult to distinguish from the real thing. There is a real risk that the quantity and quality of fabricated evidence will place a heavy burden on parties to litigation, and on the courts. If expert assistance is needed to detect such fabrications, the cost and time involved in litigation will increase and access to justice will be impaired. But on the other hand, AI tools may assist with the identification of fabricated evidence: just where that arms race will land is not currently possible to predict.

Courts have managed to apply their long-standing approach to testing evidence and finding facts in the context of technological innovation over many centuries, including the strides in digital technology that occurred between (say) 1970 and 2020. There are further challenges ahead – but for the present, at least, there is room for optimism that the approach adopted by the courts to determining facts is basically sound, and capable of rising to new challenges.

[21] P Bloom, *Psych: The Story of the Human Mind* (New York, Harper Collins, 2023) ch 7.

[22] ibid 189.

[23] See *Gestmin SGPS (SA) v Credit Suisse (UK) Ltd* [2013] EWHC 3560 (Comm) [15]–[20]; and T Bingham, *The Business of Judging – Selected Essays and Speeches* (Oxford, Oxford University Press, 2011) ch 1.

III. The Limits of Common Law Courts' Epistemological Claims

The provisional and qualified nature of the claim to epistemological authority made by common law courts is underscored by the law's treatment of factual findings made by a trial court.

It has long been recognised that fact-finding processes may go awry for a number of reasons. A finding of a trial court can in most jurisdictions be called into question on appeal on the basis that the fact-finding process miscued, casting doubt on the reliability of the conclusions reached. For example, the court may have received inadmissible evidence or wrongly excluded admissible evidence. In some jurisdictions an appeal may be available on the grounds of error of fact. Where appeals on questions of fact are not available, there will usually be a right of appeal or review where findings are made that were not open to a reasonable fact-finder on the basis of the evidence before them. In some contexts, there may be more than one right of appeal on questions of fact or on mixed questions of law and fact.

It bears mentioning that the existence of rights of appeal does not provide a guarantee that all decisions that are not appealed are accepted as correct by all parties. Appeals can be expensive and slow. Litigants may run out of money, or time, or patience. A pragmatic resolution may be agreed by the parties. And, of course, an appeal does not guarantee that the right answer will be reached on appeal – hence the familiar quip that final appellate courts are right because they are final, not final because they are right.

The common law limits the preclusive effect of findings of fact to the parties to the proceeding (and their privies). As already mentioned, the only persons who are entitled to call evidence, and be heard on the findings that the court should make, are the parties. The court makes its decision on the basis of the evidence that those parties choose to put forward. There may be other relevant evidence that the court did not receive, whether because it was not available to those parties or as a result of strategic decisions. For reasons of both principle and pragmatism, an issue estoppel will arise between the parties (and their privies) in relation to findings of fact that were necessary for the court's decision. That fact cannot be called into question in subsequent proceedings between the same parties (or their privies). But common law courts do not claim to have reached a conclusion that should be accepted as objectively true by everyone. A person who was not a party to the proceeding (or a privy of a party) is free to relitigate matters of fact determined in the earlier proceeding.

Indeed, the judgment of a court in an earlier proceeding is (with certain exceptions) generally treated as inadmissible in subsequent proceedings, as the findings made are simply the opinion of the judge in those proceedings formed on the basis of the evidence called in those proceedings. A subsequent court is not merely free to disregard the findings made by the earlier court – it has a positive duty to do so.

It follows that we should not be unduly concerned about court decisions being perceived as disputable sources of information. The legitimacy of judicial decisions seems more likely to be called into question if we make overly ambitious claims about what it is that the courts are doing and suggest that their findings are *indisputable* sources of information. The parties, who have had every opportunity to put relevant evidence before the court, cannot dispute its findings – at least, once all rights of appeal are exhausted. Others can.

Indeed, it can be very much in the public interest for court decisions to be disputed in certain circumstances. Courts can and do reach incorrect conclusions, for reasons that may be specific to a particular case or may be systemic.

Most, if not all, jurisdictions have experience of miscarriages of justice in particular cases that have been addressed many years later, sometimes as a result of the efforts of a small group and sometimes as the result of a public outcry. A party may succeed in misleading the court: the courts' fact-finding methodology is not infallible, as explained above. Judges and jurors are human, and human decision-making is prone to error: our decisions are often 'noisy' and sometimes biased.[24] Relevant evidence may not be placed before the court because of inadequate disclosure, a failure to appreciate its significance, or an inability of then-current scientific knowledge and techniques to evaluate that evidence.[25] The common law trial process is designed to reduce those risks, but cannot eliminate them.

More problematically still, in most, if not all, jurisdictions there are systemic issues that can result in errors and injustices. One notable recent example is the British Post Office scandal: between 1996 and 2018, many hundreds of subpostmasters were convicted of theft, fraud and false accounting based on faulty computer system data. The individuals affected did not have the resources and expertise to challenge the reliability of the data that provided the foundation for the allegations against them. Some were persuaded to plead guilty. Others were convicted despite their denial of any wrongdoing. It was only when investigations into the 'Horizon' computer system used by the Post Office revealed the scale of the flaws in that system that an independent inquiry was established by the UK Government, and convictions began to be quashed in the courts. Legislation was recently enacted providing for exoneration of people convicted of relevant offences during the period when the Horizon system was in use.[26]

This saga illustrates a pervasive problem with fact-finding by courts in all common law systems. Because those systems rely on the evidence provided by the parties, they can work effectively only where each party has sufficient knowledge and resources to identify the issues on which evidence is needed, and to obtain and adduce that evidence. That requires legal knowledge that individual litigants typically lack. Most people need legal representation to participate effectively in proceedings – but the cost is often prohibitive, and publicly funded legal aid schemes are often inadequate. Ensuring that relevant evidence is put before a court is dependent on sufficient skill and resources to locate and brief witnesses of fact, and (where appropriate) to retain experts to provide advice and give evidence. The ability to review and challenge novel forms of expert evidence – such as the 'bite mark evidence' that was deployed in criminal trials in the US and elsewhere from the 1970s onwards, but has recently been discredited and identified as a contributing factor in numerous wrongful convictions – depends on skilled legal

[24] D Kahneman, O Sibony and CR Sunstein, *Noise: A Flaw in Human Judgment* (New York, Little, Brown Spark, 2021).

[25] See, for a recent example of evidence that was only able to be evaluated using techniques developed many years after trial, and also of material failures of disclosure by the prosecution contributing to an unsafe (and almost certainly incorrect) verdict, *Malkinson v R* [2023] EWCA Crim 954.

[26] Post Office (Horizon System) Offences Act 2024 (UK).

representation and sufficient funding to access competing expert assistance.[27] The ability to effectively seek and review disclosure provided by another party – in particular, by a prosecutor in criminal proceedings – also depends on access to legal representation and money.

The public should not accept uncritically the outcomes of court proceedings that are affected by idiosyncratic failures, or by systemic weaknesses – whether in the court system itself, or as a product of wider social inequities that lead to inequality of arms between parties. Rather, a healthy democracy with a well-functioning public sphere should encourage debate about the reliability of court findings and the underlying causes of problematic outcomes, and about how such issues might be addressed.

This is not to suggest that court decisions should be disregarded by the public. To the contrary, it is important for the health of free and democratic societies that the courts can be trusted to administer justice according to the law. That requires trust in the courts' fact-finding process as a reasonable method for determining facts relevant to a proceeding: not infallible, but sufficiently reliable for the purpose in hand. However, this chapter argues that it is the court *process* that needs to enjoy – and maintain – public trust and confidence, rather than the findings that are made in particular cases. And public trust in the courts will be enhanced, not diminished, if we acknowledge the difficulty of ascertaining facts in an uncertain world, the limits on the confidence with which even the best process can ascertain facts, the factors that impede reliable fact-finding in our courts, and the inevitability that mistakes will be made.

Court decisions in particular cases can and do contribute to the development of a fact-based public sphere. As members of the public, we cannot ascertain each and every fact relevant to that sphere for ourselves. Some sources can be treated as generally trustworthy and provisionally reliable, precisely because of the process that those trusted sources adopt to establish matters of fact. Well-functioning court systems that make findings of fact using the evidence-based approach described above are one of those generally trustworthy sources. Findings made by a court can reasonably be taken as the best available source of truth on an issue that the court has determined unless there is good reason for concern about the court process in that case, or some other evidence that was not before the court has become available that calls into question the finding made by the court. Indeed, it seems unreasonable for a person to disregard a finding made by a court following a hearing involving parties with a strong interest in that finding and the resources to contest it, unless that person has identified some good reason to call that finding into question. But the common law does not claim that such findings are conclusive for all purposes and for all persons: the respect that such findings command, while real, is necessarily qualified and provisional.

[27] For the rise and fall of bite mark expert evidence, and other dubious forms of forensic evidence, see National Research Council, *Strengthening Forensic Science in the United States: A Path Forward* (Washington DC, The National Academies Press, 2009), available at www.ojp.gov/pdffiles1/nij/grants/228091.pdf; and K Sauerwein et al, *Bitemark Analysis: A NIST Scientific Foundation Review* (Gaithersburg, MD, National Institute of Standards and Technology, 2023), NIST Interagency Report (IR) NIST IR 8352, available at doi.org/10.6028/NIST.IR.8352; and MC Fabricant, *Junk Science and the American Criminal Justice System* (Brooklyn, Akashic Books, 2022).

IV. Conclusion

Common law courts have for many hundreds of years approached their forensic task of finding facts by adopting a neutral, open-minded, transparent, evidence-based approach which enables each party to put forward their own account of disputed facts, and to test and respond to competing accounts. Primary reliance is placed on accounts given by those directly involved in the relevant events. Second-hand (hearsay) evidence and opinion evidence may be received in certain circumstances, but the limits of such evidence are expressly acknowledged. Evidence of little probative value that invites illegitimate inferences (for example, because it evokes strong emotional responses) may be excluded, to reduce the risk that rational decision-making will be distorted.

In light of the evidence adduced in a particular proceeding, the fact-finder (judge or jury) decides whether they can reach a view about the facts with the requisite level of confidence. If not, no finding at all need be made: it is sufficient to say that the allegations were not made out to the relevant standard on this occasion. If a finding is made, no claim is made to certainty in respect of that finding. And as explained above, the epistemological authority claimed by the common law in respect of any findings made is limited and provisional.

The increasing volumes of disinformation and misinformation that are enabled by digital technology, and spread through the internet, pose real challenges for the courts. But – answering the first limb of the question posed at the start of this chapter – the basic fact-finding task remains the same, the common law approach to fact-finding has in the past enabled courts to respond to disinformation and misinformation in a manner that has commanded broad acceptance, and no better approach has been identified by any commentator to date. So we have little choice but to continue broadly as we are. However, we should not rest on our laurels: we need to keep our fact-finding processes actively under review, and make any changes required to bring those processes into line with the best available evidence about the workings of human perception and memory, and human decision-making.

Turning to the second limb of the question posed, we should frankly acknowledge that court decisions are indeed a disputable source of information. Provisionally reliable, as explained above, but disputable where there is good reason to do so. This acknowledgement, properly framed, seems likely to enhance the legitimacy of the courts as compared with a strategy of claiming an authority for court findings in the public sphere that exceeds the authority that they are accorded by the common law itself. An acknowledgement of fallibility in particular cases, and systemic weaknesses in certain contexts, can also stimulate a productive discussion about how best to respond to the factors that put court fact-finding at risk: most notably, the extent to which many participants in court proceedings lack the knowledge and resources required to participate effectively in those proceedings by bringing forward their own evidence and testing the evidence of other parties. If we acknowledge and tackle those challenges, we will enhance both the actual and perceived legitimacy of court processes and court decisions.

Unfortunately this is not a simple story to tell in an era of soundbites and TikTok videos. And in most societies, no-one much is telling it. So the task falls to the courts to engage in more effective outreach to ensure that the public is better informed about the role of the courts, and how they go about performing that role.

Finally, there is a very important lesson that the courts can provide to a wider audience in the face of disinformation, misinformation and truth decay. It is the same lesson that Professor Shapiro describes the courts as providing some 400–500 years ago – a lesson about the processes that are the necessary prerequisite for making reliable claims about matters of fact. The lesson is relevant to those who make claims about facts, and to those who are invited to accept those claims. Before one accepts as reliable a claim that another person makes, one should ask whether the claim has been tested through a rigorous process that:

(a) requires the person making the claim to identify the primary evidence/sources on which they rely, and to explain why those sources are sufficiently reliable for the purpose in hand;

(b) enables people with contrary views to be included in the conversation, and to have a meaningful opportunity to test the claims made and the evidence relied on and to draw attention to other reliable evidence that should be taken into account; and

(c) requires the person to be open and transparent about the process by which their view of the facts has been reached, the confidence with which that view is held, and the existence and extent of remaining uncertainty.

If these tests are not met, there is no rational basis for accepting a claim as reliable – regardless of who makes it, and regardless of how confidently it is made.

All too often people's beliefs owe more to emotion, and the desire to identify with a particular group, than to evidence. But if courts can continue to encourage people to adopt the approach outlined above, through example and through outreach, that would be a truly significant (continuing) contribution to the wider public sphere in our societies.

13

Truth Decay and its Implications for the Judiciary: An Australian Perspective

ANDREW BELL AC*

I. Introduction – Truth and the Courts

Truth, as a subject of philosophical discourse, is one that has gripped thinkers from at least the time of classical antiquity. It is a value and concept which is at the heart of judicial systems. Witnesses must swear to tell 'the truth, the whole truth, and nothing but the truth'.[1] As Lord Denning put it in *Harmony Shipping Co SA v Davies*,[2] 'the primary duty of the court is to ascertain the truth by the best evidence available'.

Truth is closely associated with honesty. Drawing upon rules of professional ethical responsibility in New South Wales, which have their analogues in other common law jurisdictions, lawyers, in the discharge of their duty to the court and to the administration of justice, must not engage in conduct that is dishonest,[3] and must not knowingly or recklessly mislead the court[4] nor make false or misleading statements to an opponent.[5] Lawyers must not advise witnesses to provide false or misleading evidence, or coach witnesses about which answers they should provide to certain questions.[6] Lawyers must refuse to take further part in cases where their client has lied to the court, falsified documents, or suppressed material evidence for which there was a duty to disclose.[7]

* The author acknowledges the considerable assistance he has obtained in the preparation of this chapter from various research associates, Mr Sam Cass, Ms Meghan Malone and Mr John Lidbetter. The comments of Justices Peter Garling and Sarah McNaughton of the Supreme Court of New South Wales on an earlier draft of this chapter are also acknowledged.

[1] Evidence Act 1995 (NSW) (Evidence Act), s 21, sch 1.

[2] *Harmony Shipping Co SA v Davies and others* [1979] 3 All ER 177, 181.

[3] For barristers, see Legal Profession Uniform Conduct (Barristers) Rules 2015 (NSW) (Barristers Rules), r 8(a); for solicitors, see Legal Profession Uniform Law Australian Solicitors' Conduct Rules 2015 (NSW) (Solicitors Rules), rr 4.1.2, 5.

[4] For barristers, see Barristers Rules, r 24; for solicitors, see Solicitors Rules, r 19.1.

[5] For barristers, see Barristers Rules, r 49; for solicitors, see Solicitors Rules, r 22.1.

[6] For barristers, see Barristers Rules, r 69; for solicitors, see Solicitors Rules, r 24.1.

[7] For barristers, see Barristers Rules, r 79; for solicitors, see Solicitors Rules, r 20.1.

Prosecutors must 'fairly assist the court to arrive at the truth'.[8] Lawyers are also obliged to assist investigative and inquisitorial tribunals fairly to arrive at the truth.[9]

Within the Australian judicial system, a transformative consumer protection statute first passed in the 1970s and extended at state levels and applicable to trade and commerce generally as well as to corporate activity proscribes conduct that is misleading or deceptive, or likely to mislead or deceive.[10] Critically for present purposes, the statute is not directed solely towards intentionally deceptive conduct but operates at an objective level. It is a most important piece of normative legislation which is underpinned by the notion that misleading or deceptive conduct, whether intentional or not, will not be tolerated. It has resulted in Australian courts being placed in a role of peculiar responsibility for policing conduct that objectively deviates from factually accurate positions. It is enforceable in civil suits and is routinely invoked.

Returning to the topic more generally, equivalence between truth and the objectives of a mature judicial system is not absolute or coterminous, and there may be a difference or a degree of difference in this regard between the adversarial system of justice in the common law tradition and judiciaries in the civilian tradition with their focus on inquisitorial justice. While it is the case that, in the eyes of the public, a primary function of a contested trial – if not *the* primary function – is to conduct a search for truth through the mechanism of the adversarial system,[11] in reality, of course, this is an oversimplification of the role of a court. In the adversarial tradition, the objective of the judicial function is not necessarily to find the truth *in all cases* or *at all costs*. The fact-finding objective is balanced against other equally important considerations, often derived from exclusionary rules of evidence, some of which exist to serve policy objectives extraneous to the 'pursuit of truth' or at least which are conscious of the imperfections of human nature and human memory.

James Spigelman, a former Chief Justice of New South Wales, recognised that at times 'the untrammelled search for truth may impinge upon other public values'.[12] He gave as examples exclusionary rules of evidence and rules of practice and procedure that result in potentially relevant evidence not being taken into account or received by the tribunal of fact.[13] These included:

- restrictions on the admissibility of fresh evidence on appeal;
- the exclusion of involuntary or unknowing confessions;
- restrictions on the use of tendency or coincidence evidence;
- the exclusion of hearsay evidence;
- the exclusion of lay opinion evidence; and
- the exclusion of evidence after balancing prejudice and probative value.

[8] For barristers, see Barristers Rules, r 83; for solicitors, see Solicitors Rules, r 29.1.

[9] For barristers, see Barristers Rules, r 97; for solicitors, see Solicitors Rules, r 29.13.

[10] Trade Practices Act 1974 (Cth), now the Australian Consumer Law.

[11] So much is reflected in Lord Eldon's sentiment that 'Truth is best discovered by powerful statements on both sides of the question': *Ex parte Lloyd* (1822) Mont 70, 72, reported as a note to *Ex parte Elsee* (1832) Mont 69.

[12] J Spigelman, 'Truth and the Law' [2011] *Bar News (Winter)* 99, 102. See also MS Moore, 'The Plain Truth about Legal Truth' (2003) 26 *Harvard Journal of Law & Public Policy* 23. As an illustration, consider *La Rocca v R* [2023] NSWCCA 45, in which the conduct of law enforcement agencies resulted in a permanent stay of proceedings, frustrating any 'pursuit of truth'.

[13] Spigelman (see n 12 above) 103.

A similar view had been expressed by Professor William Twining, who observed that 'the pursuit of truth as a *means* to justice under the law commands a high, but not necessarily an overriding, priority as a social value.'[14]

Further, to the extent that the judicial process involves a pursuit of truth, the particular *kind* of truths ventilated in courtrooms tend to be highly specific to the parties to the dispute. While high-profile litigation may touch upon social issues about which there is intense factual disagreement,[15] the role of a judge rarely involves reaching conclusions about wide-ranging truths of application to the community as a whole. Rather, a judge's typical role is only to find the facts necessary to resolve the particular dispute between the parties.

And findings of fact by reference either to the civil or criminal standard equally recognise that 'finding' absolute and objective truth is at best elusive and at worst impossible. Courts, of necessity, operate by reference to the balance of probability and beyond reasonable doubt standards in civil and criminal cases, respectively.

Chief Justice Stephen Gageler has recently reflected on the historical and philosophical interrelationship between the concept of truth within the common law system and the concept of justice according to the rule of law.[16] With elegant simplicity, he noted that:[17]

> The rule of law postulates the existence of a legal rule and postulates imposition of a legal sanction for breach of that legal rule. The link between the rule and the sanction is the fact of breach. Whether or not there is a breach of the rule is a question of fact. … *maintenance of the rule of law is dependent on the ability of our system to generate reliable findings of fact.* … our legal system needs to be able to determine with integrity in respect of a past event, the occurrence of which is contested and the occurrence of which is uncertain, that the event either happened or did not happen, or more accurately is either proved to have happened or not proved to have happened. (emphasis added)

He argued that:

> our concept of justice is reliant on our concept of truth. Second, our concept of truth is not absolute but a matter of degree. Third, truth for us is relative. True or untrue is proven or unproven, and proven or unproven is ultimately believed or not believed with the requisite degree of intensity.[18]

The statement that 'truth for us is relative' is one that gives me some pause unless, by that expression, the Chief Justice was simply making the point that courts do not deal with absolute truths but with probabilities. So much may be accepted, but concepts such as 'my truth' or a particular person's 'truth' are often morally problematic, self-serving and often defiant. Words and phrases such as 'misspoke', 'alternative facts' and 'fake news' also evidence the vice of relativism in this area.

Accepting the complexity of the matter, with all its philosophical nuances, including those brought out so deftly by David Goddard in the previous chapter, it may

[14] W Twining, *Rethinking Evidence: Exploratory Essays* (Northwestern University Press, 1994) 72–74, quoted in Gageler (see n 16 below).

[15] Consider, eg, *Djokovic v Minister for Immigration, Citizenship, Migrant Services and Multicultural Affairs* [2022] FCAFC 3 and *Kassam v Hazzard; Henry v Hazzard* [2021] NSWCA 299 (which involved various actions taken by governments to mitigate the risks posed by unvaccinated persons during the COVID-19 pandemic).

[16] S Gageler, 'Truth and Justice, and Sheep' (2018) 46 *Australian Bar Review* 205.

[17] ibid 207.

[18] ibid 208.

nevertheless be said that there is an extremely close connection between the concepts of truth, justice, and honesty. Any suggestion, therefore, of truth decay is one that should be of deep concern to judges, to all those involved in the administration of the law and justice, and indeed to all those with an interest in civil society.

Before turning to the scourge of truth decay, it may also be observed that the association of courts and judges with the ascertainment of 'truth' may be seen in the appointment of current and former judicial officers to conduct public commissions of inquiry into what are often matters of high controversy or scandal. Although these are not judicial bodies, they co-opt the characteristics and processes of the judiciary, together with personal and institutional reputations for impartial, robust ascertainment of the facts. Royal Commissions, for example, are independent from government, have coercive evidence-gathering powers, and are required in Australia to adhere to judicial norms of procedural fairness and natural justice. They are also typically staffed by a small army of solicitors and counsel. This is done for the precise reason that the qualities inherent in the legal profession and the judicial method are well suited to a forensic and impartial pursuit of truth – and therefore endow the inquiry with public legitimacy.[19]

This 'borrowing' of institutional legitimacy makes commissions and inquiries very versatile for the executive branch. In some cases, it allows commissions and inquiries to effectively wade into territory with contentious party-political implications, while maintaining balance and impartiality. It may also provide an appropriate vehicle for revealing 'truths' of a broader, more systemic nature than could be revealed in a conventional legal dispute.[20]

II. Truth Decay

In their book, *Truth Decay: An Initial Exploration of the Diminishing Role of Facts and Analysis in American Public Life*,[21] Jennifer Kavanagh and Michael D Rich focus on trends in public discourse in the US. The extent of this phenomenon may vary from country to country, but it is one that must be taken extremely seriously. As highlighted in the previous two chapters, the authors outline four trends that they argue characterise truth decay in the US over the past two decades, the last of which being 'declining trust in formerly respected sources of factual information'.[22]

An immediate example of this may be seen in the fact that, notwithstanding that myriad courts in the US have categorically rejected the claim that the presidential election in 2020 was 'rigged' or 'stolen', it is frequently reported that up to 30 million

[19] See generally K Hayne, 'On Royal Commissions', speech at the Centre for Comparative Constitutional Studies Conference, Melbourne (26 July 2019); J Tjandra, 'From Fact Finding To Truth-Telling: An Analysis Of The Changing Functions Of Commonwealth Royal Commissions' (2022) 45 *University of New South Wales Law Journal* 341.

[20] As seen in, for example, the Australian Royal Commission into Institutional Responses to Child Sexual Abuse, or the recent Special Commission of Inquiry into LGBTIQ Hate Crimes conducted in New South Wales.

[21] J Kavanagh and MD Rich, *Truth Decay: An Initial Exploration of the Diminishing Role of Facts and Analysis in American Public Life* (Santa Monica, RAND Corporation, 2018).

[22] ibid x–xi.

Americans accept this claim.[23] Implicit in that reported statistic is that a significant percentage of the population is either ignorant of the rulings of multiple courts or simply does not accept such rulings. Neither explanation is comforting.

As a general and trite observation, any decline in trust of judicial institutions is a matter of note and concern. To the extent that the courts are viewed as 'sources of factual information', the fourth trend pointed out by Kavanagh and Rich in relation to declining trust focuses the mind and provokes thought about how such a trend may be resisted and reversed.

In Australia, during the Australian Law Reform Commission's recent review of judicial impartiality and the law on bias, the Commission conducted a survey which indicated that, in 2020, trust in Australian courts had actually increased over the past 10 years, and was higher than trust in federal parliament, business and industry, and the news media (second only to university research centres among the bodies surveyed).[24] Evidently, notwithstanding the frequent and at times unwarranted public attacks on the judiciary, there is a 'large reservoir of respect for the fairness of the Courts'.[25] There is, however, no room for complacency, and, as explained below, courts have real vulnerability to the pernicious effects and reach of truth decay.

Kavanagh and Rich identify four drivers, or potential causes of truth decay:

- 'Characteristics of cognitive processing such as cognitive bias';
- 'Changes in the information system', including the rise of social media, the transformation of the media market and the wide dissemination of disinformation and misleading or biased information;
- 'Competing demands on the educational system that limit its ability to keep pace with changes in the information system'; and
- 'Political, sociodemographic, and economic polarization'.[26]

They then go on to argue that the consequences of truth decay are enormous and include 'the erosion of civil discourse', 'political paralysis', 'alienation and disengagement of individuals from political and civic institutions' and 'policy uncertainty at the national level'.[27]

The phenomenon of truth decay may be exacerbated by the advent of generative artificial intelligence (GenAI). In September 2023, the Australian Defence Force Chief, General Angus Campbell, drew attention to this, when he said the following:

> As these technologies quickly mature, there may soon come a time when it is impossible for the average person to distinguish fact from fiction, and although a tech counter response can be anticipated, the first impression is often the most powerful …

[23] J Viala-Gaudefroy, 'Why do millions of Americans believe the 2020 presidential election was "stolen" from Donald Trump?' (*The Conversation*, 3 March 2024), available at theconversation.com/why-do-millions-of-americans-believe-the-2020-presidential-election-was-stolen-from-donald-trump-224016; M Pengelly, 'More than a third of US adults say Biden's 2020 victory was not legitimate' (*The Guardian*, 2 January 2024), available at www.theguardian.com/us-news/2024/jan/02/poll-biden-2020-election-illegitimate.

[24] Australian Law Reform Commission, 'Without Fear or Favour: Judicial Impartiality and the Law on Bias' (Final Report, No 138, December 2021) 146.

[25] R Beech-Jones, 'The Dogs Bark but the Caravan Rolls On: Extra Judicial Responses to Criticism', speech at the Conference of South Australian magistrates, Adelaide (8 May 2017) 12.

[26] *Truth Decay* (see n 21 above) at xiii–xiv.

[27] ibid xvi.

> This tech future may accelerate truth decay, greatly challenging the quality of what we call public 'common sense', seriously damaging public confidence in elected officials and undermining the trust that binds us.[28]

It is sobering to reflect that Kavanagh and Rich's thought-provoking book preceded by some four to five years the public and widespread emergence of GenAI, at least as a readily available tool to members of the public, including the legal profession.

This is a topic which the second half of this chapter addresses, but it may be observed here that in at least one Australian case, the rise of GenAI has led to concerns about the authenticity of documents tendered on sentence,[29] and sooner or later (but most likely sooner), deepfakes will inevitably pose huge challenges for courts determining matters which turn on photographic or audiovisual evidence.[30] The broader point to be made about deepfakes is that their use in society at large by criminal syndicates and in fraudulent activity more generally will itself be likely to generate a wave of work for the judiciary in their endeavours to separate true fact from fiction. The scope for malicious disinformation is enormous and will test the skill of courts throughout the world.

At a macro level, judicial inability to cope with this phenomenon may undermine respect for and reliance upon the courts and the role they play as arbiters (however imperfect) of the truth in our societies.

III. Vulnerability to Truth Decay

There are at least five reasons why courts are particularly vulnerable to truth decay before one even reaches the challenges presented by GenAI.

First, the judiciary is more dependent than perhaps any other public institution on the confidence of the public and of other arms of government.[31] As is often noted, the judiciary 'has no influence over either sword or the purse',[32] and therefore *respect* for the work of the courts in a very practical sense is central to ensuring the efficacy of that work. As the fourth Chief Justice of New South Wales, Sir James Martin, put it so eloquently almost 150 years ago:

> A Supreme Court like this … is the appointed and recognised tribunal for the maintenance of the collective authority of the entire community. …. Without armed guards, or any ostentatious display - with nothing but its common law attendant, the sheriff, and its humble officials

[28] A Greene, 'Defence Force Chief Angus Campbell Warns Deepfakes and AI will Drive Era of "truth decay"' (*ABC News*, 15 September 2023), available at www.abc.net.au/news/2023-09-15/angus-campbell-warns-about-deepfakes-artificial-intelligence/102860418; D Hurst, 'Democracies Face "truth decay" as AI Blurs Fact and Fiction, Warns Head of Australia's Military' (*The Guardian*, 14 September 2023), available at www.theguardian.com/australia-news/2023/sep/14/democracies-face-truth-decay-as-ai-blurs-fact-and-fiction-warns-head-of-australias-military.

[29] *Director of Public Prosecutions (ACT) v Khan* [2024] ACTSC 19, para 39ff (Mossop J). This decision is referred to at greater length later in this chapter.

[30] See R Pfefferkorn, '"Deepfakes" in the Courtroom' (2020) 29 *Boston University Public Interest Law Journal* 245; E Dudley, '"The Camera Does Lie": Concerns over AI in NSW Courts' (*The Australian*, 21 January 2024), available at www.theaustralian.com.au/business/legal-affairs/the-camera-does-lie-concerns-over-ai-in-nsw-courts/news-story/b4c2ec40cb611c00f278803e7f8cb4a1.

[31] See generally AR Blackshield, 'The Legitimacy and Authority of Judges' (1987) 10 *University of New South Wales Law Journal* 155.

[32] A Hamilton, 'Federalist No 78' in A Hamilton, J Madison and J Jay (eds), *The Federalist Papers* (New American Library, 1961) 465.

> the court-keepers and tipstaffs, *it derives its force from the knowledge that it has the whole power of the community at its back. This is a power unseen, but efficacious and irresistible, and on its maintenance depends the security of the public.*[33] (emphasis added)

Second, although empirical evidence suggests that most members of the public have little understanding of what courts and judges do,[34] their decisions are capable of provoking intense and emotive public responses. What understanding the public does have tends to be derived from courtroom dramas, word of mouth, and the handful of sensational cases that make national news each year. In a speech given several years ago, Tom Bathurst observed that, because so few members of the public read the reasons that judges write – and even fewer can assess the technical validity of those reasons – confidence in the judiciary relies on the public making a 'leap of faith'.[35]

Third, and as a result, judges are almost entirely reliant on news media – with its own set of commercial and professional incentives – to translate and explain their decisions to the public.[36] While technological advancements theoretically facilitate direct access to judicial decisions at a scale never seen in the past,[37] the professional media (increasingly complemented by social media) retain a critical role as 'intermediaries between the legal system and the people it serves'.[38]

Fourth, despite limited public understanding of the judicial function, courts hold a prominent place in the public imagination, and their decisions frequently involve matters that engage the interest and passions of the public. Decisions involving, for example, crime and punishment, the care and custody of children, migration and asylum, and sexual assault and harassment are capable of evoking visceral emotive reactions and lend themselves to sensationalism. They also tend to involve issues and factual scenarios that are – at least on their face – relatively easy to understand, and about which members of the public may have preconceived views.

Fifth, judges are limited in their ability to publicly defend themselves, their decisions and their institutions from erroneous or ill-informed (whether deliberately or otherwise) public attacks.[39] Particularly in the common law tradition, judges have historically not been active participants in public debate. While this norm has partially diminished over time, there remains – and rightly – a reticence on behalf of judges to engage in public discussion about contentious contemporary issues.

The cumulative effect of at least the first, second and fifth of these factors is that members of the public have little ability independently to scrutinise or verify assertions made by others – and particularly by public figures – about the judiciary and its work, both in a general sense and in the context of particular decisions.

[33] *In re "The Evening News" Newspaper* (1880) 1 LR (NSW) 211, 237.

[34] I Nielsen and R Smyth, 'What the Australian Public Knows About the High Court' (2019) 47 *Federal Law Review* 31.

[35] TF Bathurst, 'Trust in the Judiciary' (2021) 14 *The Judicial Review* 263, 264.

[36] See generally M Groves, 'Judges and the Media' in G Appleby and A Lynch (eds), *The Judge, the Judiciary and the Court: Individual, Collegial and Institutional Judicial Dynamics in Australia* (Cambridge, Cambridge University Press, 2021) 259.

[37] See M Warren, 'Open Justice in the Technological Age' (2014) 40 *Monash University Law Review* 45.

[38] B McLachlin, 'The Relationship Between the Courts and the Media', speech at Carleton University (31 January 2012).

[39] See, eg, M Kirby, 'Attacks on Judges: A Universal Phenomenon' (1998) 72 *Australian Law Journal* 599; PA Keane, 'The Idea of the Professional Judge: The Challenges of Communication' (2015) 12 *Judicial Review* 301; Beech-Jones (see n 25 above).

Unfounded or inaccurate criticism of courts has important consequences in and of itself: it may lead to a loss of public confidence in courts and judges, which compromises the effectiveness of the courts. However, an arguably more concerning risk is that ill-informed perceptions of the judiciary, in turn, may shape the development of public policy on issues of law and justice – or, in the worst case, may be actively encouraged and eventually invoked to justify a weakening of the administration of justice, including judicial independence.

This is not to suggest that the courts should not be subject to legitimate, reasoned criticism. The powers exercised by judges in the name of the community have significant human consequences. Like all democratic institutions, courts must be subject to scrutiny and made publicly accountable to the communities which they serve. It was this fundamental importance of open justice which led Jeremy Bentham to describe 'publicity' – rather poetically – as 'the very soul of justice' and 'the surest of all guards against improbity'.[40]

Yet in order to serve the purpose of promoting democratic accountability, criticism of the judiciary must be based on an accurate understanding of the work of the courts, be rational and measured in balance, and not treat the exceptional as the typical. The concern is not with the 'disinfectant' of open justice nor with reasoned public criticism of judicial outcomes, but with a particular brand of populist, ill-informed or exaggerated criticism of courts and judges that is liable dangerously to undermine confidence in the judiciary.

There is also the fact that the ubiquity of social media and informational tools such as Google is increasingly prompting concern about the integrity of the fact-finding process in jury trials.[41] Modern jurors have in their mobile phones and other devices access to a vast volume of information which is not evidence in a case (and which may or may not be accurate) but which, notwithstanding judicial directions not to do so, they will be tempted to draw upon to discharge their responsibilities. This is an increasing problem, corrupting the role traditionally played by jurors in the determination of the facts. A recent amendment to the Juries Act 1967 (ACT) has created, by s 42BA, a criminal offence for a juror to make an inquiry, including by conducting internet research, for the purposes of any matter relating to the trial in which the juror is participating.

Courts have already been affected by elements or manifestations of truth decay in ways additional to the example earlier given by reference to the 2020 US Presidential Election. That is to say, public commentary on judges and courts has been increasingly coloured by emotive or anecdotal attacks, factual inaccuracies and a lack of engagement with the reality of how judicial decisions are made.[42]

A. An Illustrative Example: Criminal Justice and Sentencing

One area of judicial activity which has long attracted emotionally charged public incomprehension, perhaps more than any other, is the work of sentencing judges. At its core, this lack of comprehension stems from factual misapprehensions about crime, a lack of

[40] J Bowring (ed), *The Works of Jeremy Bentham* (Simpkin, Marshall, 1843) 316.

[41] See A Dale and F Silva, 'Future Proofing the Jury System' (2023) 3 *Law Society Journal* 40.

[42] See, K Mack, S Anleu and J Tutton, 'The Judiciary and the Public: Judicial Perceptions' (2018) 39 *Adelaide Law Review* 1, in which the authors draw on a range of interviews with and surveys of judicial officers. Judicial officers consistently reflected on often aggressive and ill-informed public commentary they received.

understanding of what judges do, and, often, a very shallow engagement by the media with the sentencing process.

The tendency for public perceptions of crime and criminal justice to be out of step with reality has been observed in a number of developed countries.[43] Indeed, it is one of the key examples relied upon by Kavanagh and Rich in their foundational book on truth decay. They cite evidence indicating that, until around the year 2000, public attitudes about the prevalence of crime in the US corresponded closely with the reality – which was that violent crime rates had steadily decreased since 1993. However, after around 2000:[44]

> … an increasing number of respondents reported that they perceived *more* crime in the United States than in the previous year, despite clear evidence to the contrary. In other words, an increasing number of respondents question existing data on trends in crime even as data collection and documentation methods become more advanced.

Similar findings have been made in the Australian context. Since the early 2000s, a growing body of evidence has demonstrated a substantial mismatch between public perceptions of criminal offending and the data collected by government agencies.[45] In particular, 'a substantial proportion of the population incorrectly believe crime rates are increasing [even] when, in fact, they are stable or declining'.[46] Tellingly, respondents tend to be more concerned about an increase in crime rates at the state or territory level than at the local level, and often do not perceive an increase in criminal offending in their *own* neighbourhood.[47]

The concern about these beliefs is not so much that they are often inconsistent with empirical evidence. It is that, increasingly, the public debate about criminal offending does not appear to be *concerned* with empirical evidence. Public perceptions of crime and criminal justice are primarily driven by anecdotal reasoning, emotive and incomplete media coverage, and a strong selection bias favouring particularly gruesome, shocking or unusual offending.

The paradox underlying this trend is that, in the age of 'big data', the collection, analysis and accessibility of data about criminal offending is more advanced than ever before. Clearly, the issue is not that the relevant evidence is not readily available. This reflects the essence of truth decay: a culture of public discourse driven by emotion, anecdote and tribalism rather than fact.

Of course, it is unrealistic to expect that the public and the media will take a sudden interest in the thousands of unexceptional cases of criminal offending when they could, instead, read and write about shocking crimes involving tragic, unprovoked violence,

[43] See, eg, B Davis and K Dossetor, '(Mis)perceptions of Crime in Australia' (Trends and Issues in Crime and Criminal Justice: Research Paper No 396, Australian Institute of Criminology, July 2010) and the sources cited therein.

[44] *Truth Decay* (see n 21 above) 25–26.

[45] See, eg, D Weatherburn and D Indermaur, 'Public Perceptions of Crime Trends in New South Wales and Western Australia' (2004) 80 *Crime and Justice Bulletin: Contemporary Issues in Crime and Justice* 1; Davis and Dossetor (see n 43 above); L Roberts and D Indermaur, 'What Australians Think about Crime and Justice: Results from the 2007 Survey of Social Attitudes' (Research and Public Policy Series No 101, Australian Institute of Criminology, July 2010); K Warner et al, 'Public Judgement on Sentencing: Final Results from the Tasmanian Jury Sentencing Study' (Trends and Issues in Crime and Criminal Justice: Research Paper No 407, Australian Institute of Criminology, February 2011) 3.

[46] Davis and Dossetor (see n 43 above) 1.

[47] ibid 2.

mysterious disappearances, or organised crime groups. The front pages of newspapers will never be occupied solely by comprehensive dashboards of statistics. It is in our nature to be drawn to stories of individual human intrigue. Yet there is no reason why stories of human intrigue cannot be counterbalanced against, or placed in the perspective of, accepted evidence about broader trends in criminal justice and public safety.

This complaint about the way in which sentencing decisions are conveyed to the public is not a novel one and has been made by the three immediate predecessors of this author.[48] More recent data confirms that sentencing remains the judicial function in which the public has the least trust. Although, as already observed, the Australian Law Reform Commission's 2021 survey indicated that overall trust in Australian courts has increased over the last ten years, the same survey also showed that over 40 per cent of respondents had 'very little confidence' or 'no confidence' in the ability of judges to 'give appropriate sentences to those who have committed crimes'.[49] Similarly, surveys indicate that, when asked to assess general sentencing patterns, between 70 and 80 per cent of the public reply that sentences are too lenient.[50]

Yet in a study conducted in Victoria between 2013 and 2015 among jurors who had returned a guilty verdict – the members of the public with perhaps the most intimate understanding of the facts of a criminal offence – some 62 per cent suggested a sentence *more* lenient than that ultimately imposed by the judge.[51] These results were broadly consistent with the results of a previous study conducted in Tasmania in which 90 per cent of jurors considered the sentence imposed by the judge to be appropriate.[52]

This discrepancy reveals the lie in the tired and misconceived yet stubbornly popular view that courts are 'soft on crime' or that sentencing outcomes are out of step with community expectations. It indicates that perceptions of *general trends* in judicial outcomes are starkly at odds with the views of community members who are given complete and objective information about a *particular judicial decision*.

Of course, in the modern information ecosystem, the public is generally *not* given complete and objective information about judicial decisions and the way they are made. This difficulty is made more intractable in the age of the online 'attention economy', characterised as it is by a breakneck digital news cycle, the decentralisation of news media to a variety of online forums, the subtle effects of online algorithmic curation, and the inexorable rolling commentary of 'X' (formerly Twitter). Faced with powerful incentives to make news short, engaging and 'shareable', it seems that the inherent complexity involved in judicial decision-making is rarely conveyed in public debate.

[48] AM Gleeson, 'Who do Judges Think They are?' (1998) 22 *Criminal Law Journal* 10, 15; J Spigelman, 'The Power of Twelve: A New Way to Sentence for Serious Crime' (2005) 86 *Australian Law Reform Commission Reform Journal* 51; and TF Bathurst, 'Community Confidence in the Justice System: The Role of Public Opinion', speech at the Opening of NSW Law Term Address, Sydney (3 February 2014).

[49] Australian Law Reform Commission (see n 24 above) 148.

[50] Warner et al (see n 45 above) 181.

[51] ibid 186. In some cases, this discrepancy may be partially explained by the presence of prior relevant convictions (which are taken into account by sentencing judges but are not in evidence at trial). However, even where the defendant had no relevant prior convictions, 57% of jurors recommended a sentence more lenient than was imposed by the sentencing judge.

[52] Warner et al (see n 45 above). In this study, participants were invited to hear the submissions on sentence before completing the survey.

IV. Limited Insulation Against Truth Decay

It has been said that 'discussions of judicial legitimacy in Australia have a prophylactic, rather than a defensive tenor'[53] and several features of courts and the judicial system provide some form and degree of insulation from the corrosive effects of truth decay.

In the common law tradition, judicial method itself involves an analytical, Socratic approach that necessarily prioritises fact and reasoned analysis and requires the balanced consideration of arguments in favour of and against a position before a final conclusion is reached. Extensive rights of appeal are directed to the correction of both factual and legal errors. Judges are also expected to retain at all times their independence and impartiality such that their conclusions are not 'subjective or personal to [him or her] but … the consequence of [his or her] best endeavour to apply an external standard'.[54] It should be acknowledged that this statement was made many decades before more recent scholarship relating to considerations of subconscious bias.

Courts are also to some degree shielded from truth decay by the sometimes-painstaking strictures of courtroom procedure, the ethical rules to which reference has already been made and the rules of evidence. For example, the opinion rule draws a strong distinction between evidence of facts and opinions and only allows for the admissibility of opinions in certain narrow circumstances, including where those opinions are given by experts with specialised training or experience.[55] The stringent requirements of procedural fairness upheld in Australian courts, principally the fair hearing rule and the rule against bias, also have important work to do in ensuring that the courts remain a respected source of factual and legal information,[56] the outcome of whose determinations has not been distorted by procedural irregularity.

Another aspect of the topic is the way in which the law and the judiciary may be enlisted in support of public efforts to mitigate the harms of misinformation. So much is illustrated by recent public debate about the regulation of online discourse, sparked by the release in Australia of the draft consultation Communications Legislation Amendment (Combatting Misinformation and Disinformation) Bill 2023. Another example may be seen in proposals for 'truth in political advertising' laws at the federal level within Australia. While these proposals typically involve a non-judicial body having primary responsibility for enforcing restrictions (such as the Australian Communications and Media Authority or the Australian Electoral Commission), some form of appeal or judicial review will inevitably lie to the courts. These proposals may raise difficult questions about the institutional competence of courts when adjudicating disputes about truth and dishonesty in the political arena.

[53] J Gleeson, 'Advancing Judicial Legitimacy: The Stakes and the Means' (2023) 15 *Journal of the Judicial Commission of New South Wales* 1, 4 citing M Gordon, 'The Integrity of Court: Political Culture and a Culture of Politics' (2020) 44 *Melbourne University Law Review* 863.

[54] O Dixon, 'Concerning Judicial Method' (1956) 29 *Australian Law Journal* 468, 471.

[55] Evidence Act, ss 76, 78 and 79.

[56] R French, 'Procedural Fairness – Indispensable to Justice?', speech at the Sir Anthony Mason Lecture, University of Melbourne Law School (7 October 2010) 1.

V. Maintenance of Public Confidence in the Work of the Courts

Maintaining public confidence in the work of the courts is another antidote to truth decay. The efficacy of judicial institutions inevitably depends on the confidence of the public, and of other branches of government. Among public institutions, the judiciary

> is … the most dependent upon habitual conformity to its decisions on the part of the community and the other branches of government. That habit of conformity only exists because the public have a certain attitude towards judicial power, and those who exercise it; an attitude we describe as confidence.[57]

When this 'habit of conformity' disintegrates, the consequences can be calamitous. Al Gore knew this in 2000 when, in the wake of the 5-4 majority decision of the US Supreme Court in *Bush v Gore*,[58] he ordered his supporters, 'don't trash the Supreme Court'.[59] The outcome was largely accepted without violence or social unrest. A year and a half later, on this side of the Pacific, Chief Justice Murray Gleeson would remark:[60]

> Doubts about the electoral process were resolved by recourse to law, and the nation accepted the result. Dissatisfaction with the outcome on the part of about half of the voters, and criticism of the decision of the court, co-existed with peaceful acceptance of the consequences of that decision.

There is an obvious contrast with what occurred in the US with regard to the Presidential election some 20 years later. This also corresponds to current reported low levels of public confidence in the US Supreme Court. At the same time, there have been vicious attacks on judges of lower courts who have been described as 'tyrannical and unhinged', a 'fully biased Trump Hater', a 'radical left judge' and a 'so-called judge'. Such comments, of which these are a minute selection, and the relative silence in terms of the defence of the judges attacked, can only result in the corrosion of respect for the judiciary as a whole.

There is some irony in that the branch of government which was described as the 'least dangerous' by one of the architects of Western democracy, Alexander Hamilton,[61] is often treated by modern populist movements across the world as if it were the *most* dangerous branch. This irony is perhaps best explained by Professor Wojciech Sadurski, in a recent book surveying illiberal populism and constitutional turmoil in democratic countries including Hungary, Poland, Turkey, Slovakia, Israel, and the US. He writes:[62]

> … the same factors that render judges and courts the least dangerous branch at the same time make them the most defenseless in the face of executive assault. … After being elected, populist rulers almost invariably take on the courts, often with fervor and unusual animus.

[57] M Gleeson, 'Public Confidence in the Judiciary', speech at the Judicial Conference of Australia Colloquium, Launceston (27 April 2002). See also A Bickel, *The Least Dangerous Branch: The Supreme Court and the Idea of Progress* (New Haven, Yale University Press, 1962) 258: 'Broad and sustained application of the [US Supreme] Court's law, when challenged, is a function of its rightness, not merely of its pronouncements.'

[58] *Bush v Gore* 531 US 98 (2000).

[59] S Breyer, *The Authority of the Court and the Peril of Politics* (Cambridge, MA, Harvard University Press, 2021) 28.

[60] Gleeson (see n 57 above).

[61] Hamilton (see n 32 above).

[62] W Sadurski, *A Pandemic of Populists* (Cambridge, Cambridge University Press, 2022) 106.

Sadurski offers two related reasons why attacks on independent judiciaries occupy such a prominent place in the ideological agendas of populist movements. First, they offer the most feasible *alternative* legitimacy to popularly elected leaders, by providing a channel for citizens to air their grievances against governments.[63] Second, the existence of *any* independent check on the 'will of the people' is incompatible with populist ideology;[64] therefore, in the eyes of the populists, members of the judiciary become anti-democratic 'elites'. To this may be added the practical reality that populist leaders tend to be elected on grand platforms of anti-establishment social or institutional reform – proposals of the kind that are likely to engage the close scrutiny of constitutional courts, particularly where they touch on civil liberties or involve attempts to alter the structure or powers of state entities or compromise judicial independence.

The references to events in the US should not be taken to suggest that Australia has been immune from attacks on its judiciary in ways which highlight how confidence in the courts as independent and competent arbiters of 'truth' can be eroded.

Concerns about a mounting hostility towards the Australian judiciary by media and public figures first began to be expressed in earnest by leaders of the legal profession towards the end of the twentieth century.[65] From 1992 on, the focal point for this criticism became a series of decisions of the High Court, including *Mabo v Queensland (No 2)* (*Mabo (No 2)*),[66] *Wik Peoples v State of Queensland*,[67] and a number of decisions concerning implied constitutional rights which are now well-established features of the Australian constitutional apparatus.[68] *Mabo (No 2)* was, at the time, particularly controversial, as it exploded the legal myth of *terra nullius* by recognising the truth that the lands of Australia were not 'practically unoccupied' in 1788 at the time of white settlement.

Much ink has been spilt about the sustained and vehement response to these decisions by public figures and the media, especially in the 1990s.[69] The febrile media environment at the time had many of the characteristics of truth decay; it was described as an instance in Australian public life when 'facts were swallowed by opinions'.[70] As one academic noted at the time:[71]

> The strident criticism of the Court left many with the impression that the judgments were not supported by extensive and careful legal reasoning. This helped create an environment in which misinformation could thrive.

[63] ibid 108.

[64] ibid 109.

[65] See, eg, A Mason, 'Judicial Independence and the Separation of Powers - Some Problems Old and New' (1990) 13 *University of New South Wales Law Journal* 173, 180–81; M Kirby, 'Judges under Attack' (1994) *New Zealand Law Journal* 365, 366; G Brennan, 'The State of the Judicature' (1998) 72 *Australian Law Journal* 33; Kirby (see n 39 above).

[66] *Mabo v Queensland (No 2)* (1992) 175 CLR 1.

[67] *Wik Peoples v State of Queensland* (1996) 187 CLR 1.

[68] See, eg, *Theophanous v Herald & Weekly Times Ltd* (1994) 182 CLR 104, *Australian Capital Television v Commonwealth* (1992) 177 CLR 106; *Lange v Australian Broadcasting Corporation* (1997) 89 CLR 520; *Dietrich v The Queen* (1992) 177 CLR 292.

[69] See generally T Josev, *The Campaign Against the Courts: A History of the Judicial Activism Debate* (Annandale, NSW, Federation Press, 2017), chs 4 and 5, and the sources referred to therein.

[70] P Keyzer, 'What the Courts and the Media Can Do to Improve the Standard of Media Reporting of the Work of the Courts' (1999) 1 *UTS Law Review* 150, 151.

[71] ibid. See also Kirby (see n 39 above) 600.

Attacks on the judiciary are, of course, not limited to any one side of the ideological spectrum. In 2011, the decision of the High Court of Australia in *M70/2011 v Minister for Immigration and Citizenship* – better known as the *Malaysian Declaration Case* – attracted the ire of members of the federal executive.[72] The Chief Justice was said by an unnamed cabinet member to have 'zero credibility',[73] and the decision was criticised as a 'missed opportunity … to send a very strong message of deterrence to people smugglers'.[74] As was said by Justice Philip McMurdo at the time, in his capacity as President of the Judicial Conference of Australia:[75]

> To suggest that a court has missed an opportunity to achieve a certain policy outcome is a completely misguided comment about what courts do. They do not look for opportunities to further matters of policy whether that be government policy or otherwise.

More recently, criticism of Australian judges by the executive returned to sharp focus in 2017, when three federal ministers launched verbal attacks at the Victorian Court of Appeal relating to an appeal against a sentence for terrorism charges. After oral argument was heard on the appeal – but before the decision was delivered – a front-page story in *The Australian* quoted the three ministers as variously saying that Victorian judges were 'hard-left activist judges' who were 'divorced from reality' and conducting 'ideological experiments'.[76] The President of the Judicial Conference of Australia, Justice Robert Beech-Jones, released a statement condemning these remarks as a 'threat to the rule of law' and having 'no evidentiary foundation'.[77] The ministers narrowly avoided being charged with contempt of court after issuing a full apology.[78]

Six months later, the Law Council of Australia and the Law Institute of Victoria released similar public statements after another minister criticised the 'jokes of sentences being handed down' by Victorian courts for violent offending.[79] These instances illustrate the growing importance of representative professional bodies in protecting the independence and reputation of the judiciary and the legal profession.

Truth decay in the context of the work of the courts will only be hastened by attacks on independent judiciaries and judges. It is incumbent on courts and the legal profession more broadly to develop strategies for maintaining confidence in their vital work and resisting, or at least mitigating, the erosion of rational, fact-based public discourse. Extensive civic education about the role and importance of an independent judiciary is critical.

[72] See R French, 'A Voice for Judges: 30 Years on Truth to Power in a Post Truth Era', speech at the 30th Anniversary Lecture of the Australian Judicial Officers Association, Sydney (16 June 2023).

[73] G Brandis, 'Julia Gillard Attack Offensive and her Defender Lame' (*The Australian*, 9 September 2011), available at www.theaustralian.com.au/business/legal-affairs/julia-gillard-attack-offensive-and-her-defender-lame/news-story/4e66638f7ce0678ebbc473d11e183ad3.

[74] J Thompson, '"Rewriting of Act" puts offshore deals in doubt' (*ABC*, 1 September 2011), available at www.abc.net.au/news/2011-09-01/gillard-says-ruling-puts-offshore-processing-in-doubt/2866956.

[75] Judicial Conference of Australia, 'The Prime Minister's Criticism of the High Court' (Media Release, September 2011).

[76] Judicial Conference of Australia, 'Grossly Improper and Unfair Attack on Victorian Judiciary' (Media Release, 13 June 2017).

[77] ibid.

[78] Supreme Court of Victoria, 'Announcement of the Court of Appeal in Terrorism Matters' (Media Release, 23 June 2017).

[79] Law Council of Australia, 'Vital the rule of law is upheld despite warring words' (Media Release, 15 January 2018).

The vulnerability of the courts to misrepresentation and unfounded criticism raises age-old questions about the role of the judiciary in public debate. In particular, it raises questions about what body or office is best placed to defend the courts against inaccurate or unfair criticism, and whether – or in what circumstances – courts should publicly 'correct the record'.[80] Much has changed since the days of what were known as the Kilmuir Rules – which were, in fact, not rules at all, but a letter written in 1955 by the UK Lord Chancellor to the Director-General of the BBC, in which Viscount Kilmuir said that 'as a general rule it is undesirable for judges to broadcast on the wireless or appear on television'.[81]

It is now accepted that judges may be contributors to public discussion, provided that they are always careful not to attract controversy or undermine the independence of their office. Within these overriding constraints, the freedom of judges to contribute to public discussion is reflected in, for example, the United Nations' Basic Principles on Independence of the Judiciary[82] and the Australasian Institute of Judicial Administration's Guide to Judicial Conduct.[83] Yet the prevailing tendency remains for judges to be reticent to engage in public commentary. As was said by Sir Anthony Mason 35 years ago, 'Judicial reticence has much to commend it ... Judges are not renowned for their sense of public relations.'[84]

The more specific question which arises in the context of the present discussion is this: against the background of an erosion of reasoned, factual public discourse, what role do judges and courts have to play in responding to or correcting inaccurate, ill-informed public criticism of their work? In the age of digital platforms, on which misinformation can spread at lightning speed unless swiftly countered, should the judiciary take a more muscular approach to defending itself from unfair criticism?

These questions should be considered against a background of shifting political norms involving the role of the Attorney-General as the traditional 'defender' of the judiciary. The increasingly belligerent criticism of judges towards the end of the twentieth century also coincided with a well-observed contraction of the willingness of many Attorneys-General to defend the judiciary in the political arena and in the public domain.[85] In a speech delivered in 1989, Sir Anthony Mason, after referring to the tradition of Attorneys-General representing the interests of the judiciary, said:[86]

> But the old framework has been largely dismantled: The Judiciary, in common with other institutions, is not immune from criticism; nor should it be. But somebody must defend the

[80] For two thoughtful explorations of this topic, see K Mason, 'A Time to Keep Silence, and a Time to Speak', speech to the NSW Bar Association (12 May 2000) and M McMurdo, 'Should Judges Speak Out?', speech at the Judicial Conference of Australia, Uluru (April 2001).

[81] See also Groves (see n 37 above) 260. J Rozenberg, 'The Embattled Judge' in J Copper (ed), *Being a Judge in the Modern World* (Oxford, Oxford University Press, 2017) 59.

[82] Adopted by the 7th United Nations Congress on the Prevention of Crime and the Treatment of Offenders (6 September 1985), clause 8 of which provides:

> In accordance with the Universal Declaration of Human Rights, members of the judiciary are like other citizens entitled to freedom of expression, belief, association and assembly; provided, however, that in exercising such rights, judges shall always conduct themselves in such a manner as to preserve the dignity of their office and the impartiality and independence of the judiciary.

[83] Australasian Institute of Judicial Administration, *Guide to Judicial Conduct*, 3rd edn (2023) cl 5.7.

[84] Mason (see n 65 above) 181.

[85] Groves (see n 36 above) 262ff; Beech-Jones (see n 25 above) 14ff; McMurdo (see n 80 above) 3; LJ King, 'The Attorney-General, Politics and the Judiciary' (2000) 74 *Australian Law Journal* 444; D Williams, 'The Role of the Attorney-General' (2002) 13 *Public Law Review* 1252.

[86] Mason (see n 65 above) 181.

> Judiciary. Attorneys-General are today more conscious of the advantages of political expedience. A politician does not win votes by defending judges or public servants. *An Attorney-General no longer feels that he needs to defend the judges or their decisions in the face of every critic. The critics will include his own political colleagues. In recent years members of Parliament and media personalities have been prepared to criticise judges and judicial decisions to a greater extent than formerly.* Many politicians - I speak of the Australian variety - do not understand judicial independence and its value. (emphasis added)

Over past decades, courts have developed a number of strategies to pre-empt and respond to ill-informed public commentary. First, from the 1990s, courts around Australia began to appoint 'Public Information Officers' (now often known simply as media managers or media liaison officers), tasked with publicly communicating the work of the courts to the journalistic profession and facilitating requests for information.[87] It has since become routine for courts to issue judgment summaries in cases of particular public interest or complexity, with the primary purpose of assisting journalists to report accurately under the deadline-driven, time-poor conditions of modern journalism. And in the past decade, courts have begun to 'us[e] the internet to speak directly to the public'[88] by live-streaming certain court proceedings online and posting judgments and judgment summaries on social media accounts. On the whole, live-streaming of cases of public importance is valuable and a natural extension of the commitment to open justice. Such streaming will demonstrate to the public the nature of judicial work and, in the delivery of judgment, the natural sifting of evidence and systematic, structured and careful working through of arguments. Care must, however, be taken where possible to avoid the sensationalisation of solemn hearings. That will not always be in the court's hands.

In Australia, perhaps the most significant development has been the emerging role of the Australian Judicial Officers Association (AJOA), together with other legal professional bodies, as the primary defenders of the judiciary. It has been noted that the inception of the AJOA in 1993 (then the Judicial Conference of Australia) coincided with public debate about the proper body to defend the judiciary from attacks,[89] and the AJOA now 'fills the role that many Attorneys-General used to perform but no longer do'.[90]

There may also be occasions when a reply by the court itself is warranted. So much is acknowledged in rule 5.7.2 of the Guide to Judicial Conduct issued by the Australian Council of Chief Justices, which states:

> On occasions decisions of a court may attract unfair, inaccurate or ill-informed comment. Many judges consider that, according to the circumstances, the court should respond to unjust criticism or inaccurate statements, particularly when they might unfairly reflect upon the competence, integrity or independence of the judiciary. Any such response should be dealt with by the Chief Justice or other head of the jurisdiction.

[87] See J Johnston, 'A History of Public Information Officers in Australian Courts: 25 Years of Assisting Public Perceptions and Understanding of the Administration of Justice (1993–2018)' (Research Paper, Australian Institute of Judicial Administration, April 2019) 1. This development was pioneered by the Family Court in 1983, and began to be adopted in other courts a decade later.

[88] Warren (see n 37 above) 57.

[89] See R French, 'Seeing Visions and Dreaming Dreams', speech at the JCA Colloquium, Canberra (7 October 2016) 3.

[90] Beech-Jones (see n 25 above) 16.

The question of when it will be necessary, or indeed helpful, for a head of jurisdiction to issue a public statement to 'correct the record' is a delicate one. The guiding considerations should always be whether the criticism has the capacity to seriously undermine public confidence in the court, and whether a public statement will in fact mitigate the damage or merely compound it. There is always a risk that by responding directly to unfounded criticism, the dominant effect will be merely to amplify that criticism. One must also be conscious of the likelihood that the statement will be conveyed to the public under sensationalist headlines such as 'Court Hits Back at Minister'.[91] As with many decisions that fall to judges, this is an area in which there are no hard and fast rules; a decision must be made on a realistic assessment of all the circumstances.

A statement by a head of jurisdiction is most likely to be the appropriate response where an unwarranted attack is mounted against the competence of a particular court, as opposed to the court system as a whole. In this context, it should be noted that attacks on the judiciary do not always take the form of criticism of particular decisions or perceived patterns in judicial outcomes. They may also take the form of unfounded criticism of a particular court's competence, including its accessibility to the public, the efficiency and expense of its processes, and the expertise of its judges.

Commentary of this kind was recently made in the New South Wales Legislative Assembly in support of a Bill to establish a new Industrial Court. It was stated – incorrectly – that industrial law proceedings in the New South Wales Supreme Court generally took several years, required the cost of briefing Senior Counsel, and were determined by judges who often do not have a background in industrial law. The Court responded to these comments via a brief public statement published on its website, which addressed the factual errors in what had been said in Parliament.[92] It took the view that false statements about the work of the Court could not, and should not, go uncorrected.

As for steps that judges may take to encourage factual, reasoned debate about the courts and their decisions, attention should also be given to other ways in which courts and judges may proactively promote broader public engagement in, and respect for, the work of the courts. The presence of courts on social media platforms and the livestreaming of judicial proceedings are two elements of this broader effort. Not to be forgotten in the context of maintaining confidence in and respect for the legitimacy of our judicial system is the important role played by juries in criminal matters: the daily occurrence of hundreds of our citizens sitting in court, all day, day after day, participating in our system of justice, including observing and being guided by our judges in close detail, and then being entrusted to judge their fellow citizens in matters as serious as murder.

This chapter now turns to a more recent threat to the ascertainment of truth in the sense and to the extent that courts are involved in its ascertainment, although, as the current Master of the Rolls, Sir Geoffrey Vos, would caution, it is important not to take

[91] See R French (see n 72 above) 5.

[92] Supreme Court of New South Wales, 'Statement on Behalf of the Supreme Court of New South Wales' (Media Statement, 30 November 2023).

a reflex, uniformly negative response to GenAI across the board.[93] There is real potential for its valuable application, albeit real caution is required in its embrace. Others have been rather more alarmist about algorithmic justice, raising existential questions about the future of law and the legal profession.[94] Their views are worthy of the greatest respect and reflection.

VI. Generative AI and Truth Decay

The vulnerability of courts to truth decay is perhaps most graphically illustrated by the emergence and rise in the use of GenAI within the legal system.

There is no doubt that GenAI may be hugely valuable in certain tasks, what Professor Tania Sourdin has described as 'supportive technology' or 'supportive AI'.[95] Notwithstanding its undoubted potential advantages, a real concern with the advent of GenAI is the extent to which it will 'deskill' lawyers (including judges) and undermine or erode the development and maintenance of their analytical abilities and capacity for the critical testing of legal and factual propositions. The combination of cost, efficiency and laziness may generate disproportionate or even overwhelming reliance on GenAI in the judicial and wider legal system in a way that not only exposes it to abuse but more fundamentally has the capacity to alter the high regard in which judges, and their judgments, are currently generally held by the broader community to the extent that their decisions may be viewed as little more than another output or result of GenAI.

There are several ways in which the use of GenAI programs may contribute to the phenomenon of truth decay. First, it has been well documented that GenAI is prone to generating incorrect or false information. This is obviously a matter of serious concern. These errors are sometimes a consequence of a 'garbage in, garbage out' problem whereby outputs merely reflect false information contained in the dataset upon which

[93] G Vos, 'AI – Transforming the work of lawyers and judges', keynote speech at the AI Conference 2024: Transforming the Legal Landscape, Manchester (9 March 2024) 3. In this speech, Vos said:

> … we all owe a duty to those we serve … to make constructive use of whatever technology is available if it helps to provide a better, quicker and more cost effective service to clients and the public, if you are a lawyer, and to provide a better, quicker and more cost effective dispute resolution process if you are a judge.
>
> … it is [also] an integral part of the adoption of new technologies that we need to do all we can to protect the very same citizens and businesses from their adverse effects. That means that, where appropriate, we need to promote effective regulation, rule-making, data protection, the protection of confidential material, and the minimisation of cyber-crime and cyber-fakes…
>
> But none of that means that we should forsake new technologies and the benefits they bring … [T]he simple fact is that we would not be properly serving either the interests of justice or access to justice if we did not embrace the use of new technologies for the benefit of those we serve.

[94] See, eg, D Hunter 'The Death of the Legal Profession and the Future of Law' (2020) 43 *University of New South Wales Law Journal* 1199; see also T Endicott and K Yeung, 'The Death of Law? Computationally Personalised Norms and the Rule of Law' (2022) 72 *University of Toronto Law Journal* 373.

[95] T Sourdin, 'Judge v Robot? Artificial Intelligence and Judicial Decision-making' (2018) 41 *University of New South Wales Law Journal* 1114; T Sourdin, *Judges, Technology and Artificial Intelligence* (Cheltenham, Edward Elgar, 2021).

AI is trained.[96] That also highlights the dependency of users of the underlying datasets upon or by reference to which a GenAI program operates. It also highlights the huge power enjoyed by those that control and can manipulate the underlying datasets. While it may be expected that the problem of GenAI 'hallucination' discussed further below may be seen by some as a 'teething problem' and one that may to a certain extent be expected to be addressed as GenAI becomes more refined, the more fundamental point remains and is one that has profound implications for the efficacy in terms of 'truth' and 'accuracy' of GenAI.

Error-riddled AI outputs may also be a product of the program being trained on outdated information. For instance, the free version of ChatGPT, ChatGPT-4o, only draws on information available up until October 2023, which means that, in a legal context, developments in the law that have occurred since that time are not reflected in ChatGPT's outputs.[97] Equally, GenAI may also only be trained on a dataset from a particular geographic area. ChatGPT draws predominantly from American data, so it is more likely to make errors in providing legal information in other jurisdictions.[98]

GenAI programs may additionally produce 'hallucinated' outputs. Hallucinated outputs are those outputs which contain false information, but which are presented as if they were facts. ChatGPT may produce hallucinations in a number of situations, including where it does not understand the prompt it has been given or where there are gaps in its dataset, and the possibility of errors is expressly stated in ChatGPT's Terms of Use.[99] That said, in relation to the summarising of short documents, it should be noted that ChatGPT's hallucination rate is estimated to be around 1.7 per cent, which is low when compared with some other GenAI chatbots.[100] For instance, the Claude 3.7 Sonnet system offered by Anthropic has been reported as having a hallucination rate of around 4.4 per cent,[101] although the quality of the underlying technology is being continually refined and updated so that statistics and information more generally in this sphere may rapidly become out of currency.

Associate Professor Blayne Haggart recently wrote the following in *The Conversation* in relation to GenAI hallucinations and their relationship with truth:[102]

> ChatGPT, and other machine-learning, large language models may seem sophisticated, but they're basically just complex autocomplete machines. Only instead of suggesting the next word in an email, they produce the most statistically likely words in much longer packages. …

[96] F Bell et al, 'AI Decision-Making and the Courts: A Guide for Judges, Tribunal Members and Court Administrators' (*Australian Institute of Judicial Administration Inc*, December 2023) 15.

[97] S Kerner, 'ChatGPT Search: Details About OpenAI's Search Engine' (*TechTarget*, 13 December 2024), available at www.techtarget.com/whatis/feature/SearchGPT-explained-Details-about-OpenAIs-search-engine.

[98] See, eg, UK Courts and Tribunals, 'Artificial Intelligence (AI) – Guidance for Judicial Office Holders' (12 December 2023) 2, available at www.judiciary.uk/wp-content/uploads/2023/12/AI-Judicial-Guidance.pdf (UK Judicial Guideline on AI).

[99] OpenAI, 'Terms and Conditions', available at openai.com/policies/row-terms-of-use.

[100] Vectara, 'Leaderboard Comparing LLM Performance at Producing Hallucinations when Summarizing Short Documents' (*Github*, 13 March 2025), available at github.com/vectara/hallucination-leaderboard.

[101] ibid.

[102] B Haggart, 'Unlike with Academics and Reporters, You can't Check when ChatGPT's Telling the Truth' (*The Conversation*, 31 January 2023), available at theconversation.com/unlike-with-academics-and-reporters-you-cant-check-when-chatgpts-telling-the-truth-198463.

> The justification for these outputs can never be truth. Its truth is the truth of the correlation, that the word "sentence" should always complete the phrase "We finish each other's…" because it is the most common occurrence, not because it is expressing anything that has been observed.
>
> Because ChatGPT's truth is only a statistical truth, output produced by this program cannot ever be trusted in the same way that we trust a reporter or an academic's output. It cannot be verified because it has been constructed to create output in a different way than what we usually think of as being "scientific".
>
> You can't check ChatGPT's sources because the source is the statistical fact that most of the time, a set of words tend to follow each other.
>
> One particular vice of GenAI is the plausibility of its output and the language employed, that is to say, propositions are expressed with great confidence and clarity of language, features which it has in common with the most accomplished of fraudsters.

A. Use by Lawyers

It has been suggested that, as AI continues to develop and improve, in some instances and subject to local rules of professional ethics, use of AI by lawyers will not be optional. Large firms already have their own proprietary GenAI systems which are used internally. Clients may not wish to pay for what they could produce themselves using AI or for what could be done more efficiently by lawyers using AI. In fact, Sir Geoffrey has suggested that there may be future professional negligence cases which will concern the liability of persons, including lawyers, for *non-use* of AI![103] However, as highlighted by a number of cases internationally in which ChatGPT has been relied upon by lawyers in the preparation of litigation, the issues with GenAI highlighted above are matters of serious concern.

In the highly publicised[104] case of *Mata v Avianca*,[105] a Southern District of New York District Court decision which involved a claim by Mr Mata for damages after a metal serving cart struck his knee during a flight operated by Avianca, submissions were filed which included 'non-existent judicial opinions with fake quotes and citations created by the artificial intelligence tool ChatGPT'.[106] After judicial orders called the existence of the fake opinions into question, the two lawyers responsible for drafting and approving the submissions used ChatGPT to generate copies of the provably fake cases, which they then filed.

District Judge Kevin Castel described one of the fake decisions filed as showing 'stylistic and reasoning flaws that do not generally appear in decisions issued by United States Courts of Appeals'. He went on to characterise its legal analysis as 'gibberish'.

[103] G Vos (see n 93 above) 7, 9.

[104] See, eg, M Novak, 'Lawyer Uses ChatGPT in Federal Court and it Goes Horribly Wrong' (*Forbes*, 27 May 2023), available at www.forbes.com/sites/mattnovak/2023/05/27/lawyer-uses-chatgpt-in-federal-court-and-it-goes-horribly-wrong/?sh=7565cf383494 and D Carrick and S Kesteven, 'This US Lawyer Used ChatGPT to Research a Legal Brief with Embarrassing Results. We Could All Learn from his Error' (*ABC News*, 24 June 2023), available at www.abc.net.au/news/2023-06-24/us-lawyer-uses-chatgpt-to-research-case-with-embarrassing-result/102490068.

[105] *Mata v Avianca Inc* 22-cv-1461 (PKC).

[106] ibid 1.

A number of other features also alerted Judge Castel to the fact that the decision may have been falsified. They included that the procedural history outlined in the fake opinion bordered 'on nonsensical', the presence of often unpaired quotation marks, the lack of a conclusion to the judgment, the fact that the docket number in fact corresponded with another decision of the court and the inclusion of internal citations and quotes that were themselves non-existent.[107]

In discussing the consequences of the law firm's use of ChatGPT in this manner, Judge Castel acknowledged that lawyers obtain the assistance of a variety of sources in the preparation of submissions and there was 'nothing inherently improper about using a reliable artificial intelligence tool for assistance'. However, he went on to highlight the relationship between GenAI use by lawyers and 'truth decay' in courts by reasoning as follows:[108]

> Many harms flow from the submission of fake opinions. The opposing party wastes time and money in exposing the deception. The Court's time is taken from other important endeavours. The client may be deprived of arguments based on authentic judicial precedents. There is potential harm to the reputation of judges and courts whose names are falsely invoked as authors of the bogus opinions and to the reputation of a party attributed with fictional conduct. It promotes cynicism about the legal profession and the American judicial system. And a future litigant may be tempted to defy a judicial ruling by disingenuously claiming doubt about its authenticity.

Ultimately, Judge Castel found that the two lawyers who were primarily involved in the preparation of the submissions and their law firm were jointly and severally liable for a breach of Rule 11 of the Federal Rules of Civil Procedure (US),[109] and sanctions were imposed.

Although this decision illustrates the corrosive effect that GenAI use by lawyers in the preparation of litigation *may* have in terms of producing reliable, trustworthy outputs, it also demonstrates that the rules of procedure with which lawyers must comply may be an important safeguard against 'truth decay'. Apart from defamation, malicious prosecution, false imprisonment, trespass to the person, death and personal injury proceedings, pleadings in the Supreme and District Courts of New South Wales, for example, must be verified by an affidavit.[110] This may discourage lawyers from relying on ChatGPT in the preparation of pleadings without confirming that some or all of the outputs produced are supported evidentially or are or can be verified by the person taking responsibility for the pleading. Similarly, in the Federal Court of Australia, pleadings must be accompanied by a certificate signed by the lawyer that any factual and legal material available to the lawyer provides a proper basis for each allegation, denial and

[107] ibid 5–6.
[108] ibid 1.
[109] Rule 11 provides that: '(a) Signature. Every pleading, written motion, and other paper must be signed by at least one attorney of record in the attorney's name … (b) Representations to the Court. By presenting to the court a pleading, written motion, or other paper – whether by signing, filing, submitting, or later advocating it – an attorney or unrepresented party certifies that to the best of the person's knowledge, information, and belief, formed after an inquiry reasonable under the circumstances: … (2) the claims, defenses, and other legal contentions are warranted by existing law or by a nonfrivolous argument for extending, modifying, or reversing existing law or for establishing new law.'
[110] Uniform Civil Procedure Rules 2005 (NSW) rr 14.22–14.24.

non-admission in the pleadings.[111] Reliance on the fact that GenAI was used would not be likely to be accepted as a satisfactory explanation to justify a departure from this requirement.

In appeal proceedings, submissions must be signed by the barrister or solicitor who prepared them.[112] Assumption of professional responsibility in this way will be an important means of dissuading lawyers from uncritically using ChatGPT or any other GenAI product to generate material filed in proceedings. Adverse costs sanctions against practitioners supply an additional means of institutional protection.

Where, like in *Mata v Avianca,* ChatGPT-generated material is filed in court which includes fictitious cases, this author's view is that very strong sanctions should be imposed and an answer or purported explanation that it was what was produced by ChatGPT should not be accepted as satisfactory.

In the Canadian context, the case of *Zheng v Chen,*[113] which was decided in the British Columbian Supreme Court in 2024, bears a strong resemblance to that of *Mata v Avianca.* It concerned the insertion by counsel of two cases into a notice of motion which were discovered to have been invented by ChatGPT.

In reaching his conclusions as to the sanctions to be imposed upon the offending lawyer, DM Masuhara J noted the 'express warning' on the ChatGPT website that its outputs could be inaccurate and that ChatGPT should not be used as a substitute for professional advice.[114] He also had reference to a notice sent out by the Canadian Law Society in July 2023 regarding the risks of generative AI.[115] Further guidance was then issued to the profession in November 2023 which urged lawyers to 'review' content generated using AI 'carefully and ensure its accuracy'.[116]

Although special costs orders were not made against the offending lawyer,[117] she was ordered to review all of her files and advise the court and opposing counsel if any materials filed or handed up in any other case contained case citations or summaries which were obtained using generative AI tools.[118] Masuhara J also held that it would be 'prudent' to 'advise the court and the opposing parties when any materials [submitted] to the court include content generated by AI tools such as ChatGPT'.[119]

Zheng v Chen highlights the utility of professional ethical obligations to regulate, to some extent at least, the use of GenAI in relation to litigation. It may be that lawyers and experts should be required expressly to state the extent to which they have relied on GenAI in the preparation of materials for trial, and to formally certify that they have personally checked all references which have been thrown up by the use of such technology. It should be a breach of the obligation borne by solicitors and barristers not to

[111] Federal Court Rules 2011 (Cth) r 16.01.
[112] ibid rr 51.12, 51.13, 51.36 and 51.45.
[113] *Zheng v Chen* [2024] B.C.J. No. 305.
[114] ibid para 36.
[115] ibid para 34.
[116] ibid para 35.
[117] ibid para 32.
[118] ibid para 44.
[119] ibid para 45.

mislead the court to file documentation in proceedings which includes hallucinated or error-riddled information generated by ChatGPT.[120]

Guidelines have also been issued by the legal profession which outline how AI may be used in a manner consistent with a lawyer's ethical and professional obligations. The Professional Support Unit of the New South Wales Law Society released in the Law Society Journal in November 2023 a 'guide to responsible use of artificial intelligence'.[121] It highlighted a number of the Solicitors' Conduct Rules that may be breached where solicitors have inappropriately used AI.[122]

The New South Wales Bar Association has also released a guideline, Issues Arising from the Use of AI Language Models (including ChatGPT) in Legal Practice, which aims to provide 'guidance for barristers in relation to the consideration of use of AI language models, including ChatGPT, in their practice'.[123] The guideline draws attention to several of the Barristers Rules that may be infringed by uses of ChatGPT or another GenAI product.[124] The Bar Association described those rules as cumulatively reflecting the expectations of the community that barristers, as specialist advocates, will 'apply their own skill and exercise their own independent judgment when performing work for a client' and 'exercise reasonable care and skill'.[125]

The Bar Association also included the following in the guideline:[126]

> A barrister should be transparent with clients about their use of AI tools and their use to assist in legal representation. This should include disclosing to the client the nature of the AI tool the barrister proposes using and acknowledging the known limitations of the use of AI in legal practice. A barrister should always remain entirely accountable for any legal work based on AI-generated information.

The New Zealand and UK judiciaries, seemingly in response to the decision in *Mata v Avianca* and the public attention it received, have produced guidelines on AI use in courts and the steps that judicial officers may take to ensure that AI is not misused in the judicial system. However, those guidelines have not yet recommended the disclosure of GenAI use in all cases.

New Zealand led the way. On 7 December 2023, the New Zealand judiciary issued the Guidelines for Use of Generative Artificial Intelligence in Courts and Tribunals:

[120] See, eg, Barristers Rules, r 64 which prevents barristers from alleging any matter of fact in any court document, submission or address unless the barrister believes on reasonable grounds that the factual material available provides a proper basis to do so.

[121] Professional Support Unit, 'A Solicitor's Guide to Responsible Use of Artificial Intelligence' (*Law Society Journal*, 14 November 2023), available at lsj.com.au/articles/a-solicitors-guide-to-responsible-use-of-artificial-intelligence.

[122] They include rule 4, which concerns a solicitor's duties of competence, integrity and honesty, rule 17, which concerns a solicitor's independence, and rule 37, which pertains to the expectations of a solicitor who is charged with supervising the legal practice of others.

[123] New South Wales Bar Association, 'Issues Arising from the Use of AI Language Models (including ChatGPT) in Legal Practice' (12 July 2023) 1.

[124] Including rr 4, 8, 11, 13, 23, 24, 35 and 42.

[125] ibid 2.

[126] ibid.

Lawyers (NZ Lawyers Guidelines).[127] These guidelines emphasise the fundamental ethical and professional obligations of all legal professionals in New Zealand and stipulate at the outset that '[a]ny use of GenAI chatbots in the context of court and tribunal proceedings must be consistent with the observance of lawyers' obligations'.[128] Before using GenAI applications, the guidelines encourage lawyers to 'have a basic understanding of their capabilities and limitations'. In particular, they caution that 'even if the output looks convincing, it may not be factually correct' and highlight that existing GenAI applications have limited familiarity with New Zealand law and procedure.[129]

In addition to warning lawyers about potential biases in the outputs produced by GenAI, the guidelines mandate that all outputs generated by GenAI should be checked by an appropriately qualified person for accuracy before they are referred to in court or tribunal proceedings.[130] Nevertheless, the guidelines provide that where all procedures set out in the guidelines are complied with, it will not be necessary to disclose use of a GenAI chatbot, unless asked directly by a court or tribunal.[131]

On 12 December 2023, the UK judiciary issued judicial guidance on the use of AI (UK Judicial Guideline on AI). It provides the following in respect of potential uses of GenAI by legal practitioners:[132]

> Some kinds of AI tools have been used by legal professionals for a significant time without difficulty…
>
> All legal representatives are responsible for the material they put before the court/tribunal and have a professional obligation to ensure it is accurate and appropriate. Provided AI is used responsibly, there is no reason why a legal representative ought to refer to its use, but this is dependent upon context.
>
> Until the legal profession becomes familiar with these new technologies, however, it may be necessary at times to remind individual lawyers of their obligations and confirm that they have independently verified the accuracy of any research or case citations that have been generated with the assistance of an AI chatbot.

More recently, Singapore[133] and New South Wales[134] have issued guidelines on the use of GenAI which differ both from the New Zealand and UK models and from each other,

[127] Courts of New Zealand, 'Guidelines for Use of Generative Artificial Intelligence in Courts and Tribunals: Lawyers' (7 December 2023), available at www.courtsofnz.govt.nz/assets/6-Going-to-Court/practice-directions/practice-guidelines/all-benches/20231207-GenAI-Guidelines-Lawyers.pdf (NZ Lawyers Guidelines). At the same time, Courts of New Zealand, 'Guidelines for Use of Generative Artificial Intelligence in Courts and Tribunals: Judges, Judicial Officers, Tribunal Members and Judicial Support Staff' (7 December 2023) (NZ Judicial Guidelines on AI) were released.

[128] NZ Lawyers Guidelines (see n 127 above) 1.

[129] ibid 2.

[130] ibid 4.

[131] ibid.

[132] UK Judicial Guideline on AI (see n 98 above) 5.

[133] Supreme Court of Singapore, Registrar's Circular No 1 of 2024, 'Guide on the Use of Generative Artificial Intelligence Tools by Court Users' (23 September 2024), available at www.judiciary.gov.sg/docs/default-source/circulars/2024/registrar's_circular_no_1_2024_supreme_court.pdf.

[134] The Chief Justice of New South Wales, Supreme Court Practice Note SC Gen 23, 'Use of Generative Artificial Intelligence (Gen AI)' (28 January 2025), available at supremecourt.nsw.gov.au/documents/Practice-and-Procedure/Practice-Notes/general/current/PN_SC_Gen_23.pdf.

in the case of New South Wales, proscribing the use of GenAI in the generation of affidavits and witness statements and regulating the use of GenAI by expert witnesses and counsel.

B. Use by Self-Represented Litigants

The use of GenAI to prepare for litigation, including by conducting legal research and drafting submissions, is not restricted to lawyers and law firms. Rather, GenAI programs may be even more heavily relied upon by self-represented litigants. This is because programs like ChatGPT *may* be able to promote access to justice in that they may allow those who are not otherwise able to access legal representation to, for instance, identify if they have a claim, become familiar with legal processes and complete court documentation. In this respect, GenAI has obvious benefits for the efficiency and fairness of the justice system. However, GenAI's lack of a 'truth filter' may have the same insidious effect on the justice system when used by self-represented litigants as when used by legal representatives.

This issue emerged in a recent decision of the Federal Circuit and Family Court of Australia[135] in which an interlocutory application to restrain legal practitioners from acting for the respondent in the proceedings was refused. The applicant, a self-represented litigant, filed 24 authorities and corresponding summaries which she said were examples of cases where MinterEllison had been restrained from acting for their clients. Some of those cases did not exist, others had citations which corresponded with cases that had different names than those provided by the applicant, and others were not as the applicant had described them.

When asked by Judge Riley to provide the correct citations, the applicant had explained that she had been provided with the list of cases by another person, was rushing, so had not had time to verify them and 'did not know what ChatGPT was'.[136]

Similar issues arose in the UK First-Tier Tribunal Tax Chamber when a self-represented litigant sought to appeal against a penalty imposed on her as a consequence of her failure to notify the Commissioner of Revenue of her liability to capital gains tax.[137] The applicant had provided the tribunal with the names, dates and summaries of nine other tribunal decisions in which she claimed that an applicant had been successful in showing that a reasonable excuse existed for failing to notify.

In addition to the applicant's concession that it was 'possible' the document had been created using AI and the fact that none of the judgments could be found using legal databases, the tribunal took a number of factors into account in making a finding of fact that the cases were generated by 'an AI system such as ChatGPT'.[138]

The tribunal found that the applicant was not aware that the cases were fabricated and 'did not know how to locate or check case law authorities'.[139] However, it also

[135] *Finch v The Heat Group Pty Ltd* [2024] FedCFamC2G 161.
[136] ibid para 137.
[137] *Harber v The Commissioners for His Majesty's Revenue and Customs* [2023] UKFTT 1007 (TC) (*Harber*).
[138] ibid para 21.
[139] *Harber*, para 22.

acknowledged the role that GenAI, by falsifying authorities, may play in perverting the course of justice. The tribunal considered, with reference to the decision of Judge Castel in *Mata v Avianca*, that the applicant's conduct generated considerable harm to the courts and legal profession, and particularly to respect for the doctrine of precedent, on the basis that the tribunal's decisions are 'persuasive authorities' which later tribunals would be expected to follow.[140]

Unlike solicitors and barristers who use GenAI in a manner which results in falsifiable information being put before the court, self-represented litigants are not subject to the same professional conduct rules. This generates complexity for courts in ensuring that GenAI use by self-represented litigants promotes efficiency in and access to the justice system, rather than leaving it vulnerable to fabrication and distortion.

The UK Judicial Guideline on AI provides that:[141]

> AI chatbots are now being used by unrepresented litigants. They may be the only source of advice or assistance some litigants receive. Litigants rarely have the skills independently to verify legal information provided by AI chatbots and may not be aware that they are prone to error. If it appears an AI chatbot may have been used to prepare submissions or other documents, it is appropriate to inquire about this, and ask what checks for accuracy have been undertaken (if any).

Alternatively, guidance and information directed to unrepresented litigants may be issued by courts with a view to assisting them in navigating appropriate uses of GenAI in court proceedings. This course of action has been taken in New Zealand where a dedicated Guideline for Non-Lawyers on the Use of GenAI in Courts[142] has been issued.

That guideline instructs non-lawyers that GenAI chatbots may help by 'identifying and explaining laws and legal principles that might be relevant to a situation' and in drafting 'basic legal documents' or 'helping … organise the facts into a clearer structure or suggesting suitable headings'.[143] However, it also warns that GenAI programs have limited training in New Zealand law and court procedure, cannot 'understand the unique fact situation in a specific case', 'understand culture and emotional needs', 'understand the broader Aotearoa New Zealand social and legal context', 'predict the chance of success or the outcome of a case', 'be trusted to always provide legal or other information that is relevant, accurate, complete, up-to-date and unbiased' or 'reach logical conclusions, even when given relevant facts'.[144] As such, the guideline encourages non-lawyers to seek legal assistance and to thoroughly check any material generated by GenAI chatbots on the basis that such programs have a propensity to produce 'fake material' which 'can look as though it has been taken from a real source even when it has not'.[145]

Nonetheless, as with uses of GenAI by lawyers, the guideline provides that disclosure 'by default' of GenAI chatbot use is not necessary 'unless asked by the court or tribunal'.

[140] ibid para 24.
[141] UK Judicial Guideline on AI (see n 98 above) 5.
[142] Courts of New Zealand, 'Guidelines for Use of Generative Artificial Intelligence in Courts and Tribunals: Non-lawyers' (7 December 2023), available at www.courtsofnz.govt.nz/assets/6-Going-to-Court/practice-directions/practice-guidelines/all-benches/20231207-GenAI-Guidelines-Non-Lawyers.pdf.
[143] ibid 1.
[144] ibid.
[145] ibid 4.

Rather, it suggests that where non-lawyers have appropriately checked the accuracy of information in accordance with the guideline, the risks of GenAI use will have been sufficiently mitigated such that disclosure will not be necessary.[146]

C. Use by Judges

Use of GenAI by judges themselves also has the potential to compromise the judicial method, which has thus far guarded the courts from the worst of the effects of truth decay. There are now at least three reported cases internationally of judges using ChatGPT in the drafting of judgments.[147]

The first reported case of use of ChatGPT by a judge was in Cartagena, Colombia. Judge Juan Manuel Padilla included a conversation with ChatGPT in his judgment which concerned the entitlement of an autistic child to have his medical treatment entirely compensated by insurance.[148] Judge Padilla asked ChatGPT the following four questions, which he recorded in his judgment:

1. Is an autistic child exempt from co-payments for therapy?
2. Should tutela [constitutional] actions in these cases be granted?
3. Is requiring a co-payment in these cases a barrier to access to health services?
4. Has the jurisprudence of the constitutional court made favourable decisions in similar cases?

The answers provided by ChatGPT have been described as 'poorly justified' and lacking 'nuance', with the chatbot citing a law only tangentially relevant to the case on one occasion and then failing to cite specific Constitutional Court cases on another. Although the judge recorded in his reasons that the answers provided by ChatGPT would be 'corroborated', nothing in the text of the judgment confirms that the answers provided by ChatGPT were verified elsewhere before the judge relied upon them in reaching his conclusions.[149] In respect of his reasons for using ChatGPT, the judge outlined that 'including these AI-produced texts is in no way to replace the judge's decision. What we are really looking for is to optimise the time spent drafting judgments after corroborating the information provided by AI.'[150]

ChatGPT was also used in 2023 in the Punjab and Haryana High Court to collate relevant legal principles applicable to the bail plea of an accused charged with rioting,

[146] ibid.

[147] A Smith, A Moloney and A Asher-Schapiro, 'Are AI Chatbots in Courts Putting Justice at Risk?' (*Context*, 4 May 2023), available at www.context.news/ai/are-ai-chatbots-in-courts-putting-justice-at-risk.

[148] The judgment can be accessed at the following link: forogpp.files.wordpress.com/2023/01/sentencia-tutela-segunda-instancia-rad.-13001410500420220045901.pdf.

[149] JD Gutierrez, 'ChatGPT in Colombian Courts: Why We Need to have a Conversation about the Digital Literacy of the Judiciary' (*Verfassungsblog: On Matters Constitutional*, 23 February 2023), available at verfassungsblog.de/colombian-chatgpt.

[150] L Croft, 'Use of ChatGPT in Courts Should be "approached with great caution"' (*Lawyers Weekly*, 13 February 2023), available at www.lawyersweekly.com.au/the-bar/36657-use-of-chatgpt-in-courts-should-be-approached-with-great-caution.

criminal intimidation, murder, and criminal conspiracy.[151] Ultimately, in dismissing the bail petition, Justice Chitkara made clear that 'any reference to ChatGPT and any observation made is neither an expression of opinion on the merits of the case nor shall the trial Court advert to these comments; this reference is only intended to present a broader picture on bail jurisprudence, where cruelty is a factor'.[152]

In a third case, which received less media attention, Bolivian Constitutional Court judges consulted ChatGPT during an online hearing which concerned three journalists accused of posting photos of a victim of violence without her permission in circumstances where the journalists argued they had obtained the victim's consent. The judges asked ChatGPT whether there was any 'legitimate public interest' in journalists posting photos of a 'woman showing parts of her body' without her consent, to which ChatGPT responded that it was a 'violation of the person's privacy and dignity'. Orders were ultimately made for the photos to be removed and although the Court said that ChatGPT only assisted by 'clarifying certain concepts', the journalists' representative described the use of ChatGPT in the hearing as 'arbitrary'.[153]

Some have argued that use of GenAI by judges could promote public trust in the judiciary and combat truth decay by reducing the appearance of corruption, partiality or bias.[154] However, as already discussed, GenAI also has the potential to *introduce* bias, undermine the judiciary's independence and produce significant errors which will undermine confidence in the courts.[155] Despite this, neither the New Zealand nor UK guidelines to judicial officers on GenAI discussed below entirely warn against uses of GenAI in the judgment production process. In Canada, the Federal Court issued Interim Principles and Guidelines on the Court's Use of Artificial Intelligence on 20 December 2023 which provided that

> the Court will not use AI, and more specifically automated decision-making tools, in making its judgments and orders, without first engaging in public consultations. For greater certainty, this includes the Court's determination of the issues raised by the parties, as reflected in its Reasons for Judgment and its Reasons for Order, or any other decision made by the Court in a proceeding.[156]

The NZ Judicial Guidelines on AI issued on 7 December 2023 outline that 'GenAI chatbots … have been developed to assist judges, judicial officers, tribunal members and judicial support staff who may wish to use such tools in the course of their work' but caution that any such use 'must be consistent with the judiciary's overarching obligation to protect the integrity of the administration of justice and court/tribunal processes.'[157]

[151] J Sandhu, 'In a First, Punjab and Haryana HC Turns to ChatGPT for View on Bail in Murder Case' (*Indian Express*, 28 March 2023), available at indianexpress.com/article/cities/chandigarh/in-a-first-hc-turns-to-chatgpt-for-view-on-bail-in-murder-case-8522544.

[152] ibid.

[153] Smith, Moloney and Asher-Schapiro (see n 147 above).

[154] M Zalnieriute, 'Technology and the Courts: Artificial Intelligence and Judicial Impartiality' (Submission, Australian Law Reform Commission Review of Judicial Impartiality, 4 June 2021) 2.

[155] ibid 3–4.

[156] See Federal Court, 'Interim Principles and Guidelines on the Court's Use of Artificial Intelligence' (20 December 2023), available at www.fct-cf.gc.ca/en/pages/law-and-practice/artificial-intelligence.

[157] Zalnieriute (n 154) 1.

Warnings to judicial officers about appropriate and inappropriate uses of GenAI are given and were subsequently emulated by those offered by their UK equivalent referred to below. In particular, it is emphasised that GenAI should not be used for legal research and legal analysis. The NZ Judicial Guidelines on AI also stipulate that judicial officers do not need to declare the use of GenAI in judgment preparation. Later in the guidelines, sample prompts for effectively using AI in judgment preparation are offered.

The UK Judicial Guideline on AI cautions judges that GenAI tools have the potential to 'make up fictitious cases, citations or quotes, or refer to legislation, articles or legal texts that do not exist', 'provide incorrect misleading information regarding the law or how it might apply' and 'make factual errors'. The guideline also warns judges that there are enormous privacy concerns associated with inputting information into GenAI chatbots which is not already in the public domain, as this information may form part of the dataset which those chatbots utilise to answer the questions of future users.

The guideline goes on to recommend that AI may be 'potentially useful' in 'summarising large bodies of text', 'writing presentations, eg to provide suggestions for topics to cover' and 'administrative tasks like composing emails and memoranda'. However, the guideline is clear that all judges who use AI should understand what it does and does not do. Importantly, it sets out that AI use is 'not recommended' for legal research or legal analysis.[158] Rather, it suggests that AI 'may be best seen as a way of obtaining non-definitive confirmation of something, rather than providing immediately correct facts'.[159]

VII. AI Generated Evidence[160]

Another way in which GenAI may mask or obscure what is true and false is where AI is used for the purposes of generating evidence which is then relied upon in proceedings. This is particularly problematic.

Already AI has been used by some art historians and conservators to verify the authenticity of works, although such evidence is yet to be adduced in court proceedings.[161] Similarly, AI might be used by police to conduct facial comparisons between an image and a suspected offender.[162]

However, as has already been highlighted, applications like ChatGPT are able to generate text which, in many cases, will be indistinguishable from that written by a human. It is thus possible for ChatGPT to be used to produce written statements or affidavits that are then adduced in proceedings under the false pretence of having been made by a witness or party to the proceedings.

[158] NZ Judicial Guidelines on AI (see n 127 above) 6.

[159] ibid 3.

[160] See, generally, D Seng and S Mason, 'Artificial Intelligence and Evidence' (2021) 33 *Singapore Academy of Law Journal* 241.

[161] A Kushnir and M Schaumann, 'Friend or Foe? How Artificial Intelligence is Challenging the Law's Approach to Art' (*LexisNexis*, 12 July 2024) available at www.lexisnexis.com.au/en/insights-and-analysis/practice-intelligence/2023/friend-or-foe-how-artificial-intelligence-is-challenging-the-laws-approach-to-art.

[162] Lord Sales, 'Artificial Intelligence and Evidence', speech at the Seminars in Law and Technology, Singapore (15 September 2021), referring to Seng and Mason (see n 160 above).

This problem is illustrated by a recent highly publicised[163] decision of the Australian Capital Territory Supreme Court, *Director of Public Prosecutions (ACT) v Khan*.[164] In that case, Mossop J held that little weight could be given to a character reference supplied by an offender's brother in relation to the offender's subjective circumstances for the purposes of sentencing on the basis that, when read as a whole, the language of the reference was strongly suggestive of the document having been generated using a 'large language model program, such as ChatGPT'.[165]

An obvious risk of GenAI relates to its potential and malign use to generate sophisticated deepfakes. By using AI, it is possible to create a 'deepfake', an image, video or piece of audio which makes real people appear to do and say things that were never done or said.

In 2023, the Federal Court of Australia was presented with Australia's first litigation concerning deepfakes. Civil penalty proceedings were brought against a man who the eSafety Commissioner alleged posted 'intimate images' of several Australian public figures on a website called MrDeepFakes.com. In a decision concerning the imposition of penalties for contempt of court as a result of the man's failure to remove the images, Derrington J said the following in relation to 'deepfakes':[166]

> Deepfakes are digitally manipulated forms of visual media in which one person's likeness is replaced convincingly with that of another so as to depict circumstances that never existed. Unfortunately, the material before the Court suggests that deepfakes are not especially difficult to create. Programs presently available on the internet enable the face of one person to be fixed to the body of another person with considerable precision to create a false or misleading image, the synthetic nature of which is difficult to detect…

There have already been cases of deepfake evidence being adduced in proceedings internationally, including in UK family law proceedings where a deepfake audio recording of a purported phone call between the parties was introduced into evidence and later excluded.[167]

Courts have always had to deal with forgeries, but modern technology, in its sophistication and reach, magnifies that age-old challenge to courts charged with determining civil and criminal disputes. If AI technology reaches a point where courts are unable to discern if evidentiary material is genuine or not, the forensic future is bleak.[168]

Some existing rules of evidence may prevent the potentially corrosive effects of AI-produced evidence on the justice system. For instance, in criminal proceedings, evidence which is alleged to be a deepfake or the product of GenAI may be inadmissible

[163] See, eg, C Caulfield, 'Judge's Ruling a Warning to Lawyers Tempted by ChatGPT' (*Lawyerly*, 28 February 2024), available at www.lawyerly.com.au/judges-ruling-a-warning-for-lawyers-tempted-to-use-chatgpt-to-write-court-docs.

[164] [2024] ACTSC 19.

[165] *Director of Public Prosecutions (ACT) v Khan* (see n 29 above) para 39.

[166] *eSafety Commissioner v Rotondo (No 3)* [2023] FCA 1590, para 7.

[167] See B James, 'Why You and the Court should not Accept Audio or Video Evidence at Face Value: How Deepfake can be Used to Manufacture Very Plausible Evidence' [2020] *International Family Law Journal* 43, 43. See also MR Grossman et al, 'The GPTJudge: Justice in a Generative AI World' (2023) 23 *Duke Law & Technology Review* 1, 17.

[168] M Maras, 'Determining Authenticity of Video Evidence in the Age of Artificial Intelligence and in the Wake of Deepfake Videos' (2019) 23(3) *International Journal of Evidence and Proof* 255.

where a judicial officer considers that the risk of unfair prejudice created by the potential origins of the evidence outweighs the probative value of the evidence.[169]

In some cases, there may be obvious signs that evidence is inauthentic and may have been generated by AI, to which the parties and judicial officers will be attuned. Tell-tale signs that an image or video is a deepfake or has been generated by AI can include discolouration of images, problems with the blinking rate of people depicted in videos, issues with hand movements or obvious inconsistencies with aural texture and synch. Metadata programs may also be used to see what software was used to create or edit a piece of evidence where the original file is available to the parties or to the court.[170]

Generally, however, the emergence of deepfake and AI-created evidence may impose significant evidentiary hurdles on both the proponent of the actual or suspected GenAI-produced or deepfake evidence and on those who challenge its authenticity. In some cases, eyewitness testimony may be relied upon to verify the origins of audio-visual evidence adduced in proceedings. The possibility of using AI itself to detect AI-synthesised evidence has also been raised. A machine-learning algorithm called XceptionNet can distinguish between videos which use a face swap and videos without AI modification. However, the same algorithm can also be used to improve AI-generated evidence thereby making it harder to detect.[171]

Additionally, there may be an increasing demand for, and courts may need to place enormous reliance upon, the evidence of GenAI experts in distinguishing between fact and fiction where disputed GenAI evidence is sought to be adduced in proceedings.[172] This is exemplified by a US securities case in which the plaintiff sought leave to file an expert report which it said explained that many of the videos on which the defendants sought to rely may have been the product of deepfake technology.[173] Courts have long drawn on the expertise of digital media forensics experts. However, experts in image and video forensic analysis may soon need to be well-versed in AI, and even then, expert testimony may not be enough to verify the authenticity of evidence as the ability of AI to modify audio-visual evidence becomes more advanced.[174]

VIII. Expert Evidence

The possibility of greater reliance needing to be placed on experts to distinguish between real and artificially generated written and audio-visual evidence presents further issues. Expert witnesses enjoy a special status in legal proceedings in that, unlike lay witnesses, they are able to express opinions on matters within their expertise. In order to enable experts to assume their privileged position in the courtroom, strict criteria are placed on the admissibility of their evidence. Importantly, an expert must have specialised

[169] Evidence Act, s 137.
[170] James (see n 167 above) 44–45.
[171] Maras (see n 168 above).
[172] Grossman et al (see n 167 above) 24.
[173] *Valenti v Dfinity USA Research LLC* 21-cv-06118-JD (8 May 2023).
[174] Maras (see n 168 above).

knowledge based on their training, study or experience, and any opinion they express must be based wholly or substantially on that knowledge.[175]

Questions arise as to the use by experts of AI in the preparation of their research and any underlying research and analysis.

Just as expert reports may in certain circumstances have input from people in addition to the expert,[176] it is obvious that an expert may seek to draw upon the assistance of GenAI. Even if an expert has genuine expertise, it is not difficult to envisage a situation in which he or she may rely on AI to generate the whole, or part of, the expert opinion. This risk is exemplified by events that took place in November 2023 when a group of academics were forced to publicly apologise to the Big Four consultancy firms after it came to light that they had used Google Bard AI, another large language model (LLM) system similar to ChatGPT, to generate research relied upon in part of a submission to a Commonwealth parliamentary inquiry. The submission levelled several false accusations against the Big Four firms. Although the academics apologised for the error, they contended that the substance of their recommendations, and the rest of their research, was appropriately supported by evidence. The incident is the first time (so it is understood) that a parliamentary inquiry has received a submission with false AI-generated information.[177]

An expert who deliberately lies to or misleads the court in respect of their qualifications or the origins of their report may be guilty of contempt of court or could be prosecuted for perjury. In New South Wales and other Australian jurisdictions, experts are bound to adhere to a Code of Conduct. Clause 2 of the Code applicable in New South Wales provides that an expert has a 'paramount duty … to assist the court impartially'. Pursuant to cl 3, an expert report must also include, among other things, 'the assumptions and material facts on which each opinion expressed in the report is based' and 'the reasons for and any literature or other materials utilised in support of each such opinion'.

IX. Conclusion

The rise of GenAI exposes Australian courts to considerable truth decay risks. Its prospective use by lawyers, self-represented litigants, judges and experts alike, as well as the scope for its malign use in the fabrication of evidence, will expose courts to serious new challenges in ensuring that they remain respected arbiters of the truth, and discriminators between fact and fiction in the years to come.

More generally, and as discussed in the first part of this chapter, the courts already have a number of tools with which the corrosive effects of truth decay may be resisted,

[175] Evidence Act, s 79. See also *Honeysett v The Queen* (2014) 253 CLR 122; [2014] HCA 29 and *R v Tang* (2006) 65 NSWLR 681; [2006] NSWCCA 167.

[176] See, eg, *R v Pabon* [2018] EWCA Crim 420. See also E Freer, 'Experts and Pretenders: Examining Possible Responses to Misconduct by Experts in Criminal Trials in England and Wales' (2020) 24 *The International Journal of Evidence & Proof* 180, 181.

[177] H Belot, 'Australian Academics Apologise for False AI-generated Allegations against Big Four Consultancy Firms' (*The Guardian*, 3 November 2023), available at www.theguardian.com/business/2023/nov/02/australian-academics-apologise-for-false-ai-generated-allegations-against-big-four-consultancy-firms.

but it is a task which demands eternal vigilance and a degree of proactivity on the part of leaders of superior courts in defending them and their work from unprincipled and misinformed attack. In the area of GenAI, it is essential that judges are educated as to the potential and potency of this technology, which has rightly been described as transformative. It carries both benefits but also serious challenges for judiciaries and raises fundamental questions about the nature and future of the judicial process.

PART IV

Climate Change

14

Introduction to Climate Change

ANDREW BELL AC, NALLINI PATHMANATHAN
AND GOH YIHAN

I. Introduction

This chapter will first introduce the Intergovernmental Panel on Climate Change (IPCC) and its Sixth Assessment Report (Report),[1] as well as the current state of climate change and the turn to international courts, tribunals and quasi-judicial bodies. It will then offer a commentary on the subject, before briefly introducing the two other chapters in this section of the book – 'Climate Change and Legal Responsibility' (by James Allsop) and 'A Sentinel's Toil in Climate Action: Significance of the Judicial Role (with emphasis on the role of the Indian Supreme Court)' (by Arjan Sikri).

II. IPCC and its Sixth Assessment Report

A. Overview of the IPCC

The IPCC was established in 1988 by the United Nations (UN). Its role is to 'assess on a comprehensive, objective, open and transparent basis the scientific, technical and socio-economic information relevant to understanding the scientific basis of risk of human-induced climate change, its potential impacts and options for adaptation and mitigation'.[2]

In short, the IPCC is an intergovernmental body that evaluates the scientific basis of climate change. Importantly, the IPCC is not international but intergovernmental, meaning that its 195 member states control its operations, rather than international entities. Member states appoint national focal points who attend the plenary sessions. As such, IPCC reports are neutral with respect to policy, although they will deal objectively with scientific, technical and socio-economic factors relevant to the application of specific policies.

[1] H Lee et al, *Climate Change 2023: Synthesis Report* (Intergovernmental Panel on Climate Change, 2023).
[2] IPCC, 'Principles Governing IPCC Work' (2018) para 2, available at www.ipcc.ch/site/assets/uploads/2018/09/ipcc-principles.pdf.

In terms of leadership and work organisation, the IPCC elects a bureau that provides scientific leadership. This bureau includes a Chair, three Vice-Chairs, and Co-Chairs of three Working Groups focusing on different aspects of climate change: (a) Working Group I: physical science underpinning climate change; (b) Working Group II: impacts, adaptation, and vulnerability; and (c) Working Group III: mitigation of climate change. The IPCC has an executive committee, a subset of the bureau, to make urgent decisions between plenary meetings.

As for its report production process, the IPCC's assessment reports, which are accessible to the public, take around three years to complete and follow a structured process. First, scoping: governments and organisations suggest topics, and scientists draft a framework outlining the report's structure. Second, author selection: governments and organisations nominate experts. Third, draft preparation and review: authors draft the chapters, which are then reviewed by experts and governments in multiple stages. Finally, final draft and approval: the final draft is prepared, and a summary for policymakers is approved.

B. Highlights of the Sixth Assessment Report

The Report surveyed current global warming trends. Alarmingly, the Report confirmed significant warming since 1900, with projections indicating a rise of 1.4°C to 4.4°C by the end of the century, depending on actions taken.[3] More specifically, the Report found that North America and Europe accounted for around 40 per cent of historic carbon dioxide emissions, with North America dominating *per capita* emissions. Meanwhile, Southeast Asia, the Pacific, and Africa produced a smaller share of emissions.[4]

By way of mitigation, the concept of a carbon budget represents the maximum cumulative emissions permissible to limit warming to a specific level. The remaining carbon budget for 1.5°C will soon be exhausted, and for 2°C, largely depleted.[5] That said, positive developments include a significant reduction in the cost of renewable energy technologies such as solar and wind power, leading to an increase in renewable energy adoption.

There are obviously long-term climate and development futures, of which the following two are emphasised. First, renewable energy and barriers: while renewable energy adoption has increased, challenges remain in Sub-Saharan Africa and parts of Asia due to high investment risks and inadequate infrastructure.[6] Second, current and future climate risks: at around 1.2°C warming, moderate risks are appearing in ecosystems like permafrost, biodiversity, and coral reefs.[7] Indeed, extreme temperature poses significant challenges, particularly in low-altitude regions. The key adaptation and mitigation strategies include, first, near-term reductions by 2030: opportunities include solar and wind energy for electricity supply, reducing methane leakage, bioenergy with carbon capture and storage, and improved soil management in agriculture.[8] Second, policy and

[3] Report 12.
[4] Report 45.
[5] Report 20.
[6] Report 33.
[7] Report 17.
[8] Report 27.

framework support: individual choices require supportive policies and infrastructure, such as charging stations for electric vehicles.[9]

Ultimately, the Report stressed that climate action should align with the UN's Sustainable Development Goals. For instance, adopting green and blue infrastructure in urban areas can help with adaptation and mitigation.

C. Key Insights and Messages

Several key insights and messages, arising from the IPCC and the Report, were discussed at the Fourth Judicial Roundtable:

(a) First, the IPCC's intergovernmental structure ensures that the reports are scientifically rigorous while reflecting the political realities of climate negotiations.

(b) Second, the Report underscores the urgency of immediate, radical action to reduce emissions. Delays will diminish the likelihood of limiting warming to 1.5°C.

(c) Third, despite progress in renewable energy and mitigation policies, global emissions continue to rise. The Report emphasises the need for stronger climate policies, financial investment, and international cooperation.

(d) Fourth, climate action needs to balance mitigation and adaptation while considering the social and economic implications, particularly for vulnerable regions that have contributed least to global emissions but face disproportionate risks.

(e) Fifth, structural shifts in energy, transportation, and food systems are essential for achieving climate goals. This requires cooperation across governments, the private sector, and civil society.

(f) Sixth, the most vulnerable populations are those who have contributed the least to climate change. Equity and justice should underpin climate policies, ensuring that the burden of mitigation and adaptation is shared fairly.

The Report paints a stark picture of the climate crisis but also outlines a pathway to a sustainable future. With the seventh cycle expected to conclude in 2029 or 2030, governments have a crucial window to implement ambitious climate policies and accelerate the transition to a net-zero world.

III. Climate Change and the Turn to International Courts, Tribunals and Quasi-Judicial Bodies

The Roundtable also featured a discussion on: (a) the current state of climate change; and (b) the turn to international courts, tribunals and quasi-judicial bodies. (Indeed, the latter development has intensified since the Roundtable. In particular, the International Court of Justice and the International Tribunal for the Law of the Sea have issued landmark advisory opinions in July 2025 and May 2024, respectively,

[9] Report 105.

which clarified and affirmed the obligations of states to take proactive steps to mitigate and adapt to climate change.[10])

On the first point, the Earth has undergone numerous climatic changes throughout its 4.5-billion-year history. It has experienced five major ice ages, along with several minor glacial and interglacial periods in the last 800,000 years. The most recent ice age concluded about 11,700 years ago. These climatic shifts largely resulted from subtle variations in the Earth's orbit.

In more contemporary times, with the advent of the Industrial Revolution in the mid-nineteenth century, unprecedented warming of both oceans and land was recorded. Such accelerated warming has not been observed for the past 10,000 years. Indeed, extensive evidence confirms that the current rise in global temperatures is primarily due to carbon dioxide and other greenhouse gases from industrial activities, which trap heat in the atmosphere. The scientific community overwhelmingly agrees on the correlation between greenhouse gas concentrations and global warming.

Turning then to the second point about the turn to international courts, tribunals and quasi-judicial bodies, the background context is that the tracking of climate litigation is challenging due to the sheer volume of ongoing cases. Two significant reports – one by the UN Environment Programme and another by the London School of Economics' Grantham Research Institute – catalogue the rapidly growing number of climate-related legal cases worldwide, providing plaintiffs and the judiciary with vital information. Between 2017 and 2022, the number of climate change cases more than doubled from 884 to 2180, which signals an increased engagement with climate litigation.[11]

More particularly, international courts play a crucial role in these matters, as they possess jurisdiction across regions. There has been a surge in related claims arising from UN human rights conventions, especially in jurisdictions lacking robust domestic legal protections. Many claims emerge from various jurisdictions and are presented jointly.

For example, in *Teitiota v New Zealand*,[12] Teitiota, a Kiribati citizen, sought refugee status in New Zealand due to rising sea levels and environmental degradation in his home country. New Zealand's courts denied his application, as the risks did not meet the strict definition of persecution required for refugee status. The UN Human Rights Committee found that New Zealand acted within its rights, though it acknowledged climate change significantly affects vulnerable small island nations like Kiribati.

Similarly, in *Sacchi et al v Argentina, Brazil, France, Germany, and Turkey*,[13] youth climate activists filed a complaint with the UN Committee on the Rights of the Child, alleging that these countries failed to mitigate climate change. The committee recognised states' obligations but dismissed the case due to a lack of exhaustion of domestic remedies. Despite this, the case underscored states' extraterritorial responsibilities in addressing climate change.

[10] International Court of Justice, Obligations of States in respect of Climate Change, Advisory Opinion of 23 July 2025; International Tribunal for the Law of the Sea, Request for Advisory Opinion Submitted by the Commission of Small Island States on Climate Change and International Law, Advisory Opinion of 21 May 2024.

[11] M Burger and MA Tigre, *Global Climate Litigation Report: 2023 Status Review* (Sabin Center for Climate Change Law, Columbia Law School and United Nations Environment Programme, 2023) 12.

[12] *Ioane Teitiota v New Zealand*, CCPR/C/127/D/2728/2016.

[13] *Sacchi et al. v Argentina et al*, CRC/C/88/D/104/2019.

Finally, in *Daniel Billy et al v Australia*,[14] Torres Strait Islanders filed a complaint against Australia, alleging that the government's inadequate climate measures violated their fundamental rights. The United Nations Human Rights Committee ruled in favour of the claimants, establishing a historic precedent linking climate change to human rights. The ruling underscored the international community's obligation to protect vulnerable populations.

Apart from international courts, there are also concerns arising from the European Convention of Human Rights (ECHR). In this regard, because climate change affects everyone, once a disaster strikes, its impact is universal. In *Union of Swiss Women for Climate Protection v Swiss Federal Council and others*,[15] four senior women claimed that climate change disproportionately affected them. They argued that inadequate Swiss climate policies violated their rights under the ECHR. The case established that climate change claims could be made under the ECHR, potentially holding states liable for insufficient climate action. However, the ECHR is wary of an overflow of cases. Typically, plaintiffs must exhaust domestic remedies before approaching the European courts.

IV. Commentary

On a jurisprudential basis, addressing climate change is an integral part of environmental justice. While environmental justice as we know it is largely confined to national and domestic jurisdictions, climate justice has expanded this to become a global issue. Indeed, transboundary disputes comprise the core of climate justice litigation and adjudication. This transnational aspect will require a new construct or approach to the relatively narrow boundaries of the law as we understand it under our current common law and civil law systems.

This has already begun to happen. Differing approaches are utilised across the globe, the bright line division being the approaches adopted by the Global North as compared to the Global South. It is useful to consider these seemingly disparate approaches in turn.

In examining climate change, the identity of the 'wrongdoer' or 'polluter' is not always clearly ascertainable and often falls outside the national jurisdiction. What legal process is to be adopted to redress and penalise or restrain the wrongdoer? The Global North and Global South have adopted disparate approaches to deal with this issue.

At the risk of oversimplification, in the Global North, climate change action and litigation centres on a *statutory regime premised on commitments undertaken by states under various international instruments*. To that extent, national legislatures bear the primary responsibility to ensure that such commitments are made mandatory on a national level and adhered to. However, it is the courts that have the role of ensuring and enforcing these commitments, such that the essential climate change commitments achieve their full objective on a practical level. In short, the law in this area is essentially regulatory. From that starting point, the broader effects of public and private responsibility for regulation become the essence of climate litigation.

[14] *Daniel Billy et al. v Australia*, CCPR/C/135/D/3264/2019.
[15] *Verein KlimaSeniorinnen Schweiz et al. v Switzerland*, App No 53600/20.

Case law discloses that even in recent times, issues such as jurisdiction and standing comprised obstacles to a full adjudication of a dispute on its merits.[16] However, there are signs that the courts are starting to take a less stringent approach to ensure that these cases are dealt with on their merits, in recognition of the alarming implications of climate change. In *Milieudefensie v Royal Dutch Shell*,[17] the District Court assessed the claim on the basis of the following:

1) unwritten standards of care;
2) private business enterprises have a duty to respect human rights; and
3) the responsibility on the part of private enterprises to take appropriate action on the basis of their findings and assessments.[18] Appropriate action would include an obligation by a private enterprise to take the necessary steps to prevent an adverse human rights impact. The necessary steps encompass methods to cease or reduce the enterprise's contribution, and where it has the ability to affect change, to mitigate any remaining impact as far as possible.

This case expanded the scope of the duty of care in relation to climate action claims to private enterprises. The court and the parties acknowledged that the twin challenges facing the world are the reduction of carbon dioxide emissions to prevent further deterioration of climate change, while meeting, on the other hand, the global energy demand of the growing world population.[19]

While this case signals the new way forward, it is to be noted that the claims of the NGO ActionAid and the individual claimants were denied for procedural reasons. The court also held that other collective claims were not allowed, as this would involve recognising the interests of the entire world population, which was not feasible.

On appeal, the Hague Court of Appeal overturned the District Court's decision. However, the Court of Appeal maintained that companies like Shell, which contribute to the climate problem significantly, have an obligation to limit carbon dioxide emissions to counter dangerous climate change. It is important to note that it departed from the District Court in that it did not see that there was sufficient scientific consensus to set a specific reduction level for Shell. However, the Court of Appeal did affirm the emerging case law on the legal duties of corporations like Shell to address climate change.

In *Okpabi v Royal Dutch Shell*,[20] the UK Supreme Court allowed a jurisdictional appeal where the issue was whether the claimants had an arguable case against a UK-domiciled parent company, as a necessary and proper party to the proceedings, in respect of an oil spill occurring as a result of the acts or omissions of the parent company's foreign subsidiary. This in turn turned on whether it could be said that the UK parent company owed the claimants a common law duty of care to found such jurisdiction. The UK Supreme Court allowed the claim to proceed against the UK parent company. This decision again marks the expansion of the common law duty of care, not incrementally as

[16] *Sharma by her litigation representative Sister Marie Brigid Arthur v Minister for the Environment* [2021] FCA 560; *Minister for the Environment v Sharma* [2022] FCAFC 35.

[17] *Milieudefensie et al. v Royal Dutch Shell plc*, ECLI:NL:RBDHA:2021:5339.

[18] JJ Cheema, *Climate Change: The Policy, Law and Practice*, 1st edn (London, Thomson Reuters, 2024) 504.

[19] ibid 509.

[20] *Okpabi and others v Royal Dutch Shell Plc and another* [2021] 1 WLR 1294; [2021] UKSC 3.

detailed in the traditional common law approach epitomised in *Caparo*,[21] but allowing for a more expansive approach to be undertaken in relation to tort-based claims relating to climate change litigation transnationally.

And in *R v Finch*,[22] the UK Supreme Court set an important precedent, stipulating that the climate impact of fossil fuel projects must be assessed when deciding whether such projects should be approved. It further noted that the law governing environmental impact assessments in the UK did not impose a geographical limit on impacts and that there was no justification for limiting the scope of assessment to effects which occur at or near the site.

These cases exemplify how the courts in the Global North, in response to climate change dangers, have leapfrogged the traditional approach – requiring an incremental expansion of the duty of care and the narrow confines of company law in relation to the separate legal identity of companies – to accept and apply the far wider concept of a duty of care transcending national borders, as well as the concept of a single global corporate identity in certain circumstances, in order to meet and afford redress to the serious and adverse consequences of climate change claims.

In the Global South, climate change litigation has not always been recognised as such, because the case law is categorised differently such that it is aligned to an encroachment of human rights, the public trust doctrine, or rights-based arguments.

One approach, which is commonly used in Africa and to a lesser extent in Asia, relies on a cause of action premised on a challenge against a government's failure to implement environmental impact assessment (EIA) requirements. The African EIA climate cases provide a potential growth area for climate litigation.[23]

The common law doctrine of the public trust, which is widely used in India, stipulates that the state holds natural resources in trust and therefore, as a trustee, is required to utilise such resources for the benefit of the citizenry as a whole. This basis for this cause of action has been widely accepted, particularly in the environmental jurisprudence of both India and Pakistan, as well as some common law countries.[24]

Perhaps of greatest prevalence and uniquely distinct to the Global South is the use of environmental constitutional rights claimed under constitutional bills of rights, seeking cessation, mitigation or adaptation against violative actions or omissions in relation to the environment.[25] This is in contrast to the Global North jurisdictions, where the possibilities of rights-based claims are more constrained.

Other significant and innovative developments in the prosecution of climate change claims in the Global South include the invocation of a *parens patriae* jurisdiction where, in accordance with the 'rights of nature approach', nature (albeit in the form of a forest, a river, or the ocean) is considered a juristic person enjoying the corresponding rights,

[21] *Caparo Industries plc v Dickman* [1990] 2 AC 605 (HL).

[22] *R (on the application of Finch on behalf of the Weald Action Group) (Appellant) v Surrey County Council and others (Respondents)* [2024] UKSC 20.

[23] J Peel and J Lin, 'Transnational Climate Litigation: The Contribution of the Global South' (2019) 113 *American Journal of International Law* 679, 704.

[24] ibid 709.

[25] *Datuk Bandar Kuala Lumpur v Perbadanan Pengurusan Trellises & Ors and Other Appeals* [2023] 3 MLJ 829.

duties and liabilities of a living person in order to preserve and conserve them (see *A Periyakaruppan v Principal Secretary to the Government and another*).[26]

The legislature of New Zealand has recognised this approach by granting the Whanganui River legal personality[27] as has the Supreme Court of Colombia in recognising that the Amazon River has rights deserving of protection.[28] These decisions recognise the increasing awareness to adopt a different approach to the protection of the environment and therefore climate change.

V. Overview of Chapters 15 and 16

Against that background, we turn to the two subsequent chapters in this section of the book. In chapter fifteen, James Allsop discusses a selection of key climate change cases, including actions against the state and actions against emitters. In respect of the former, the author discusses the cases of *The Netherlands v Urgenda*[29] and *Sharma*,[30] highlighting that the differing outcomes could be justified by the relevant legal frameworks, which were not as straightforward in *Sharma* and lacked the underlying constitutional and legal clarity in *The Netherlands v Urgenda*. In respect of actions against emitters, the author discusses a trio of decisions from the Netherlands, Italy and New Zealand, noting that they illuminate strands of reasoning or approaches that may bear upon cases against state parties and public authorities. The author then discusses issues such as the relationship between causation and judicial policy, and the basis for attributing liability to parent companies for the actions of their subsidiaries.

In chapter sixteen, Arjan Sikri highlights the significant increase in climate-related litigation in recent years, pointing to the growing public awareness of environmental rights. He notes the emerging role of courts in addressing climate change and explores in detail the key judgments of the Supreme Court of India. In particular, he outlines a number of key developments in India's approach to environmental law: (a) treating the right to a clean environment as a fundamental right; (b) extending the use of public interest litigation (or PIL) to encompass environmental litigation; (c) adopting an inquisitorial approach to the collection of evidence and the analysis of cases; and (d) inventing the concept of the continuing mandamus to address ongoing environmental issues. However, we should be cautious not to assume universal applicability of these innovative measures, especially when one considers the unique constitutional context that underpins the decisions of the Indian Supreme Court. A cautious and measured approach may be necessary, in recognition of the limitations of judicial activism and the need to uphold environmental principles within constitutional bounds.

[26] *A Periyakaruppan v Principal Secretary to the Government and another* (2022) SCC Online Mad 2077.

[27] K Warne, 'A Voice for Nature' (*National Geographic*), available at www.nationalgeographic.com/culture/graphics/maori-river-in-new-zealand-is-a-legal-person.

[28] Decision of the Supreme Court of Colombia in STC4360-2018, available at www.cortesuprema.gov.co/corte/wp-content/uploads/2018/04/STC4360-2018-2018-00319-011.pdf.

[29] *The State of The Netherlands (Ministry of Economic Affairs and Climate Policy) v Urgenda Foundation* ECLI:NL:HR:2019:2007, Hoge Raad, 19/00135.

[30] See n 16.

VI. Conclusion

Climate change, which is inextricably tied with climate justice, is premised on science. It responds to science and acknowledges the need for the equitable distribution and utilisation of the world's resources. Today it has become a complex global problem, and the law serves to enforce the scientific responses required to preserve and maintain the environment. This area of law therefore requires as seamless an evolution as possible to provide the best responses to the disturbing trend of climate events that currently subsist and will continue.

From the varied range of approaches adopted both in the Global North and Global South, it is timely that jurisdictions globally work together and coordinate their responses on a global basis to meet this threat to the world. A climate disaster in one part of the world should be understood as being a matter of devastating concern for all jurisdictions. This requires a unification of approaches which would allow for a common mode of addressing climate change litigation.

15

Climate Change and Legal Responsibility

JAMES ALLSOP

I. Introduction

Questions of the response of public power, and in particular, judicial power, to climate change raise deep and important questions, which for their answer require an understanding of substantive and procedural law and of judicial technique, and of the process of change of the former by the latter.

There have been thousands of law cases brought in many countries seeking to advance the case 'of the environment' by means of seeking various legal remedies against governments, emitters of greenhouse gases (GHGs), directors of corporations, and financial institutions with relationships with perceived culprits in relation to the emission of GHGs.

II. Some Assumptions

It is helpful to remind oneself of some important working assumptions that are common to civil law and common law legal systems.

One should commence with the role of the courts in society. Most systems of government built on non-autocratic power do not conceive of judges and courts as mere instruments of governmental power wielded at the behest of the ruling power of the day. If courts were such, they would likely behave in a manner reflective of the dictates of that ruling power. In such a case, no distinction need be made between governmental and judicial power, as the latter would serve, or be a function of, the former. There would be no cause to agonise over 'the role of the courts' in respect of climate change.

The difficulty (and interest) comes with the posited role of the courts as based upon independent and impartial resolution of disputes between citizen and citizen, and citizen and state (using those terms in a broad and constitutionally neutral sense) based on the evidence before and accepted by the court.

This assumption illuminates something of importance for the discussion: that the essence of judicial power is *protective* in character. It is a unique form of power in that regard. It protects the individual, the group and the society by declaring and enforcing rights and obligations and by repairing wrongs through orders for compensation or orders to enforce lawful conduct, and to restrain unlawful conduct. In significant part, that protection is about the control of power, whether private or public power.

III. Some Considerations of Jurisprudence and Judicial Technique

Within that expressed framework is the place of the material against, or on the basis of, which courts decide to act, namely, the law, and the material or evidence upon which to apply the law. That apparently simple binary dichotomy between law and fact can be deceptive. There is an expression that is sometimes used in explaining the task of the first instance judge: the law oozing out of the facts.

The law is not a complete and comprehensive matrix of self-referential rules capable of mechanical application to every factual set of circumstances raised by any dispute. In resolving disputes, there is a daily interplay between rules, principles and values, between text and context, and between the explicit and the implicit. The adaptability and development of the law are to be recognised, whether in interpreting generally expressed or open-textured rules or principles, or in developing common law principles, or in interpreting codes to adapt to changing circumstances. Law, and its development, are ridden with opposites or antinomies. The law is not static, but it is stable. It grows and develops. As Benjamin Cardozo said on the first page of the second volume of his great trilogy (*The Growth of the Law*[1] in 1924; after *The Nature of the Judicial Process*[2] in 1921; and before *The Paradoxes of Legal Science* in 1928[3]), the enduring conflict is between stability and progress, mediated by a philosophy of change, informed or supplied by a principle of growth. And, as the same jurist said towards the end of the third volume, 'dichotomy is everywhere':[4] freedom and restraint, the individual and the group, as part of the wider opposites of the one and the many and rest and motion, which are at the heart of all being.

The relevance of these considerations of a jurisprudential kind and of the philosophical penumbra of judicial technique, will perhaps become clearer after one examines the material or evidence on climate change or global warming. For now, it perhaps suffices to say that legal policy to develop the law, drawn in part from the necessities of society to adapt, will always be present in the judicial task.

IV. The Subject Evidence

A perusal of the scientific evidence brought before the courts in the cases discussed below reflects the underlying *factual* scientific concerns. In the field of climate science, there is a remarkable scientific consensus as to the topic. The word 'topic' and not 'problem' is used in recognition of the political controversy in many countries as to the reality

[1] BN Cardozo, *The Growth of the Law* (New Haven, Yale University Press, 1924).
[2] BN Cardozo, *The Nature of the Judicial Process* (New Haven, Yale University Press, 1921).
[3] BN Cardozo, *The Paradoxes of Legal Science* (New York, Columbia University Press, 1928).
[4] ibid 132.

or seriousness of the 'problem', and whether it is exaggerated or whether, and if so how, its resolution should affect activity or policy in the manner suggested by some. This controversy requires that the manner of approach by courts to the resolution of legal disputes relating to climate science display the highest judicial technique in how to develop legal principle.

There appears to be a broad and clear scientific *consensus*. It may be shown ultimately to be wrong in, or to, some degree; but that is within the realm of the inevitable uncertainty of life. Courts cannot ignore scientific consensus of the kind placed before them.

The Climate Change 2023: Synthesis Report[5] of the Intergovernmental Panel on Climate Change (the IPCC) is a summary for policy makers. From it can be drawn the following. Human activities from unsustainable energy use, land use, and patterns of consumption and production since 1850 have caused global surface temperature to rise 1.1°C above 1850–1900 levels in 2011–20, by the emission of GHGs.[6]

This has caused widespread and rapid changes in the atmosphere, ocean, cryosphere and biosphere, which has led to weather and climate extremes, such as heatwaves, heavy rainfall, droughts and cyclones, in all regions in the world.[7]

Substantial damage, with increasingly irreversible losses in ecosystems and species, has occurred.[8] Based on nationally determined contributions announced by October 2021, it is *likely* that global surface temperature warming will exceed 1.5°C above 1850–1900 levels during the twenty-first century.[9] Depending upon the volume of GHG emissions in the twenty-first century, the best estimates are that a 1.5°C temperature rise will occur in the near-term, and warming for 2081–2100 spans a range from 1.4°C for very low GHG emissions, to 2.7°C for intermediate GHG emissions, and 4.4°C for very high GHG emissions.[10]

With every additional increment of global warming, changes in extremes become larger, affecting precipitation, drought, loss and degradation of carbon sinks of forests and oceans, loss of permafrost, seasonal snow cover, glaciers, ice sheets and sea ice.[11] Hazards associated with these changes include increases in heat-related mortality, food or water or insect or other organism-borne diseases, flooding, loss of ecosystems and biodiversity, and sea level rise.[12]

Linear progression of risk is present, and some future changes, though unavoidable, can be limited by GHG reduction. For instance, sea level rise is unavoidable for centuries or millennia to come because of deep ocean warming and the melting of ice sheets, but deep, rapid and sustained GHG emission reductions would limit further sea level rise acceleration. Relative to 1995–2014 sea levels, the *likely* global mean sea level rise is from 0.15–0.23m by 2050 and 0.28–0.55m by 2100 in the 'very low' GHG emissions

[5] H Lee et al, *Climate Change 2023: Synthesis Report* (Intergovernmental Panel on Climate Change, 2023).
[6] ibid 4.
[7] ibid 5.
[8] ibid 5.
[9] ibid 10.
[10] ibid 12.
[11] ibid 12–13, 23.
[12] ibid 15.

scenario, to 0.20–0.29m by 2050 and 0.63–1.01m by 2100 in the 'very high' GHG emissions scenario.[13]

The risks are, however, not only linear. Abrupt and/or irreversible changes may occur, triggered by 'tipping points', such as the melting of the permafrost and the loss of ice sheets. There is a greater likelihood of such tipping points as global mean temperature rises.[14]

Limiting human-caused global warming requires net zero anthropogenic CO2 emissions. The cumulative total of carbon emissions until net zero CO2 is reached determines whether warming can be limited to 1.5°C or 2°C above 1850–1900 levels. Every GHG emission affects rising temperature and consumes part of the carbon budget that would be necessary to limit temperature rise to 1.5°C to 2°C.[15] There is an urgency to near-term action in the face of the threat to human well-being and the health of the planet.[16]

All these abstract expressions of the matter can be transformed into language-evoking experiences: the risk of drought, heatwave, wildfire, torrential rain, flooding, landslides, sea-level rise and inundation; forced large-scale migration; the spread of disease; the drying of the land; the loss of crops and agricultural resources; the loss of habitat, ecosystems, animals, species and natural resources; and the likely rise in the risk of famine, death, and violence and war over resources and migration.

If these are the facts of risk in the future directly related to past, present and future human conduct causing the emission of GHGs, what law will ooze out of them?

V. Climate Change Litigation

The range of litigation that has taken place is broad. Importantly, there have been advisory opinions issued by international tribunals: the International Tribunal for the Law of the Sea, the Inter-American Court of Human Rights and the International Court of Justice. Some adversarial cases challenge government policy responses; others challenge corporate policy responses; others seek to force climate considerations into public and private decisions; others are directed to preventing finance for emitters or emitting projects; others seek to make government or corporations adapt operations for the risk of climate change; others seek compensation; others challenge inaccurate statements about corporate responses and conduct.

There is an increasing emphasis on human rights, especially those protecting personal health, safety and life, in particular, in demanding appropriately adapted *prospective* policies.

These human rights are the very stuff of old traditional common law actions in tort or delict and private and public nuisance.

[13] ibid 81.
[14] ibid 18.
[15] ibid 82.
[16] ibid 92, 95.

This chapter will discuss a small selection of cases: *The Netherlands v Urgenda*[17] and *Sharma*[18] being actions against the state; *Milieudefensie v Royal Dutch Shell*,[19] *Smith v Fonterra*[20] and *Greenpeace v ENI*[21]being actions against emitters; after which, this chapter will say something of judicial policy and causation, and the relationship between human rights and the common law; and then *Vedanta Resources*[22] and *Okpabi v Royal Dutch Shell*[23] in relation to corporate form and liability and modern corporate management; and finally, it will say something of corporate responsibility, directors' duties and the interests of creditors.

A. Actions Against the State

i. *The Netherlands v Urgenda*

The Netherlands v Urgenda was decided by the Hoge Raad (the ultimate appeal court of the Netherlands in the fields of civil, criminal and tax law). The decision is remarkable for its clarity and directness. It came to the Court by way of cassation. The issue in the case went to the core of governmental response to climate change: whether the Dutch state was (legally under Dutch law) obliged to reduce GHG emissions originating from Dutch soil by 2020 by at least 25 per cent compared to 1990, and whether the courts could order the state to do so.[24]

One can see the two basal issues concerning the relationship of the state (through the relevant Minister of Economic Affairs and Climate Policy) and the courts:

1. Was climate policy binding upon the state under domestic law?
2. Could the courts enforce such an obligation so central to government policy?

Both the District Court and the Court of Appeal answered these questions in the affirmative.[25] On cassation, the Supreme Court found no error, agreeing with the lower courts that the state had an enforceable legal obligation as to the reduction of GHGs.[26]

[17] *The State of The Netherlands (Ministry of Economic Affairs and Climate Policy) v Urgenda Foundation* ECLI:NL:HR:2019:2007, Hoge Raad, 19/00135 (*The Netherlands v Urgenda*).

[18] *Sharma by her litigation representative Sister Marie Brigid Arthur v Minister for the Environment* [2021] FCA 560 (*Sharma No 1*); *Minister for the Environment v Sharma* [2022] FCAFC 35 (*Sharma No 2*).

[19] *Vereniging Milieudefensie and Others v Royal Dutch Shell plc* ECLI:NL:RBDHA:2021:5339, The Hague, C/09/571932/HA ZA 19-379 (*Milieudefensie v Royal Dutch Shell*); *Shell plc and Others v Vereniging Milieudefensie and Others* ECLI:NL:GHDHA:2024:2100, The Hague, 200.302.332/01 (*Shell v Milieudefensie*).

[20] *Smith v Fonterra Co-Operative Group Ltd* [2021] NZCA 552 (*Smith v Fonterra* (CA)); *Smith v Fonterra Co-Operative Group Ltd* [2024] NZSC 5 (*Smith v Fonterra* (SC)).

[21] *Greenpeace Italy v ENI SpA, the Italian Ministry of Economy and Finance and Cassa Depositi e Prestiti SpA* (*Greenpeace v ENI*).

[22] *Lungowe and others v Vedanta Resources plc and another* [2017] EWCA Civ 1528 (*Vedanta Resources* (CA)) *Lungowe and others v Vedanta Resources plc and another (International Commission of Jurists and others intervening)* [2019] UKSC 20 (*Vedanta Resources* (SC)).

[23] *HRH Emere Godwin Bebe Okpabi and others v Royal Dutch Shell plc and another* [2018] EWCA Civ 191 (*Okpabi v Royal Dutch Shell* (CA)); *HRH Emere Godwin Bebe Okpabi and others v Royal Dutch Shell plc and another (International Commission of Jurists and others intervening)* [2021] UKSC 3 (*Okpabi v Royal Dutch Shell* (SC)).

[24] *The Netherlands v Urgenda* (n 17) 2.

[25] ibid [2.3.1]–[2.3.2].

[26] ibid [5.10], [7.6.1]–[7.6.2].

The factual material based on climate science was not the subject of dispute. The Court summarised the position in a way consistent with the description above.[27]

The legal foundation of the Netherlands' domestic law obligation was that the European Convention on the Protection of Human Rights and Fundamental Freedoms (ECHR) requires state parties to the Convention to protect the rights and freedoms so established for their inhabitants. Articles 2 and 8 of the ECHR were engaged: Article 2 expresses the right to life, and Article 8 expresses the right to respect for private and family life. Case law of the European Court of Human Rights (the ECtHR) provided that a Contracting State is then obliged to take suitable measures if a real and immediate threat to people's lives or welfare exists and the state is aware of the risk. Those at risk are not limited to individuals or groups but extend to a population as a whole, and even if the hazards will only materialise over the long term. Articles 2 and 8 cannot result in an impossible or disproportionate burden on the state but do require measures that are suitable to avert imminent danger as much as reasonably possible.[28]

The power of the courts in the ECHR comes from Article 13: a national law must offer a legal remedy against a violation or imminent violation of rights safeguarded by the ECHR. National courts then must be able to provide effective legal protection.[29]

Critically, under Articles 93 and 94 of the Dutch Constitution, Dutch courts are obliged to apply the ECHR in accordance with the interpretation of the ECtHR.[30] The enforceability of human rights thus judicialised the fact-finding about climate change: from the circumstances and detail of its reality and existential hazards and risks, to the human rights concerned, to the steps necessary to be taken to mitigate those hazards and risks in the future.

Though it was facing a world problem, as a party to the United Nations Framework Convention on Climate Change (UNFCCC), the Netherlands was obliged to act in accordance with the premise of the UNFCCC: that all member countries must take measures to prevent climate change in accordance with their responsibilities. Each country is then responsible for its own share of the problem. The Dutch state was therefore obliged to reduce GHG emissions from its territory in proportion to its share of the global responsibility.[31]

It was necessary, however, to deal with what was the legal manifestation of this concept of '*doing its share*': that is, giving substantive content to the positive obligation imposed on the state by Articles 2 and 8. It was at this next stage that scientific consensus, and the international agreement and consensus based upon it, moulded the shape of the legal obligation.

The Court recognised that the views of the IPCC had moved to the view that global warming should be limited to 1.5°C, from an earlier view of 2°C. But even to achieve a limitation to 2°C, developed countries were required to reduce their GHG emissions from 1990 levels by 25–40 per cent in 2020 and by 80–95 per cent in 2050. The Court

[27] ibid [4.1]–[4.8].
[28] ibid [5.2.1]–[5.4.3].
[29] ibid [5.5.1]–[5.5.3].
[30] ibid [5.6.1].
[31] ibid [5.7.2]–[5.8].

said that this conclusion was drawn from 'a great degree of consensus' on the urgent necessity for developed countries so to act.[32]

The dispute before the Court arose from the fact that after 2011, Netherlands government policy changed from one to reduce GHG emissions by 2020 by 30 per cent compared to 1990, to one for a reduction of 20 per cent.[33] The lower courts had ruled that the state must comply with a 25 per cent reduction mandate. This was an obligation based on the factual conclusion of necessity to protect the rights under Articles 2 and 8, based on the accepted scientific consensus.[34]

At this point the Supreme Court confronted the question of policy.

The state argued that it was not for the courts to undertake the political considerations necessary for a decision on the level of reduction of GHG emissions.[35] The force of this was recognised, to a point, by the Supreme Court accepting that the government had a large degree of discretion to make the political choices involved in *how* this was to be done, but not *whether* it must be done. The role of the courts was, by the mandate of the Constitution, to apply the provisions of the ECHR in accordance with the interpretation of the ECtHR.[36] The Court's view was that the current policy was not meeting the requirements of Articles 2 and 8. This was based on factual conclusions of the lower courts from the scientific consensus. It was then for the state to ascertain the specific measures to be taken to comply with the order of the court.[37] The Court was not ordering legislation or acts of any particular nature or content. The state, however, had a legal obligation to act to undertake acts (legislative or executive) to bring about the required reduction, but was free to choose the legislative or other power of these acts. The state was recognised to have a large degree of choice. The Court's role was to decide whether the state's actions within that choice were within the 'limits of the law'.[38] The 'limits of the law' were shaped by Articles 2, 8 and 13 of the ECHR, made enforceable by the courts by Articles 93 and 94 of the Constitution. The apparent political nature of the state decisions could not oust the direct role of the courts, by force of the Constitution and the binding character of the ECHR.

ii. Sharma

Sharma was heard by the Federal Court of Australia at first instance and on appeal. There was no application to appeal to the High Court of Australia (the ultimate appellate court of Australia). Ms Sharma, a minor, was the lead applicant in a group of minors in a class action brought by a tutor on behalf of a class of people, being those born in Australia after a particular date and all being under 18 years of age.[39] It was a deliberately intergenerational case. The application sought two primary remedies: first, a declaration that the Commonwealth (that is national) Minister for the Environment owed, in relation

[32] ibid [6.1]–[7.3.6].
[33] ibid [7.4.1]–[7.4.2].
[34] ibid [2.3.1]–[2.3.2].
[35] ibid [3.5].
[36] ibid [8.3.2]–[8.3.3].
[37] ibid 6.
[38] ibid [8.3.2].
[39] *Sharma No 1* (n 18) [4]; *Sharma No 2* (n 18) [104].

to making a decision under the legislation in question, the Environment Protection and Biodiversity Conservation Act 1999 (Cth) (EPBC Act), to approve the extension of operation of an existing coal mine which would result in an increase in GHG emissions, a duty of care at common law to take reasonable care to avoid causing harm (personal injury or death) to the applicant and the children in the class. Secondly, an injunction to prevent a feared breach of the posited duty that would effectively prevent approval being given to the extension of the mine.[40] The Court at first instance refused the injunction but declared that the duty of care at common law existed.[41] The Full Court of the Federal Court allowed an appeal and set aside the declaration of the duty of care.[42] The three members of the Full Court were unanimous in their view that the duty should not be imposed, but differed in their reasons.

The legal framework was not as straightforward and lacked the underlying constitutional (and so, legal) clarity as that in *The Netherlands v Urgenda*. The relevant Commonwealth legislation (the EPBC Act) provided for Commonwealth (national) authority on specific environmental issues referable to treaties adopted by Australia and incorporated into domestic law. Climate change conventions were *not* such conventions. The EPBC Act provided for co-operative and co-ordinated decision-making between the Commonwealth and the states,[43] the latter having their own authoritative powers in relation to environmental questions. Indeed, here, the relevant state (New South Wales) authority had responsibility for examining (and did examine) the expansion of the mine and its effect on climate change. In the exercise of that responsibility, the state authority, working on the premise, conformable with Australia's responsibilities under the United Nations Framework Convention on Climate Change Paris Agreement 2015 (Paris Agreement), that Scope 3 emissions (that is, emissions from the burning of coal, and explained in greater detail in the footnote[44]) were the responsibility of the country that burnt the coal and not of the country that mined it, found Australia's emissions were not increased, and, in fact, there was a small reduction by operational improvements in the carrying on of the overall mining.[45] That critical assumption as to Scope 3 emissions and its conformity with the Paris Agreement was a central part of Australian and New South Wales government policy on climate change, adopted to seek to reach Australia's targets in the future. By contrast, the Commonwealth Minister's statutory responsibility under the EPBC Act was limited to questions of the effects of the expansion of the mine on particular species of animals, communities and water resources.[46]

This chapter does not aim to traverse all the reasoning in the judgments. They dealt with the incoherence and inconsistency of the duty of care with the limited statutory

[40] *Sharma No 2* (n 18) [15], [20], [104].
[41] *Sharma No 1* (n 18) [513].
[42] *Sharma No 2* (n 18) [7].
[43] ibid [5].
[44] There are three 'scopes' set out in the GHG Protocol Corporate Accounting and Reporting Standard. Scope 1 emissions are *direct* 'emissions from operations that are owned or controlled by the reporting company'; Scope 2 emissions are *indirect* 'emissions from the generation of purchased or acquired electricity, steam, heating, or cooling consumed by the reporting company'; and Scope 3 emissions are 'all indirect emissions (not included in scope 2) that occur in the value chain of the reporting company, including both upstream and downstream emissions'. See Greenhouse Gas Protocol, 'Scope 3 Frequently Asked Questions', available at ghgprotocol.org/scope-3-frequently-asked-questions-0.
[45] *Sharma No 2* (n 18) [27], [38].
[46] ibid [24].

function of the Commonwealth Minister and the governmental (Commonwealth and state) framework; the indeterminacy of liability upon the Minister for future damages; the lack of control of the Minister over the harm; a lack of proportionality between the small increase in risk and the indefinite liability; and the lack of foreseeable harm *caused* (under traditional conceptions of causation) by the decision.

Importantly, for two of the three judges (the author and Wheelahan J), the duty was one which, on the evidence and in the way the content of the duty was framed, was core governmental policy involving questions which were the domain of the non-judicial branches of government, and not such as to be coherently assessed through the process of litigation and the lens of negligence.[47] Such policy embodied the most appropriate way to fulfil Australia's global responsibilities to contribute to limiting the rise of temperature levels that could cause global environmental catastrophe. We considered that this question was not the domain of the courts in civil action for personal injury. It should be noted for later discussion that there was reference in *Sharma*[48] to the similar view of the New Zealand Court of Appeal in *Smith v Fonterra*[49] as to the political character of the matter involved (a view not shared by the Supreme Court on appeal,[50] after *Sharma*).

That said, there is, or would be, nothing novel or controversial in the courts' scrutiny of government decision-making for legality under statutory or regulatory provisions, or even under the general prerogative or executive power, in respect of the exercise of power that may exacerbate global warming. The nature of such review would depend on the statute and context, but it would always be conducted against the background of the growing consensus on the risk of existential damage to humanity from the problem, and the increasing sophistication of science to attribute effects *in the future* to particular measured present activity and causes. It is also worth noting in this context that in Australia (conformably with similar notions in other countries), the factual background to a decision may be so clear or overwhelming that a government decision which results in physical harm, or the risk of physical harm, may be *legally unreasonable* and vulnerable to being set aside.

B. Cases Against Non-Public Entities – Emitter Corporations

By way of introduction, it can be said that the three cases that will be discussed (only one of which has been decided) illuminate strands of reasoning or approaches that may bear upon cases brought against state parties and public authorities.

i. District Court in Milieudefensie v Royal Dutch Shell

In May 2021, The Hague District Court delivered judgment in a case brought by a Dutch association with the chartered purpose of contributing to the solution and prevention of climate problems and like aims, namely, Vereniging Milieudefensie, in a class action representing other Dutch climate organisations, including Greenpeace, against Royal

[47] ibid [247], [868].
[48] ibid [255].
[49] *Smith v Fonterra* (CA) (n 20).
[50] *Smith v Fonterra* (SC) (n 20).

Dutch Shell plc (RDS), the ultimate parent of the Shell Group since a 2005 restructuring, which was incorporated in England, though having its head office in The Hague.[51]

The activities of RDS included the holding of shares in intermediate parent companies, meeting its obligations to shareholders from its three listings in New York, London and Amsterdam and, importantly, determining the Shell Group's general corporate policy.[52]

The framing of the dispute was direct. Milieudefensie et al requested a ruling: that the aggregate annual volumes of CO2 emissions (Scopes 1, 2 and 3) of RDS and the Shell Group constitute an unlawful act and that RDS must reduce the emissions relative to the emissions level in 2019 in accordance with the temperature target of Article 2 paragraph 1 of the Paris Agreement and in accordance with the best available UN climate science; and that RDS will act unlawfully if:

(a) it fails to reduce the Shell Group's CO2 emissions (Scopes 1, 2 and 3) by at least net 45 per cent relative to 2019 levels by the end of 2030; or

(b) by at least 35 per cent; or

(c) by at least 25 per cent; and

an order that RDS limit or cause to be limited the group's CO2 emissions to those amounts by the end of 2030.[53]

The basis of the legal obligation involved, breach of which was said to be unlawful, was said by Milieudefensie et al to be the unwritten standard of care pursuant to Book 6 Section 162 of the Dutch Civil Code (set out below) to contribute to the prevention of dangerous climate change through its corporate policy for the Shell Group. This obligation rested on criteria identified in earlier Dutch Supreme Court authority, human rights, in particular the rights to life and for private and family life (Articles 2 and 8 of the ECHR), and soft law endorsed by RDS, in particular the UN Guiding Principles and Guidelines, such as the UN Principles on Business and Human Rights, the UN Global Compact and the OECD Guidelines on Multinational Enterprises.[54]

In allowing the claim, the District Court dealt with standing, choice of law, the source of the obligation, the obligation itself and its enforceability.

The applicants were held to have standing to bring the class action in the public interest and in the interests of Dutch residents.[55] Dutch law was applicable by reference to Articles 7 and 4 of Rome II.[56] Involved in this choice of law question was a debate about what was the event that gave rise to the damage. Shell said it was the emissions themselves, and therefore there was a myriad of legal systems around the world (but not the Netherlands) involved; Milieudefensie et al said the (or an) event was the formation and adoption of corporate policy by RDS in The Hague. The Court said that every emission around the world for which Shell was said to be responsible contributed to

[51] *Milieudefensie v Royal Dutch Shell* (n 19) [2.1]–[2.2].
[52] ibid [2.2.3].
[53] ibid [3.1].
[54] ibid [3.2].
[55] ibid [4.2].
[56] Regulation (EC) No 864/2007 of the European Parliament and the Council of 11 July 2007 on the law applicable to non-contractual obligations.

the imminent environmental damage in the Netherlands. Further, the policy made in the Netherlands was not prefatory or preparatory. That was too narrow a view given the nature of, and characterisation of responsibility for, this kind of damage, the imminence of the damage and the necessary concept of protection underlying the choice of law rule in Article 7 of Rome II. The adoption of policy in the Netherlands constituted an independent cause of the damage, which could contribute to environmental damage to Dutch residents.[57]

The source of the obligation was Book 6 Section 162 of the Dutch Civil Code and the unwritten standard of care laid down:[58]

> Article 6: 162 Definition of a 'tortious act':
>
> 1. A person who commits a tortious act (unlawful act) against another person that can be attributed to him, must repair the damage that this other person has suffered as a result thereof.
> 2. As a tortious act is regarded a violation of someone else's right (entitlement) and an act or omission in violation of a duty imposed by law or of what according to unwritten law has to be regarded as proper social conduct, always as far as there was no justification for this behaviour.
> 3. A tortious act can be attributed to the tortfeasor [the person committing the tortious act] if it results from his fault or from a cause for which he is accountable by virtue of law or generally accepted principles (common opinion).

The interpretation of the provision and the finding of an obligation was a multifactorial analysis after an assessment of all the relevant circumstances. This is very similar to the technique used in the common law, certainly in Australia, for the identification of the circumstances in which a duty to take reasonable care will be imposed.

The Court took into account the following factors. Firstly, the facts showed that RDS determined the general policy of the Shell Group.[59]

Secondly, the Shell Group was and is responsible for significant CO2 emissions (Scopes 1, 2 and 3) all over the world, exceeding the emissions of many states, including the Netherlands. These emissions contribute to global warming in the Netherlands.[60]

Thirdly, global warming may or will cause serious and irreversible consequences for the Netherlands and, in particular, the Wadden region, including risks for all Dutch citizens.[61]

Fourthly, these hazards affect and threaten the human rights in Articles 2 and 8 of the ECHR and Articles 6 and 17 of the International Covenant on Civil and Political Rights (ICCPR). These are not binding on RDS directly, but the existence of the rights and the values within them are relevant to the interpretation of the written standard of care, especially in light of *The Netherlands v Urgenda* and the responsibility of the Dutch state.[62]

[57] *Milieudefensie v Royal Dutch Shell* (n 19) [4.3].
[58] ibid [4.4].
[59] ibid [4.4.4].
[60] ibid [4.4.5].
[61] ibid [4.4.6].
[62] ibid [4.4.9]–[4.4.10].

Fifthly, the Court took into account 'soft law' instruments. The UN Guiding Principles and the OECD Guidelines for Multinational Enterprises, set out in 'soft law', are the responsibilities of states and businesses in relation to human rights. While these instruments recognise that the responsibility of states is more wide-ranging than businesses, the respect for human rights is a global standard to be expected of all businesses. The Court recognised an 'internationally propagated and endorsed need' for businesses (and so Shell Group) to take responsibility for Scope 3 emissions to the extent that (here) the Shell Group or RDS, through policy, could control them.[63]

Sixthly, the Court recognised RDS's control over the Shell Group, including as to Scope 3 emissions.[64]

Seventhly, the Court took into account that international agreements such as the Paris Agreement recognised that the climate change challenge requires the need for action by non-state actors.[65]

Eighthly, the Court recognised that the pathways for reduction were contained in IPCC reports. The Special Report on Global Warming of 1.5°C required a 45 per cent reduction of CO2 emissions in 2030 relative to 2010 levels in order to yield a 50 per cent chance of limiting global warming to 1.5°C and an 85 per cent chance of limiting global warming to 2°C.[66] From this, the Court concluded as part of its interpretation of the unwritten standard of care:[67]

> the Court deduces that reduction pathways aiming for a net 45% reduction of CO_2 emissions in 2030, relative to 2010 levels, offer the best possible chance worldwide to prevent the most serious consequences of dangerous climate change.
>
> …
>
> … there is a widely endorsed consensus that in order to limit global warming to 1.5°C, reduction pathways that reduce CO_2 emissions by net 45% in 2030, relative to 2010 levels, and by net 100% in 2050, should be chosen.

The Court also accepted that the permanent role for some fossil fuels during and after energy transition, the lack of a uniform approach, the presence of uncertainties, and many other factors were part of the pathways.[68]

From all the circumstances, the Court accepted that the nature of the problem was worldwide, that RDS cannot solve it alone, and that the obligation contains and recognises mutual dependencies and the need for cooperation. But the consensus to be accepted is that reaching net zero by 2050 requires non-state party cooperation. From the consensus as to the need for net zero by 2050 and as to the need for cooperation of non-state actors to achieve it, RDS is to be expected to play its part as a major emitter. The Court emphasised the 'individual partial responsibility' on RDS to contribute to the

[63] ibid [4.4.11] –[4.4.19].
[64] ibid [4.4.19].
[65] ibid [4.4.26].
[66] ibid [4.4.27]–[4.4.29].
[67] ibid [4.4.29].
[68] ibid [4.4.31].

fight against climate change, which threatens the Netherlands and its citizens, *according to its ability*.[69]

Once the principle that the unwritten standard of care could impose a legal obligation on RDS and the Shell Group to contribute to climate change reduction, the scientific consensus as to pathways was used to formulate the content of the obligation to meet the standard, the Court saying, 'in its formulation of the Shell group's corporate policy, RDS should take as a guideline that the Shell group's CO2 emissions (Scope 1, 2 and 3) in 2030 must be net 45% lower relative to 2019 levels'.[70]

The Court concluded (similarly to the Supreme Court in *The Netherlands v Urgenda* in dealing with the question of the political domain) that RDS had a legal obligation to take steps to reduce and to exercise best efforts to reduce GHG emission, and, importantly, recognised that '[a] consequence of this significant obligation may be that RDS will forego new investments in the extraction of fossil fuels and/or will limit its production of fossil resources.'[71]

The Court concluded that the Dutch standard of care required that:[72]

> RDS must do its part with respect to the emissions over it has control and influence. It is an individual responsibility that falls on RDS, of which much may be expected … Therefore, RDS must do more than monitoring developments in society and complying with the regulations in the countries where the Shell group operates. … RDS' responsibility differs as regards (a) the Shell group (obligation of results) and (b) the business relations of the Shell group (significant best-efforts obligation)… RDS does bear an individual responsibility, which it can and must effectuate through its corporate policy for the Shell Group.

The Court recognised the economic effects on Shell's business:[73]

> The court assumes that the reduction obligation will have far-reaching consequences for RDS and the Shell group. The reduction obligation requires a change of policy, which will require an adjustment of the Shell group's energy package…This could curb the potential growth of the Shell group.

The essential element of the judgment is that within the obligation not to cause harm to others framed by the right to life or respect for private and family life as human rights, the law imposes an obligation to change emission-causing businesses, notwithstanding that they are being otherwise lawfully conducted.

ii. Court of Appeal in Shell v Milieudefensie

The Court of Appeal quashed the District Court's judgment. Importantly, however, it did not disagree with the District Court's conclusion that a private party such as Shell owed an obligation, described as a social duty of care, to contribute to the mitigation of dangerous climate change[74] and, as a major participant in the fossil fuel industry for

[69] ibid [4.4.33]–[4.4.37].
[70] ibid [4.4.32].
[71] ibid [4.4.39].
[72] ibid [4.4.52].
[73] ibid [4.4.53].
[74] *Shell v Milieudefensie* (n 19) [7.55].

100 years, more would be expected of Shell than others in that contribution.[75] Oil and gas companies such as Shell are expected under this duty of care to take into account the negative consequences of investing in new oil and gas fields.[76]

Thus, the primary question of the existence of a duty of care as found by the District Court was not denied by the Court of Appeal. The Court, however, after an intense examination of the material before it, refused to accept the claim that Shell was obliged to reduce its GHG emissions by any certain percentage.

It is instructive to outline the approach of the Court in a little detail as reflective of the careful judicial method employed.

The Court began by recognising the uncontested nature of the underlying facts on climate change.[77] It outlined existing climate change conventions, the climate policy of the European Union (EU) and Dutch climate legislation. It examined the nature of Shell and the Shell Group. In particular, it examined in some detail Shell's climate goals and policies.[78] The lack of treatment of these goals and policies of Shell by the District Court was a key plank in Shell's appeal. Central to Shell's goals and policies was Shell becoming a net zero energy business by 2050. In this examination of Shell's business, the Court examined Shell's projected sales of energy products, projected production and investment in fossil fuels as well as low-carbon energy solutions, and the regional distribution of Shell's oil and gas production and sales.[79]

The Court conducted an intense investigation of Milieudefensie's claim that Shell was acting unlawfully by examining the facts and circumstances for itself. This was not cassation, but a re-examination of all material placed before the Court.

The Court dealt with the appeal in seven sections: (a) climate change and human rights; (b) the so called 'horizontal effect' of human rights in their effect on private relationships (as opposed to so called 'vertical effect' in their effect on relationships of government with society); (c) an examination of the EU's climate legislation; (d) an interim review based on the above three factors as to whether Shell had a legal obligation to limit its GHG emissions; (e) whether new investments in oil and gas violate the (found) social duty of care; (f) Shell's obligations regarding Scope 1 and Scope 2 emissions and whether the claims of Milieudefensie on Scope 1 and Scope 2 emissions were made out; and (g) Shell's obligations regarding Scope 3 emissions, whether Shell was obliged to adhere to a global average reduction of 45 per cent, whether an oil and gas sectoral standard applicable to Shell could be formulated, and whether Milieudefensie's claims on Scope 3 emissions were made out.

There was no doubt about the relevance of human rights to the establishment of the social duty of care.[80] Such conclusion came from the *Urgenda* judgment,[81] recent jurisprudence of the ECtHR,[82] a review of case law outside Europe,[83] the approach of

[75] ibid.
[76] ibid [7.62].
[77] ibid [3.1]–[3.13].
[78] ibid [3.25]–[3.41].
[79] ibid [3.42]–[3.54]
[80] ibid [7.06]–[7.27].
[81] ibid [7.7]–[7.8].
[82] ibid [7.9]–[7.11].
[83] ibid [7.12].

the UN,[84] and guiding non-binding principles concerning business behaviour.[85] The conclusions as to these were powerfully expressed.[86] The Court concluded at [7.27] by stating:

> In summary, the court of appeal is of the opinion that companies like Shell, which contribute significantly to the climate problem and have it within their power to contribute to combatting it, have an obligation to limit CO2 emissions in order to counter dangerous climate change, even if this obligation is not explicitly laid down in (public law) regulations of the countries in which the company operates. Companies like Shell thus have their own responsibility in achieving the targets of the Paris Agreement.

The Court then examined the climate legislation of the EU and the greenhouse gas emissions trading scheme and other applicable rules in the EU.[87] It rejected Shell's submissions that its compliance with its legal obligations under legislation was necessarily an answer to any social duty of care. Such did not preclude a duty of care based on a social standard of care to reduce the GHG emissions, although such compliance was relevant to any question of breach.

In dealing with the topic of fresh investment in oil and gas fields and thus Scope 3 emissions, the Court noted the so-called carbon lock-in effect.[88] It accepted that such may be a breach of the duty, but the Court maintained focused on the claims in the proceedings: whether an obligation can be imposed on Shell to reduce its Scope 1, 2 and 3 emissions by 45, 35 or 25 per cent. The fact that companies like Shell were expected (as a matter of law) to take into account the negative consequences of new oil and gas fields by expanding supply could not lead to the granting of any part of the claims in the case. The Court then separately examined Shell's obligations as to Scope 1 and 2 emissions, and concluded that there was no pending violation of the legal duty.[89] As to Shell's obligations as to Scope 3 emissions the Court rejected the general IPCC-based 45 per cent reduction as a legal obligation with which Shell had to comply.[90] It was a generalised obligation and was not circumstance specific. This could be shown by simply realising that the supply of gas by Shell to a consumer which had been using coal as an energy source would reduce and not increase the GHG emissions of that customer. The Court insisted on more than obligations from averages, stating at [7.80] by reference to the United Nations IPCC report:

> The fact that that expert report, as well as other documents, states that companies should make maximum efforts to reduce their emissions as soon as possible is not sufficient to turn an average global reduction standard into a general, binding standard for Shell.

The Court further found that the available material by reference to the oil and gas sector was inadequate to provide support for an obligation upon Shell to reduce GHG emissions by a certain percentage by 2030.[91]

[84] ibid [7.13]–[7.17].
[85] ibid [7.18]–[7.27].
[86] ibid [7.24]–[7.27].
[87] ibid [7.28]–[7.54].
[88] ibid [7.58]–[7.62].
[89] ibid [7.63]–[7.66].
[90] ibid [7.67]–[7.81].
[91] ibid [7.82]–[7.96].

Further, the Court accepted that reducing Shell's sale of oil and gas would not necessarily lead to a reduction of GHG emissions.[92]

The judgment reveals an intense and demanding factual analysis of the claims based on the material placed before the Court. The approach displays a judicial technique that recognised the phenomenon of climate change and the need for the law to respond to it by placing obligations on private parties and not just public institutions. But it also reflected the difficulty of extracting meaningful orders upon a company that was not otherwise breaking the written law of the country in question based on general propositions and general guidelines and averages from worldwide climate reports. It reveals, perhaps even more starkly than *Sharma*, the difficulties involved in using the legal process (rather than the political process) to deal with a public policy question by broad strokes which are not supported by fine analysis of the particular circumstances of the case that is necessary for ascription of liability by the judicial process.

iii. Greenpeace v ENI

In May 2023, Greenpeace began proceedings in the Civil Court of Rome against the Italian energy major ENI S.p.A., the Italian Ministry of the Economy and Finance and the Cassa Depositi e Prestiti S.p.A. (the Italian Development Bank owned by the Ministry of the Economy and Finance).

The initiating process is 137 pages in length. It repays careful reading in full.

Importantly, it contains a clear description of what is referred to as 'attribution science', described in the preamble to the application as:[93]

> The science that makes it possible to attribute to a specific subject a specific quantity of emissions that do not comply with the values set at international level. In particular, it is possible to ascertain, among other things, the quantity of ENI's emissions … and to ascertain that ENI is responsible at global level for a volume of greenhouse gas emissions that is greater than that of Italy as a whole, thus being one of the main contributors to the climate change underway.

Section 17 of the pleading described the conclusions of 'attribution science' in reconstructing the contribution (and so historical responsibility) of individual companies for climate change. One study cited claimed that '62% of global industrial emissions of carbon dioxide and methane from 1751 to 2015 can be traced back to the activities of 100 '*carbon majors*' – basically companies operating with fossil fuels (oil, gas and coal) – currently active'.[94]

Another citation stated that 'emissions from these companies accounted for 91% of global industrial emissions and over 70% of all anthropogenic GHG emissions in 2015'.[95]

These figures, of course, include Scope 3 emissions.

Section 23 deals with international sources of the responsibility of the respondents, in particular human rights, as relevant to the responsibility of not only state, but also non-state actors.[96]

[92] ibid [7.97]–[7.110].
[93] Writ of Summons of *Greenpeace v ENI* 3.
[94] ibid 43–44.
[95] ibid 44.
[96] ibid 82–90.

The basis of the claim rests upon Article 2043 of the Italian Civil Code dealing with the causing of 'unjust damage' to others, including the violation of Articles 2 and 8 of the ECHR, and upon Articles 2050 and 2051 concerning damage for dangerous activity and things in one's possession.[97]

Importantly, the initiating process recognises and discusses the legal and conceptual difficulty of causation caused by acts affecting the environment, even though the causal relationship between the use of fossil fuels and climate change is not in dispute. Nevertheless, in this regard, reliance is placed on *The Netherlands v Urgenda* and the rejection by the Hoge Raad of causation arguments, at least prospectively.[98]

iv. Smith v Fonterra

In February 2024, the New Zealand Supreme Court overturned the decision of the Court of Appeal in *Smith v Fonterra Co-operative Group Ltd*,[99] to which the Full Court in *Sharma* (at [255]) had referred in support of the proposition that '[c]ourts are… ill-equipped to address the issues that the claim raises', which calls for 'a level of institutional expertise, democratic participation and democratic accountability that cannot be achieved through a court process'.[100]

It was a strike-out application, thus not an action on the merits. The claims were made by a Māori elder claiming customary interests in land, water and resources and as a representative of the family or kin group or clan.[101]

Fonterra was a dairy co-operative, and the six other respondent companies were energy, dairy, steel, infrastructure and/or mining companies. All were significant emitters of GHGs, whether by burning fossil fuels, or raising methane-emitting animals.[102] The case was pleaded under the common law and under customary Māori law. The claims were in public nuisance, negligence, and a proposed (new) climate system damage tort.[103]

The Supreme Court refused to strike out (any of) the pleadings and said the Court of Appeal had been wrong to do so.[104]

After a detailed review of the law of public nuisance, the Supreme Court stated (at [145]):[105]

> The rights to public health, public safety, public comfort, public convenience and public peace – fall tenably within (or bear sufficient relation to) the particular rights identified … as providing foundation for a public nuisance pleading: i.e. public rights to life, health, property or comfort.

If (as the Supreme Court held) there is no requirement in public nuisance to prove the acts complained of to be otherwise unlawful, one can see here the common law equivalent of interference with the human rights in Articles 2 and 8 of the ECHR.

[97] ibid 4, 98–100, 109–13.
[98] ibid 113–21.
[99] *Smith v Fonterra* (CA) (n 20).
[100] ibid [26], [116]; *Sharma No 2* [255].
[101] *Smith v Fonterra* (CA) (n 20) [3]; *Smith v Fonterra* (SC) (n 20) [3], [50].
[102] *Smith v Fonterra* (CA) (n 20) [3]; *Smith v Fonterra* (SC) (n 20) [51]–[52].
[103] *Smith v Fonterra* (SC) (n 20) [4].
[104] ibid [2].
[105] ibid [145].

As was said in the criminal appeal *Karim v The Queen* about the relationship between the common law and human rights, albeit in a different context: '[t]he norms and conceptions inhering in the exercise of judicial power incorporate from their roots in the common law the norms that now characterise international human rights'.[106]

The Court touched on 'special damage' and standing in public nuisance and said it required 'reconsideration in a 21st century context'.[107] The Court also referred to causation, though without exploring or dealing with 'attribution science', but it left open how causation would be dealt with in this context, doubting the appropriateness of a 'but for' test in public nuisance.[108]

VI. Causation

At this point, something should be said of causation and the development of the common law. It is a basal proposition in relation to the common law, and causation in it, that the approach to asking and answering such a question depends on the relevant rule of responsibility and the context in which, and the reason why, the question is being asked. Considerations of justice and the appropriateness of fashioning rules that facilitate the just remedying of disputes by the courts come into play. One can see that in the rules governing responsibility for personal injury and sickness in industrial settings. The abandonment, in appropriate contexts, of a 'but for' analysis and the requirement only to show a material contribution to a condition, as in *McGhee v National Coal Board*,[109] reveal this. There has been debate whether this was only the display of a 'robust and pragmatic'[110] approach to the inferential fact-finding of material contribution or perhaps, that only causing a material increase in risk was an adequate causal link, or that no relevant distinction should be drawn between materially increasing the risk and materially contributing to the injury. Leaving that debate to one side, the alleviation of the burden of a 'but for' analysis, that but for the impugned act the injury or sickness would not have occurred, leads to the intrusion of pragmatic and principled policy. The requirements of 'but for' proof in such circumstances might reveal the law as unable to adjust to the realities of life and as unable to give effective and just remedies.

This policy element in the rules of liability and causation was starkly illuminated in the House of Lords in *Fairchild v Glenhaven Funeral Services*[111] and *Barker v Corus (UK) plc*.[112] The context was the contraction of the shockingly painful and fatal disease of mesothelioma caused by exposure to asbestos (particularly blue asbestos) dust. There were often multiple defendant tortfeasor culprits, and also innocent actors or circumstances. Science said it was exposure to the asbestos dust that caused the disease, but science was unable to say who was responsible for the pieces of fibre that, over 20 years, worked their way from the inner surface of the lung to the outer wall, there causing a

[106] *Karim v R; Magaming v R; Bin Lahaiya v R; Bayu v R; Alomalu v R* [2013] NSWCCA 23 [119].
[107] *Smith v Fonterra* (SC) (n 20) [151].
[108] ibid [165]–[166].
[109] *McGhee v National Coal Board* [1973] 1 WLR 1.
[110] *Wilsher v Essex Area Health Authority* [1988] AC 1074, 1090 (Bridge J).
[111] *Fairchild v Glenhaven Funeral Services* [2002] UKHL 22.
[112] *Barker v Corus (UK) plc* [2006] UKHL 20.

tumour or tumours which grew, gradually filling the cavity at the outer lung, which prevented, eventually, any breathing and suffocated the person in excruciating pain. The defendants said in unison to the court as they looked (metaphorically and literally) at the dying plaintiff, 'True it is that we each negligently exposed you to asbestos fibre and dust some of which fibre and dust has or may have brought about your disease and your imminent death; but the cause of your disease might be one or more of us; and you cannot prove which of us has or have caused your condition and your imminent (and painful) death. So, you are without a remedy.'

The law responded with an explicit change to the applicable causal rules by expressly requiring only a material increase of risk of injury by the tortious conduct. The Law Lords thought that it would be an affront to justice to require more of a plaintiff than a material increase in risk as the relevant causal or factual involvement upon which to find responsibility. As this author said about *Fairchild* in a paper on causation:[113]

> Very much at the root of this policy decision was an aspect of underpinning legal theory referred to extra-curially by Justice McLachlin that tort law, as an aspect of the rule of law, is concerned with righting wrongful conduct. If, what are (by legitimate human perception) self-evident wrongs are not recognized by the law's rules and thus go unremedied, people who legitimately feel themselves victims will be left with a sense of injustice. A legitimate sense of injustice should not be the product of the rule of law. The place of justice and fairness was both explicit and central in the reasoning of Lord Bingham, Lord Nicholls, Lord Hoffmann and Lord Rodger.

Whether common law rules of causation on attribution of responsibility should be amended, and for what purpose, in dealing with legal responsibility for one of the greatest challenges facing mankind is riddled with such policy. The common law adapts over time through incremental, and sometimes large, steps to meet felt necessities of the day and to remedy legitimate sources of injustice.

The lack of a human rights regime in a common law country may not crimp the law of public nuisance, nor may rules of locus or standing designed for other purposes in other ages, nor should intellectually constructed rules of causation in a field of practical human engagement and affairs be designed to remedy harm caused. Judges are not philosophers or metaphysicians. Causation is a practical matter to the law; it is part of the just attribution of responsibility and of compensation for, or restraint of, conduct which 'causes' injury or damage.

One feature of causation should be noted. Whilst causal responsibility for past conduct for the present predicament is difficult to sheet home to any party, such causal responsibility for the future by prospective emissions is not as fraught, given the position in which the scientific consensus says we now find ourselves and the development of 'attribution science'.

[113] J Allsop, 'Causation in Commercial Law' in S Degeling, J Edelman and J Goudkamp (eds), *Torts in Commercial Law* (Sydney, Thomson Reuters, 2011) 323–24.

VII. The Corporate Form, the Group, and Legal Responsibility of the Parent[114]

Relevant to the consideration of corporate responsibility (whether compensatory or by way of prospective restraint) is the corporate form and responsibility for the group. These matters were present in *Milieudefensie v Royal Dutch Shell*. The strain upon the corporate form and upon the modern multinational group where national or sector-specific subsidiaries are used, but overall policy (often of operational matters) is controlled by the board of the parent or specific executives of the parent, can be seen in a number of recent cases. Even under orthodox current common law principles, the responsibilities of parent companies for the activity of their subsidiaries may be made out, not as some manifestation of the metaphor 'piercing the corporate veil', but by reason of their control of, or influence over, the operations of the group of which they are the parent.

As *Milieudefensie v Royal Dutch Shell*, *Greenpeace v ENI* and *Smith v Fonterra* reveal, it is important for the claimant to be able to sue the central arm of a group, whether parent or main asset holding company or chief operating company of any large group. Throughout the world the separateness of limited liability companies is a feature of company law and the legal landscape. Actions can always be brought against subsidiaries where such are the actual emitting companies, but the vulnerability of parent and senior corporations in a group can be seen in some recent cases about physical pollution and personal injury. These developments have not been an illustration of the metaphorical 'piercing of the corporate veil', where the parent might be forced to stand for the liabilities of the subsidiary. Rather, they are stark illustrations of the potential liability of parent companies for their own actions in respect of damages which may be directly physically caused by subsidiaries.

The legal structure of parent and subsidiary, and of separate legal personality, may not reflect the organisational and management structure of a group, which might be based on functions, lines of business or any number of structures or modes of organisation of a business or its operations. Head office may play (by choice or business necessity) a key role in supervising and directing lines of business or functions. Within this potential variety, there intrudes public expectations of responsible and decent behaviour, and often a corporate desire (by the importance in consumer capitalism of reputation or 'brand') to be seen as fulfilling those expectations. These are the kinds of considerations which weighed so heavily with the Dutch courts. These questions are sometimes looked at narrowly in time: as to value for present shareholders, without due regard for likely future perceptions of, and impositions of legal liability by, future generations. Social responsibility in the form of regard to climate change is, perhaps, better viewed by a board, not as involving matters extraneous to the interests of shareholders, but with the eye of an underwriter of long-tail liability business looking at future risk and the possible (present) incurring of (future) liability of the indefinitely continuing company affecting possibly present, but certainly future, shareholders.

[114] This section reproduces and develops part of J Allsop, 'Piercing the Corporate Veil: Recent International Developments', address at the Banking and Financial Services Law Association 2022 Conference (26 August 2022).

If a parent is found liable, it is liable in its own right as a tortfeasor by reason of its own acts, not those of its subsidiary. A finding of liability resulting from the application of orthodox principles of the law of torts does not entail disregarding a parent's separate legal personality; to the contrary, the legal personhood of the parent company is the very foundation of its liability.

A. *Chandler v Cape*

As early as 2012, in *Chandler v Cape*,[115] the Court of Appeal looked at personal responsibility for the parent company. Mr Chandler was employed as a brick loader by Cape Buildings Products Ltd (Cape Products) in the 1950s and 1960s and was exposed to asbestos in the course of his employment. He later suffered from asbestosis. By that time, however, Cape Products no longer existed. Mr Chandler brought an action against Cape Products' parent company, contending that the parent owed him a duty of care as an employee of its subsidiary to ensure a safe system of work. It was common ground at trial that there was 'nothing to justify' the piercing of the corporate veil, and the plaintiff's counsel urged that the 'right course' was to apply tort principles to resolve the case.[116]

The leading judgment of the Court of Appeal was delivered by Lady Justice Arden, who, applying the *Caparo* test,[117] found that the imposition of a duty of care was merited. As later decisions showed, this was not the appropriate test, as the category of duty of care was not novel: it concerned the infliction of personal injury. In this case, the business of the parent and subsidiary was the same, with the parent 'clearly in the practice' of issuing instructions to its subsidiary, with the subsidiary unable to incur capital expenditure without approval; the parent had superior knowledge on matters of work health and safety, having conducted considerable research on the health risks of asbestos products; the parent knew that its subsidiary's system of work was unsafe; and the parent ought to have foreseen that the subsidiary would rely on its knowledge in relation to health and safety.[118]

B. *Vedanta Resources*

This concerned a mass tort claim brought by poor Zambian citizens against a parent company domiciled in the UK for loss and damage suffered as a result of the operations of a copper mine owned and operated by the parent's subsidiary in Zambia.[119] The plaintiffs alleged that the UK-based parent, Vedanta Resources plc (Vedanta), owed them a duty of care because of the high level of supervision and control it maintained over its subsidiary, its knowledge of the likelihood that the activities of its subsidiary would cause environmental harm, and its assumption of responsibility for

[115] *Chandler v Cape plc* [2012] EWCA Civ 52 *(Chandler v Cape)*.
[116] ibid [37], [39].
[117] *Caparo Industries plc v Dickman* [1990] 2 AC 605.
[118] *Chandler v Cape* (n 115) [73]–[80].
[119] *Vedanta Resources* (SC) (n 22) [1]–[2] (Briggs SCJ). Note that the Zambian subsidiary, Konkola Copper Mines plc, is the second defendant in this case.

the environmental standards of its related companies in published material.[120] Vedanta challenged the jurisdiction of the courts of England and Wales to hear the dispute.[121] In 2019, the Supreme Court upheld the decision of the Court of Appeal that the claim disclosed a triable issue and that the case should proceed to trial in England.[122] In doing so, the Supreme Court clarified the appropriate principles to be applied.

The Court rejected the proposition that this case involved the assertion of a novel and controversial new category of case for the recognition of a common law duty of care, thus calling for the application of *Caparo*.[123] The wrong alleged was the poisoning of a waterway, injuring people and poisoning land: the stuff of torts.[124] In relation to multinational group companies, the Court said:[125]

> … there is nothing special or conclusive about the bare parent/subsidiary relationship, it is apparent that the general principles which determine whether A owes a duty of care to C in respect of the harmful activities of B are not novel at all. They may easily be traced back as far as the decision of the House of Lords in *Dorset Yacht Co Ltd v Home Office* [1970] AC 1004, in which the negligent discharge by the Home Office of its responsibility to supervise Borstal boys working on Brownsea Island in Poole harbour led to seven of them escaping and causing serious damage to the moored yachts in the vicinity, including one owned by the plaintiff.

The Court stressed that whether a duty of care should be imposed in a particular case depends to a large degree on the evidence (often documentary) concerning the level of a parent company's intervention in, and assumption of responsibility for, the affairs of its subsidiary, which are questions of fact.[126]

C. *Okpabi v Royal Dutch Shell*

In the 2021 decision of *Okpabi v Royal Dutch Shell*, the UK Supreme Court drew similar conclusions. Much like *Vedanta Resources*, this case involved proceedings brought by Nigerian communities against both RDS, a UK-domiciled company, and The Shell Petroleum Development Company of Nigeria Ltd, a subsidiary of RDS, in connection with environmental damage resulting from oil spills allegedly negligently caused by the Nigerian subsidiary, or by third parties acting illegally, which activities ought to have been prevented by Shell.[127] The plaintiffs claimed that RDS owed them a common law duty of care because it exercised significant control over its subsidiary's operations and/or assumed control for those operations, including by the 'promulgation and imposition' of mandatory environmental policies, standards and manuals.[128] The primary

[120] ibid [55].
[121] ibid [4].
[122] ibid [102].
[123] ibid [49]–[50]; approving the statement of Sales LJ in 2018 in *AAA v Unilever plc* [2018] EWCA Civ 1532 [36].
[124] *Vedanta Resources* (SC) (n 22) [60].
[125] ibid [54].
[126] ibid [44].
[127] *Okpabi v Royal Dutch Shell* (SC) (n 23) [4]–[6], [33].
[128] ibid [7].

judge and the Court of Appeal found that the plaintiffs had no arguable case that RDS owed them a duty of care.[129] The plaintiffs appealed that finding to the Supreme Court.

In allowing the appeal, the Supreme Court took the opportunity to reiterate the findings of the Court in *Vedanta Resources*. In particular, the Supreme Court stressed that:

It is incorrect to approach cases alleging that a parent company owed a plaintiff a duty of care by reference to the threefold *Caparo* test for establishing a novel duty because the liability of parent companies in relation to the activities of their subsidiaries is not novel. Earlier cases have considered it and the principles involved in determining that liability are themselves neither novel nor distinctive: the harm was the alleged infliction of physical damage and personal injury.[130]

There is 'no special test applicable to the tortious responsibility of a parent company for the activities of its subsidiary'.[131]

The question of whether a parent company has sufficiently intervened in, controlled, supervised or advised the management of a subsidiary in connection with some relevant aspect of its operations is a 'pure question of fact', and consequently, internal corporate documents evidencing operational matters are critically important.[132]

The Court made an important point as to the relevance of the structure of a corporate group in the application of tort principles. For the Master of the Rolls in the Court of Appeal, the manner in which RDS had structured its foreign operations was relevant to his finding that no duty of care was owed:

> … it would be surprising if a parent company were to go to the trouble of establishing a network of overseas subsidiaries with their own management structures if it intended itself to assume responsibility for the operations of each of those subsidiaries. The corporate structure itself tends to militate against the requisite proximity.[133]

However, the Supreme Court cautioned against making presumptions on the basis of corporate structure. As Lord Briggs SCJ noted in *Vedanta Resources*, there is 'no limit to the models of management and control which may be put in place within a multinational group of companies', and what is relevant is not the specific structure adopted but the extent to which a parent in fact took over or shared the management of the relevant activity with its subsidiary.[134]

There is nothing new in these cases. In New Zealand and Australia, parent responsibility in tort for defective products and personal injury has been found in *James Hardie Industries plc v White*,[135] *CSR Ltd v Wren*[136] and *CSR Ltd v Young*.[137] In these cases, the courts made clear that there was no special rule for parent companies. If they exercised enough supervision and control with relevant knowledge, they could be held tortiously directly liable.

[129] ibid [14], [18].
[130] ibid [24]–[25].
[131] ibid [27].
[132] ibid [129], [132].
[133] *Okpabi v Royal Dutch Shell* (CA) (n 23) [196], quoted in *Okpabi v Royal Dutch Shell* (SC) (n 23) [86], [150].
[134] *Okpabi v Royal Dutch Shell* (SC) (n 23) [150], citing *Vedanta Resources* (SC) (n 22) [51].
[135] *James Hardie Industries plc v White* [2018] NZCA 580 [1].
[136] *CSR Ltd v Wren* (1999) 44 NSWLR 463.
[137] *CSR Ltd v Young* (1998) Aust Torts Reports 81–468.

All these considerations are brought into sharp relief in the context of climate change and the urgency of emission reduction by non-state actors. As the Dutch courts have said, with the attention that corporations are paying (and properly so) to matters of economic and social responsibility and governance, and climate change considerations in particular, it is important to be cognisant of the potential ramifications of having (and not having) such policies in terms of exposure to tortious liability.

There is a real possibility, as shown by *Milieudefensie v Royal Dutch Shell*, *Greenpeace v ENI* and *Smith v Fonterra* and by the development of 'attribution science', if found to be acceptable, that private corporations will be held responsible for past and future damage caused by their GHG emissions.

All this raises the spectre of directors' duties and the possible future liability of the company for present or future wrongs caused by failing to alter the business model of a company sufficiently to meet GHG emission targets in accordance with known scientific consensus.

Such liabilities, or their possibility, are unlikely to be presently accounted for. Such compensatory claimants may be future creditors. It is entirely arguable that corporations have a responsibility not to cause injury and harm to people (even by acts that are otherwise lawful), at least in the jurisdiction in which they are incorporated. If so, and if they can be sued for negligence or nuisance, directors may be seen to have an obligation to the company as a whole to adapt the company's business to lower emissions, not as an act of 'good corporate citizenship' in the public interest, but as an exercise in dutiful self-interest to avoid the risk of incurring liability from contribution to global warming.

VIII. Directors' Duties: Not Social Responsibility, Just Future Creditors

Here we are not dealing with the topic of discussion in recent years of social responsibility and directors' duties.[138] Rather, this is a simpler and more familiar problem: the question as to how directors should consider their company's possible liability to suit for causing damage to others (from the company's contribution to climate change).

The fiduciary and statutory duties are not a narrow concern for only present shareholders. The corporation is an indefinitely continuing entity. Directors must take into account the interests of future shareholders through the long-term consequences of their acts or omissions.[139]

Thus, climate change plaintiffs as prospective climate change creditors may well fall for consideration by directors in the consideration of present and future shareholders in the company or the group companies in the company not acting unlawfully or in a manner that is or may be found to be compensably tortious.

The spectre of such liability is beginning to hover.

[138] eg, The Future of the Corporation programme launched in 2017 by The British Academy; The British Academy, Net Zero Governance, 'Governance for Net Zero' (February 2024).

[139] eg, Companies Act 2006 (UK), s 172(1)(a).

The extent of 'long-arm' jurisdiction of national courts is important. The variety of connecting factors to a particular country to ground jurisdiction of its courts in tort differs. One such factor is of significance: damage suffered within the jurisdiction, whether to persons or property within the jurisdiction.

If it can be demonstrated, through 'attribution science' or otherwise, that significant emissions have been, are or will be made by the putative defendant, such may provide a foundation for service *ex juris* upon the foreign putative defendant.

If such long-arm jurisdiction is available, the question of submission to the jurisdiction will arise. Not to appear would place at least property within the jurisdiction in jeopardy of default judgment. Appearance only to challenge service and jurisdiction may fail. Thus, the assets of emitting companies within the jurisdiction may be at risk depending upon the terms of service *ex juris* provisions in countries other than their own.

IX. Final Comments

The place of judicial decision-making in the formulation and effectuation of climate change policy response will likely generate both controversy in relation to the role of the courts, legal policy, and the reconsideration of fundamental principles by, at least, courts of final appeal.

The obligation to deploy judicial technique does not mean that significant change in doctrine cannot, or will not, come about.

The most important of the considerations that courts must grapple with is the propriety of judicial power being exercised in an area of policy and power which is certainly the domain of executive and legislature power. That it is the latter does not mean that it cannot be the subject of the former: judicial power, which power, after all, and subject to national constitutional considerations (such as in the Netherlands), can be limited by valid legislative acts.

Yet, if the facts are to be drawn from the scientific consensus before the courts in *The Netherlands v Urgenda, Milieudefensie v Royal Dutch Shell, Greenpeace v ENI, Smith v Fonterra* and *Sharma*, variation to legal principle in relation to such matters as standing, causation, justiciability, and the elements of public nuisance may well occur.

16

A Sentinel's Toil in Climate Action: Significance of the Judicial Role (with emphasis on the role of the Indian Supreme Court)

ARJAN SIKRI

I. Introduction

> We stand now where two roads diverge. But unlike the roads in Robert Frost's familiar poem, they are not equally fair. The road we have long been travelling is deceptively easy, a smooth superhighway on which we progress with great speed, but at its end lies disaster. The other fork of the road — the one 'less travelled by' — offers our last, our only chance to reach a destination that assures the preservation of our earth.[1]
>
> Rachel Carson, *Silent Spring*

The above-quoted extract from the famous book of Rachel Carson, said in a similar context, highlights the worldwide effects and ramifications of climate change and how it is having an increasing impact on our economies and communities. In fact, climate change has become the global commons issue posing difficult questions for various stakeholders, which legislators and policymakers have been debating for about 50 years. What was once a topic of academic discussion has now become a global reality, albeit with varying degrees of immediate impact.

There is now unequivocal scientific evidence that human activity is responsible for almost all of the global warming that has occurred over the past 200 years.[2] The entire planet is warming faster than it has in at least the last two millennia due to greenhouse gas emissions from human activities. The average temperature of the Earth's surface is currently 1.2°C warmer than it was in the late 1800s, before the industrial revolution, and warmer than it has ever been in the previous 100,000 years.[3] The most recent

[1] R Carson, *Silent Spring* (New York, Mariner Books, 2002) 277.

[2] United Nations, 'What is Climate Change', available at www.un.org/en/climatechange/what-is-climate-change, citing Intergovernmental Panel on Climate Change, 'Climate Change 2021: Summary for All' (12 December 2022).

[3] ibid.

decade (2011–20) was the warmest on record, and since 1850, every decade since then has been warmer than the one before it.[4]

While scientists and government reviewers have concurred in a number of United Nations (UN) reports that keeping the rise in global temperature to 1.5°C would help avoid the worst effects of climate change and retain a climate that is liveable, present practices indicate that temperatures will climb by up to 3.1°C by the end of the century.[5] Current plans call for the world to adhere to the Paris Agreement's unconditionally nationally determined contributions (NDCs) in order to keep global warming to 2.9°C over pre-industrial levels this century. To lower this to 2.5°C, full implementation of conditional NDCs would be required.[6]

Undeniably, every country in the world contributes to climate change through emissions and, thus, is responsible for the malaise. However, some countries are creating pollution far in excess of others. It is a harsh reality that about half of all greenhouse gas emissions worldwide in 2020 came from the top seven emitters – China, the US, India, the European Union, Indonesia, Russia, and Brazil.[7]

However, the footprint of climate change, along with evolving scientific understandings, is forcing new possibilities in law. Necessity, therefore, is truly the mother of invention. With courage, conviction, and candour, there might just be a glimmer of hope. Here the author is reminded of what the Atharva Veda[8] 12.1-15 says:

> Born of Thee, on Thee move mortal creatures;
>
> Thou bearest them-the biped and the quadruped;
>
> Thine, O Earth, are the five races of men, for whom Surya (Sun),
>
> As he rises spreads with his rays the light that is immortal.[9]

The reference to the Atharva Veda underlines a deep-rooted spiritual acknowledgement of the Earth and all its inhabitants as sacred and interconnected. This ancient Indian scripture embodies a view prevalent in many religious traditions, which sees the environment not merely as a resource but as a manifestation of the divine.[10] Such spiritual frameworks offer profound ethical imperatives for environmental stewardship, suggesting that humanity's relationship with nature transcends utilitarian concerns and is instead grounded in moral and spiritual obligations. The concept of Brahman in ancient India, depicting the universe and everything within it as aspects of the divine, further emphasises the sanctity of the natural world, presenting a holistic approach to understanding and engaging with our environment.[11]

[4] ibid.

[5] ibid.

[6] United Nations Environment Programme, 'Emissions Gap Report 2023: Broken Record – Temperatures Hit New Highs, Yet World Fails to Cut Emissions (Again)' (2023).

[7] See n 2 above.

[8] RTH Griffith, *The Hymns of the Atharva-Veda* (Benares, EJ Lazarus & Co, 1895).

[9] ibid Hymn 12.1-15.

[10] See generally RS Gottlieb, *This Sacred Earth: Religion, Nature, Environment*, 2nd edn (New York, Routledge, 2003).

[11] NR Acharya, 'Brahman: Scientific Exploration of The Divine Through Vedic Wisdom' (2023) 2 *Towards Unification of Sciences* 65.

However, notwithstanding the current awareness of international climate discussions and the necessity of reducing carbon emissions, comprehending the trajectory of climate reform remains a multifaceted and continuous undertaking, with several lacunae in the policy frameworks of both national and international entities. Discussions regarding the various aspects of climate change include a broad spectrum of topics, including economic, political, topographical, cultural, population, health, and reproductive rights. The existing policy gap on these issues necessitates critical discourses on the socio-legal dimensions of climate change, to develop mitigative and constructive strategies that could harness the potential of law and policies.

This chapter will focus on the public enforcement of environmental standards by the courts. It will elaborate on this concept by discussing the Indian Supreme Court's notable judgments, which have been the torchbearers on the subject matter. It will discuss some of the innovative techniques that the Supreme Court has adopted, including an inquisitorial approach to developing this concept by way of a special mechanism called public interest litigation (PIL). In this process, the Court also came up with a tool in the form of the continuing mandamus to ensure the effective implementation of its judgments.

II. The Emerging Role of Courts

It is now universally accepted that human beings are just custodians of this planet, and there is intergenerational equity between generations. This means that the current generation is obligated to consider the needs of the future generation when designing and implementing current policies. The public trust doctrine, in essence, protects certain components of the natural environment from exploitation. These components, often referred to in this context as natural resources or properties, are held in trust by the state for the people, who are, in a sense, the real owners and beneficiaries of the same.

Legislators around the world have tried, often unsuccessfully, to pass meaningful climate change legislation. Against this, there has been an expansion of litigation-related activity.[12] Research from the Grantham Research Institute on Climate Change and the Environment and the Centre for Climate Change Economics and Policy reveals that since 2015, courts worldwide have received over 1,000 lawsuits related to climate change.[13] The same report found that only 800 cases were filed in the last 30 years before 2015.[14] These trends confirm the fact that courts are looked at to provide climate action leadership.

For instance, in the field of tort law, the question of whether public authorities have a duty of care to citizens to prevent harm from carbon emissions has attracted attention

[12] DC Smith, 'Courts Must Provide Climate Change Leadership in the Absence of Law-Making Progress' (2021) 39 *Journal of Energy & Natural Resources Law* 385.

[13] ibid; J Setzer and C Higham, 'Global Trends in Climate Change Litigation: 2021 Snapshot' (Grantham Research Institute on Climate Change and the Environment and the Centre for Climate Change Economics and Policy, July 2021).

[14] Setzer and Higham (n 13) 4.

in recent years.[15] A number of significant cases, such as *Minister for the Environment v Sharma*[16] and *The Netherlands v Urgenda*[17] have explored the extent to which public bodies can be held accountable for their failure to lessen the effects of climate change. These cases, which have been discussed by James Allsop in the previous chapter, highlight various aspects of the prospects and legal obstacles associated with climate litigation. It is against this background that this chapter discusses the PIL, a unique mechanism created by the Indian Supreme Court since the 1980s.

III. Innovative Techniques for Preservation of Environment by the Indian Judiciary

A significant portion of the environmental law in India has evolved via rigorous judicial thought in the Supreme Court, High Courts, and, since 2010, the specialised tribunal known as the National Green Tribunal (NGT). The Supreme Court and High Courts have been instrumental in interpreting Article 21[18] – which guarantees the fundamental right to protection of life and personal liberty – for the purpose of addressing environmental issues, utilising their authority under Articles 32 and 226 of the Indian Constitution, respectively. In order to interpret the Constitution and statutes, the courts have successfully developed indigenous legal theories by incorporating a variety of international environmental doctrines,[19] and combined this with a liberal perspective that ensures that social justice and the protection of human rights are part of India's environmental jurisprudence.[20]

The jurisprudence developed is premised on the following pillars:

1. Treating the right to a clean environment as a fundamental right.[21]
2. Extending the use of PIL to encompass environmental litigation.
3. Adopting an inquisitorial approach while dealing with such cases.
4. Inventing the concept of continuing mandamus.

Two umbrella cases: an amalgam of continuing mandamus with the inclusion of fresh environmental cases.

[15] W Bonython, 'Tort Law and Climate Change' (2021) 40 *University of Queensland Law Journal* 421; D Kysar, 'What Climate Change can do about Tort Law' (2011) 41 *Environmental Law* 1.

[16] *Minister for the Environment v Sharma* (2022) 400 ALR 203.

[17] *The State of The Netherlands (Ministry of Economic Affairs and Climate Policy) v Urgenda Foundation* ECLI:NL:HR:2019:2007, Hoge Raad, 19/00135.

[18] See generally MP Singh, *VN Shukla's Constitution of India*, 14th edn (Lucknow, Eastern Book Company, 2022).

[19] For more literature and discussion on cases, see generally, S Divan and A Rosencranz, *Environmental Law and Policy in India: Cases and Materials* (Oxford, Oxford University Press, 2023).

[20] H Koli, 'Public Interest Litigation in Environmental Cases', paper presented at Session 7 of the Fifth ASEAN Chief Justices' Roundtable on Environment in 2015, para 1. See generally G Austin, *Working a Democratic Constitution: A History of the Indian Experience* (Oxford, Oxford University Press, 2003).

[21] *Virender Gaur v State of Haryana* (1995) 2 SCC 577.

A. Treating the Right to a Clean Environment as a Fundamental Right

Part III of the Indian Constitution,[22] which includes Articles 12–35, contains many fundamental rights (human rights) guaranteed to Indian citizens. Some of these rights are available to every 'person' in India, including those who are not Indian citizens.[23] Article 21 is one of them, and it states the following on the protection of life and personal liberty:[24]

> No person shall be deprived of his life or personal liberty except according to procedure established by law.

Article 21 encompasses two freedoms, namely, the 'right to life' and the 'right to personal liberty' – both these expressions have been very widely construed by the Indian Supreme Court.[25] When it comes to the 'right to life', the Court has held that it includes within its sweep not only physical existence, but also the quality of life with human dignity.[26] On this foundation, as many as 40 rights have been carved out using the concept of the right to life.[27]

This interpretation treats ecology as an aspect of Article 21[28] – which is based on the public trust doctrine – and extends it to natural resources such as rivers, forests, seashores, and air, with the aim of protecting the ecosystem and the right to a clean environment.[29] As a result, the protection of the environment is accorded the status of a fundamental right. Because fundamental rights are enforceable, the Supreme Court and the High Courts have the authority to uphold environmental and climate rights and issue appropriate writs and directions to ensure environmental protection. As discussed hereinafter, in this process, PIL has become the most distinctive tool for implementing Indian environmental law.[30] Since 1985, pro bono advocates have filed the majority of environmental cases in India as writ petitions with the courts. Since environmental matters involve the rights of the community rather than the individual, this structure is typically more effective in handling them.[31]

[22] PM Bakshi, *The Constitution of India*, 19th edn (London, LexisNexis, 2023).

[23] See A Padmanabhan, 'Rights: Breadth, Scope, and Applicability' in S Choudhry, M Khosla and PB Mehta (eds), *The Oxford Handbook of the Indian Constitution* (Oxford, Oxford University Press, 2016).

[24] See S Gardbaum, 'Horizontal Effect' in S Choudhry, M Khosla and PB Mehta (eds), *The Oxford Handbook of the Indian Constitution* (Oxford, Oxford University Press, 2016).

[25] For a detailed discussion about the intertwining of rights under Part III of the Indian Constitution, see AK Sikri, 'Human Dignity: A Purpose in Perpetuity' (*Scottish Council of Law Reporting*, 23 March 2023), available at www.scottishlawreports.org.uk/publications/macfadyen-lectures/human-dignity-a-purpose-in-perpetuity-23-march-2023.

[26] *DK Basu v State of West Bengal* (1997) 1 SCC 416; *Sunil Batra v Delhi Administration* (1980) 3 SCC 488.

[27] For detailed discussion on this aspect see Part I of AK Sikri, *Constitutionalism and the Rule of Law: In a Theatre of Democracy* (Lucknow, Eastern Book Company, 2023).

[28] *MK Ranjitsinh v Union of India* 2024 INSC 280.

[29] *MC Mehta v Kamal Nath* (1997) 1 SCC 388.

[30] For a detailed discussion on PIL in environmental cases, see 'Public Interest Litigation' in S Divan and A Rosencranz (eds), *Environmental Law and Policy in India: Cases and Materials*, 3rd edn (Oxford, Oxford University Press, 2023).

[31] L Rajamani, 'Public Interest Environmental Litigation in India: Exploring Issues of Access, Participation, Equity, Effectiveness And Sustainability' (2007) 19 *Journal of Environmental Law* 293.

B. PIL

PIL in India is a judicially created tool that eases the *locus standi* requirements,[32] and which diverges from the 'proof of injury' requirement.[33] Originally, this remedy was devised as a means of ensuring access to justice for people who were unable to approach the court due to poverty or illiteracy.[34] The main idea was to accord social justice to the marginalised section of society, giving liberty to any public-spirited person to approach the court on behalf of such a community, thereby waiving the *locus standi* requirement. Since it was done to achieve the larger *public* interest, it came to be known as PIL. However, over a period of time, two more facets were covered by the Supreme Court within the realm of PIL, namely, the promotion of environmental concerns, and accountability in governance.

The Supreme Court of India traced the beginnings and development of PIL in the notable case of *State of Uttaranchal v Balwant Singh Chaufal.*[35] Three general phases have been identified. They are as follows:

Phase I: This dealt with cases from the Supreme Court where rulings and directions were mostly given to preserve the fundamental rights of the marginalised groups and parts of society under Article 21, who were unable to access the Supreme Court or the High Courts due to extreme poverty, illiteracy, or ignorance.

Phase II: This phase related to cases pertaining to the preservation and protection of the environment, forests, wildlife, marine life, mountains, rivers, historical monuments, and forests.

Phase III: This phase concerned the court's directives for upholding the integrity, probity, and transparency of governance.

Over the last 25 years, environmental law in India has developed quickly.[36] The Indian judiciary, in particular the higher judiciary comprising the Supreme Court, the High Courts, and the NGT, is largely responsible for this development.[37] They have integrated numerous international environmental doctrines into Indian environmental jurisprudence.[38] As a result, the evolution of PIL has made it easier for people from all social classes to obtain justice.[39]

In fact, the evolution of PIL led to the judicial acknowledgement of vital elements of international environmental law:

The polluter pays principle: In *Indian Council for Enviro-Legal Action v Union of India*,[40] the Supreme Court observed that, the polluter pays principle 'has now come

[32] S Divan, 'Public Interest Litigation' in S Choudhry, M Khosla and PB Mehta (eds), *The Oxford Handbook of the Indian Constitution* (Oxford, Oxford University Press, 2016).

[33] A Bhuwania, *Courting the People: Public Interest Litigation in Post-Emergency India* (Cambridge, Cambridge University Press, 2017) 17.

[34] ibid 80.

[35] *State of Uttaranchal v Balwant Singh Chaufal* (2010) 3 SCC 402, para 45.

[36] PK Singh, *A To Z of Public Interest Litigation (PIL)*, 2nd edn (Burari, Whitesmann, 2024).

[37] MG Faure and AV Raja, 'Effectiveness of Environmental Public Interest Litigation in India: Determining the Key Variables' (2017) 21 *Fordham Environmental Law Review* 239.

[38] Bhuwania (n 33) 203–08.

[39] M Rao, *Public Interest Litigation in India: A Renaissance in Social Justice* (Lucknow, Eastern Book Company, 2002).

[40] *Indian Council for Enviro-Legal Action v Union of India* (1996) 3 SCC 212.

to be universally accepted as a sound principle and that according to this principle, the responsibility for repairing the damage is that of the offending industry'.[41]

Precautionary principle: Then in *Vellore Citizens' Welfare Forum v Union of India*,[42] the apex Court held that much like the polluter pays principle, the precautionary principle is also a 'part of the environmental law of the country'.[43] The Court further noted that 'this requires the government to address environmental degradation before it occurs'.[44]

The principle of intergenerational equity: In the case of *State of Himachal Pradesh v Ganesh Wood Products*,[45] the Supreme Court found that 'the present generation has no right to deplete all the existing forests and leave nothing for the next and future generations'.[46]

Public trust doctrine: In *MC Mehta v Kamal Nath*,[47] the apex Court remarked that 'our legal system – based on English common law – includes the public trust doctrine as part of its jurisprudence and State as a trustee is under a legal duty to protect the natural resources'.[48]

On various occasions, the Court has itself taken cognisance of the hazards of illegal and indiscriminate mining of minerals,[49] the discharge of toxic effluents into water bodies,[50] the deteriorating quality of air,[51] and the damage done to the ecology on account of industrial or construction activity.[52] In all these cases, the Supreme Court has emphasised that while industrial development is critical to the economic growth of the country, the environment and the ecosystem must also be preserved. The Court has also highlighted that sustainable development with equal emphasis upon ecology is the way forward.

In addition to its ever-growing body of environmental law, India has seen the rise of cases that are either based on the concept of climate change or in which the courts have used it to justify their positions on other environmental matters.[53] In respect of the former, the case of *Ridhima Pandey v Union of India*[54] marks a significant advancement in the use of climate change as a foundation for the claim. The petitioner sought

[41] ibid para 67.

[42] *Vellore Citizens' Welfare Forum v Union of India* (1996) 5 SCC 647.

[43] ibid paras 11–14.

[44] ibid para 20.

[45] *State of Himachal Pradesh v Ganesh Wood Products* (1995) 6 SCC 363.

[46] ibid para 51.

[47] *MC Mehta v Kamal Nath* (1997) 1 SCC 388.

[48] ibid para 34.

[49] See judgments of the Supreme Court of India in *Goa Foundation v Union of India* (2014) 6 SCC 590; *Rural Litigation and Entitlement v State of Uttar Pradesh* (1989) Supp 1 SCC 537; *MC Mehta v Union of India* (2004) 12 SCC 118.

[50] See *Vellore Citizens' Welfare Forum v Union of India* (1996) 5 SCC 647 wherein the Supreme Court imposed a fine on tanneries discharging untreated effluent into agricultural fields, road-sides, waterways and open lands.

[51] See *MC Mehta v Union of India* (1997) 2 SCC 353 wherein the Supreme Court directed 292 industries located near the Taj Mahal to stop the use of coal and coke and switch to Compressed Natural Gas.

[52] See *MC Mehta v Kamal Nath* (1997) 1 SCC 388. In this case the Supreme Court levied exemplary fine on a motel that damaged an ecologically fragile area around the river Beas in an attempt to change the river's natural course.

[53] U Varottil, 'Directors' Liability and Climate Risk: White Paper on India' (Commonwealth Climate and Law Initiative, 4 October 2021) 14.

[54] *Ridhima Pandey v Union of India*, Order dated 15.01.2019 of the National Green Tribunal, Principal Bench, New Delhi in Original App No 187/2017.

the intervention of the NGT to direct the government 'to take effective, science-based action to reduce and minimize the adverse impacts of climate change in the country'.[55] The Principal Bench of the NGT declined to get involved in the merits of the case and instead chose to defer the matter to the executive branch of the government.[56] The petitioner has appealed the decision of the NGT before the Supreme Court.

In the latter category of cases, the courts have acknowledged the necessity of the sustainable development and ecological preservation of eco-sensitive areas, even if doing so results in a downturn in local economic growth or a decrease in state revenue. An example of this is the judgment of the Supreme Court in *Bombay Dyeing and Mfg. Co. Ltd. v Bombay Environmental Action Group*,[57] where the Court held thus:

> **251.** [W]ith major threats to the environment, such as climate change, depletion of natural resources, the eutrophication of water systems and biodiversity and global warming, the need to protect the environment has become a priority. At the same time, it is also necessary to promote development. The harmonization of the two needs has led to the concept of sustainable development, so much so that it has become the most significant and focal point of environmental legislation and judicial decisions relating to the same. Sustainable development, simply put, is a process in which development can be sustained over generations.[58]

The Supreme Court again ruled in *Karnataka Industrial Areas Development Board v C. Kenchappa*[59] that the litigant must fully understand any potential negative environmental effects before purchasing any land for industrial use. The Court emphasised the significance of sustainable development in the following manner:

> **102.** Sustainable use of natural resources should essentially be based on maintaining a balance between development and the ecosystem. Coordinated efforts of all concerned would be required to solve the problem of ecological crisis and pollution. Unless we adopt an approach of sustainable use, the problem of environmental degradation cannot be solved.
>
> **103.** The concept of sustainable development was propounded by the 'World Commission on Environment and Development', which very aptly and comprehensively defined it as '*development that meets the needs of the present without compromising the ability of future generations to meet their own needs*'. Survival of mankind depends on following the said definition in letter and spirit.[60] (emphasis added)

In many cases, the courts have given significant directions from time to time by applying the aforesaid principles. In many judgments, it has invoked the doctrine of accountability of public authorities in tort law as well as corporate accountability, which is akin to jurisprudence developed in other countries. The experience has shown that the Indian courts, while dealing with these environmental issues invoking the extraordinary writ jurisdiction by the constitutional courts (ie, the Supreme Court and the High Courts), have faced two hurdles. The first relates to the scope and power of the courts while exercising writ jurisdictions. Normally, the courts are not supposed to go into the disputed

[55] See III of the petition filed in *Ridhima Pandey v Union of India*.
[56] *Ridhima Pandey v Union of India* para 2.
[57] *Bombay Dyeing and Mfg. Co. Ltd. v Bombay Environmental Action Group* (2006) 3 SCC 434.
[58] ibid para 251.
[59] *Karnataka Industrial Areas Development Board v C. Kenchappa* (2006) 6 SCC 371.
[60] ibid paras 102–03.

questions of facts. But sometimes, environmental issues coming before the court may involve some 'disputed facts', and some fact-finding enquiry becomes necessary. The second problem which is encountered relates to the enforcement of the orders. It hardly needs elaboration that in order to ensure effective justice, implementation monitoring becomes an essential function when handling environmental cases. Merely restating the law in court will rarely result in change if there is no effective implementation of the directions, leaving us with the same dilemma of 'rights without remedies'.[61]

To redress both the aforesaid impediments, the courts have devised a unique methodology. When it comes to dealing with environmental issues even in writ jurisdiction, in order to gather the correct factual matrix, the courts have adopted an inquisitorial approach. Likewise, to ensure that the directions issued by the courts are properly implemented, the courts have assumed the authority to supervise regulatory enforcement actions, guaranteeing the observance of environmental rules and due process. This is known as continuing mandamus. These two approaches are explained further below.

C. Inquisitorial Approach

In response to the complexities of environmental challenges, legal systems around the world have developed various approaches to address them effectively.[62] The inquisitorial approach in environmental law signifies a departure from traditional legal frameworks by emphasising judicial investigation and intervention, which may be contrasted with the adversarial system's reliance on parties presenting evidence and arguments.[63] In environmental law, this approach is particularly relevant due to the complexity and interconnectedness of environmental issues. Environmental problems often involve multiple stakeholders and intricate scientific evidence, and have more long-term impacts, thus necessitating a more thorough and holistic examination.[64]

The application of the inquisitorial approach can be seen in the famous case of *Research Foundation for Science, Technology and Natural Resource Policy v Union of India*.[65] Before the Supreme Court, the petitioners argued that the Ministry of Environment, Forests, and Climate Change's (MoEF) ability to allow the import of toxic wastes from industrialised nations should be invalidated because it was dangerous for the environment and human health.[66] It was brought to the Court's notice that MoEF was not complying with international covenants and the Hazardous Wastes (Management and Handling) Rules, 1989.[67]

[61] M Poddar and B Nahar, 'Continuing Mandamus - A Judicial Innovation to Bridge the Right-Remedy Gap' (2017) 10 *NUJS Law Review* 555, 587; PS Karlan, 'What's a Right Without a Remedy?' (*Boston Review*, 1 March 2012), available at www.bostonreview.net/articles/pamela-karlan-supreme-court-rights-legal-remedies.

[62] S Cassotta, 'The Development of Environmental Law within a Changing Environmental Governance Context: Towards a New Paradigm Shift in the Anthropocene Era' (2019) 30 *Yearbook of International Environmental Law* 54.

[63] For a detailed discussion, see 'Judicial Remedies and Procedures' in S Divan and A Rosencranz (eds), *Environmental Law and Policy in India: Cases and Materials*, 3rd edn (Oxford, Oxford University Press, 2023).

[64] DT Rogers, *Fundamentals of Environmental Law and Compliance* (Boca Raton, CRC Press, 2022).

[65] *Research Foundation for Science Technology National Resource Policy v Union of India* (2005) 10 SCC 510.

[66] ibid para 21.

[67] ibid para 52.

The Court, after considering the arguments, constituted a high-powered committee of experts to provide findings and recommendations on many facets of hazardous waste management.[68] The committee was also given the responsibility of supervising the orders of the Court that had to be implemented by a specified time.[69] After taking into account the reports of the committees and experts, as well as international standards, the Court gave directions to the Central and State Pollution Control Boards, and made recommendations for the drafting of legislation to address the transboundary movement of hazardous wastes, with provisions for punishing illegal trafficking.[70]

The Court also instructed the recycling or destruction of garbage based on its hazardous character, under the watchful eye of the monitoring committee.[71] In 2012,[72] the Court disposed of the writ petition and reiterated its previous interim orders, requiring the government to align its regulations with international agreements and prohibit the importation of hazardous wastes classified under the Basel Convention.[73]

D. Continuing Mandamus

One of the primary obstacles to achieving effective relief in environmental matters has been the non-implementation of rulings,[74] such as when court directions are disregarded.[75] However, under a PIL, the writ of mandamus has a broader scope. The device adopted by the courts is not to dispose of the matter after issuing the necessary writ and/or directions. Instead, the court monitors the implementation of its orders, thereby discharging a 'supervisory role'. In the process, the court also keeps on issuing further mandamus from time to time depending upon the contingencies of the situation. That is why it is known as a 'continuing mandamus'.

The origin of the continuing mandamus is not traced to environmental issues before the courts. In fact, it started with the other types of cases in PIL which primarily relate to Phase III mentioned in *Balwant Singh Chaufal*,[76] namely, ensuring the integrity, probity and transparency of governance. The courts have been using PIL and the continuing mandamus to broaden their purview and assume the authority of the legislature and executive branches in specific instances where they believe the other branches of government are underperforming relative to their legal obligations.

[68] ibid para 53.

[69] ibid para 22.

[70] ibid paras 23–24.

[71] ibid para 29.

[72] *Research Foundation for Science v Union of India* (2012) 7 SCC 769.

[73] ibid paras 42–43.

[74] *MC Mehta v Union of India* (1986) 2 SCC 176. In this case which is also known as the *Oleum Gas Leak* decision, the Court articulated the notion of absolute liability, clarifying the strict liability premise established in *Rylands v Fletcher*. The public remedy concept was also advanced by the Court, which gives rise to the right to reimbursement under writ jurisdiction. However, the victims of the gas leak are now only able to seek conventional remedies by suing for damages.

[75] The orders of the Court issued in the Ganga River pollution case have never been enforced. In the cases of the tanneries in Kanpur and Calcutta, the Court had ordered stringent measures against the polluting industries, although the tanneries are still in operation. See P Singh, 'Bridging the Ganga Action Plan: Monitoring Failure at Kanpur' (2006) 41 *Economic and Political Weekly* 590.

[76] See n 35 above.

The notable case of *Vineet Narain v Union of India*[77] serves as a manifestation of this, as it defined continuing mandamus for the first time in Indian legal history. Speaking on behalf of the Court, Chief Justice JS Verma stated that in some situations it was preferable to keep the case open while investigations were ongoing and make sure that this was accomplished by periodically monitoring the authorities and issuing orders in this regard, rather than hearing the case, issuing a simple mandamus and expecting them to follow it.[78] It was determined that issuing a writ of mandamus to the agencies would be futile in certain cases, so it was decided to issue directions on a regular basis and keep the matter pending, requiring the agencies to report the progress of the investigation so that the court could monitor it and ensure its continuation.[79] This act was referred to as a 'continuing mandamus'.[80]

In order to guarantee compliance in environmental disputes, the apex Court has attempted on multiple occasions to start court-monitored proceedings. In *Vellore Citizen's Welfare Forum v Union of India*,[81] the Supreme Court addressed a writ petition against tanneries in Tamil Nadu that were contaminating groundwater with untreated effluents. The Court ordered the Central Government to establish an authority to handle the case,[82] and it also instructed the Madras High Court to establish a Green Bench to handle the case and keep an eye on the committee's and the tanneries' operations.[83] As such, even before its formal designation as a 'continuing mandamus', persistent monitoring was an acceptable procedure in environmental proceedings.[84]

E. Two Umbrella Cases: Amalgam of Continuing Mandamus with the Inclusion of Fresh Environmental Cases

Two significant environmental cases, which started in 1986 and 1997 respectively, are still pending before the apex court, where a slew of directions have been given.

In *MC Mehta v Union of India*,[85] the Supreme Court employed the writ of continuing mandamus for the first time to address the resistance and indifference towards environmental issues, even in the face of court orders and recognition of rights abuses. In this case, the Court continued to consider the petition after rendering a decision. As a result, this case included other recent environmental cases.[86] This guaranteed the timely and efficient execution of environmental-related concerns on the ground, since the Court was keeping an eye on the proceedings.

[77] *Vineet Narain v Union of India* (1998) 1 SCC 226.
[78] ibid paras 7–9.
[79] ibid paras 13–14.
[80] ibid para 29.
[81] *Vellore Citizens' Welfare Forum v Union of India* (1996) 5 SCC 647.
[82] ibid para 20.
[83] ibid para 26.
[84] D Sinha et al, 'Courting The Environment: Implementation of Environmental Judgments' (Vidhi Centre for Legal Policy, April 2021), available at vidhilegalpolicy.in/wp-content/uploads/2021/04/Courting-the-Environment-Full-Report.pdf.
[85] *M.C. Mehta v Union of India* (1986) 2 SCC 176.
[86] ibid para 26.

For example, the Court revisited MC Mehta's PIL about Delhi's air pollution from 1985[87] in the *Delhi Vehicular Pollution* case[88] and issued several orders as continuing mandamus.[89] The Court justified the case's supervision as being necessary in order to guarantee Article 21 compliance, by helping authorities understand their statutory obligations and averting the frustration of legislative intent.[90] It mandated routine vehicle emissions tests and had the authority to revoke the registration certificates of cars that were not working properly.[91] In addition, the Court ordered the Ministry of Environment to form an expert committee to examine administrative, legal, and technological approaches to reduce pollution.[92] Between 1991 and 1997, almost 30 reports were sent to this committee.[93]

The *Omnibus Forests* case,[94] often referred to as the *Godavarman* case, is the next umbrella case falling under 'continuing mandamus'. In 1995, an environmental activist, TN Godavarman Thirumulpad, filed a writ petition in the Supreme Court to protect the Nilgiris forest land from devastation by illicit timber activities.[95] The Court taking cognisance of the issue passed an order revising the definition of 'forest' under the Forest (Conservation) Act of 1980.[96] The Court has been hearing arguments in this case for the past 28 years, and instead of disposing of the petition, it continues to issue orders and directives in an effort to keep an eye on how the executive is implementing the orders.[97] The impact and repercussions of this case for India's forest governance and management have been enormous. It now includes not only woods mentioned in government records, but also all regions that are forests in the dictionary definition of the term, regardless of ownership or categorisation.[98]

F. Judicial Activism Coupled with Global Approach

Two significant aspects of the judicial approach which have contributed to the creation of the unique environmental jurisprudence in India are, namely, judicial activism and the liberal incorporation/reliance on recognised principles of international environmental law. Adverting to the second aspect in the first instance, it is undeniable that climate change is a global issue which transcends geographical boundaries. There have

[87] *M.C. Mehta v Union of India* (1991) 2 SCC 353.
[88] *M.C. Mehta v Union of India* (2002) 4 SCC 356.
[89] ibid para 47.
[90] ibid para 48.
[91] ibid para 47.
[92] *M.C. Mehta v Union of India* (1991) 2 SCC 353 para 15.
[93] GN Gill, 'Human Rights and the Environment in India: Access through Public Interest Litigation' (2012) 14 *Environmental Law Review* 200.
[94] *T.N. Godavarman Thirumulpad v Union of India* (1997) 2 SCC 267.
[95] M M-Rao, 'The Woods' (*Fifty Two*, 3 December 2020), available at fiftytwo.in/story/the-woods.
[96] ibid paras 3–4.
[97] PK Manohar, 'T.N. Godavarman Thirumulpad: The Architect of an Omnibus Forest-Protection Case' (*The Hindu*, 4 July 2016), available at www.thehindu.com/opinion/open-page/The-architect-of-an-omnibus-forest-protection-case/article14470903.ece.
[98] S Upadhyay, S Chohan and A Vaidya, 'India's Forest and The Judiciary: The Godavarman Case' (*World Wide Fund for Nature*, December 2009), available at awsassets.wwfindia.org/downloads/indias_forests_and_the_judiciary_2.pdf.

been attempts on the part of national courts across jurisdictions to effectively deal with climate change. In the process, many fundamental principles to protect the environment have been developed which are universally recognised as well, like the polluter pays principle, the precautionary principle, the principle of intergenerational equity and the public trust doctrine. The judiciaries of different jurisdictions can learn from the experiences of others. So far as the Indian judiciary is concerned, it has recognised the importance of a transjudicial approach, and foreign precedents are liberally followed and incorporated by Indian courts to deal with complex global questions of law that may arise in the context of environmental laws.

Coming to the first aspect mentioned above – judicial activism by the Indian Supreme Court – generally, it has faced accolades and admiration as well as severe criticism at the same time. The irony is that whereas on the one hand, environmental activists remark that the Indian judiciary is not doing enough, the government agencies feel that the judiciary unnecessarily interferes and, at times, unjustifiably stalls development projects that are necessary for economic growth, on the grounds that these projects would have an adverse impact on the environment.

Eschewing this debate, it would be sufficient to remark that the criticism of judicial activism may be justified to some extent when the judiciary transgresses into the executive domain in 'policy' matters. However, in the context of human rights and environmental laws, the judicial approach has received more appreciation than criticism.

IV. Moving Towards the Era of Environmental Rule of Law

In international environmental jurisprudence, the idea of the environmental rule of law is becoming more and more prominent.[99] So far as India is concerned, the courts have played a leading role in defining environmental rights and obligations broadly and in bringing international environmental legal principles into Indian jurisprudence.[100] In a similar vein, the judiciary has supported the concept of the 'environmental rule of law'.[101]

Recent rulings from the Supreme Court of India have brought this to light twice. The apex Court examined the environmental rule of law in great detail in the case of *Hanuman Laxman Aroskar v Union of India*,[102] ordering the expert appraisal committee to reevaluate its recommendations for the granting of clearance while hearing an appeal against a decision of the NGT granting environmental clearance to a greenfield

[99] See generally, 'As a New Era of Environmental Rule of Law Takes Shape, UN Recommends Good Practices' (*UN Environment*, 22 November 2023), available at www.unep.org/news-and-stories/press-release/new-era-environmental-rule-law-takes-shape-un-recommends-good. See also Rogers (n 64); S Cassotta, 'The Development of Environmental Law within a Changing Environmental Governance Context: Towards a New Paradigm Shift in the Anthropocene Era' (2019) 30 *Yearbook of International Environmental Law* 59–63.

[100] G Devarhubli and A Shrivastava, 'The Advancement of Environmental Procedural Rights in India: An Analysis of Issues, Problems and Prospects' (2024) 10 *Cogent Social Sciences*.

[101] M Nirula, 'Guest Blog: Pioneering Decision from the Indian Supreme Court Recognizing Freedom from the Adverse Effects of Climate Change as a Fundamental Right' (*Climate Law Blog*, 28 August 2024), available at blogs.law.columbia.edu/climatechange/2024/08/28/guest-blog-pioneering-decision-from-the-indian-supreme-court-recognizing-freedom-from-the-adverse-effects-of-climate-change-as-a-fundamental-right.

[102] *Hanuman Laxman Aroskar v Union of India* (2019) 15 SCC 401.

airport in Goa.[103] The Court held that, '[f]undamental to the outcome of this case is a quest for environmental governance within a rule of law paradigm'.[104] It also recognised that the 'environmental rule of law provides an essential platform underpinning the four pillars of sustainable development – economic, social, environmental and peace',[105] and that '[i]t imbues environmental objectives with the essentials of rule of law and underpins the reform of environmental law and governance'.[106]

More recently, the Indian Supreme Court again defined the term 'environmental rule of law', which includes climate risk, in the case of *Himachal Pradesh Bus Stand Management and Development Authority v The Central Empowered Committee.*[107] Speaking for the Court, the Chief Justice of India, Dr Justice DY Chandrachud observed thus:

> **49.** [T]he environmental rule of law seeks to facilitate a multi-disciplinary analysis of the nature and consequences of carbon footprints and in doing so it brings a shared understanding between science, regulatory decisions and policy perspectives in the field of environmental protection. ... it seeks to draw within the fold all stakeholders in formulating strategies to deal with current challenges posed by environmental degradation, climate change and the destruction of habitats ....[108]

This shows that, in order to identify areas that require reform, the environmental rule of law can provide a valuable foundation for a critical review of the Indian environmental legal and regulatory system, and the courts have become the North Star of this endeavour.

V. Conclusion

In *Municipal Corporation of Greater Mumbai v Ankita Sinha*,[109] the Indian Supreme Court stated that judges ought to take the initiative and take *suo motu* cognisance of environmental, social and governance (ESG) related issues.[110] The Court in *Ankita Sinha* held that the NGT had the authority to consider environmental matters on its own initiative.[111] The Court opined that 'the role of the watchdog can't remain only ornamental due to procedural nit-picking and hair-splitting'.[112] Furthermore, 'it is vital for the well-being of the nation and its people, to have a flexible mechanism to address all issues pertaining to environmental damage and resultant climate change so that we can leave behind a better environmental legacy, for our children'.[113]

In a rapidly evolving world, it is important for judges to be prepared and proactive while handling a variety of ESG litigation concerns. Consider the charge of greenwashing

[103] ibid para 162.
[104] ibid para 142.
[105] ibid para 144.
[106] ibid para 144.
[107] *H.P. Bus-Stand Management & Development Authority v Central Empowered Committee* (2021) 4 SCC 309.
[108] ibid para 49.
[109] *Municipal Corpn. of Greater Mumbai v Ankita Sinha* (2022) 13 SCC 401.
[110] ibid paras 44–48.
[111] ibid paras 49–52.
[112] ibid para 100.
[113] ibid para 94.

(from stakeholders like regulators, shareholders, and the general public), which may grow as green marketing and ESG commitments become more significant to consumers.[114] Furthermore, as investors and astute businesspeople come under closer scrutiny for their funding, the scope of climate change litigation will only expand.[115] Public and private entities will need to adhere to their publicly committed commitments, or they are likely to face litigation from a variety of sources. All these issues can be missed by the parties, or the parties are so much engrossed in dealing with substantial challenges, that the parties may not argue this.

The role of the judiciary is pivotal in addressing climate change, and judges have to be aware of existing trends in climate change litigation to ensure that the courts are well-equipped to effectively adjudicate ESG-related cases. Commercial courts can play an instrumental role in robust ESG governance and can contribute to the development of an effective global response to climate change.[116] The pattern of adjudication has the potential to create a system of norms and beliefs about the relevance of climate change. However, in order to fight the battle of climate change, all the stakeholders and all relevant institutions have to join in the mission and contribute to this mission.

[114] United Nations, 'Greenwashing – the Deceptive Tactics behind Environmental Claims | United Nations', available at www.un.org/en/climatechange/science/climate-issues/greenwashing.

[115] B Merkt et al, 'Greenwashing: Green claims in Commercial Communications' (*Lenz & Staehelin*, 21 July 2023), available at www.lenzstaehelin.com/news-and-insights/browse-thought-leadership-insights/insights-detail/greenwashing-green-claims-in-commercial-communications.

[116] V Vadi, 'Beyond Known Worlds: Climate Change Governance by Arbitral Tribunals?' (2021) 48 *Vanderbilt Law Review* 1285.

CONCLUSION: COURTS IN AN INTERCONNECTED JUSTICE ECOSYSTEM

SUNDARESH MENON, ANSELMO REYES AND NALLINI PATHMANATHAN

In today's rapidly evolving world, society faces unprecedented challenges – a confluence of digital transformation, environmental crises, and shifting global interdependencies – that demand an evolution in the role of the judiciary. Courts are no longer regarded solely as isolated adjudicators operating solely within jurisdictional siloes but are essential nodes within a comprehensive justice ecosystem that transcends national boundaries. This ecosystem integrates multiple modalities of dispute resolution, engages robustly with other branches of government, and actively participates in transnational dialogues for legal development. Based on the discussions during the 4th Judicial Roundtable on the Future of Justice and this book's chapters, this conclusion envisages the potential future of justice through the lens of an interconnected system where courts, far from being mere arbiters, are dynamic nodes that help shape, inform, and even transform the dispute resolution landscape.

I. Courts as a Component of a Comprehensive Dispute Resolution Ecosystem

A. From Confrontation to Collaboration

Historically, dispute resolution relied heavily on power-based methods.[1] Early systems often settled conflicts through power and coercion. Later, legal evolution introduced rights-based adjudication, replacing brute force with the application of rules. However, a purely rights-based approach will not address the intricate realities of contemporary disputes, which frequently involve multiple parties, long-term relationships, and overlapping interests requiring alternative sustainable solutions.[2]

[1] WL Ury, JM Brett and SB Goldberg, *Getting Disputes Resolved: Designing Systems to Cut the Costs of Conflict* (Hoboken, Jossey-Bass, 1988) ch 1.

[2] ibid.

Contemporary practice recognises that interest-based methods are a vital complement to traditional rights-based dispute resolution, permitting early conflict prevention. Courts, rather than serving solely as final arbiters, should become dynamic hubs that channel disputes into appropriate resolution mechanisms.[3] Digital tools such as decision trees and diagnostic platforms need to be integrated to offer litigants early guidance regarding their legal standing and anticipated outcomes.[4] These systems will help to defuse potential conflicts by directing parties toward mediation, negotiation, neutral evaluation, and other cooperative modes of alternative dispute resolution (ADR) before formal adversarial processes become necessary. In essence, these front-end services will aim at 'dissolving' disputes before they fully materialise, thereby saving time and costs and preserving symbiotic relationships.[5]

This evolution from confrontation to collaboration, aided by technological innovation and innovative adjudicative models, is central to reimagining the role of courts.[6] Rather than being vestiges of an old adversarial system, courts become dynamic service providers. They integrate and coordinate diverse pathways – ranging from digital triage and early dispute resolution platforms to structured mediation processes – ensuring that the justice system is accessible, efficient, and tuned to the real-world complexities of modern conflicts.

B. Embracing Technological Innovation with Systemic Responsibility

The digital era has brought transformative changes to every sector. The administration of justice is no exception. Advances in AI are reshaping judicial processes. The emerging concept of 'legal singularity' looks to a future in which judicial systems deliver near-instantaneous and reliable resolutions to complex disputes.[7] By harnessing technologies such as machine learning, natural language processing, and data analytics, AI can facilitate and accelerate how courts manage and analyse information. This will streamline legal research, enhance evidence synthesis, and assist with (to the extent needed in the absence of consensual resolution) the drafting of judgments.

Modern digital tools should enable parties to interact with user-friendly interfaces that simplify and demystify the law. For instance, interactive decision trees and automated diagnostic systems can offer early assessments that direct parties towards more time-efficient and cost-effective non-adversarial modes of dispute resolution.[8] These front-end interventions can reduce court waiting lists and empower parties with a

[3] F EA Sander, *Address by Frank EA Sander, Bussey Professor of Law at Harvard University, at the National Conference on the Causes of Popular Dissatisfaction with the Administration of Justice (7–9 April 1976)* (reprinted in *The Pound Conference* 70 F.R.D. 79, 111 (1976)); W Burger, 'Address to ABA Midyear Meeting' [24 January 1982] (1982) 68 *American Bar Association Journal* 274–76.

[4] R Susskind, 'The Future of Courts' (*Harvard Law School Center on the Legal Profession*, 2020) clp.law.harvard.edu/knowledge-hub/magazine/issues/remote-courts/the-future-of-courts.

[5] ibid.

[6] R Susskind, *Online Courts and the Future of Justice* (Oxford, Oxford University Press, 2019).

[7] B Alarie and A Aidid, *The Legal Singularity: How Artificial Intelligence Can Make Law Radically Better* (Toronto, University of Toronto Press, 2023) 5.

[8] ibid.

clearer understanding of their rights and obligations. These innovations represent a shift from over-reliance on lengthy, resource-intensive litigation processes to more accessible preventive measures.

Yet the effective integration of such technology requires a robust framework. For example, emerging challenges in data protection and privacy – evident in complex litigations involving cross-border data flows and AI-generated evidence – underscore the need for systematic governance.[9] Courts must ensure that these digital innovations, such as AI-driven tools, are uniformly subject to transparent oversight, rigorous quality checks, and clearly defined benchmarking criteria.[10] This structured approach will not only guard against the risk of algorithmic opacity and inadvertent bias but also underscore the importance of protecting data integrity and privacy.[11]

In short, as disputes become increasingly complex – often involving sophisticated technical and scientific evidence – courts must evolve their procedures accordingly.[12] There is a responsibility to adopt new procedures and innovative practices that streamline complex legal disputes. Incorporating mediation protocols, AI-enhanced evidence organisation, and real-time digital tracking systems can all contribute to a holistic dispute resolution process that is efficient and responsive to the multifaceted dynamics of modern conflicts. By fostering an environment where innovation is balanced with accountability – and where continuous learning and adaptation are embedded into judicial processes – courts can enhance their operational capacity and protect fundamental human values such as empathy, creativity, and moral judgment. This dual commitment to advancing technology responsibly to streamline dispute resolution, while safeguarding individual rights, is essential to maintaining public trust and ensuring that justice remains accessible and equitable in the rapidly evolving digital landscape.

C. Integrating a Bespoke Judicial Model for Complex Disputes

Environmental adjudication under the current adversarial framework faces notable limitations.[13] Traditionally, courts have focused on remedying past harms – typically through compensation or injunctive relief – while being reactive in nature. This approach often misses the opportunity to probe the underlying causes of environmental degradation and to promote sustainable practices. Moreover, the conventional model does little to enforce environmental standards in a proactive manner or to address the cumulative impacts of disputes involving significant public interests.[14]

In response to these challenges, there are alternative pathways worth considering. One such alternative is a public enforcement or inquisitorial approach, similar to the

[9] See chs 8–10.

[10] See chs 1–7; see also N Guha et al, 'LegalBench: A Collaboratively Built Benchmark for Measuring Legal Reasoning in Large Language Models' (26 September 2023) papers.ssrn.com/sol3/papers.cfm?abstract_id=4583531.

[11] See chs 1–10.

[12] See, eg, S Menon, 'Judicial Excellence in a Challenging World: The Centrality of Trust', speech at the International Association for Court Administration Conference (12 November 2024).

[13] See chs 14–16.

[14] ibid.

mechanism adopted by the Supreme Court of India through Public Interest Litigation.[15] This model empowers courts to initiate early investigations to enforce environmental standards, shifting their role from passive adjudicators to proactive stewards of public welfare.

Another approach is for courts to anchor judicial mandates in established scientific consensus (for example, as evidenced by the IPCC reports), transforming scientific data into legally binding directives.[16] This approach supports proactive and preventive rulings – exemplified by decisions such as *Netherlands v Urgenda* – thereby reinforcing human rights and public health.[17] Additionally, evolving doctrinal methods, which move beyond overly rigid 'but-for' tests in assessing contribution to environmental harm, can empower courts to deliver remedies (such as declarations, injunctions or orders of mandamus) that respond to long-term environmental risks and require states, corporations or individuals to adhere to their legal duties to reduce greenhouse gas emissions.[18]

A third potential approach involves integrating therapeutic justice principles, drawing inspiration from practices in family law.[19] This model introduces a proactive, collaborative dimension by instituting a judicial system that, in addition to its core duty to 'say what the law is', prioritises early intervention. For instance, judges can lead early case triage and direct disputes to multidisciplinary teams composed of technical, scientific, and social experts to uncover the underlying causes and cumulative impacts of environmental conflicts. This approach would aim not so much at determining fault but at restoring balance, promoting sustainable practices, and reducing the deadlock often seen in complex, multi-party conflicts. By complementing the traditional adversarial process rather than replacing it, this therapeutic framework can transform entrenched positions into opportunities for long-term, mutually beneficial resolutions. It exemplifies a shift from confrontation to collaborative engagement. Although this idea remains exploratory – and was not a central theme of the discussions at the 4th Judicial Roundtable – it represents a promising avenue for reimagining dispute resolution in addressing our evolving legal landscape.

II. Courts Interacting with Other Branches: Executive, Legislative, and Constitutional Dialogue

A. Upholding the Core Adjudicative Mandate

Despite the call for innovation and the integration of new dispute resolution tools, the fundamental judicial duty remains unchanged. Judges are supposed to 'say what the law is'.[20] This constitutional mandate, rooted in the timeless principles of judi-

[15] ch 16.

[16] ch 15.

[17] *The State of The Netherlands (Ministry of Economic Affairs and Climate Policy) v Urgenda Foundation* ECLI:NL:HR:2019:2007, Hoge Raad, 19/00135.

[18] ch 15.

[19] S Menon, 'A New Perspective on Climate Disputes: Lessons from Therapeutic Justice', speech delivered at the Asia Pacific Judicial Convening on Environment and Climate Law Adjudication (2 December 2024).

[20] *Marbury v Madison* 5 US 137 (1803) 177.

cial review, serves as the cornerstone of the legal system's integrity and stability. The application of established legal rules ensures that judicial decisions are predictable, equitable, and anchored in the rule of law.[21]

While modern reforms can expand the modalities of dispute resolution and improve access to justice, the impartial and principled interpretation of the law will continue to be the essential task of the judiciary. Even as digital innovation transforms the mechanisms for resolving conflicts, the core function of translating written law into fair outcomes must endure as the guiding light for all judicial activity.

B. Engaging in Constitutional Dialogue Without Overreach

The interaction between the judiciary and other governmental branches forms a complex but essential system of checks and balances within the constitutional framework. Through measured dialogue with the executive and legislative branches, the judiciary contributes expert insights on emerging challenges such as digital privacy, cybersecurity, and environmental regulation. But this form of inter-branch dialogue remains distinctly advisory; it respects the separation of powers by refraining from dictating policy.[22]

Judicial contributions in constitutional dialogues are characterised by thoughtful, reasoned observations that guide legislative reform without encroaching on the policymaking domain.[23] As rapid technological advances and environmental challenges blur the boundaries between traditional legal disputes and long-term public policy concerns, a symbiotic governance framework ensures that accountability is maintained and that legal standards evolve to mitigate future harm. For instance, in matters of environmental regulation, courts translate robust scientific consensus into clear legal obligations without dictating policy.[24] Courts can adopt a mode of inquiry that invites parties to articulate key environmental issues at an early stage – thereby de-escalating potential conflicts before they evolve into full-blown disputes.[25] Maintaining a balanced dialogue is critical to preserving the independence and legitimacy of the judiciary. The reflective commentary provided in judicial opinions and public addresses offers valuable input for systemic reform, while upholding the impartiality that is essential for public trust.

[21] S Menon, 'The Role of the Judiciary in a Changing World', Supreme Court of India Day Lecture, Supreme Court of India (4 February 2023).

[22] ibid.

[23] PJ Yap, *Constitutional Dialogue in Common Law Asia* (Oxford, Oxford University Press, 2015).

[24] See ch 15.

[25] A Reyes, 'The Use of Domestic Law to Regulate the Conduct of Individuals, Corporations and Governments Extraterritorially' in *Collected Courses of The Hague Academy of International Law, Tome 441* (Leiden, Brill, 2025).

III. Courts Interacting with Other Judiciaries: Judicial Diplomacy and a Transnational System of Justice

A. Embracing Global Engagement in an Interconnected World

In an increasingly globalised society, many legal disputes extend well beyond national borders. Conflicts related to cross-border trade, digital data management, and environmental protection necessitate coordinated responses among diverse legal systems. Recognising that contemporary challenges are inherently transnational, the judiciary must cultivate robust channels for global judicial engagement.[26] International judicial engagement is not simply a matter of exchanging ideas or citing foreign precedents – it is about forging partnerships that facilitate a convergence of substantive and procedural norms across jurisdictions.

Global judicial engagement reinforces the notion that justice is a shared responsibility. It enables courts to harmonise approaches to complex matters – including digital and data governance, climate litigation, and cross-border commercial disputes – reducing legal uncertainty and building mutual trust among jurisdictions. The collective efforts of an international judicial community fortify the integrity of the global legal order and ensure a coordinated response to challenges that transcend any one nation's borders.

B. Building a Robust Transnational Justice Framework

This vision of a robust transnational justice system involves constructing institutional mechanisms that enable national courts to coordinate effectively on disputes spanning multiple jurisdictions.[27] Such a framework would facilitate the sharing of legal precedents, the mutual recognition of judicial decisions, and the harmonisation of procedural norms.

The development of this framework is not intended to erase distinct legal traditions but to provide a flexible structure that accommodates diversity while upholding universal values. By converging procedural standards in areas such as commercial, data protection, and environmental litigation, the transnational framework can reduce the costs and uncertainties associated with cross-border disputes. Digital technologies play a pivotal role in this endeavour by enabling virtual conferencing, the establishment of shared databases, and platforms that enhance real-time legal communication and information exchange.

C. Ensuring Global Legitimacy Through Judicial Diplomacy

Legitimacy is a cornerstone of any judicial system and is strengthened through domestic consistency and international recognition. Judicial diplomacy serves as a critical tool for building domestic and international legitimacy.[28] Engaging in proactive judicial

[26] S Menon, 'Reimagining the Rule of Law: A Renewed Conception', speech delivered at the Singapore Courts – Conversations with the Community (20 September 2024).

[27] ibid.

[28] ibid.

diplomacy reinforces the public trust towards legal institutions and promotes a culture of accountability and mutual respect on the global stage.

International forums, bilateral exchanges, and judicial workshops – such as the Judicial Roundtable on the Future of Justice – provide practical platforms for discussing common challenges and sharing innovative practices. These initiatives not only enhance the technical competencies of domestic courts but also build enduring networks of trust and cooperation. Such global partnerships demonstrate that legal challenges – from digital privacy to climate change – require collective responses that transcend jurisdictional interests.

However, caution is warranted when relying on external capacity-building efforts, which may compromise the perceived impartiality of judges.[29] Instead, judicial capacity building should aim towards being self-organised and intrinsically integrated into the judicial structure. This approach ensures that courts, especially in emerging economies, develop and sustain the necessary expertise to navigate complex disputes – including those involving environmental challenges – without compromising their independence or integrity.[30]

In an era marked by rapid digital transformation, courts confront the problem of truth decay – where widespread misinformation, disinformation, and declining trust in institutions undermine public confidence in judicial processes.[31] Judicial engagement with the public can serve as a vital counterbalance to this trend. By reaffirming their commitment to transparent, evidence-based adjudication and actively communicating the rationale behind their decisions, courts should aim to rebuild and sustain public trust.

IV. Conclusion: A Unified Vision for the Future of Justice

The future of justice requires a reconceptualisation of the role of courts. Rather than operating as isolated entities, the judiciary must become dynamic components of an interconnected ecosystem that integrates advanced digital innovations, restorative dispute resolution methods, and effective engagement with governmental institutions and international legal communities. This multifaceted approach ensures that justice is accessible, efficient, and responsive to the evolving challenges of the digital age, environmental imperatives, and global interdependence.

This transformation requires a commitment to early intervention and streamlined processes. Courts should integrate digital tools – ranging from AI-driven evidence organisation to real-time tracking systems – within a robust framework of regulation and oversight. Such a framework ensures that technological advances are balanced with rigorous quality controls, transparent decision-making, and respect for individual rights. Moreover, sustained dialogue with other branches of government and

[29] A Reyes, 'The Limits of Private International Law in Cross-Border Environmental Disputes' (Symposium on Environment, Corporations and PIL, Singapore Management University, 6–7 February 2025) [NOTE: This will be published in a forthcoming volume within the *Hart Studies in Private International Law: Asia* series].

[30] ibid.

[31] See chs 11–13.

international partners will help align judicial practices with rapidly changing societal needs without compromising the rule of law.

On an international scale, judicial diplomacy and the development of a transnational justice framework are essential strategies for addressing cross-border disputes. By building robust cooperative networks, sharing best practices and harmonising procedural standards, judiciaries can contribute to a global rule of law that is as resilient as it is just.

Ultimately, this vision affirms that justice is a collective endeavour – one that must evolve continuously to meet contemporary challenges while remaining anchored in the timeless principles of the rule of law. By becoming accountable, collaborative and nimble institutions that operate within interconnected systems, courts can enhance public trust, address complex legal challenges, and shape a legal landscape that meets the demands of today and tomorrow.

LIST OF PARTICIPANTS IN THE 4TH JUDICIAL ROUNDTABLE ON THE FUTURE OF JUSTICE, APRIL 2024

Judges

Chief Justice Andrew Bell AC, Supreme Court, New South Wales
Lady Jill Black, formerly Justice, UK Supreme Court
Dr Dhananjaya Y Chandrachud, formerly Chief Justice, Supreme Court, India
Judge Du Weike, Deputy Chief Judge, Intellectual Property Court of the Supreme People's Court, China
Justice Gao Xiaoli, Vice-President, Supreme People's Court, China
Justice David Goddard, formerly Judge, Court of Appeal, New Zealand; currently International Judge, Singapore International Commercial Court (SICC)
Deputy Attorney-General Goh Yihan, formerly Justice, Supreme Court, Singapore
Justice Philip Jeyaretnam, President, SICC
Justice Sanjeev Sudhakar Kalgaonkar, Madhya Pradesh High Court, India
Justice G S Kulkarni, Bombay High Court, India
Judge Kwon Bowon, Intellectual Property High Court, Republic of Korea
Justice Godfrey Lam, Court of Appeal, Hong Kong SAR
Justice Syamsul Maarif, Supreme Court, Indonesia
Chief Justice Sundaresh Menon, Supreme Court, Singapore
Justice Hri Kumar Nair, Supreme Court, Singapore
Lord David Neuberger, formerly President, UK Supreme Court; currently International Judge, SICC
Justice Bernd Odörfer, Federal Court of Justice, Germany
Justice Matthew S R Palmer, Court of Appeal, New Zealand
Tan Sri Nallini Pathmanathan, formerly Judge, Federal Court, Malaysia
Justice Anselmo Reyes, International Judge, SICC
Justice Eric M Runesson, Supreme Court, Sweden
Justice Arjan Sikri, formerly Judge, Supreme Court, India; currently International Judge, SICC
Justice Yashwant Varma, Allahabad High Court, India
Justice K V Viswanathan, Supreme Court, India

Academics, Policymakers, Practitioners and Assistants

Dr Roberta Bassi, Senior Commissioning Editor, Hart Publishing
Assistant Professor Chen Jielei, Law School, Tongji University, China
Professor Chen Lei, Deputy Dean, Durham Law School, Durham University, UK
Assistant Professor Damian Clifford, LSE Law School, London School of Economics and Political Science, UK

Associate Professor Ylli Dautaj, Durham Law School, Durham University, UK
Assistant Professor Can Eken, Durham Law School, Durham University, UK
Associate Professor Ronán Feehily, Durham Law School, Durham University, UK
Assistant Professor Dirk Hartung, Yong Pung How School of Law, Singapore Management University
Mr Huang Jiahui, Barrister, Twenty Essex
Dr Shashi Jayakumar, Executive Director, SJK Geostrategic Advisory, Singapore
Professor Jiang Huiling, Dean, Law School, Tongji University, China
Ms Latha Kunjappa, Senior Assistant Director, Supreme Court, Singapore
Associate Professor Luo Tianxuan, Law School, Tongji University, China
Mr Adrian Mak, Anselmo Reyes KK, Japan
Professor Petra Minnerop, Durham Law School, Durham University, UK
Mr Gordon Moodie, formerly Chief Product Officer, Harvey AI; currently Partner, Debevoise & Plimpton, New York, US
Professor Volker Roeben, Dean, Durham Law School, Durham University, UK
Sir Jim Skea, Chair, Intergovernmental Panel on Climate Change
Dr Aria Suyudi, Chairman, Jentera Law School, Indonesia
Mr Tan Ee Kuan, formerly Assistant Registrar and Special Assistant to the Chief Justice, Supreme Court, Singapore
Mr Jacob Turner, Barrister, Fountain Court Chambers
Professor Christina Voigt, Faculty of Law, University of Oslo, Norway
Associate Professor Jia Wang, Durham Law School, Durham University, UK
Mr Yeong Zee Kin, Chief Executive, Singapore Academy of Law

INDEX

www.ingramcontent.com/pod-product-compliance
Ingram Content Group UK Ltd.
Pitfield, Milton Keynes, MK11 3LW, UK
UKHW030855310826
474961UK00001B/4

9 781509 984398